KU-281-284

Transactional analysis psychotherapy

Transactional Analysis Psychotherapy: An Integrated Approach is the first advanced textbook for psychotherapists and counsellors who use the theory and techniques of Transactional Analysis in their practice. It provides a comprehensive guide to goal-setting and clinical planning for every stage of treatment; problems of technique are illustrated throughout by clinical vignettes and case material.

At the theoretical level, the author represents Transactional Analysis as a contemporary psychotherapy based on the classical work of Eric Berne and predecessors such as Federn, Fairbairn, and Klein, which integrates humanistic/existential philosophy with behavioural pragmatism. This is not only a practical textbook relevant to modern developments in supervision, but one which makes a new and original contribution to ways of thinking about transference and countertransference, the theory of self, and the process of psychotherapeutic change. It is intended as a bridge between Transactional Analysis and other theories of psychotherapy and is of particular relevance in today's climate of interdisciplinary communication.

Transactional analysis psychotherapy

An integrated approach

Petrūska Clarkson

U.M.C.
New Cross

UNIVERSITY OF WOLVERHAMPTON
LEARNING RESOURCES

2051172   CLASS

CONTROL

0415026546   616.8914
CLA
DATE   SITE   T   CS8
16/9/96   NEW

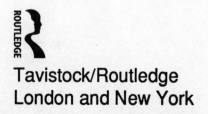

Tavistock/Routledge
London and New York

First published in 1992
by Routledge
11 New Fetter Lane, London EC4P 4EE

Simultaneously published in the USA and Canada
by Routledge
a division of Routledge, Chapman and Hall Inc.
29 West 35th Street, New York, NY 10001

First published in paperback in 1992

© 1992 Petrūska Clarkson

Laserprinted from author's disks by LaserScript, Mitcham, Surrey
Printed and bound in Great Britain by
Mackays of Chatham PLC, Chatham, Kent

All rights reserved. No part of this book may be reprinted or reproduced or utilized in
any form or by any electronic, mechanical, or other means, now known or hereafter
invented, including photocopying and recording, or in any information storage or
retrieval system, without permission in writing from the publishers.

British Library Cataloguing in Publication Data

Clarkson, Petrūska
    Transactional analysis psychotherapy: an integrated approach.
    1. Transactional analysis
    I. Title
    158.2

Library of Congress Cataloging in Publication Data

Clarkson, Petrūska, 1947–
    Transactional analysis psychotherapy: an integrated approach/by
    Petrūska Clarkson.
    p. cm.
    Includes bibliographical references and index.
    1. Transactional analysis. I. Title.
RC489.T7C58 1992
616.89'145–dc20   90-47735
                                                                              CIP

ISBN 0-415-02454-4
     0-415-08699-X (pbk)

Contents

Illustrations

TABLES

Contributors

Petrūska Clarkson, Ph.D., M.A., A.F.B.Ps.S., is a Chartered Clinical Psychologist and a practising psychotherapist, supervisor and OD consultant. She is a Clinical Teaching and Supervising Transactional Analyst of the International Transactional Analysis Association (ITAA). She has served on the ITAA Board of Trustees, on the Editorial Board of the Transactional Analysis Journal, and on national and international Training Standards Committees for Transactional Analysts. She has served on the Level I and Level II examining boards of the ITAA and co-ordinated several successful Training Endorsement Workshops on international sites. She has published more than twenty-four papers on transactional analysis, been translated into eight languages, and conducted workshops in many countries. She has been nominated for several awards and won the 1990 European Association for Transactional Analysis award for her paper 'Script cure? A diagnostic pentagon of types of therapeutic change'. She is a past Chairperson of the Personal, Sexual, Family and Marital Division of the B.A.C. and member of the British Psychological Society's Counselling Section and Clinical Psychology Division. She has served on the Registration Subcommittee of the United Kingdom Standing Conference for Psychotherapy and currently serves on the Board of Examiners of the British Psychological Society Psychology Counselling Diploma. She is Chairperson of the Gestalt Training Institute of Great Britain and co-ordinator for the British Institute for Integrative Psychotherapy (affiliated to S.E.P.I. International). She also draws on extensive psychoanalytic and Jungian training and experience. She has been active in the training and supervision of counsellors, psychotherapists, clinical psychologists and organisational consultants for more than twenty years and is a founder director of *metanoia* Psychotherapy Training Institute which offers, among other approaches to psychotherapy, a major professional TA Psychotherapy Training Programme which draws visitors and students nationally and internationally.

Sue Fish, B.Soc.Sc., Dip. Ed., Dip. Speech and Drama, Dip. N.L.P., is a Certified Clinical Teaching and Supervising Transactional Analyst (ITAA) and Teaching Member of the Gestalt Psychotherapy Training Institute of Great Britain. She has extensive training and experience in remedial and therapeutic work with children and young people including several years as the head of a unit for disturbed adolescents. She is a founder director of *metanoia* Psychotherapy Training Institute where she conducts psychotherapy with children, families and adults as well as doing training, and supervision in TA and Gestalt. She is one of the directors of the Child Psychotherapy Training Programme at *metanoia*.

Maria Gilbert, M.A. (Clin. Psych.), B.A. Hons. (English), Accredited Supervisor (B.A.C.), is a Chartered Clinical Psychologist, a Clinical Teaching and Supervising Transactional Analyst and a Teaching Member of the Gestalt Psychotherapy Training Institute of Great Britain. She has fifteen years' experience in adult education and individual, couple, and group psychotherapy, as well as in the supervision and training of psychotherapists and psychotherapists' supervisors in Transactional Analysis, Gestalt Therapy and Integrative Psychotherapy. She is co-author with Petrūska Clarkson of 'Transactional analysis' in *Handbook of Individual Therapy in Britain* (edited by Windy Dryden) and 'The training of counselling trainers and supervisors 'in *Counselling in Action* (edited by Windy Dryden). She is the Director of Clinical Training at *metanoia*.

Fran Lacey, B.Sc., C.Q.S.W., comes from a background of youth and community work. She is a Certified Transactional Analyst and Provisional Clinical Teaching and Supervising Transactional Analyst working in private practice in London and is a tutor on the *metanoia* Counselling Diploma course and assistant trainer on the *metanoia* TA Psychotherapy Programme. She has been widely involved with programmes for personal development and, with Elana Leigh, has devised and run workshops on various aspects of growth and communication. She is the co-author of a training manual for trainers and has contributed to various youthwork publications and national reports. She is a member of the Institute of Transactional Analysis Council.

Phil Lapworth, Cert. Ed., Dip. Counselling skills, Dip. Systemic Integrative Psychotherapy, came to psychotherapy through his work in Special Education in London as deputy headteacher in a school for children and adolescents with learning disorders and as Senior Teacher at the Maudsley Psychiatric Hospital. He is a Certified Transactional Analyst and currently runs a psychotherapy and supervisory practice in West London. He is the Director of Clinical Services at *metanoia* Psychotherapy Training Institute.

Elana Leigh, B.Soc. Sc., trained, qualified and worked as a social worker specialising in group-work in South Africa, Australia and Britain. Her interest in the areas of personal growth and development has extended from leading, for example, multicultural workshops in South Africa on 'Burn-out' to conference workshops on 'Friendship' (with Fran Lacey) in Britain and Europe. She is a

Certified Transactional Analyst and an assistant trainer on the *metanoia* TA Psychotherapy Training Programme and runs a private psychotherapy practice in North London. She is a member of the Institute of Transactional Analysis Council in Britain and serves on the Ethics Sub-committee.

David Schofield, L.R.P.C., M.R.C.S., D.R.C.O.G., M.R.C.G.P., is a General Practitioner in Abingdon and a tutor in the Department of Public Health and Primary Care, University of Oxford. He was previously an approved trainer of G.P. trainees. He is currently in TA Psychotherapy training at *metanoia* Psychotherapy Training Institute, London, and is developing a private psychotherapy practice based in Abingdon.

Acknowledgements

A version of Chapter 2 appeared in *Transactional Analysis Journal*, 1988, 18: 211–19, as 'Script Cure? A diagnostic pentagon of types of therapeutic change'. A version of Chapter 3 appeared in *Transactional Analysis Journal*, 1988, 18: 20–9, as 'Berne's original model of ego states: therapeutic considerations' (P. Clarkson and M. Gilbert). A version of Chapter 4 appeared in *Transactional Analysis Journal*, 1989, 19: 45–50, as 'Metaperspectives on diagnosis'. A version of Chapter 5 appeared in *Transactional Analysis Journal*, 1988, 18: 51–9, as 'Rechilding: creating a new past in the present as a support for the future' (P. Clarkson and S. Fish). A version of Chapter 9 appeared in *ITA News*, 1988, 20: 4–16, as 'Group imago and the stages of group development: a comparative analysis of the stages of the group process'. A version of Chapter 10 appeared in *Transactional Analysis Journal*, 1988, 18: 123–32, as 'Systemic assessment and treatment considerations in TA child psychotherapy' (P. Clarkson and S. Fish). The last section of Chapter 10 appeared in *Transactional Analysis Journal*, 1988, 18: 85–93 as a section of the article 'Ego state dilemmas of abused children'. A section of Chapter 11 appeared in *ITA News*, 1988, 9: 4–8 as 'Burnout'. A section of Chapter 11 appeared in *Transactional Analysis Journal*, 1987, 17: 82–7 as 'The bystander role'. A section of Chapter 11 appeared in *The British Psychological Society Counselling Section Review*, 1987, 2: 11–13 as 'One model for the training of supervisors' (P. Clarkson and M. Gilbert). A section of Chapter 11 appeared in *ITA News*, 1987, 16: 7–10 as 'Post level I clinical certification training or "Is there life after level I?"' (P. Clarkson and M. Gilbert). A version of Chapter 12 appeared in *British Journal of Psychotherapy*, 1990, 7: 148–63 as 'A multiplicity of psychotherapeutic relationships'.

Routledge gratefully acknowledges permission to reproduce material previously published elsewhere. Dr John Dusay allowed use of Figure 1 (Figure 6.1 in this volume) from 'Egograms and the "constant hypothesis"', *Transactional Analysis Journal*, 2: 37–41.) Kenneth Mellor granted permission for reproduction of Figure 1 (Figure 6.6) from 'Impasses: a developmental and structural understanding', *Transactional Analysis Journal*, 10: 213–20. Dr Stephen B. Karpman allowed use of the diagram, Drama Triangle (Figure 11.5) from 'Fairy tales and script drama analysis', *Transactional Analysis Bulletin*, 7: 39–43. Mary

Goulding and Robert Goulding granted permission for reproduction of the diagram, Third Degree Impasse (Figure 6.8) from 'Injunction, decisions and redecisions', *Transactional Analysis Journal*, 6: 41–8. Andre Deutsch Ltd, Random House Inc and Alfred A. Knopf Inc allowed use of Figure 1 (Figure 8.1) from *Games People Play* by Eric Berne. Muriel James granted permission for the reproduction of the diagram, Ego states in the individual self being energized by inner core energy, (Figure 8.7) from *A New Self* by M. James and L. Savary. Penguin Books Ltd allowed use of Figure 2.2 (Figure 8.8) from *A Psychology with a Soul: Psychosynthesis in Evolutionary Context* by Jean Hardy. International Universities Press Inc granted permission for reproduction of the diagram, The Clinical Rhombus, (Figure 11.2) from *Teaching and Learning Psychotherapy* by R. Ekstein and R.S. Wallerstein. Pamela Levin and Health Communications allowed use of a compilation of diagrams (Figure A.1) from *Cycles of Power* and *Becoming the Way We Are*. The International Transactional Analysis Association granted permission for the reproduction of the *ITAA Statement of Ethics* as Appendix C. Every effort has been made to obtain permission to reproduce copyright material throughout this book. If any proper acknowledgement has not yet been made, the copyright holder should contact the publisher.

Preface

This book is the end result of a long journey. As a qualified clinical psychologist and practising psychotherapist well schooled in existential/phenomenological and psychodynamic psychotherapy with a Tavistock-trained Freudian analysis behind me, I was searching for a way to help liberate people's minds from the shackles of cultural, ideological and psychological determinism. What I was learning and discovering in psychology of the individual's responsibility and the possibility of change seemed to me to be so precious that I wanted to share it with many others so that it could help them as much as it had helped me.

In South Africa, lacking much international contact, books were my most valued intellectual companions. I came across a hard-cover book called *The Book of Choice* by Thomas Harris (1970) published by Jonathan Cape from Great Britain. Perhaps if I had met the same book under its other title, *I'm OK, You're OK* I would never have picked it up and this book would never have come to pass. I immediately started studying Eric Berne's books. In our isolation from the American popularity wave, I found that the concepts of multiple states of consciousness under the direction of an integrated Adult ego state shorn of harmful influences or introjects from significant childhood figures and free from the re-experiencing of pain or limits of the past, matched my current thinking and practice very well. In 1975 I met my first American TA person, Dr Dorothy Jongeward, who led an introductory course to transactional analysis in Johannesburg. Thank you Dorothy for first showing me a good way to teach TA. I then commenced one of the most fruitful personal and colleagial collaborations of my life with Maria Gilbert, another psychotherapist and clinical psychologist who shared my intellectual curiosity, my passion for engaging in a struggle for consciousness and liberty (in whatever domain) and my joy in co-operative endeavour with talented and authentic companions. Technically Maria appears as co-author on several chapters, psychologically she has supported and encouraged me on my whole journey and I take this opportunity to express my heartfelt gratitude to her. We started teaching the material we had learned to mixed-race groups in Johannesburg and were seriously involved in one of the major centres for liberal humanistic adult education which challenged the institutionalised devaluation of human beings – Wilgepruit. Some psychologists who lit their TA fire from ours, such as Professor Diana Smukler, have continued to be active in professional and other ways in the struggle for humanistic reform in the South African situation.

In 1976 in Entschede in Holland I attended my first international TA conference and passed an exam with a group of international teaching members assembled to test my knowledge of transactional analysis before officially endorsing me as a 101 (TA Introduction) instructor. I also met Dr Richard Erskine (five of whose workshops – some co-led by Rebecca Trautman – I went on to attend) and Shea Schiff, with whom I did most of my supervised supervision hours for my eventual Clinical Teaching Member examination, among many other fine people who became my teachers, colleagues and friends. Thank you very much. If I listed all, space would be exceeded. However, the names of most influences appear throughout the text as references – please consider this due mention as I thank you for your stimulation and your kindness to me. Val Chang, Lois Johnson, Margery Friedlander, Dr Carlo Moiso, Mary and Dr Bob Goulding, Dr Muriel James, Denton Roberts, Dr Guido Stellemans, Marilyn Zalcman and others have nurtured my heart or taught me about detail, encouraged, supported and challenged me. To all the people who participated in this production, particularly Edwina Welham, Margaret Renouf, Rita Cremona, Peter Keogh, Matthew Gilbert, Sarah Lermit, Lynda Townsend and Barbara Kulesza, my sincere appreciation. I have studied and still teach several other approaches to psychotherapy, but TA has a special place. This volume is a kind of culmination of my work in transactional analysis, honouring it as an integrative approach in its own right.

Sue Fish and the late child and adolescent psychiatrist, Dr Brian Dobson (who with Maria formed the core group of *metanoia* Psychotherapy Training Institute in London) have over many years made contributions of the mind and heart which I value every day I live. Without our generations of *metanoia* TA trainees (and curious delegates at international conferences) who kept asking the questions, I would not have believed that I could make a worthwhile contribution and this book would never have been attempted. Your curiosity and talent were its midwives. This is also true for all the many supervisors we have trained and supervised over the years. The way you delighted in learning, discovering and testing was my motivation. The manner in which you kept proving the material valuable and useful in your everyday psychotherapy practice, supervision and training, in discussion with colleagues and in your personal lives, provided me with the conviction which has seen me through some of the difficult times in bringing a major project like this to fruition. Your stories and those of your clients (with suitably disguised identities) represent not only your lives but more particularly your practice at many junctions in this work. Phil Lapworth, Ian Stewart, Charlotte Sills, Elana Leigh, Fran Lacey, Renee Walinets, Dr David Schofield, Jenny Mackewn, Katherine Murphy, among many others, made particular contributions.

Finally I would like to acknowledge that my greatest debt is to my own psychotherapy supervisees, supervisor trainees and clients who have been so 'patient' with me over all these years while I have learned and continue to learn from them about them, about me, about the human struggle and, no matter what the pain or the confusion, about the eternal recurrence of *Physis* in all our lives.

Chapter 1

Transactional analysis as an integrated approach to psychotherapy

Let knowledge grow from more to more,
  But more of reverence in us dwell;
  That mind and soul, according well,
May make one music as before.

(Alfred, Lord Tennyson, 1869)

Transactional analysis can be a multi-faceted system of psychotherapy. Berne's emphasis on the interactional aspect of communication is reflected in the name *transactional* analysis. He saw it as an extension to the in-depth emphasis of psychoanalysis with its singular focus on intrapsychic dynamics. Transactional analysis as a theory of psychotherapy, however, integrates intrapsychic dynamics with interpersonal behaviours in an innovative reactive manner within a humanistic/existential framework of values.

Eric Berne, the founder of transactional analysis, was born Eric Lennard Bernstein (1910–1970) – a Canadian-born psychiatrist who originally trained as a psychoanalyst at the New York Psychoanalytic Institute.

He wrote prolifically about transactional analysis in a creative and original style with enormous popular appeal. Many introductory and basic books on transactional analysis have sold millions. Along with Berne's wit, accessibility, humour and common sense, there is also a depth of wisdom and clinical experience that lends an impressive character to his written work. He made a genuine contribution to twentieth-century psychology which is often unacknowledged. However, his influence is manifested in the ubiquitous references, for example to 'the child' in the person, which have been absorbed into popular vocabulary and mainstream psychotherapy. TA terms often occur unacknowledged in Gestalt literature and in modern psychoanalytic works.

Since the 1950s transactional analysis psychotherapy has shown tremendous growth throughout the world. The International Transactional Analysis Association now has 8,000 members in 52 countries in the world. The major current focus in terms of numbers of trainees, organisational development and theory building has significantly shifted to Europe. With this drift, some of the New-World gloss has been rubbed off and TA has gained in philosophical richness and realism. Yet it has retained a vision of humankind's possibilities for good tempered by an acknowledgement of our capacity for evil and destruction.

Although popular and introductory texts have flourished, there has been a dearth of advanced texts to guide experienced psychotherapists or to reflect the depth of accumulated wisdom and clinical experience which can characterise transactional analysis as an integrated psychotherapy. This book is intended to begin to fill the gap and discuss TA at a level that assumes familiarity with the basic ideas as well as the basics of psychotherapy itself.

It is not intended to be another introductory manual, nor another cookbook of practical TA but, in response to the requests of trainees and colleagues, an advanced text for the practising, thinking, theoretically interested psychotherapist considering TA in context with other psychotherapeutic approaches.

THE PLACE OF TA IN PSYCHOTHERAPY

Transactional analysis psychotherapy finds its place in one of the major three streams of psychology which all originated around the turn of the twentieth century (see Table 1.1).

Freud's (1900) theory of psychoanalysis came to represent one major stream of psychological thinking and psychotherapy, with his first major work, *The Interpretation of Dreams*, being published in 1900. Freudian and Kleinian psychoanalytic thinking tends to view human beings as biologically determined and motivated primarily by sexual and aggressive drives (Klein, 1984/1957; Symington, 1986). For Freud (1973/1917) the purpose of psychoanalysis is exploration and understanding or 'insight', not necessarily change.

The second major group derives its theoretical lineage from Pavlov (1927), the Russian psychophysiologist who studied conditioned reflexes and other learning behaviours. Theoreticians and practitioners following in his footsteps are usually referred to as learning theorists, behaviour-modification specialists or, latterly, cognitive-behaviour therapists.

In 1962 Abraham Maslow coined the term 'third-force psychology' (p. iii) to distinguish the third grouping which did not originate from either the Freudian or Pavlovian tradition. This humanistic/existential tradition has as its intellectual and ideological grandfather the originator of psychodrama, Jacob Moreno. Moreno was arguably the first psychiatrist to put 'the patient' in a centrally responsible role in his own life drama and he worked to empower the patient to do his own healing. Moreno was applying group psychotherapy with children based on humanistic existential principles and writing about it by 1908 (Anderson, 1975).

Of course such divisions into different schools of thought are merely suggestive and are not meant to imply that individual practitioners necessarily exclusively or dogmatically adhere to rigid orientations. Indeed, skilled

Table 1.1 Summary of three schools in twentieth-century psychology

School of Therapy	Psychoanalytic	Behavioural	Humanistic/Existential
Founder	Freud	Pavlov	Moreno
Date when active	1893	1902	1900
Comments about philosophy, orientation and practice	Bio-psychological determinism. Analysand lying on couch. Therapist passive, makes interpretations from position of greater understanding. Centrality of transference	Behaviours seen as a result of learning and conditioning. Emphasis on experimental research and measurable variables. Stimulus/response chains	Centrality of responsibility. Non-interpretive concern with here-and-now. Psychotherapist as person plus transference in some approaches. Occasionally includes transpersonal. Dialogue and relationship
Application	Used particularly for neurotic illness, usually modified approach for other disorders	Used particularly for phobias and obsessive behaviours, also depression	Used for psychoses, personality disorders and neuroses, but also for growth and development
Motivation	Sexual and aggressive drives	Conditioned reflexes Biology	Biological, social and creative needs
Techniques	Free association, dream interpretation. Parapraxes, etc. Resistance and transference. Interpretation	Flooding Modelling Desensitisation Thought-stopping Role rehearsal	Wide and diverse Active Interventionist
Goal	Attaining of the depressive position (Hinshelwood, 1989) Insight	Adjustment	Self-realisation. All that you could be
Other workers	Klein (1949) Malan (1979) Anna Freud (1986) Fairbairn (1952) Federn (1977) Symington (1986)	Skinner (1953) Ellis (1962) Eysenck (1968) Lazarus (1981) Dryden (1984)	Rogers (1986) Perls et al. (1969) Maslow (1962) May (1969) Frankl (1969) Berne (1972) Rowan (1988)
Focus	Why?	What?	How?

clinicians (Erskine and Moursund, 1988) often integrate various approaches, but hopefully from within a clear conceptual and practical model. Indeed, research studies (Frank, 1982; Garfield, 1978; Malan, 1979; Parloff et al., 1978) show that client characteristics and the helping relationship are the crucial components in effective psychotherapy and not necessarily the choice of psychotherapy system. Neither empirical studies nor comprehensive reviews indicate that any one therapeutic approach used in isolation can be shown to be superior to another. Some 70 per cent of psychotherapists in the United States (Bergin and Lambert, 1978; Frank, 1979; Landman and Dawes, 1982; Luborsky *et al.*, 1975; Meltzoff and Kornreich, 1970; Sloane *et al.*, 1975; Smith *et al.*, 1980) are now identifying themselves as integrative or systematically eclectic. 'There appear to be well over a dozen different types of eclecticism referred to in the psychotherapy literature' (Dryden, 1984: 343). This trend is already beginning to show in Europe.

An integrated approach to transactional analysis psychotherapy draws on each of these three traditions. Berne originally used all three in a systematic, not haphazardly eclectic, fashion within a humanistic/existential value orientation.

THE PSYCHOANALYTIC HERITAGE – INTRAPSYCHE

From psychoanalysis, Berne drew his understanding of intrapsychic forces acting upon the person. His major works – *Transactional Analysis in Psychotherapy* (1980/1961); *Principles of Group Treatment* (1966); and *What Do You Say After You Say Hello?* (1972) – are only truly well understood given a sufficiently thorough grounding in psychoanalytic thinking. For Berne, through his background reading and training, an understanding of Freud (1973/1917), Klein (1984/1957) and Fairbairn (1952) was combined with the intrapsychic phenomenological interests of Federn (1977/1953) and the social-developmental emphases of Erikson (1950). He thus assumed in his writing familiarity with commonly known psychoanalytic, ego psychological and object-relations theories.

Federn (1977/1953) had extensively described the reality and permanence of ego states 'parts of the ego unit' (p.217) and their influence on decisions, involuntary behaviours and psychopathology. He identified the Adult ego state as potentially being the executive (most highly energised) with a primitive id at the core of the personality. Fairbairn (1952) had identified several *categories* of ego including 'Central ego', 'Libidinal ego', and 'Internal Saboteur' reminiscent of the somewhat later Berneian categorisation of ego states into Adult, Child, and Parent (1977). Heimann (quoted in Bollas, 1987) showed an awareness of these multiple presences when she asked who is this person (patient) speaking? 'At any one moment in a session a patient could be speaking with the voice of the mother, or the mood of the father, or some fragmented voice of a child self either lived or withheld from life' (p.305). Berne naturally focused on developing his more original neo-psychoanalytic contributions. Later readers, who may lack such background, may have missed some of this depth, settling instead for more superficial applications rather than a grounded understanding, contextualised in a similar idiom to that which the originator had used. Berne left much for his successors to spell out which he implicitly or sparsely indicated. Only gradually is this theoretical articulation being attempted.

Transactional analysis is none the less fundamentally a humanistic/existential psychotherapy by virtue of its primary emphasis on human freedom and autonomy. The centrality of responsibility as a philosophical notion with radically practical clinical applications is also characteristic of a third-force psychotherapy. The injudicious use of a misunderstood humanism has in the past led to humanistic psychology practices which have been criticised as superficially optimistic and also devoid of any serious attempt to deal with humankind's darker motivations. This is, however, a serious misinterpretation of both the spirit and the intent of Berne's work.

Most, if not all, of Berne's writing reflects his serious and prevailing preoccupation with the forces of death or destruction in individuals, groups, organisations and nations. What Freud (1961/1920) called the 'death instinct', Berne (1981/1969), like Federn (1977/1953), calls 'mortido'. (Weiss (1950) referred to the destructive force by the name of 'destrudo'.) There is no denial of our capacity for evil in the following statements from Berne:

> Every human being seems to have a small fascist in his head. This is derived from the deepest layers of the personality.... The small fascist in every human being is a little torturer who probes for and enjoys the weakness of his victims.... These primitive strivings became interwoven with the injunctions, precepts and permissions of the script (pre-consciously chosen life-plan) and form the basis for third-degree 'tissue' games that draw blood.... Some [people] even try to demonstrate their innocence by becoming the purposeful victims instead of the aggressors, on the principle that it is better to shed their own blood than that of others, but blood they must have.
>
> (Berne, 1972: 268–70)

The quotations are of some length to show that these are not the thoughts of a Pollyanna-minded optimist, but a doctor well versed in the nature and manifestations of *Thanatos* – the death instinct. Berne links our capacities for such evil to the perversion of mankind's earliest survival tasks, and strongly and unreservedly states their consequence:

> He who pretends that these forces do not exist becomes their victim. His whole script may be a project to demonstrate that he is free of them. But since he is most likely not, this is a denial of himself and therefore of his right to a self-chosen destiny.
>
> (Berne, 1972: 270).

Indeed, the whole body of Berne's work can be seen as a manifestation of his struggle to overcome what he had understood as 'mankind's inherent tendency to destructiveness' – the four horsemen of the Apocalypse (war or peace, famine or plenty, pestilence or health, death or life) (Berne, 1972).

Part of Berne's Freudian preoccupation with the death instinct was his fascination with the repetition compulsion. This was the term used by Freud to describe what he believed to be an innate tendency to revert to earlier conditions (Freud, 1961/1920). For Berne this became the central metaphor of life script – the notion that each person develops early in life a pre-conscious or pre-verbal life plan which they live out in a compulsive way, much as scenes and acts of a cast of characters progress towards a denouement in the stories of theatre and film. Berne defines script as a life plan developed in early childhood under parental influence which 'directs the individual's behaviour in the most import-ant aspects of his life' (Berne, 1972: 418).

Of course, different scripts are created at different developmental stages by children with different genetic predispositions, with different temperaments, and in response to different situations. This script is but an image, metaphor or tool to symbolic thinking and is not to be taken more literally than is useful. Berne viewed scripts as being potentially productive, destructive or banal. In all cases, even where individuals decide subconsciously on an apparently 'winning script', there is a lack of autonomous self-choice. As such the script militates against people's ability to take responsibility for themselves and thus ultimately for their own growth and wellbeing. As an existentialist, Berne was frequently at pains to point out that each child *decides* upon their script no matter how parental pressures or environmental factors may shape the circumstances of this choice. Some children in a family may choose to be psychotic, others may choose to become psychiatrists (Berne, 1972: 84, 95). By holding this conviction Berne was in good company. V. Frankl (1969) the existentialist psychiatrist survived Buchenwald and Dachau with the untarnished belief that even when people cannot choose their circumstances, they can choose their attitudes towards it.

Scripts therefore can be seen as an operationalised description of the untrans-formed death instinct in individual lives. Some authors like Cornell (1988) have drawn attention to the apparently reductionistic and deterministic aspects of the theory of scripts. In so far as it used to reflect psychoanalytical concepts alone, there is a measure of truth in this and he suggests that transactional analysts need significantly to challenge and broaden the current conceptualisation of script. However, Cornell in his article (1988), which is supposed to review script theory, omits a major classical Bernian drive concept and a crucial theoretical diagram which throws a whole different light on script and explains the indomitable belief in the possibility of change which is characteristic of most transactional analysts. The belief in the possibility of change is in contrast with many psychoanalysts who see the goal of psychoanalysis as insight not change (Freud, 1973/1917) or as resignation to the depressive position (Klein, 1984/1957) not necessarily creative actualisation (Maslow, 1962).

Cornell (1988) suggests that transactional analysts need significantly to challenge and broaden the current conceptualisation of script. This author suggests a rereading of Berne's original theories, which emphasise the auto-nomous aspiration of human beings to choose their destiny. These are indeed significantly his most neglected, yet most inspirational contributions (Clarkson, 1988c). This theme will be picked up again later in this chapter.

Berne accepted the other major force active in human destiny as 'libido' or *Eros* (1981/1969) – the desire for affectional closeness or emotional bonding which ranges from the earliest symbiotic attachment which fortunates receive from their earliest caretakers, to sexual intimacy, to a realisation of interconnectedness with the rest of the world (Clarkson, 1986a).

In his own life Berne, like other people of vision such as Freud, fell far short of his ideas and his ideals. Freud, the prime advocate of sexual consciousness, apparently relinquished sexual activity some thirty years before his death (1961/1920). Berne, the advocate of intimacy, in spite of several attempts, apparently never really succeeded in establishing a mutually satisfying close relationship (Jorgensen and Jorgensen, 1984). He posited intimacy as the major goal which most of us seek and 'games' as the major way in which people avoid the fear and risk and even possible satisfaction of our earliest and most urgent loving needs. This is very much in the spirit of Fairbairn (1952) who saw libidinal drives as derived from human needs for loving attachment rather than vice versa. In his discussion of Fairbairn's dissent from Freud, Symington (1986: 238) summarises it thus: 'What man seeks most deeply is emotional contact with his fellow human beings.... The fundamental trauma for the child is either that he or she is not loved or that his or her love is not received.'

In his discussion of child development Berne (1966: 265–80) had already adopted an object-relations approach, albeit with existentialist intent. Berne took from Klein (see Segal, 1986) the term 'position' to indicate an internal psychological condition, formed early in childhood and always potentially present in the personality, which also has a defensive function. This differed in emphasis from subsequent behavioural elaborations of the four basic life positions (Ernst, 1971).

The terms paranoid, depressive and schizoid are taken directly from Klein (1949), whose work we know Berne had read by 1966 since it is referenced in *Principles of Group Treatment* where he discusses them. He elaborated on these life positions in their *interpersonal* manifestation by characterising whether the self or the other is devalued. (Klein had incorporated the term 'schizoid' position from Fairbairn (1952: 8) and combined it with the paranoid position thus losing some of the differentiating power given to it by Fairbairn.)

Klein chose the word 'position' to emphasise a configuration of object relations, anxieties and defences which begin in infancy and persist throughout the rest of life, even if only as a potential mode of operation. Indeed these 'existential positions' *are* in transactional analysis the characteristic intrapsychic embodiments of the primal self–object, other–object relationship and as such permeate the quality of all the individual's relationships with significant others. The I–You transactional nature of human relationships is emphasised in the dyadic pairing of a statement about self (I) and a statement about the other (You). Transactional analysis thus provides the conceptual framework and practical tools for working with object relations as they are manifested in our interpersonal relationships and particularly in the psychotherapeutic relationship.

One of the special ways in which internal object relations are enacted in psychotherapy is in the relationship between the patient and the psychotherapist. Berne treated transference reactions as 'transactions', i.e. stimulus–response pairs. The patient offers a stimulus to the psychotherapist (generally based on their archaic childhood experiences) usually expecting the psychotherapist to react either in the same way as the original caretaker (self object) or in an idealised hope of receiving from the psychotherapist the care or structure, for example, which they did not receive in the original caretaking relationship. This transference reaction is one of the major cornerstones of psychoanalysis. 'The transference relationship is an essential part of the analytic procedure since the analysis consists in inviting the transference and gradually dissolving it by means of interpretation' (Laplanche and Pontalis, 1988/1973: 455).

Berne considered interpretation as one of the basic techniques in transactional analysis. He conceptualised interpretation as a 'crossed transaction' since the analyst or psychotherapist will avoid responding to the patient in a way that he or she is expected. 'Transactionally, this means that when the patient's Child attempts to provoke the therapist's Parent, it is confronted instead by the therapist's Adult. The therapeutic effect arises from the disconcertion caused by this crossed transaction' (Berne, 1980: 164). While the patient continues to act according to outdated patterns, the analyst's reaction conforms strictly to the actual therapeutic situation.

Countertransference is of course frequently present in transactional analysis as it is in most forms of psychotherapeutic relationships. This will be further discussed in Chapter 7. Transactional analysis has techniques and procedures for dealing with a great variety of transactions including the transferential type. However, the transference reaction or transferential therapeutic relationship is recognised, intentionally fostered and interpreted in treating *some patients* for the entire duration of their psychotherapy or for some parts thereof (Barr, 1987; Moiso, 1985). It is important to remember that the transferential relationship was emphasised in psychoanalysis but even with Freud himself it did not exclude other forms of therapeutic relating (Freud, 1912a: 105; Greenson, 1967: 389; Clarkson, 1990). Equally, exploration of the personality (especially hitherto unknown parts or hidden motivations), cognitive insight and intellectual under-standing are highly valued and fostered in transactional analysis.

According to Pine (1985) psychoanalysis has proceeded in three great waves – drive psychology, ego psychology and object-relations theory. Comparatively recent developments in psychoanalysis (Kohut, 1977; Kernberg, 1980) have also begun to pay attention to self psychology. Of course, attention to the self has been a feature of analytical psychology since Jung's earliest formulations in 1913 (1971: vi). As can be seen from the preceding discussion, transactional analysis grew from drive theory, particularly focused on ego psychology and is an attempt to place object relations in the interpersonal arena. The self also has a long, varied, and honoured place in transactional analysis. James and Savary (1977) in particular have recently further explored the concept of self. Chapter 8 uses the concept of self (primarily as used in transactional analysis) as a crucible for the development or renewal of theory, particularly in its relationship to Physis.

EXISTENTIAL PHENOMENOLOGY – HUMANISTIC VALUES

TA is a personality theory and system for understanding human behaviour. It provides a great many techniques for alleviating distress and promoting growth and self-awareness as well as methods for improving interpersonal relationships. Most importantly, it is centrally concerned with helping people change their lives in significant ways. Applications have ranged from educating youngsters in healthy ways of relating, to counselling those in life transition, to the psychotherapy of psychosis. (Schiff *et al.*, 1975).

TA places the client or 'patient' – choosing, self-determining and responsible – in the centre of the therapeutic process. For example, Berne was one of the first psychiatrists working in a state hospital who opened case conferences to patient observation and participation. His belief was if it cannot be said in front of the person concerned, it was probably not worth saying at all (Berne, 1966). The primary drives of human beings are seen as positive, striving towards health, growth and self-actualisation and appropriate social concern.

In TA clients are enabled to take responsibility for their lives and their progress in psychotherapy and counselling, although this does not absolve psychotherapists from their clinical responsibilities. The process of *how* the past distorts the here-and-now relationship with the psychotherapist or other people is the focus of the work with future goals explicitly validated. Berne (1966) wrote that the task of psychotherapy is to heal the past in the present in order to ensure the future. In transactional analysis people are generally seen as essentially capable, responsible, willing and able to use psychological information and learn about the psychotherapeutic process so that 'mystification' is actively discouraged. Since the intention is to make psychological – and emotional – health information available to clients, it has attempted to keep the language actually used in psychotherapy simple, colloquial and easy to understand. Berne was in tune with his time. The spirit of Berne compels an up-to-date language for psychotherapy. It may therefore require relinquishing some of the favourite but outdated terms of the past such as 'racket' and, for example, substituting for it 'intrapsychic analysis' (Zalcman, 1990: 16).

The psychotherapist using TA often engages in a person-to-person encounter with the client. TA values insight, provided it is accompanied by safe expressiveness of emotions and a close and harmonious relationship with the physical self or bodily ego. Psychotherapy is mobile, people move about. Touching is usually important although used with extreme discretion. Fortunately, some psychoanalysts are also now beginning to acknowledge that psychotherapists need to and do touch their patients and that they ignore the role of touch in psychotherapy 'at their peril' (Woodmansey, 1988). TA psychotherapy is often conducted in groups, although it is also frequently used in conjunction with or separately as individual psychotherapy.

Affective health or 'emotional literacy' (Steiner, 1984), psychophysiological emotional expressiveness (Goulding and Goulding, 1979) and catharsis of archaic repressed feelings (Childs-Gowell and Kinnaman, 1978) are, depending on the skill and personal experience of the psychotherapist, vitally important parts of theory and therapy in transactional analysis. Berne differentiated (in the writer's opinion more clearly than most other psychoanalytic authors) between genuine, authentic feelings and inauthentic feelings which he called 'rackets' (Berne, 1972: 139). These are those feelings (English, 1971, 1972) learnt and reinforced in early childhood, often substituting (subconsciously) for other feelings, which are used in a conditioned reflex manner to manipulate others (for example, an hysteric tantrum or a passive–aggressive sulk). An intrapsychic analysis of such feelings and their related phenomena will be used in Chapter 11.

Although originating in the idealism of the 1960s, theory, training and professional practices in TA are now gaining recognition and parity with other psychotherapeutic trainings throughout the world. As a caution against misunderstandings due to superficial exposure to TA the following anecdote may be illuminating. The man sitting next to Berne on a flight to New York asked him his name and occupation. Berne said: 'I am Eric Berne, a psychiatrist who has developed transactional analysis.' The man said, 'Oh, I know all about TA. It's I'm OK. You're OK!' Then Berne asked the man about himself. 'I'm a professor of astronomy' he said. And Berne replied, 'Oh, I know all about astronomy – it's twinkle, twinkle little star!' (Clarkson, 1986b).

Berne saw transactional analysis as a 'systematic phenomenology' which could usefully fill a gap in psychological theory (Berne, 1980/1961: 270–1). Phenomenology as a philosophical approach values the importance of the person's subjective experience above any interpretation, prejudgement or preconceived theories or ideas (Spinelli, 1989). Berne's phenomenology concerned the description of ego states as phenomena which people experience subjectively and which he personally and clinically observed and intuited. The hypnotherapist Watkins (1978) has also extensively documented the phenomenological reality of the ego states which Federn (1977) first elaborated. Ego states were not metaphors or hypothetical constructs for Berne or Federn but phenomenologically real phenomena, as will be discussed in greater detail in the next chapter.

Throughout his life, Berne never minimised the destructive potential of people as individuals and nations, but he also adhered to his belief in the person's inner drive to health and growth, which places him firmly in the humanistic tradition.

As already mentioned, Berne accepted the importance of the two major Freudian (and Federnian) drives, 'mortido' (the death instinct) and 'libido' (the sexual instinct). However, he added *Physis* (the force of nature), a general creative force which eternally strives to make things grow and to 'make growing things more perfect' (Berne, 1981/1969: 98).

Heraclitus held that the nature of life and existence is perpetual change itself. 'All things and the universe as a whole are in constant, ceaseless flux; nothing is, only change is real, all is a continuous passing away' (Runes, 1962: 124). *Physis*, then, was the 'workings' or 'mechanism' of that change. Change is spontaneous or at the very least originates internally within that which has changed. There must be the capability of and proclivity for change in that which changes. The Stoics saw all existence as part of the flux whose nature is change; we are born from it and re-enter upon death. Change as *Physis* comes spontaneously from within as part of a greater and general 'fire'.

Change *must* occur because change *is* life. *Physis*, then, is the all-powerful force for both physical growing and aging and mental/emotional change which is characterised as that which gives us life (our spirit so to speak). It has no *telos*, there is nothing normative about the concept, it is simply change as flux or state of being. The nature of the change that occurs is determined by outside circumstances and ourselves. The Stoics identified *Physis* with god and the active principle, while the Epicureans saw it as consisting of atoms and the void (Edwards, 1967).

Berne refers to *Physis* in his first major work *A Layman's Guide to Psychiatry and Psychoanalysis* (1981/1969), in *The Structure and Dynamics of Organisations and Groups* (1963) as well as in *What Do You Say After You Say Hello?* (1972), so it is one of his most enduring and unchanging core concepts accompanying all the developments of his theory and practice in transactional analysis.

Physis as a verb means 'to grow' or 'to be' – 'what things really are' (Edwards, 1967). The concept, developed by the pre-Socratic Heraclitus, originally meant 'change or growth which comes from the spirit within the person'.

In Aristotle:

'Nature' means: ... that iminent thing from which a growing thing first begins to grow.... The source from which the primary notion in every natural object is induced in that object as such.

(Metaphysics. 1014b 18: 19)

In other words, Aristotle perceives nature as being self-realising through its own activity. Spontaneous growth and action are self-activating. Further, he sees nature as the unconscious or conscious striving for perfection. 'Nature as a whole tends towards the good' (Phys. 230b 20, 198b 10–199b 34, 1970).

Twentieth century psychology since Freud has particularly emphasised the *unconscious* influences of Eros and Thanatos. In this process perhaps the person's unconscious (id based?) striving towards health, wholeness and creative evolution has been neglected (except by Jung, along with most humanistic psychologists).

Physis is Berne's unique addition to the other two great, unconscious forces (Eros and Thanatos) in human life, and he sees all three as the background of psychological life,

the growth force of nature, which makes organisms evolve into higher forms, embryos develop into adults, sick people get better, and healthy people strive to attain their ideals. Possibly it is only one aspect of inwardly directed libido, but it may be a more basic force than libido itself.

(Berne, 1981: 369–70)

The importance of *Physis* as a generalised creative drive towards health in TA is only equalled by its neglect in the theoretical literature since Berne. Perhaps unwittingly (and certainly without due acknowledgement since it has not been referenced by any other TA author this author has been able to trace) Berne stumbled on the mythical notion, comparable to Eros and Thanatos in evocative power and transformative potential, which could act as a unifying symbol for the whole of third-force psychology. *Physis* is nature, coming from the deepest biological roots of the human being and striving towards the greatest realisation of the good. Berne postulates that the autonomous aspiration of individual human beings rises from the depths of the somatic Child (oldest ego state) and transcends the limit-inducing downward pressures of the script which is shaped in the matrix of love and death in our earliest relationships. The script-matrix diagram (see Figure 1.1) showing the aspiration arrow has been, as far as the author is aware, omitted (excluded?) from the standardised international intro- duction to transactional analysis (also called the 101) and is nowhere listed as essential teaching nor has it ever yet been referenced. Yet it contains in schematic form the exact symbolic juxtaposition of predetermining forces predicated by attachment

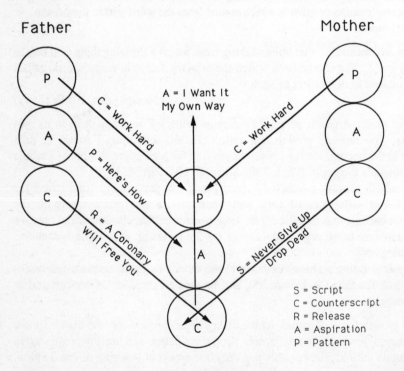

Figure 1.1 Script matrix showing aspiration arrow

Source: Berne, 1972: 128

(parental love) and despair (parental and existential restriction) counterbalanced by the primary, deeper (and higher), force for change and individual transformation as a natural process of human aspiration.

The script matrix is a simplified diagrammatic representation of the origin of the script messages/influences and prohibitions from the parents or significant others in the child's life showing in this example how mother and father influenced the person's script. S (Script) refers to the negative inhibiting messages from parents or other authorities, e.g. do not have satisfactory intimate relationships; C (Counterscript) refers to the precepts or positive instructions from significant others about how to live, e.g. work hard; R (Release) refers to an outside intervention or condition by which the individual is released from the script, e.g. a heart attack in a young stockbroker; A (Aspiration) refers to the individual's autonomous aspirations, e.g. the drive to health and intimacy; P (Pattern) refers to the modelling of significant others as to how to deal with life. The author postulates that the aspiration arrow represents the dynamic force of *Physis*.

Basic to TA theory and philosophy is Berne's image of the fundamental worth of the human being, for which his shorthand was 'OKness'. This concept embraces valuing and respecting human beings and is not to be confused with blanket approval of all of their behaviour. It is, however, predicated upon the assumption that the infant is born with the basic drive for health and growth fuelled by *Physis*, and a need for loving (libidinal) recognition.

Berne did not see a person's basic life position adopted in childhood as *necessarily* defensive or negative, as did Klein, nor did he agree with Klein's view of the person.

> In her descriptions of the early stages of the child's emotional life, Klein presents us with a portrait of a wicked infant in which she fails to show the connections between the infant's violent feelings (such as hate, envy or greed) and the unconscious of the parents, as well as the humiliation, mistreatment and narcissistic wounds the latter inflict on the child.
>
> (Miller, 1985: 60)

Berne identified the three not-OK, or potentially limiting, if not destructive, basic positions as paranoid (I'm OK – You're not OK), depressive (I'm not OK – You're OK) and schizoid (I'm not OK – You're not OK). Berne also emphasised the decisional nature of these positions predicated on the child's basic OKness (Clarkson, 1988a). Elaboration and revision is vitally important theoretically, clinically and philosophically since it allows for a position of health and value where both self and others are respected. Berne also emphasised the existentially chosen nature of these characteristic life positions. Since children choose a life position, they can later change that decision about the expected pattern of their self-object relations in life. Symington, a modern psychoanalyst, suggests a similar move: the need to move to what can be termed the 'tragic position', the existential realisation that we all – children, parents and healers alike – share *la condition humaine* (1986). This is surely the true ground of the 'I'm OK – You're OK' basic existential life position, and is what this author understands by it.

One's neighbour is loved as oneself, neither better, nor worse, but both are loved (affirmed to have worth). Berne's unique contribution was the addition of life position number one, I'm OK – You're OK. He regarded this position as intrinsically constructive and existentially possible. It is not intended to deny our capacity for destruction, but to affirm our capacity for transcendence. In this way Berne envisaged the nature of the person as having an inborn potential, available from birth, for fulfilment and self-actualisation. Transactional analysts believe that it is possible to maintain an existential position of OKness, valuing self *and* others in the existential knowledge of our tragic 'thrownness' in the universe (Heidegger, 1949).

The spirit of mutuality or 'equal worth' in transactional analysis is further exemplified in another modality of psychotherapeutic relationship in addition to the transference relationship. The additional dimension which its humanistic legacy brings to TA is that of the person-to-person relationship. This is characterised by an I–You quality to the existential encounter between the two people since the psychotherapist is seen (not outside the patient's field of vision, or behind the couch, for example). Therefore the real person of the psychotherapist is valued in so far as the psychotherapist's presence contributes to 'the moment of real meeting'. Of course, this does not include transforming the professional relationship into a social one. Nor does this mean that the psychotherapist seeks personal gratification from the dialogue with the patient. It resembles the person-to-person, I–You relationship which has arguably been overemphasised in some approaches to Gestalt psychotherapy, and perhaps it has been underemphasised in psychoanalysis, although several psychoanalysts have stressed the importance of the personal realness of the psychotherapist and the analyst's ability and willingness to become emotionally involved with and committed to the patient (Boss, 1979; Fairbairn, 1952; Archambeau, 1979; Greenson, 1967; and particularly Greenacre, 1959; Stone, 1961).

INTERPERSONAL FIELD – LEARNING AND REINFORCEMENT

Berne was deeply impressed by the importance of the role played by learning and reinforcement in maintaining the script. He isolated what he described as the smallest unit of human recognition and called it a 'stroke'. The fact that this word (in the Berneian sense of the term) has since been included in several major English-language dictionaries indicates how widespread its use has become amongst lay people. Identifying a primary need or motivation of human beings as a hunger for such strokes (or stimulation) has become a cornerstone in the explanation of the development and maintenance of human behaviour. Several studies (e.g. Hobbs, 1968) have shown that clients tend to adapt to the behaviours reinforced by psychotherapists. This may be out of awareness, since many psychotherapists would like to believe that they are not engaging in reinforcement schedules with their clients. Yet knowledge of the processes of projective identification or degrees of trance induction ubiquitous in everyday life as well as clinical situations, should encourage us in some very serious questioning of assumptions (Conway and Clarkson, 1987; Watkins, 1954; Casement, 1985). To the extent that such processes are out of awareness they may be destructive; if used consciously they can provide good information and facilitate therapy. Studies show that clients will tend to reproduce the behaviours which psychotherapists expect (Landfield, 1971; Beutler *et al.*, 1977). For example, the 'Mm hm' of the Rogerian therapist, in response to expressions of affect, apparently tends to increase such behaviour in the client. It is common clinical lore that the patients of Freudians tend to have Freudian dreams and Jungian analysands tend to have Jungian dreams. Transactional analysts seek to become aware of when and how they are stroking or reinforcing healthy or unhealthy behaviours and they also pay special attention to how individual stroking patterns can undermine or promote autonomous aspiration.

The biological and social importance of stroking is well supported in the literature. In a study of foundling-home infants carried out by Spitz (1945), it was shown that babies being cared for in an hygienically isolated environment – with one nurse assigned to every eight infants – showed profound physical and psychological retardation by the end of the first year of life. These babies, who had been separated from their prison-inmate mothers at age 4 months (i.e. before they were capable of establishing a love bond) were unable to sit or stand, cried frequently, never smiled and had no beginnings of speech. They were apathetic and unresponsive, caught infections easily and had a high mortality rate. This syndrome of marasmus, which can be described as death through lack of stroking, used to occur quite frequently in foundling homes where there was an absence of personalised attention.

In TA people sometimes speak of 'the spinal cord shrivelling up' and in fact there are several animal studies to support at least an analogous process. Melzack (1965) and Riesen (1965) have shown how sensory neural fibres atrophy and cannot be regenerated by subsequent stimulation if there is a significant lack in early infancy.

It is notable throughout the literature that the *kind* of stimulation necessary for healthy growth is secondary to its provision. Almost any means of stimulation, e.g. stroking, tossing, shaking or shocking, will provide the necessary stimulation for neural development, and retardation of development, often irreversible, is the almost inevitable result of neglect and stroke deprivation, as shown in animal studies.

The studies by Harlow and associates (e.g. Harlow and Harlow, 1962) of infant monkeys separated from their mothers several hours after birth and provided with cloth-covered non-feeding mother surrogates as well as wire mother surrogates who did provide food, demonstrated most movingly the need in these mammals for contact–comfort. It is likely that this same need for contact–comfort exists among other mammalian infants including human babies and lack of this interferes with the normal developmental sequence as well as later resistance to stress. Although extrapolation from animal studies to human conditions is often dubious, the fact that 'gentled' rats survive surgery better than rats which had not been handled may indicate that early stroking prepares the physiological system to cope more effectively with stress-provoking situations (Levine, 1960).

Although human studies cannot be as well controlled as those with animals, various researchers have documented retardation and serious developmental trauma related to lack of early stimulation, even where all other conditions were favourable. For example, Provence and Lipton (1962) studied babies living in institutions where they were well fed, adequately protected and their physical needs cared for, but they also showed retardation in development of vocalisation and language development. Although the differences were not as dramatic as in the marasmus studies, it was clearly shown that lack of human interaction and touching leads to progressively more serious developmental handicaps, depression and listlessness in 1-year-olds.

Schaffer (1965) found that 11- to 14-week-old infants in a baby home with a high degree of measured social stimulation showed no developmental retardation, whereas those in a hospital with a low degree of stimulation were cognitively and socially retarded. In both cases the children were admitted for only short periods and following discharge the developmental quotients in the two groups were compared. This showed that the retardation was a function of the institution and not the type of children admitted.

Goldfarb (1943a, b) compared children from a highly institutionalised nursery with a group placed in foster homes and, using a battery of tests, came to the conclusion that the well-cared-for children who were not in interaction with adults were severely handicapped when compared with the children from foster homes in terms of social-attachment behaviour, capacity for human relationships, use of visual and auditory functions, energy levels and dominant affective mood.

All these studies support the primacy of sensory stimulation as a biological necessity. Some can be used to demonstrate why even 'negative' stroking, such as beatings or criticism, is preferable to the organism than no stimulation. For example, in Harlow and Harlow's (1962) later studies, noxious air blasts were vented from the 'preferred terry-cloth mother' after the primary bond of attachment (between the infant monkey and its other-object swathed in terry cloth) was established. Following the infliction of this pain, the infant monkey clung even more tightly to his 'punishing' terry-cloth mother. Not surprisingly, humans, too, tend to prefer sensory stimulation, however negative and painful, to stimulus deprivation. Several clients have reported 'It was better when he slapped – at least I felt I existed for him after months of being ignored.' For most, even a blazing row is preferable to being 'sent to Coventry'. Even hardened criminals may endure all manner of physical punishment in preference to the punishment of solitary confinement. Here is some echo of clinical situations where destructive relationships are embraced (and sustained against all reason some-times) to avoid a fantasised vacuum of stroking.

Transactional analysts will be familiar with learning theory, including the effects of conditioning, reciprocal inhibition and systematic desensitisation, and use these in a way which is compatible with awareness, ethics and the stated contractual outcome of treatment. So, the principles of classical and operant conditioning (reinforcement, extinction, punishment, shaping, chaining, stimulus control, modelling and behavioural rehearsal) are incorporated according to the skill level of the psychotherapist. In addition transactional analysis has borrowed quite extensively, and often without due acknowledgement, from rational emotive therapy. Since the early 1950s in New York, RET has emphasised how irrational beliefs, about self, others and the world, affect activity in relation to problems, behavioural skills and the availability of options and choice and how these interact in psychopathology. Like rational emotive therapy (Dryden, 1984; 1987) transactional analysis sees the behaviour, the emotions and the thinking of individual people as a unified whole which can be discussed separately from one another for theoretical purposes, but are an indivisible unity in clinical practice.

One very important way in which psychological disturbance is induced is through the stroke exchange which happens in transactions. Berne defined a 'transaction' as the smallest unit of human *communication* consisting of a stimulus and a response. He isolated complementary and crossed transactions, but placed particular emphasis on the importance of covert or implicit concomitant of communication.

The importance of the ulterior or psychological level of communication is a cornerstone of transactional analysis in general and game and script theory in particular. This level is particularly useful in explaining the psychological level of communication in games, which precedes the role switch (and payoff), and the potential transmission of the most lethal or life-limiting script messages – the injunctions. According to Berne's (1980/1961) third rule of communication (Woollams and Brown, 1979), the outcome of a communication is determined at the psychological level. This can also be referred to as the *process* of the communication, or the 'music' of psychological-level communication (such as body language) from the 'words' of the actual social level context. In rearing children, for example, it is likely that the impact of the unspoken, non-verbal, ulterior message conveyed by a mother tensing and withdrawing when her child touches her will outweigh the overt, spoken message 'I love you, darling.' Of course, much of this happens outside of awareness.

Such temporary, occasionally quite brief, changes of 'consciousness' occur in other people who may find themselves invited, often quite powerfully, to provide the reinforcing experience which fits the sender's script. This mechanism may be best understood (Conway and Clarkson, 1987) in terms of hypnotic induction, an altered state of Adult awareness (or alternatively projective identification). In this book the term hypnosis (or trance induction) is used to mean an altered state of consciousness consisting of the temporary or intermittent loss of contact with the current consensually defined reality. (It can also be understood as a temporary decommissioning of the Adult which results in the event or material becoming 'unconscious'.)

This is a process by which the sender may, out of her or his own awareness, influence or invite behaviour that creates or reinforces life-limiting transactions and injunctions. Examples of this process include the way people may unerringly choose a partner who will respond to them or reject them just like Daddy did, or acquire bosses who berate them, even in those cases where the boss does not usually behave in such a way with other employees. Sometimes it seems as if we can 'make' people do things without their conscious awareness or consent. This is similar to the dynamics of projective identification in its interpersonal aspect.

According to *The Dictionary of Kleinian Thought*: 'In this formulation the term covers a complex clinical event of an interpersonal type: one person disowns his feelings and manipulatively *induces* [my emphasis] the other into experiencing them, with consequent visible changes in the behaviour of both' (Ogden, 1982 in Hinshelwood, 1989: 200).

If the patient projects anger onto the psychotherapist (as in Kernberg's example of 1980) and then experiences and accuses the therapist continuously as angry or attacking, he or she is attempting to invite the psychotherapist into behaving in an angry or attacking manner. If the therapist responds in the 'induced' way, a game or repetitive negative pattern plays out in the psychotherapy, often echoing the patient's childhood experiences. On the other hand, if psychotherapists use such countertransferentially 'induced' feelings as objective information potentially to be used effectively in the psychotherapy, it becomes beneficial reactive counter-transference. This will be further discussed and distinguished from other thera-peutically distorting psychotherapist feelings (countertransferential responses) stemming from the psychotherapist's own script, in Chapter 7.

It is suggested that the naturally occurring hypnotic mechanism by which this occurs (or by which Berne's third rule of communication operates) may be directly comparable to hypnotic-trance induction methods which are formally taught. It is postulated that these 'inductions' may occur naturally in the field of human behaviour, in or outside psychotherapy, with people 'entrancing' each other temporarily (either losing Adult awareness, or significantly reducing Adult processing ability) and getting 'pulled into' other people's script dramas. The notion of Adult is similar to that of Federn's formulation, 'integrated personality therefore means maintenance of control not only of the particular ego reactions but also of different ego states' (Berne, 1977: 218).

Additional instruction or continuing reinforcement of earlier injunctions may be given out or received in everyday situations as people affect each others' 'current realities'. It is hypothesised that hypnotic induction of this kind is the major method of script transmission (Steiner, 1975). In addition, it is speculated that taught techniques of 'how to hypnotise' are subconsciously derived from naturally occurring hypnotic inductions, which may be a regular feature of many of our interpersonal relationships (Conway and Clarkson, 1987).

There is support for this idea in Laing's work:

Hypnosis may be an experimental model of a naturally occurring phenomenon in many families. In the family situation however, the hypnotists (the parents) are already hypnotised (by their parents) and are carrying out their instructions ... by bringing their children up to bring their children up ... in such a way, which includes not realising that one is carrying out instructions – since one instruction is not to think that one is thus instructed. This state is easily induced under hypnosis.

(Laing, 1969: 79)

Under certain circumstances, the Adult ego state may become temporarily decommissioned, partially or completely. The conditions that have been identified (Conway and Clarkson, 1987) are: shock, pain, deliriousness, psychological 'double-binds', stimulus overload, sudden unexpected situations, self-discounting and hypnotist charisma. This phenomenon, a loss of Adult awareness, is equivalent to a spontaneously (or naturally) occurring hypnotic state. Information received by the individual in this state will not be efficiently processed by the Adult within the current reality, and may have the power of hypnotic command.

In natural everyday situations hypnotic inductions are occurring outside the awareness and consciousness of either person. This may be an important explanation of the phenomenological (or subjective) experience of people who 'find themselves' fulfilling the required role in someone else's script drama. This effect occurs frequently in everyday transactions. For example, a wife asks her husband to be particularly loving and considerate that day. Subsequently, in fulfilment of her script expectations, she gives him a number of 'hypnotic' instructions to reject her: for example, her voice becomes whiney, she implies that he would probably rather be with someone else, etc. This takes place outside the Adult awareness of both of them. The husband ends up unconsciously behaving in an unpleasant and hostile way towards his wife. Afterwards he may feel that he 'was not really himself'. The scripted transaction of rejection has been reinforced for both of them.

In formal hypnotic inductions one person is aiding another who has usually voluntarily sought aid or understanding from a trained and hopefully ethical practitioner. In the clinical setting these mechanisms may be used by therapists often outside of awareness and frequently without understanding the nature of the hypnotic phenomena involved. Further elaboration of this use of hypnotic induction in the theory and practice of psychotherapy appears to be indicated. Understanding these induction patterns may also help us become more effective in our therapeutic work of 'dehypnotising' our clients from the limitations and restrictions to which they have decisionally acceded as youngsters. 'The clinical hypnotist knows what he is doing, the family hypnotist almost never' (Laing, 1969: 71).

The interpersonal field clearly involves the working alliance between the psychotherapist and client. Transactional analysis considers the working alliance, or the contract, between psychotherapist and client as one of the most distinguish-ing features of this approach. It is usually referred to as an Adult-to-Adult contract to emphasise the responsibility of both client and psychotherapist to be clear about the changes that the client wishes to make and how the psychotherap-ist will effect this. Berne defined this as 'an explicit ... bilateral commitment to a well-defined course of action' (1966: 362). The contract is an operational description of the responsibilities of both client and therapist. Working contractually maximises individual responsibility for the outcome of the psycho-therapy and thus combines the existential principle of individual freedom with a behavioural practice of goal setting and feedback.

Transactional analysis therefore embraces major theories, concepts and techniques derived from all three of the main streams of psychology this century. An integrated practice will reflect elements of intrapsychic restructuring of personality, interpersonal communication in reinforcement systems and the interface between these two.

Transactional analysis since Berne has gone through a period where divisions into 'schools' became more important than theory-building or clinical excel-lence. An integrated approach to TA, as propounded in this book, is intended to avoid the vagaries of ideological conflicts or personal loyalties and to focus instead on a systematic recombination of good transactional analysis psycho-therapy within a theoretical system consistent with classical Berne.

According to this writer's integrated perspective, psychophysiological distur-bance can happen in at least three major ways: (a) through affective and cognitive interference in the functioning of the integrated ego (confusion model); (b) through the existence of internal conflict between different parts of the ego (conflict model); (c) through developmental deficits and inadequate parenting (deficit model) for extended periods at the time of trauma. There can be no absolute dividing line between using any of the three as the primary theoretical ground for an intervention; they obviously merge and overlap. However, at any one time maximum theoretical leverage may be derived from whichever one the therapist is using as 'figure' or focus.

In the *confusion model*, psychological health can be structurally defined as the strengthening of integrated Adult functioning. This closely accords with classical Berne. The efficiency of the Adult ego state is dependent on the quality of its information and problem-solving abilities as these are integrated into the personality. The concept of *contamination* describes the way in which effective Adult functioning is impeded by the scripting process. Contaminations can occur when Parent ego states intrude upon the Adult (e.g. prejudices) or when the Child ego states intrude upon the Adult (e.g. phobias). The notion of contamination is very similar to the RET idea of irrational beliefs (Dryden, 1987) and will be further explained in Chapter 5. 'The contaminations are not subtracted from the Adult, but peeled off, as it were. It is metaphorically like scraping the barnacles off a ship so that sailing is less clumsy afterward' (Berne, 1980: 49).

The following example focuses on decontamination in clinical practice, and integrates the other models as well, in order to illustrate how the confusion model provides the theoretical basis and treatment priority in this case. The client believed that he was evil and this self-concept incorporated from his parents and the church during early childhood coloured his entire life. In an attempt to overcome this 'evil' inherent in him, he became a doctor working 80 hours per week, never delegating tasks and rarely doing anything so 'bad' as to take time off for himself. During the course of psychotherapy he continued to blame himself, and held an irrational belief that even in fantasy, his mother needed to be protected in this way.

This is an extract from a psychotherapy session where the client is in symbolic dialogue with his mother. It shows the psychotherapist facilitating his process until he realises in Adult that he no longer needs to believe the notion that he is evil. This is accompanied by the insight that this belief originated from his mother and her own efforts to control herself.

(*C* = Client; *P* = Psychotherapist)

C: Don't want it, you can have it.
P: You're going to talk back to her?
C: It's your ... actually wait now if I think, all that evil that you're wanting me to control is actually not my evil at all, is it? It's yours. You put it, you said I had it. But if you're wrong and I am not bad, then I don't have to be responsible for any of that evil – it's all your idea and the nuns and the church and all these other bodies who say you're evil. So you're the one who can feel guilty, I don't have to feel guilty about you not controlling my evil, that's your problem.
P: Or, you not controlling your evil ...
C: Well that's right. That's your evil too. I don't have to control your evil. It's sad and I'm very sad about your evil things, I don't believe they were evil, but if you want to believe they were evil, that's your problem.
P: Tell her that you don't think she was evil to get cross with her little sister.
C: I don't think you were evil to get cross with your little sister at all. I think you were a perfectly normal, ordinary, everyday 2-year-old child who doesn't want to have a baby sister. I think you were a perfectly normal child.
P: But because you felt guilty about that and ashamed, I'll continue to feel guilty and ashamed for the rest of my life.
C: No I don't think I'm going to do that, because that's your stuff, not mine.
P: Are you willing to give it back to her?
C: Yeah, or am I? Hmm. I would like to be able to give it back to you.
P: You are able, are you willing?
C: Something is coming up which says that it would be wicked and evil to give it to a poor lady of eighty something – that's yours, not mine.
P: Tell her.

C: You're putting some kind of feeling into me now, which says you mustn't give it back because I'm a poor old lady of eighty something and I've got enough trouble.

P: And now you're not putting that feeling into me, Mum, I'm putting it in myself.

C: Yeah, and I don't actually want it.

P: Hm.

C: Maybe I can just live with that feeling. That doesn't solve anything, that just puts me back being bad. Hell, augh! It's your evil. You're the one who thinks that I am full of evil, I don't think I'm full of evil. You're the one who wants to knock it out and control it and so on, so you have it and you take charge of it and you control it and what you do with your own evil, I don't think I'm bothered about. All this evil that I'm supposed to be having is not mine at all.

P: Tell her that.

C: It's yours. It's in your head all this evil. I don't believe that I was born bad and evil and covered in sin. I simply do not believe it and I don't care what churches or popes or anything else say. And churches and popes haven't personally told me – you're the one, and all those people who you chose to bring me up, they're the ones who told me about all this evil that I'm supposed to be having. And you're the one who's put up all these controls to control it and if you want to control it, you control it.

P: The one you're trying to control is yourself, it's not me.

C: I can be in control of myself.

P: How old are you?

C: How old am I?

P: Hm.

C: Now?

P: Hm.

C: I'm 54 and I control my own evil. I'm not evil! I actually don't have evil impulses to control! I have nasty, human failings like everybody, but they're not evil. I don't have evil feelings in me!

In terms of Berne's original phenomenological model of ego states developed from Federn (1977/1953), the psychotherapeutic goal is the achievement of an integrated Adult ego state without interference from such archaic personal experiences or unintegrated ego states borrowed from significant others in – in this client's case, his mother's.

The conflict model is best represented by the impasse theory of redecision therapy (Goulding and Goulding, 1979) in TA. Psychological disturbance is usually conceptualised in terms of intrapsychic 'stuck points' between different ego states. For example, Parent or influencing ego states may be 'driving' (influencing) the person to please others and be subservient to their needs, while the Child needs to play more and express their own needs and feelings. If the early decision in the Child ego state has involved shutting down on the expression of feelings, then a conflict or 'impasse' will arise when such a person starts wanting to assert herself, for example in an abusive marital relationship. Health represents the ability to resolve such impasses within the personality and function smoothly without blocking needs, values or emotions.

The clinical example that follows has been included to demonstrate how the conflict model can be used in guiding treatment design and interventions, although it also contains elements of contamination and deficit, as would be expected in practice.

(*C* = Client; *P* = Psychotherapist)

C: I don't want women. Don't want them any more. They wouldn't … they wouldn't come when I wanted them so I don't want them now. When I wanted them they didn't come, ever.

P: Who was it you wanted to come so badly? (pause) Was it your mother?

C: Mm – yes.

P: So look at Mum now (symbolically placed on a cushion in front of him) and tell her. Tell her what it is you've decided about women because she didn't come.

C: That I don't want them now – I can do without them now.

P: So look at her and tell her that – Mum, I've decided that …

C: I can do without them now and serves you right. Teach you – I'll teach you.

P: I'll teach you.

C: It serves you right. It serves you right. This is what you made me do.

P: No, she didn't make you do it. This is what you decided to do because she didn't come when you wanted her. Tell her how angry you are.

C: I think it's your fault that I'm like this now.

P: Tell her how you are feeling.

C: I'm hurt – pained. (coughing/choking/groaning) I feel hate that you left me so long. I'll make you feel bad too.

P: So tell her how you are doing that. Tell her how you are doing that in 1988 – how you are making her feel bad in 1988.

C: By not wanting her or them or anyone else.

P: So in 1988, Mum, I am making you feel bad still by not wanting you or any other women.

C: No I can manage on my own – I don't need anyone now.

P: What I've decided is – I've decided to manage on my own without anyone now.

C: (Groaning) I won't ask for anyone now – I won't ask for anybody. No, I won't even ask anyone any more or ask anyone for anything any more.

P: What are you going to do then instead?

C: I'll stay on my own and be lonely as long as I live.

P: Well, you can carry on like that forever – as long as you live – or you can decide differently.

C: (coughs/groans)

P: So what are you going to do – are you going to change that decision or are you going to keep that one?

C: I must change it.

P: You don't 'must' change it – you want to change it or you want to keep it until you die.

C: It's too painful to stay like this – just like this. There's too much time ahead.

P: So what are you going to decide?

C: To get the loving that I want.

P: So look at Mum and tell her that.

C: I'm going to get the loving that I want.

P: Say it again.

C: I am going to get the loving that I want.

P: And again.

C: Yes, I do need other people. I do need loving. I am going to get the loving that I want.

In both the confusion and the conflict model in transactional analysis the major forms of therapeutic relationship to be used are the working alliance, the transference relationship and the person-to-person relationship. A particular contribution of the so called cathexis (or Schiffian) (Schiff *et al.*, 1975) school is the provision of a reparenting relationship, although most effective therapy in practice probably incorporates some aspects of providing for clients that which they did not receive as children at times of crisis in their lives. In *such a developmental deficit model*, psychological disturbance is conceptualised as resulting from inadequate, pathological or neglectful parenting at critical developmental stages or at the time of trauma in the child's life. For example, the children of alcoholics may need the corrective experience of a relationship where consistency of response is provided in the context of a reparative therapeutic relationship. Or, as Kohut (1977) has so eloquently shown, people with narcissistic personality disorders have often lacked the mirroring or reflecting essential for a healthy sense of self – this can be supplied in the therapeutic relationship.

The clinical vignette of integrative TA practice given next includes a significant parenting experience for illustration.

C: No, no, I just want to stop being scared.

P: My experience is that when people are scared, they need help. Is this what you did when you were little and scared? You tried to talk yourself into not being scared, all on your own?

C: I am feeling very confused.

P: Very confused and very scared.

C: One minute I want to feel, then if I feel I don't want to feel.

P: Let yourself feel your scare. Let yourself feel right now.

C: I hear what you are saying, but I just have this tremendous knot in my stomach.

P: Um.

C: (sighs and starts to agitate)

P: We have time, what would the knot be saying to you?

C: I think that's the problem, a lot of it doesn't speak.

P: It's that little it doesn't speak?

C: Um, I don't know what it wants.

P: Um, what would you do with a little child that was that frightened, that had no words, what would you do?

C: Just hold on.

P: Just hold on? Do you think that that's what you wanted when you were that frightened and there were no words?

C: Yeah, I think I wanted to be held a lot more than I was.

P: Um. This may be you as a very tiny little baby with no words.

C: Yeah, yeah, cause my mother often said I didn't cry.

P: You didn't cry?

C: And she was hurting too much to hold me.

P: Oh!

C: Cause her hands hurt.

P: What was the matter with her hands?

C: The arthritis.

P: So she couldn't hold you?

C: No, she couldn't. I think I lay there a lot. I lay just like this. (she begins to tremble and writhe trying to avoid her pain)

P: It's OK, my hands are perfectly fine, see. (she cries and wriggles. The psychotherapist holds her) You make a noise now.

C: (She cries and wants to cover her face)

P: Take your hands away now, hold me, hold my hands.

C: I was too scared to cry.

P: Too scared to cry. (the psychotherapist breathes deeply to model life)

C: (breathes deeply)

P: That must have been terrible, what a terrible, terrible thing to have happened.

C: I don't know why I was scared though.

P: You don't know why you were scared? I think it must be frightening for a baby to lie there and not cry, because there is a mother who is incompetent and can't hold her. Imagine your whole world is your mother, and this person who you must rely on for everything can't hold you. Can you imagine how frightening that must be? Um ... you don't have a base in your life.

C: Um.

P: Um? Can you understand now how you were so frightened?

C: Yeah, it certainly explains why I can't get enough of being touched.

In radical reparenting, such as developed by Schiff (1969), schizophrenics have the opportunity to regress and then to move through important childhood developmental stages while introjecting a new Parent ego state. As a result of this process the healthy person has at his/her disposal a supportive and challenging set of guiding values which he/she has autonomously integrated as the end result of good parenting. As will be shown in a later chapter it is also possible to provide fragments of 'parenting' and this is probably an important part of many effective psychotherapies. Psychoanalysts such as Ferenczi (1980), Sechehaye (1951) and Miller (1985) have found patients, times and places where they have provided developmentally needed experiences as will be discussed in the last chapter.

> That Sechehaye was far more involved personally than ever the most humanistic of therapists usually are we can infer from the accounts of how she gave instructions for her meals, saw to her baths, and in general played for Renee the nourishing mother that she had been denied as an infant. That this took an emotional toll far beyond the ordinary is evident from Renee's own account that 'Mama was extremely upset' or that she regained consciousness and found Mama weeping over her.
>
> (Friedman, 1985: 188)

In an integrated perspective on transactional analysis, these three different theoretical emphases (confusion, conflict and developmental deficit) will be systematically utilised in a coherent and unified approach to individualised treatment design. Finally in transactional analysis, as in Jungian analysis, there is an acknowledgement of the transpersonal relationship between the patient and the psychotherapist (James and Savary, 1977) which is not only healing for the client but transforming for the psychotherapist. Berne was very conscious that doctors may treat, but it is God who cures, as quoted by him: '*Je le pensay, & Dieu le guarit*' (1966). This relationship dimension of psychotherapy is difficult to describe since it is rare and much of the ordinary vocabulary of psychology falls short in articulating the nature of its presence in the therapeutic relationship. At times reference will be made to it explicitly; always it is implicit in the healing relationship.

Chapter 2

Change, 'cure' or adjustment

After a time of decay comes the turning point. The powerful light that has been banished returns. There is movement, but it is not brought about by force. The ... movement is natural, arising spontaneously. For this reason the transformation of the old becomes easy. The old is discarded and the new is introduced. Both measures accord with the time; therefore no harm results.

(Wilhelm, 1988/1951: 97)

One of the central tenets of transactional analysis is that people with psychiatric difficulties can be cured.

This means not just the mildly neurotic, but the drug abuser, the severely depressed, the 'schizophrenic', everyone with a functional psychiatric disorder .... The notion that psychiatrists could in fact 'cure' the severe emotional disturbances of the people they work with was as radical and stunning a notion as has ever been introduced ....

(Steiner, 1975: 7).

Berne saw script analysis (along with ego-state analysis, transactional analysis proper and game analysis) as the primary avenue for curing people. According to him:

Each person decides in early childhood how he will live and how he will die, and that plan, which he carries in his head wherever he goes, is called his script. His trivial behaviour may be decided by reason, but his important decisions are already made: what kind of person he will marry, how many children he will have, what kind of bed he will die in, and who will be there when he does. It may not be what he wants, but it is what he wants to be.

(Berne, 1972: 36)

Newcomers to TA often find some difficulty with this apparent contradiction between the high predictability of script outcomes and our belief in and experience of major life and personality changes. 'For the transactional script analyst, as for the play analyst, this means that if you know the plot and the character, you know what his outcome will be, unless some changes can be made' (Berne, 1972: 36).

Transactional analysis, as a fundamentally existential approach to human psychology, emphasises that our scripts were constructed by our own choice and can be restructured or abandoned by our own choosing. It is precisely *because* life scripts are so predictable that they can be brought into awareness and redecided, which makes change truly possible. The Gouldings (1979) in particular have emphasised the transformative effect of such redecisions in their book *Changing Lives Through Redecision Therapy*.

However, knowing when or if a life-script change or redecision in therapy is indeed 'script cure' has intrigued and puzzled many authors, as witness a whole issue of the *Transactional Analysis Journal* (April, 1980) devoted to the subject.

In his last public address Berne (1971: 12) said that there was only one paper to write which is called 'How to cure patients'. He might have also been interested in this chapter, which hopes to differentiate real 'cure' as he meant it, from other imposters, jokers, tricksters and clowns which masquerade as 'cure' on the psychotherapeutic stage. Five types of change are now discussed.

CURE

Berne was interested in the kind of cure which meant that people could break out of their scripts entirely and 'put his own show on the road with new characters, new roles, and a new plot and payoff. Such a script cure, which changes his character and his destiny, is also a clinical cure, since most of his symptoms will be relieved by his redecision' (Berne, 1972: 362). The metaphor he repeatedly used was to change princes and princesses (who had become 'frogs' through social and parental influences) back into princes and princesses so that they could continue their development into autonomous, intimate, spontaneous and aware individuals.

In *Metanoia: A Process of Transformation* (Clarkson, 1989) such redecisions or turning points in life and in psychotherapy are analysed.

The change that is referred to in a *metanoia* is for all practical purposes a permanently transformed state of being, whether it is a spiritual or psychological transformation .... Such turning points in life and in psychotherapy are often revolutionary, but may equally be the result of evolutionary processes.

(Clarkson, 1989: 5)

Erskine (1980) describes script cure as observable from the cessation of behaviours syntonic with the individual's script. He emphasises that such a cure involves changes at behavioural and intrapsychic levels (affective and cognitive) as well as at physiological levels. Social and spiritual reorganisation has also been observed (Clarkson, 1989). Script cure also has a number of phenomenological characteristics. Clients who have made such fundamental changes of

character and destiny often report an 'ad lib' quality to their lives and relationships. They no longer 'know what to say' and their social networks frequently
undergo considerable oscillation e.g. spouse considers personal psychotherapy or
divorce, change of friends is almost always a consequence and career or name
changes are not unusual. If script decisions determine the most important aspects
of a person's life, script redecisions will affect them too.

Often people experience some 'nostalgia' for 'the person I used to be' and
may need to do some mourning for a valued archaic self even though it is now
defunct or dangerous as a survival adaptation. 'Script change can also bring
problems of necessity, freedom of choice and absurdity, all of which were
previously evaded in some measure by living with the illusions of his script'
(Berne, 1966: 311).

The person who has changed script has a frame of reference in which changing
is experienced as satisfying and autonomous. Not only are changes imposed by
the environment or natural cycles (e.g. ageing) welcomed as learning opportunities, but such 'cured' individuals also *seek* change and growth in continuing
ways. They develop and nourish their own particular needs and levels for
stimulation and excitement, complexity and diversity which Selye (1957)
referred to as 'eustress'. The change process itself is experienced as energising
and they are pro-active and creative, seeking learning and growth.

Such people act upon their world. They have overcome the subjective 'learned
helplessness' (Miller and Seligman, 1975) which reinforces the powerlessness of
script-bound individuals and collectives such as women, ethnic minorities and
the physically handicapped. Some of these may, however, free themselves from
their individual or collective scripts. Research has shown that senior levels of
management derive satisfaction from working under 'stresses' which middle
managers may experience as 'distress'. It is hypothesised that this is due to the
feeling that their decisions actually affect the outcomes they initiate (Kiev and
Cohn, 1979). The corollary of this in everyday life is clear where the degree of
satisfaction experienced is proportional to the experienced power over one's life.

Characteristically, change after termination of psychotherapy (permanently or
temporarily) continues to be important for the individual; it is, however,
essentially post-pathological; away from cure and towards growth. It has to do
with responding adaptively and creatively to life's stresses (Holmes and Rahe,
1967) and progressing with increasing autonomy and assurance through adult
developmental stages (Erikson, 1968; Levinson, 1978).

Real and lasting script cure is achieved when the new decision e.g. 'I will still
not suicide' is stable under ordinary and extreme stresses. Some vicissitudes of
life such as bereavement, loss of jobs, natural disasters, war and concentration
camps can challenge the script change profoundly. Frankl defines the 'last of
human freedoms' vividly and poignantly as the freedom to choose one's attitude
in any given set of circumstances, even Auschwitz and Dachau:

Every day, every hour, offered the opportunity to make a decision, a decision which determined whether you would or would not submit to those powers which threatened to rob you of your very self, your inner freedom; which determined whether or not you would become moulded into the form of the typical inmate.

(Frankl, 1969: 65, 66)

People who are still following other people's directives (out of awareness) may not be able to withstand such pressures without losing their sense of integrity or autonomy.

The archetypal image is that of Odysseus transforming himself and his life on the adult voyage through life. Aristotle summarised it as follows:

A certain man has been abroad for many years, Poseidon is lying in wait for him, and he is all alone. Matters at home, too, have reached the point at which his property is being squandered and his son's death plotted by suitors to his wife. He arrives there after terrible sufferings, reveals himself, and falls upon his enemies. The story concludes with his salvation and their destruction. This is all that is proper to the Odyssey; the rest is episode.

(Aristotle, 1963: 31)

This seems a truly apt metaphor for a man who *seems* compelled by his destiny to end up lonely and dethroned, bereft of all that he holds precious while he fights other men's battles. Revealing himself, in his innate 'princeliness' under severe stress, his journey ends in triumph.

MAKING PROGRESS – NON-CHANGE

This outcome of psychotherapy (short- or long-term) is not a true change at all, but mere fluctuations which may be mistaken for real change:

The patient fights being a winner because he is not in treatment for that purpose, but only to be made into a braver loser. This is natural enough, since if he becomes a winner, he has to throw away all, or most of his script and start over, which most people are reluctant to do.

(Berne, 1972: 37)

This type of 'change' is a masquerade of living creatively within very narrow norms of maintaining what Steiner calls 'banal scripts'.

Unlike tragic scripts, banal scripts go unnoticed like water running down the drain, and those who are participants in them may have no more than a glimpse, their *anagnorisis*, as they draw their final breath, that their potentialities as human beings have in some mysterious way been betrayed and defeated.

(Steiner, 1975: 115, 116)

By moving three steps forward, two back and two steps forward, three back, the client in therapy can give impressions that there is movement or progress, but a hard contractual check over any length of time will prove that in fact no significant long-term stable change has been accomplished.

Repeatedly in his writings Berne referred scathingly to this outcome of psychotherapy e.g.: 'something called getting better, or "progress" which is in effect making more comfortable frogs' (Berne, 1966: 290). People who feel they have accomplished change but have in fact 'made progress' usually place great value on the maintenance of a single world view and tend to find reinforcing experiences which support the future avoidance of both positively and negatively valued stresses. Even in fantasy, changing (or the stimulus to change), is perceived as negative, threatening, destabilising and therefore undesirable. Their goal is homeostasis or stability within very narrow and predictable limits. Psychotherapy may end up by widening the limits somewhat, but the basic restrictions on autonomy and creativity are stretched or redefined, not changed.

However, making progress *obviously* has some value and should be encouraged where the alternative may be a destructive or tragic ending (a third-degree payoff) or a prematurely forced change against resistance which results in the therapist being in effect 'the-rapist' and the client responding by disintegration or catastrophe.

Changing requires not only the willingness to take full responsibility for your life, but also courage. After many years of virtual imprisonment in her home, an agoraphobic patient has a job, a driving licence and hope. She needs and wants to leave her kind and gentle husband who supported her incapacitation in a collusive but well-meaning way. As she is poised for 'cure', he has a stroke that leaves him paralysed. Who will judge for another what price happiness?

A characteristic response to such a change is that such a person's system is in a continual state of stress, holding in psychological energy, archaic experiences and the influence of introjected others, while at the same time avoiding true contact with the here-and-now experiences which could potentially destabilise a delicate homeostatic balance. Essentially these people who have made these kind of pseudo changes in therapy may be chronically stressed, rigid in their attitudes and may frequently experience a chronic low level of fatigue and a minimum tolerance for deviance, uncertainty or ambiguity.

The response pattern of clients who are 'making progress' is recognisably *reactive* to the initiative of others, the environment or habit. These people are not pro-active but are essentially avoidant in response to stimuli from the environment and from others and do not actualise their own lives. These may be the people Berne (1972) describes as 'waiting for rigor mortis'. They often accumulate 'awareness' at the expense of real change or speak in terms of intellectual knowledge, not really 'feeling different in the gut' as a result of it.

The archetypal image is encapsulated in the story of Echo on whom Juno cast a spell so that ever afterwards she would only repeat the other person's last words. After Narcissus rejected her love, she grieved until all her flesh shrank away and only her voice was left. Echo was doomed by her script, forever to repeat the introjected words of a significant other, never giving voice to her autonomous existence in the world (Graves, 1986a: 287).

DISILLUSIONMENT – THE LIMITS TO CHANGE

This is the outcome of psychotherapy when the client says disappointedly: 'Is that all?', much to the mystification of psychotherapists who thought that they were giving the client exactly what he wanted. (This is a paraphrasing of Berne, 1972: 153.)

Misguided utopian hope is indeed one of the problems that humanistically oriented therapies, including TA, are particularly heir to, because of their own belief in achieving the seemingly impossible (e.g. self-actualisation) and their emphasis on the possibilities (rather than the impossibilities) of changing lives. Efforts to change based on illusion can be subjectively experienced as frustrating and ultimately impossible. Much heartbreak can be avoided by recognising and then confronting wisely and in good time the realism and achievability of contracts, goals and expectations which are so out of awareness they may only become known toward the end or after the termination of the psychotherapy. This kind of disillusionment occurs where either overtly or covertly the outcome of therapy, or script cure is confused with the attainment of omnipotence, irresistibility or practical immortality. The desired change is experienced as essentially inappropriate and stressful: 'This is the most painful task which the script analyst has to perform: to tell his patients finally that there is no Santa Claus' (Berne, 1972: 153).

Furthermore even after the huge investment of time, thought, emotion, money and sacrificed treasured life beliefs required in therapeutic change, there will still be people who are unjust or unkind to him or her, trains will still break down, death and disaster may still be visited upon him, she may never achieve fashionable thinness without injury to her health, he will never achieve the easy-going phlegmatic attitudinal responses of his colleague with a constitutionally different temperament. Researchers such as Thomas *et al.*, (1977) have found that temperamental differences (which are genetically transmitted) can be identified in very young infants. In later life these temperamental traits may remain unchanged or be modified by environmental circumstances.

There is substantial independent research evidence compiled by Eysenck (1968) that people are different in terms of their neuropsychological make-up. The introvert can probably never change the biochemical–electrical activity of his cortex to resemble that of his extrovert friend (or therapist?). The task for therapists as well as friends, partners, spouses and parents is rather to value and celebrate each other's different qualities than to do violence to them according to some standard of mass conformity quoting what some expert or statistical report defines as 'normal' or 'healthy'. Temperament is defined as 'Inborn, constitutional predisposition to react in a specific way to stimuli' (Freedman *et al.*,

1975). Personality and character can be changed; temperament can but be allowed for, influenced and enjoyed.

Psychotherapists can avoid getting involved with a fruitless quest for this type of change by (amongst other procedures) clarifying contracts, checking third-party involvement, learning about the physiological bases of behaviour and forever being vigilant against the cardinal sin of the amateur psychologist – extrapolating from your own psychology.

Script is not changing *who* we are, but *how* we are in the most important aspects of our lives. This may be the cause of the confusion between people who claim that script cure is impossible when what would be accurate to say is that temperament change is highly unlikely. 'Script' is *not* that which we do not like or do not understand about other people! According to Berne, whatever behaviour fits in with the formula: early parental influence – programme – compliance – payoff – is part of the script, and 'whatever behaviour does not fit in with it is not part of script. Every script will fit this formula and no other behaviour will fit it' (Berne 1972: 419).

When people keep reaching for and attempting impossible or inhuman changes it may be that the person's psychophysiological system is simply not designed for the function required of it and so suffers despair and breakdown. Conversely, some changes people may consider impossible, but can be achieved. Plastic surgery may make noses smaller and people shorter. Ordinary human beings can walk on fire (as the author has done), but no amount of 'redeciding' can change the past or give a foolproof guarantee that other people will behave in honourable ways towards you. The world is the world and pigs don't fly. It is important therefore to be careful about what one accepts as a therapeutic contract as disillusionment could mar or ruin a possible script cure while in vain seeking to change the impossible.

The archetypal myth is that of Icarus who was given wings made by his father Daedalus to escape from Crete. Because he flew too close to the sun, the wax melted and he plummeted into the sea (*The Shorter Oxford English Dictionary*, Onions, 1973: 1012). Even in ancient myth, people might fly, but wax will still melt near the sun!

DISINTEGRATION – THERAPEUTIC CASUALTIES

This outcome of therapeutic change occurs in a system when a change is not just destabilising, but also disintegrating. A casualty is defined as 'an individual who, as a direct result of his experience in the encounter group, became more psychologically distressed and/or employed more maladaptive mechanisms of defence. Furthermore, to be so defined this negative change must not be transient, but enduring' (Lieberman *et al.*, 1973: 171). Unlike Icarus' change, the desired change is possible, but it is under the influence of 'mortido', the death instinct (Federn, 1977). The system can neither tolerate it, nor creatively respond to it. It results most frequently from mistimed interventions, inadequate protection or chaotic treatment planning. The stimulus to change is imagined as noxious, and the person may insist that unless homeostasis is maintained on her own terms, catastrophe will result. The response pattern is acting out, often at a tragic (third-degree) level, resulting in accidents, imprisonment or hospitalisation. This is the outcome of psychotherapy (or encounter groups) referred to in the popular mind and in literature as a 'therapeutic casualty'.

Berne realised the real potential of this type of change in several places in his writings, e.g. 'Well, the husband looks a little paranoid to me, and I'm afraid to cure paranoids because in my experience they often get a very serious physical disorder like perforated ulcer or diabetes or a coronary' (Berne, 1971: 10).

Change that strips away a person's defences without the simultaneous provision of protection, skills, knowledge and resources can result in such destructive disintegration. Closing (at appropriate times in the therapy process) the escape hatches, for example, making Adult–Adult contracts for 'no suicide', 'no homicide', 'no going crazy outside of the therapy room', is vitally important in avoiding the likelihood of such eventualities (Holloway, 1973). Also important would be attending to the impact of the change on the person's psychosociological network, the relearning or acquiring of developmentally impaired skills, maintenance procedures, and reinforcement practice for stability under stress.

But no matter how conscientiously a therapist honours a client's contract, there is always still the possibility that the client (or workshop participant) may be more invested in forwarding the script than in creative change.

> The demon is the jester in human existence, and the joker in psychotherapy. No matter how well Jeder [everyman] lays his plans, the demon can come in at the critical moment and upset them all, usually with a smile and a ha ha. And no matter how well the therapist plans his psychotherapy, the patient always has the upper hand. At the point where the therapist thinks he has four aces, Jeder plays his joker and his demon wins the pot. Then he skips merrily off, leaving the doctor to leaf through the deck trying to figure out what happened.
> (Berne, 1972: 122)

A person may still choose to work out her script curse non-contractually despite impeccable ethical and therapeutic procedures on the part of the therapist or workshop leader. Just about any topic may 'bring up material' which a script-bound individual could use to potentiate a script payoff to become a therapeutic casualty. This possibility is not limited to transactional analysis, but can be found in all types of psychotherapy.

The archetypal image is that of Medea who, when her husband threatened to leave her, reacted to this impending change by not accepting it, nor by working through the difficulty with him, nor by finding another man who actually wanted to be with her, but by destroying her rival (Glauke) and being responsible for the deaths of her own two children (Graves, 1986b).

COUNTERSCRIPT CURE – THE ILLUSION OF AUTONOMY

[Jeder (everyman)] carries out his script because it is planted in his head at an early age by his parents and stays there for the rest of his life, even after their vocal 'flesh' has gone for evermore. It acts like a computer tape or player-piano roll, which brings out the responses in the planned order long after the person who punched the holes had departed the scene. Jeder meanwhile sits before the piano, moving his fingers along the keyboard under the illusion that it is he who brings the folksy ballad or the stately concerto to its foregone conclusion.

(Berne, 1972: 65–6)

This is a kind of pseudo-conversion – the belief that you have changed fundamentally when it is actually a cosmetic change. Changes in the person's behaviour have an introjected quality – it seems as if they have adopted new behaviour and belief systems, even a new language (such as transactional analysis) in the service of the pathology. Their behaviour remains adapted and driven. Instead of 'hurrying up' to kill themselves, they may be 'hurrying up' to be perfectly self-actualising TA people who always ask straight for strokes and let out their 'Free Child' at parties!

The fantasy is that of having achieved autonomy and having escaped the script payoff – what I describe as 'counterscript cure' or what Freudians mean by 'flight into health' (Greenson, 1967: 276). This person may have redecided to 'be close' and 'be aware of their drivers' without a 'fundamental transformation' (*metanoia*) (Burchfield, 1976) or a re-organisation in the archaic script-driven Child or compelling Parental ego states. The person is acting *as if* change at a deep structural level has occurred.

There is the story of the family who lived in a haunted house. After much deliberation they decided to move to another part of the city to get away from the ghost. On the day of the move, having packed the van with all their furniture and goods, one of the neighbours chanced by. 'What's happening?' he asked. A skeletal hand then lifted up a corner of the tarpaulin and said: 'We're moving!'

Counterscript change can be a valuable bridge to lasting script change, but it is not to be confused with the destination. Schiff *et al.* (1975) have mentioned that overadaptation has the benefit of good thinking supporting it and as such is a better choice of passive behaviour than incapacitation or escalation into violence. The dangers of overadaptation to the therapist *as an interim measure* is often greatly exaggerated. If a client stops sexually abusing his children as an adaptation to his therapist, he may start receiving positive reinforcement of his new behaviour which acts as a powerful motivation for constructive change and possible permanent script redecision. As Berne said (1972) we all know that you can talk a man into drinking or committing suicide, and therefore you can talk him out of it. As stageposts along the way to metanoia, counterscript change is not necessarily illegitimate and may be distinctly beneficial or even life-saving.

The problem with counterscript change (where the psychotherapist's directives, permission, values and example are substituted for the original counterscript messages of one or both parents) is not that it *happens*, but that psychotherapist and client may mistake it for the goalpost. If people get stuck here and terminate psychotherapy without changing at a more fundamental 'script level', such contractual changes are unstable under stress and unreliable over time. Figure 2.1 – the 'counterscript-cure' diagram – demonstrates how this process may appear as a psychotherapy outcome.

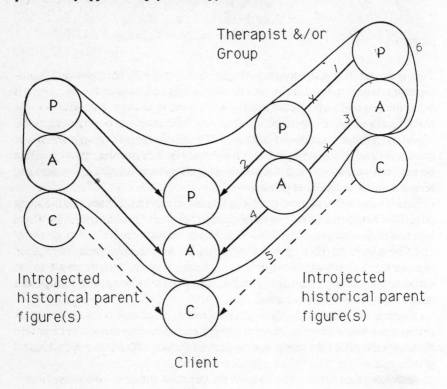

1. Original Counterscript message.

2. Substitute Counterscript message incorporated from the therapist or psychological/ideological system.

3. Old programme.

4. New samples/role models incorporated from therapist and other group members.

5. Unchanged script message manifesting payoff under stress (psychological message).

6. Area of Counterscript/Counterscript Change.

Figure 2.1 **'Counterscript-cure' diagram**

It is a development of the script matrix which usually only shows the script (5) and counterscript (1) plus programme (3) from each of the two parents (Berne, 1972). According to Steiner 'The counterscript is an acquiescence to the cultural and social demands that are transmitted through the Parent' (Steiner, 1975: 104). This diagram emphasises the potential for a client to substitute new counterscript messages (2) incorporated from the psychotherapist (or the psychological/ideological system) and/or substitute new programming (4) learned from the psychotherapist or the group which may be experienced as new sources of modelling.

Berne points out that 'The counterscript determines the person's style of life, and the script controls his ultimate destiny' (1972: 119). Therefore, although new programming and new counterscript messages may be substituted for the original ones, the original script message may still remain unchanged, manifesting the payoff under stress or contributing 'a feeling of impending doom' (Berne, 1972: 33) to the person's existence. The power of the unchanged script message is illustrated in this diagram by using broken lines to indicate this vector (5). This corresponds with the third rule of communication, which states that the outcome of transactions will be determined on the psychological level rather than on the social level. In the same way, the script outcome (which is usually transmitted at an ulterior or psychological level) will still be determined by the original psychological-level message unless the client changes this as well.

Clients have found it useful to see the area of counterscript change or 'counterscript cure' outlined as shown in Figure 2.1 (6). It has helped them to understand how they might make significant changes at the counterscript and programming level while continuing to feel threatened at a deep psychological level or regressing to script payoffs under stress. This procedure facilitates clear contract-making and treatment planning for fundamental script change and clarifies potentials for adaptation to the therapist or TA as a psychological system.

For example, a client who has been cured of vertigo, when climbing a mountain thereafter fell 'accidentally' over a cliff to her death. The underlying curse and the decision to comply might possibly have not been revoked in a therapy which paid attention primarily to change at a behavioural level or allowed premature redecisions not grounded in the total context of her life script, its supports and survival defences. Most experienced clinicians can adduce similar examples.

The compelling potency of 'script power' against 'will power' (original or new counterscript) is poignantly and chillingly illustrated in a recent newspaper report of a man who was warned by his doctor that cigarette smoking would kill him. He indeed succeeded in giving up cigarettes, but choked to death on a piece of nicotine-substitute chewing gum (*Sun*, 1986).

The symbolic or mythological archetype chosen to illustrate this type of change is that of Oedipus who believed that he had foiled his destiny. He ended up by killing his father and marrying his mother, so fulfilling a 'prophecy' made early in childhood. Aristotle also sees through the 'self-deception' of Oedipus: 'It seems unlikely that Oedipus, seeking to discover who had slain Laius, should have overlooked the clue provided by the murder which he himself had committed' (Aristotle, 1963: 27). The functional 'blindness' of Oedipus leads to the loss of his father, his mother, his wife, his kingdom and his eyes. He preserved the illusion of his autonomy but at the price of his ultimately predictable script payoff.

A summary diagram – 'The change pentagon' (Figure 2.2) – follows, which provides a precis of this material by lifting out keywords in each of the following categories: type of script change, subjective experience, characteristics, response to stress and archetype. It is hoped that this visual aid will facilitate the use and teaching of the five types of outcomes of psychotherapy and their characteristics in order to enable clients and clinicians to discriminate and differentiate between them and plan accordingly.

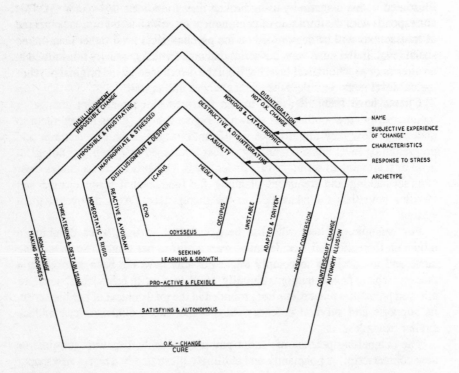

Figure 2.2 The change pentagon

I know of no better way to conclude this discussion of different types of change than to remind both client and psychotherapist of the prayer, often attributed to St Francis of Assisi, by Reinhold Niebuhr:

Grant me the serenity to accept the things I
  cannot change;
The courage to change the things I can,
And the wisdom to know the difference.

(Clinebell, 1966: 171)

SUMMARY

There are scattered references to different outcomes of psychotherapy throughout
Berne's work, but nowhere does he bring them together for comparison, contrast
and confirmation; nor does he show how possible outcomes of psychotherapy can
be systematically identified and described. In this chapter, five possible outcomes
of psychotherapy are identified: script cure, making progress, disintegration,
disillusionment and symptom relief or 'counterscript cure'. Each of these 'faces
of change' have been discussed as five separate systems with their own frames of
reference including idiosyncratic motivations for seeking/avoiding future
changes, characteristic response patterns and differing capacities in managing
stress. Each is associated with an archetypal or mythological image which may
aid the psychotherapist in distinguishing, defining and recognising the five types
of outcome so that he or she can facilitate life-script changes which are genuine,
stable under stress and provide a fertile and resilient ground for future growth.
The pentagon diagram (Figure 2.2) summarises these major points.

Chapter 3

The theory of ego states[†]

Cassius: O Brutus!
Brutus: What's the matter?
Cassius: Have not you love enough to bear
with me,
When that rash humour which my mother
gave me
Makes me forgetful?
Brutus: Yes, Cassius; and from henceforth,
When you are over-earnest with your
Brutus,
He'll think your mother chides, and leave
you so.

(Shakespeare, *Julius Caesar*, IV.i. 118–21)

FROM INTUITION TO EGO IMAGES

As shown in the introductory chapter transactional analysis as first developed by Eric Berne (1957), is an integrative theory of intra- and interpersonal psychology and psychotherapy which combines some of the clarity of behaviourism and the potential depth of psychoanalytic insight within a humanistic value system. The purpose of this chapter is to remind both the academic community and students of TA what Berne first wrote about ego states.

Berne was building on the ego psychology of Federn (one of Berne's training psychoanalysts) which was primarily intended to be a phenomenological (subjective) description of psychic life. Federn excelled in using self-observation to check the description of introspective observations of normal and mentally disturbed individuals (Weiss, 1950: 120).

Federn defined the ego phenomenologically (i.e. in a subjectively descriptive manner), as follows: 'The ego is felt and known by the individual as a lasting or

† In collaboration with Maria Gilbert

recurring *continuity* of the body and mental life in respect of time, space, and causality, and is felt and apprehended by him as a unity' (Federn, 1977/1953: 94).

Berne's contribution, in demonstrating that Parent, Adult and Child ego states are existential phenomena rather than theoretical constructs, is emphasised and elaborated upon in this chapter. Berne intended transactional analysis to be a *systematic phenomenology* which could usefully fill a gap in psychological theory (1980/1961: 244).

It is believed that because of the popularity of the behavioural implications of transactional analysis in the early years, the value of Berne's original model has been obscured. This chapter is an attempt to correct that imbalance and spell out some practical consequences of using this phenomenological model of ego states. It is not the intention here to discuss Berne's structural model in relation to the functional (behavioural) model, as this has been done extensively elsewhere (Kahler, 1978; Drego, 1981). The work of Trautmann and Erskine (1981) is valuable in this regard. It is also not the purpose of this chapter to explore and stress Berne's original model at the expense of behavioural interpretations, but rather to complement them with a strong emphasis on the phenomenological perspective.

In Berne's writing, he, like many other originators, often appears inconsistent and contradictory. It has become the task of this generation of TA clinicians to separate out the original analysis of ego states from the welter of confused models currently in use. The articulation of this model of ego states is of particular value and significance for building conceptual and practical bridges with clinicians from other traditions including psychoanalysis, Gestalt psychotherapy and Ericksonian hypnotherapy.

Berne's first interest and research for some ten years was in the field of intuition. He worked for a period in an army induction centre where he had to determine the psychiatric fitness of prospective soldiers (dressed in army dressing gowns) within 40–90 seconds. He personally extended this to 'guessing' their occupations and tabulated his results. As his interest and ability grew, he began to recognise more clearly coherent intuitive impressions which he called 'ego images', that is: 'Specific perceptions of the patient's active archaic ego state in relation to the people around him' (Berne, 1977: 102). Later in his psychotherapy practice he gave an example with his image of an adult patient Emily, as 'an infant with a dripping diaper, shrinking from her mother's disgust and tyrannical castigation and looking for an uncle to hold her as she was' (Berne, 1977: 106). Berne was impressed with the usefulness of such images for psychotherapy and contrasted the clarity of the clinician's task in experiencing the vividly phenomenological image of this writhing little girl versus labelling Emily as a passive–aggressive masochistic depressive. In 1957 Berne refers to such fixations in the person's ego state as 'ego images' (1977: 119).

EGO STATES

In the beginning of *Transactional Analysis in Psychotherapy*, Berne discusses ego states as 'states of mind and their related patterns of behaviour as they occur in nature' (Berne, 1980: 30). These 'natural psychological epochs' (ibid: 52) are distinguished from a 'traumatic ego state' (ibid: 53). 'An ego state may be described phenomenologically as a coherent system of feelings, and operationally as a set of coherent behaviour patterns, or pragmatically as a system of feelings which motivates a related set of behaviour patterns' (Berne, 1977: 123).

According to Weiss, Federn's chief exponent:

Every ego state is the actually experienced reality of one's mental and bodily ego with the contents of the lived-through period. Some ego states are easily remembered and revived even after many years, some are difficult to recall, some are strictly repressed.

(Weiss, 1950: 141)

It seems that ego states can be described as 'chunks of psychic time' – complete and discrete units of psychological reality. These natural psychological epochs do not disappear, but are preserved throughout the person's life, potentially available for the vivid re-experiencing of those ego states with the corresponding affects. Federn is convinced that the ego is more than the integrative function of the mind, or a mental abstraction, or the sum of all conscious interrelated mental phenomena. He believes that it is an experienced reality, constituted by mental and bodily ego feeling – 'an actual continuous mental experience' (Weiss, 1950: 18).

Federn maintained that ego configurations of earlier age levels are potentially available in intact adult personalities. He uses the concept of 'engrams' to connote the continuous retention of ego units related to important events, intellectual interests or personal emotional reasons, which are perpetuated in the succession of ego states in the individual. These remain available to influence the person's ordinary life for good or for ill. Federn comments on the 'normality' of this process as follows:

The permanence of previous ego states extends Freud's concept of ego fixation to the field of normal psychology. Because of its influence on symptom and resistance formation, pathological fixation was recognised earlier than this normal process. But the concept of pathological ego fixation presupposes the concept of a succession of ego states.

(Federn, 1977/1953: 218)

At first Berne used ego images to distinguish such archaic ego functioning from mature ego functioning in the patients he saw. He was clear that the 'ego images' he perceived in his psychiatric patients were reflections of the person's archaic ego states which were preserved and phenomenologically intact.

Berne followed Federn in using work on dreams, psychosis and hypnosis to substantiate the phenomenological reality and continuing accessibility of ego states formed at earlier points in time. The originality of Berne's contribution lay in integrating these findings with Penfield's (1952) studies of certain surgical procedures which demonstrated ego state regressions to earlier epochs in a person's life. Thus he also illustrated the permanence of previous ego states in pathological *and normal* functioning.

The neurosurgeon Penfield reports this phenomenon as follows:

> The subject feels again the emotion which the situation originally produced in him, and he is aware of the same interpretations, true or false, which he himself gave to the experience in the first place. Thus evoked recollection is not the exact photographic or phonographic reproduction of past scenes of events. It is the reproduction of what the patient saw and heard and felt and understood.

> (Penfield, 1952: 178)

Penfield's experiments clearly illustrate the difference between *remembering* an earlier experience and the phenomenological *reliving* thereof.

Penfield's subjects reported their reliving experiences at the same time as being aware of the operating room and Berne (1980) perceived this fact as demonstrating how two different ego states occupy consciousness simultaneously as discrete psychological entities distinct from each other. In 'reliving' the person does not only remember how they felt, they feel that way in the 'now'. There will be variations in the depth to which the physiological components of the feeling are involved in the 'reliving' experience. Clinicians are familiar with this from age regressions in clinical-practice hypnosis and dreams. Recent research continues to add to and modify Penfield's pioneering discoveries and awaits further integration of modern neurophysiology with ego-state phenomena (Aggleton and Mishkin, 1985; Mishkin *et al.*, 1984).

Modern corroboration for the hypnotic demonstrability of ego states is provided by the work of Watkins and Watkins. They use Federn's definitions of ego states as patterns of behaviour and experience organised around a common principle which are ego-cathectic, and therefore invested with self energies. They particularly use hypnosis to reach these normal segments of experience which may be partially or completely disassociated as in multiple personality. An ego state thus constitutes 'a kind of "sub-self," with its own discrete conscious- ness, which would be partially or completely separate in its awareness depending on the permeability of its boundary with the primary or "executive" state' (Watkins and Watkins, 1986: 145).

One of Berne's patients explained to him that sometimes he felt like a lawyer, as when he was being an effective professional man with family responsibilities, and sometimes he felt like a little boy, for example when he was gambling and he employed an archaic method of handling reality by a magical arithmetic of denial (e.g. 'I was prepared to lose $100 tonight and I have only lost $50, so I am really

$50 ahead and I needn't be upset' (Berne, 1977: 99). With the help of the patient, Berne identified and utilised these different aspects of the client's personality. Two different conscious ego states could be observed, one that of a mature ego, and another appropriate for a more primitive ego. Very significant is the fact that *both* were conscious and *both* belonged to the ego system.

We do know that Berne knew about Erickson's work through Weiss (whom he references in *Transactional Analysis in Psychotherapy*, 1980). Erickson records a patient's experience of age regression in a very similar way:

> He gave an account of suddenly finding himself on an unfamiliar hillside and set about trying to discover how he could be himself at 26 years of age watching himself at the age of 6 years. He soon learned that he could not only see, hear, and feel his child-self, but that he knew his innermost thoughts and feelings. At the moment of realising this, he felt the child's feeling of hunger and his wish for 'brown cookies'. This brought a flood of memories to his 26-year old self, but he noticed that the boy's thoughts were still centring on cookies and that the boy remained totally unaware of him. He was an invisible man, in some way regressed in time so that he could see and sense completely his childhood self.
>
> (Erickson, 1967: 296)

Berne realised that you don't only have to understand what kind of adult you are dealing with in psychotherapy but also what kind of child, and that these can be phenomenologically operational in the same mature grown-up body at different times, often aware of each other, one that of an adult, one that of a child. For convenience, he called these aspects of functioning 'Child' and 'Adult' respectively. In using them clinically with his patients, he spoke familiarly of the 'Adult' and the 'Child'. Only one ego state will have 'executive power' over the behaviour of the individual at any moment in time. Any ego state may be influenced by the others to a greater or lesser degree in helpful or unhelpful ways (Berne, 1980/1961: 38, 146–50).

CHILD EGO STATES

'Child ego state is a set of feelings, attitudes and behaviour patterns which are relics of the individual's own childhood' (Berne, 1980/1961: 77). When Berne writes about 'Child ego state' he is technically referring (in the Penfield and Federn sense) to a multitude of such Child ego states which represent the *entire earlier history* of an individual in vivid phenomenologically real, sensorily alive psychological units. Certain Child ego states could be distinct and circumscribed traumatic fixations which may or may not interfere substantially with secondary-process reality-testing. As a psychotherapist, Berne's main concern was with these traumatic or repeated subtraumatic fixations, as they interfered with the person's social and occupational functioning. His *examples* of 'fixated Child ego states' may have encouraged some interpreters to use part-examples as *definitions.* Such non-contextual interpretations divorce the fundamental idea of Child ego states from its phenomenological origins. Ego states were initially conceived of as vividly available temporal recordings of past events with the concomitant meaning and feelings which are maintained in potential existence within the personality (Berne, 1980/1961: 19).

However, he distinguishes from this multitude of Child ego states: (1) Child as archaic ego states and (2) Child as fixated archaic ego states. Both categories are accessible to being relived, as such, in the present by the adult person. Indeed 'Child ego states' may be a misnomer since this term suggests a repository of experiences only relating to a person's childhood whereas ego states – as normal psychological epochs – continue to be formed for the duration of a person's life. Child ego states might be better referred to as *'historical ego states'* since a person's vivid experiences of today will be stored in natural psychological epochs, archaic by tomorrow.

Berne himself considers each ego state as a phenomenological entity including other ego states which existed many years ago or a few moments previously (Berne, 1980: 39). New ego states, both fixated (e.g. in response to a rape at 60), or non-traumatic (e.g. a first real friendship at 40), are continuously being formed on a day-by-day basis, for the duration of a person's life. This is in accord with Federn (1977/1953) and Watkins (1978).

In many cases Berne does not equate fixated ego states with archaic ego states. Where he specifically defines Child ego states, as in the glossaries of his books or indexed definitions, he refers only to their 'archaic' nature. (Archaic is defined in *The Shorter Oxford Dictionary* as 'marked by the characteristics of an earlier period' (Onions, 1973: 99).) Federn also considered Child ego states in the same way – occasionally but not necessarily pathological. Archaic ego states are memories retained in their natural form – 'the temporal recording carries with it important psychical elements such as understanding of the meaning of the experience, and the emotion it may have aroused' (Berne, 1980/1961: 18).

Fixated Child ego states are therefore a subset of archaic ego states. In the following example Erickson is describing an archaic ego state which cathects a vividly re-experienced, earlier ego state which is not necessarily pathological. This is a report of a 20-year-old student nurse under hypnotic age regression:

> I could say 'Daddy'. My father was holding me. He seemed to be awfully tall. He was smiling. He had a funny looking tooth, a front tooth. His eyes were blue. His hair was curly. And it looked yellowish. Now I'm going home and tell my mother.
>
> (Erickson, 1967: 379)

She checked with her mother who corroborated all the above facts and informed her that her father had left her (the mother) when the patient was 11 months old. This 11-month-old experience represents a single Child ego state. Similarly the 3-year-old 'child' of Berne's client – the lawyer – represents a single Child ego state. There are potentially millions of these since every person has a multitude of such past ego states available. Any of these can interfere with effective Adult functioning in terms of appropriate use of the reality principle which is suited to the 'here-and-now situation', when activated by random stimuli or post-hypnotic suggestions given by parents in childhood in the form of script message or script injunctions (Conway and Clarkson, 1987).

Clinical investigation of pathological regression usually reveals earlier childhood ego states which are 'triggered' by similar or reminiscent stimuli sets in the person's present environment. In dreams and psychosis, of course, this phenomenon occurs respectively to a lesser and more seriously disturbing level. However, this spontaneous activation of earlier ego states is not considered necessarily pathological by Federn:

> Both acquired ego attitudes and past ego states are to a great extent repressed. Through their access to consciousness and to the preconsciousness they influence actual decisions. The influence of ego attitudes and ego states is helpful or disturbing, depending on their normality and fitness for present needs.
>
> (Federn, 1977/1953: 2)

When he focuses on *pathology* Berne (1980/1961: 53) emphasises that a Child ego state is like a bent penny which may skew the rest of the pile. By implication there are unbent pennies as well (Berne, 1980: 53). He states that 'ego units' are created day by day *without necessarily being traumatically fixated*.

It is particularly in the chapter on pathogenesis that Berne discusses the Child as a warped ego state that has become fixated. Specifically :

> In the case of the traumatic neuroses, the Child is that confused ego state that was fixated on the day x of the month y of the year z in that patient's infancy. In the case of the psychoneuroses, it is the unhealthy ego state which recurred day after day under similar adverse conditions from month a to month b of the year c in the patient's infancy. In either case, the number of fixated pathological archaic ego states (or series of ego states) in any one individual is very limited : one or two, and in rare cases perhaps three.
>
> (Berne, 1980/1961: 54)

In the very metaphor of the pile of coins it is clear that there are many Child ego states which are not fixated. According to both Federn and Weiss these can be easily recathected as 'the actually experienced reality of one's mental and bodily ego with the contents of the lived through period' (Weiss, 1950: 141). Already in 1958 Berne emphasised that it was not his intention to get rid of 'the Child' but to straighten out the confusion in the archaic area. 'The Child in the individual is potentially capable of contributing to his personality exactly what a happy actual child is capable of contributing to family life' (Berne, 1977: 149).

In several places in *Transactional Analysis in Psychotherapy* Berne refers to Child ego states which are not necessarily pathological and often positively enhancing to Adult effectiveness. He uses an example of how therapeutic effectiveness is enhanced by the therapist's cathecting Child while the Adult remains in the executive. 'The therapist's Child working intuitively and subconsciously (rather than deliberately and consciously like his Adult) was able to perceive accurately the instinctual connections of the gesture and its origin' (Berne, 1980/1961: 69). He also advises a client not to get rid of his Child because: 'there's a lot of good in him that could be brought out, and he's a good kid to have around' (Berne, 1980/1961: 175).

Phenomenologically people experience spontaneous 'reliving' of earlier age levels which are not pathological fixations or warped unhealthy in themselves, although they may cause temporary interruptions to Adult contact. A famous example from literature is, of course, Proust's magnum opus, *A la recherche de temps perdu* (*Remembrance of Things Past*) (1919). Most people report easy and apparently untraumatic 'reliving' of happy holiday moments triggered by smells (e.g. sea breezes, a much-loved perfume, retsina wine) which do not 'contaminate' their Adult reality processing, but which may even be *momentary* enhancements of their present experience.

In psychotherapy it is not unusual to find or to use an earlier happy Child ego state (e.g. *reliving* the experience of being warmly held and comforted) in helping a person find internal support for integrated Adult functioning (Clarkson and Fish, 1988). In NLP (Neuro-Linguistic Programming) a similar procedure is called *accessing earlier sensory/memory states* (Lankton, 1980). Dr Marty Groder (Groder, 1988) described the case of a woman where he intentionally helped her to access healthy archaic psychophysiologically complete ego states, in order to improve her integrated Adult functioning in the here-and-now. The woman, in her fourth decade, was having some difficulty in obtaining her pilot's licence. Dr Groder facilitated her 'regression' to a developmentally earlier 'Child ego state' where she was confidently, creatively and effectively dancing as a young girl. He prescribed, as a solution to the problem, that she should 'dance the plane'. By reliving this historical dancing experience, in full psychophysiological vividness, as intense as though it were happening at this moment, she was able to bring these qualities to flying the aeroplane (Erskine *et al.*, 1988).

The archaic Child ego state (which was not fixated in a pathological sense) was fully cathected to act as support for Adult functioning in terms of the current task of piloting. It subsequently became integrated into Adult, becoming reference points for 'integrated Adult piloting of the plane'. However, even this vivid reliving of archaic experiences, supportive of the here-and-now task, becomes in itself an historic memory trace, delegated to autonomic habituation, in years to come.

To summarise, Berne considers the Child as an organised state of mind which exists or once actually existed. It can be creatively used or the Child can interfere with integrated Adult functioning i.e. when it is constant or fixated (Berne, 1980/1961: 35), when it is excluded or excluding (ibid) or when it contaminates the Adult ego state (ibid: 47). These are the conditions under which Berne consistently considered the manifestations of Child ego states as 'pathological' but, as has been shown, there are many conditions, particularly when the Adult ego state is in the executive, where they are not pathological but beneficial and life-enhancing.

THE ADULT EGO STATE

'The Adult ego state is characterised by an autonomous set of feelings, attitudes and behaviours which are adapted to current reality' (Berne, 1980/1961: 76). Berne's client had one ego state wherein he felt like a grown-up lawyer and acted like a chronologically adult lawyer, and another wherein he felt like a masochistic child of a certain age and acted like such a child. At the beginning of treatment, these two ego states were overlapped and interwoven with each other. Towards the end of treatment, they had been dissected apart by the therapeutic operation which consisted of defining and strengthening the boundary between them. The clarification of the differences between these two sets of ego states coincided with a significant improvement in the patient's life and circumstances. His 'purified Adult ego state' was freed from archaic attitudes by this process of 'decontamination' and could therefore proceed on its own to respond effectively and satisfactorily to life's ongoing vicissitudes. The person was then willing and able to function 'like an adult' in the 'here-and-now'.

The Adult ego draws resources, memories and information from the Child and Parent (see next section) ego-state reservoirs. Respectively, their content can act to enhance or support healthy functioning. On the other hand, such 'ego-state programming', if it is based on pathological introjects or archaic fixations, will diminish appropriate Adult functioning in the here-and-now.

The integrated Adult ego state therefore represents a biologically mature person with fully developed adult intellectual functioning, full emotional responsivity (Pathos) and a guiding set of considered values (Ethos), all of which moderate a person's needs in response to the resources available in the environment (Berne, 1980/1961: 242). This conceptualisation corresponds with considerable accuracy to Federn's formulation:

> Integrated personality, therefore, means maintenance of control not only of the partial ego reactions but also of different ego states. This maintenance requires the reliable and strong cathexis of the lasting mature ego state .... All psychosis is ego disease, so all psychopathology is due to characteristically abnormal psycho- and organo-genesis of the ego.
>
> (Federn, 1977: 218)

Berne (1980/1961: 158) refers to a patient feeling and expressing 'the autonomous Adult anger and disappointment at her husband's behaviour'. Here, he clearly acknowledges that the Adult ego state can be appropriately emotional. He also distinguishes Child sexuality from Adult sexuality:

> The sexual fantasies seemed to be free of pregenital elements. They were intrusive, considerate, and well-adapted to the reality possibilities of each

situation; in principle they met the criteria for realistic genital sexual 'object interest', if not love, and they were based on healthy biological instinctual pressures. Since they were neither inhibitions nor archaic elements they could not be regarded as anything but Adult, free of exteropsychic and archaeopsychic influences and controlled by reality testing.

(Berne, 1980/1961: 238)

In *Born to Win* James and Jongeward explicitly discuss the integrated Adult as containing Adult feelings which are genuine responses 'to an actual situation happening now' (1971: 271). These feelings, such as outrage, respect or despair are differentiated from feelings *copied* from parental figures or feelings *previously experienced* in the person's historical infancy, childhood or, as these authors and Berne suggest, the more recent past. Gillespie (1976) also addresses the issue of feelings in the Adult ego state.

A mature person with an integrated Adult ego state therefore displays a fully developed biological sexuality and an emotional capacity for responding appropriately within the life context. For example, Mara weeps and mourns the death of a loved one, expresses anger safely and appropriately in order to mobilise energy for desired changes and experiences and expresses joy and happiness. But she expresses her feelings in a way which is consistent with a fully developed neurophysiological maturity. It is consistent with a 'bodily ego' of her current chronological age (Weiss, 1950: 18). Her anger is not a 'reliving' of an angry event at an earlier age level, since her whole neurology, physiology and motoric patterns are different, even though there may be similarities to her manner of expressing her anger as a little girl.

The activation of complete or partial Child (archaic) ego states may be an impediment to full Adult emotional and intellectual functioning – if and when they 'contaminate' (or replace) appropriate responses to current reality. Common examples of this partial or complete activation of archaic ego states which disrupt or disturb Adult functioning and feelings (e.g. excitement or pleasure) are when people feel irrationally frightened before speaking in public, examinations or job interviews; also, some people can feel inexplicably 'guilty' (with concomitant 'archaic' physiological symptoms) passing through Customs even though, as chronological adults, they are aware that they have no reason to feel that way in current reality.

PARENT EGO STATES

Later Berne (1980/1961: 75) also identified 'a set of feelings, attitudes, and behaviour patterns which resemble those of a parental figure'. These Berne called the 'Parent ego states'. This corresponds with what Weiss (1950) refers to as the 'psychic presence'. The person whose Parent predominates, habitually or at a given moment, is not acting 'like her [*sic*] mother', he or she is actually reproducing, without editing, the mother's total behaviour, including the mother's inhibitions, the mother's reasoning, the mother's impulses, as well as the mother's fixated archaic or Child ego states. The reproduction of the mother's ego states may be a whole object representation, that is the mother in a person's psychological totality. Equally well, any set of such behaviour, feelings, or attitudes, could represent the mother's Adult or Parent ego states, that is part object reproduction. These partial or complete phenomenological representations would correspond to the psychoanalytic concepts of whole- or part-objects (Klein, 1984/1957), but frequently their activation constitutes interferences with good contact with current reality. This could only be confirmed by additional historical or phenomenological investigation. For example, when a person is crying he or she may be cathecting one of their own Child ego states (reliving an historical event in which they actually cried), or they may be cathecting one of their Parent ego states (e.g. reproducing the archaic crying behaviour of one of their parents). Third, the person may be in Adult, weeping in response to pain in the here-and-now reality with feelings, behaviours and psychophysiological motoric expression consistent with that of a grown-up person.

There are many Parent ego states which may be more-or-less complete representations of the significant parental others from the person's childhood. Such Parent ego states are taken on through various processes – incorporation, internalisation, identification as well as introjection (Berne, 1966: 296). Weiss (1950) discusses the differences between these concepts in Chapter 10 of his book *Principles of Psychodynamics*.

By acknowledging the intrapsychic phenomenological reality of incorporated Parent ego states and developing a methodology for directly treating such Parent ego states, transactional analysis has made a unique and enormous contribution to psychotherapy (Dashiell, 1978; McNeel, 1976; Mellor and Andrewartha, 1980a, b). One of the most important repercussions of working with the reality of 'borrowed egos' (Weiss, 1950) in the person's Parent ego states, is that the clinician can differentiate between different diagnoses and developmental histories for different parts of the ego. (For example, the Child ego state may have an histrionic adaptation, whereas the Paternal introject may be diagnosed as a manic-depressive.) This greatly clarifies and facilitates differential treatment planning for different phases of a person's psychotherapy.

Fairbairn in 1952 had already formulated a theory of a tripartite ego – the libidinal ego (seeking the exciting and fulfilling object), the anti-libidinal ego (the critical internal saboteur or persecutory object) and the central (observing and experiencing) ego, 'assuming a dynamic pattern in relation to one another', (Fairbairn, 1952: 171). Weiss (1950: 97) highlights the fact that 'the super-ego itself is an ego state, since it is constructed of ego identifications – that is of 'egotized formations'. Our understanding of this dynamic relationship is that it is equivalent to the internal dialogue between different sets of ego states, and of particular value in explaining what Berne called the 'Parental influence' (Berne, 1980/61: 76). A Parent ego state 'may function as a directing influence (the Influencing Parent) or be directly exhibited as parental behaviour (the Active Parent)' (Berne, 1972: 444).

Berne, like Federn and Weiss, appreciated that the Parent ego state was not always sabotaging but could also be supportive and protective. In this way he also followed the opinion of Federn and Weiss: 'Psychic presences exist and are effective prior to the ego's awareness of them. They may have an approving or even a consoling character, as well as a censorious one, and play an important role in determining behaviour' (Weiss, 1950: 70). One way of describing this dynamic relationship (or internal dialogue) is that it consists of intrapsychic transactions between different introjected part- and whole-objects and other endopsychic ego structures.

It is instructive to compare Berne's ideas with a recent statement from the British School of Psychoanalysis regarding the role of the ego in current thinking:

> The new, observing and reflective self can identify now more with one end of the composite unity of self-and-mother, now more with the other; and re-establishes a two-term relationship by making either identification. Pathology would start from an inability, or from a lessened ability, to take up any one of the three positions; *the normal ego is able to move between them*.
>
> (Padel, 1986: 159, Petrūska Clarkson's emphasis)

Berne stressed that these ego states, (i.e., Parent, Adult and Child) are three *categories* of existential phenomena, not theoretical constructs. 'Parent, Adult and Child represent real people who now exist, or who once existed, who have legal names and civic identities' (Berne, 1980/1961: 32). Parent or Child can be voluntarily or involuntarily activated at any moment in time and experienced as a current reality with the same vividness that attended the original experience. Such a reliving of the past in the present can be to the detriment or enhancement (e.g. intuition) of accurate Adult reality-testing.

Berne suggests that these three types of ego states are phenomenological manifestations of three conceptual entities that he calls psychic organs, extero-psyche, neopsyche and archaeopsyche. At times Berne uses the terms ego states and psychic organs interchangeably. At other times he distinguishes the psychic organs as the structural organisers and the ego states as the phenomenological manifestations of the activity of these organs. It would appear most useful to consider the psychic organs as structural concepts and the analysis of ego states as phenomenological.

This would both correspond to and be congruent with the psychoanalytic, scientific and phenomenological subjective epistemology from which TA as a psychotherapy grew. Each of these organs has its own idiosyncratic patterns of organised behaviour (executive power), each is capable of adapting its behavioural responses to the immediate social situation (adaptability), the responses of each are modified as a result of natural growth and previous experiences (biological fluidity) and each of these mediate the phenomena of experience (mentality).

It should therefore be clear that each type of ego state, i.e. Adult as well as Parent or Child, is capable of adapting to the immediate social situation as well as being modifiable over time (Berne 1980: 75). Therefore Parent ego states, Child ego states and Adult ego states are open to growth, development and change for the duration of an individual's life. This is consistent with the work of major TA theorists such as Goulding and Goulding (1979), Schiff *et al.* (1975) and James (1974) who all describe techniques which are intended to change existing ego states. This concept is also developed further by Clarkson and Fish (1988).

For Watkins and Watkins: 'The goal is to reduce internal conflict between the various ego states by internal diplomacy aimed at making more permeable their separating boundaries and bringing them into a more cooperative arrangement within the personality structure' (Watkins and Watkins, 1986: 150).

Of all the post-Freudian analysts, Berne devoted the greatest part of his professional life to articulating the interface between the internal (intrapsychic) and external (interactional) processes. He focused on the interplay between internal objects and their external counterparts in reality. In this sense, transactional analysis makes a major contribution to object relations theory (Klein, 1984/1957) and continues a tradition of ideas initiated by Federn (1977/1953) and Fairbairn (1952).

A quotation from Alice Miller demonstrates this correspondence with TA theory and practice:

> There is a big difference between having ambivalent feelings towards someone as an adult and, after working back through much of one's previous history, suddenly experiencing one's self as a two-year-old who is being fed by the maid in the kitchen and thinking in despair: 'Why does mother go out every evening? Why does she not take pleasure in me? What is wrong with me that she prefers to go to other people? What can I do to make her stay at home? Just don't cry, just don't cry.' The child could not have thought in these words at the time, but in the session on the couch, this man was both an adult and a two-year-old child, and could cry bitterly.
>
> (Miller, 1983: 34–5)

Correct and discriminating usage of nomenclature for ego states should obviate some of the misunderstandings in and about transactional analysis which have arisen. It is important when using ego-state theory to understand and specify clearly which model of ego states is being referred to. For example, when a person is seen to be showing anger, in functional terms, she could be described as exhibiting Child ego-state *behaviour* but in structural or phenomenological terms it is not necessarily a Child ego state which is being expressed. Whether it is a Parent, Adult or Child ego state diagnostically, and therefore operationally (in practice) depends on an accurate application of all four diagnostic criteria (behavioural, social, historical and phenomenological) as spelt out by Berne himself in *Transactional Analysis in Psychotherapy* (1980/1961: 75). The accusation 'You're in your Parent' that some people make toward others who shake their fingers is simply not universally true (James, 1974). 'The pointed index finger may be a Parental admonition, an Adult indicator, or a Child's accusation' (Berne, 1966: 312).

In addition, to speak without further qualification of 'three ego states' is technically, theoretically and clinically erroneous. Within the model as Berne articulated it, there are vast numbers of ego states which can be classified in terms of three categories or types of ego states: Parent ego states, Adult ego states and Child ego states (Berne, 1966: 220). This view corresponds with the thinking of Federn (1977), Horowitz (1979) and Watkins (1978)

According to this model, if a psychotherapist is utilising a Parent ego state in working with a patient, *without integrated Adult monitoring*, she or he may be working from a non-assimilated, non-integrated 'borrowed' ego state originating from their personal past and therefore not in good contact with the here-and-now existential reality of the therapeutic encounter. Equally, the therapist may be working from a Child ego state outside of Adult awareness. 'The supportive therapist approaches his patients in a Parental ego state (or if he is resentful of them, he may approach them in a Child ego state playing a parental role, very much like a little boy playing doctor)' (Berne, 1966: 105). However, if the therapist has his or her Adult in the executive, Parent and Child ego states may be used creatively in the therapeutic process.

In terms of the original model, the psychotherapeutic goal is the achievement of a fully integrated Adult ego state without complete or partial interference from archaic personal experiences or unintegrated ego states 'borrowed' from significant others. In Gestalt-existential terms this is understood to be similar to achieving in the here-and-now organismic *Dasein* (beingness) (Heidegger 1949) without resorting to interruptions to contact with self or relationship which are archaic or fixed Gestalten (Perls *et al.*, 1969).

There have been considerable advances in the clinical applications of this model of ego states in the United States, England and Europe. These advances are only recently being articulated in writing.

SUMMARY

This chapter discusses Berne's original idea of ego states, as derived from Federn (1977/1953) and Penfield (1975), clarifying in particular the author's understanding of integrated Adult ego states and their relationship to both Parent and Child ego states. In terms of this perspective on ego states, the psychotherapeutic goal would be the achievement of a fully integrated Adult ego state without complete or partial interference from archaic personal experiences or unintegrated 'psychic presences' of significant parent figures from the past. The main focus of this chapter is on Berne's view of the phenomenological reality of ego states. Berne's contribution resides in the recognition that Parent, Adult and Child ego states are three categories of existential phenomena, not theoretical constructs. The importance of establishing an uncontaminated Adult ego state in the mature personality is emphasised. It is also acknowledged that each type of ego state (whether Parent, Adult or Child) can influence any of the others in helpful or harmful ways and is modifiable over time. It is believed that this bridges a theoretical gap in transactional analysis theory between apparently opposed views of ego states.

Chapter 4

Diagnosis

Alice took up the fan and gloves, and, as the hall was very hot, she kept fanning herself all the time she went on talking. 'Dear, dear! How queer everything is today! And yesterday things went on just as usual. I wonder if I've been changed in the night? Let me think: *was* I the same when I got up this morning? I almost think I can remember feeling a little different. But if I'm not the same, the next question is, "Who in the world am I?" Ah, *that's* the great puzzle!'

(Lewis Carroll, 1987/1865: 25)

INTRODUCTION

This chapter is intended to provide some new perspectives on the interface between the traditional diagnostic and the more intuitive approaches to psycho-therapy. Diagnosis can be used to destructive or beneficial effect. Clinicians who have seriously addressed this apparent polarity have found the perspective presented here useful for training, practice and supervision. This paradigm is intended to validate both a humanistic, person-oriented therapeutic relationship and to make the best possible use of information and patterns that have accrued from our historical and scientific predecessors in the field of psychotherapy and psychiatry. It provides a model based on left-hemispheric and right-hemispheric consciousness to differentiate between these two emphases of treatment. It also suggests that a dynamic 'Gestalt' model of figure and background (or foreground and background) can provide a useful way of balancing and integrating these functions in the practice of psychotherapy.

In *The Shorter Oxford English Dictionary* 'diagnosis' is defined as 'Determin-ation of a diseased condition; identification of a disease by investigation of its symptoms and history' (Onions, 1973: 538–9). In *A Critical Dictionary of Psychoanalysis*, Rycroft defines it as follows: 'The art of attaching labels to illnesses, of deducing the nature of the illness from the signs and symptoms presented by the patient' (1972: 34).

THE CASE AGAINST DIAGNOSIS

Transactional analysis is a humanistic/existential psychotherapy which considers the *client* as radically 'OK'. It originated in the iconoclastic 60s, at least partly in rebellion against the traditional psychoanalytic and psychiatric labels and practices of that time. Berne was one of the first psychiatrists to hold case conferences in front of patients, saying: 'Anything that's not worth saying in front of a patient is not worth saying at all' (cited in Steiner, 1974: 6). In a radical departure from his original psychoanalytic training, Berne pioneered openness and honesty in the treatment process, inviting the patient to an equal partnership in the healing.

Steiner – a major figure in radical psychiatry – declared: 'Everything diagnosed psychiatrically, unless *clearly* organic in origin, is a form of alienation' (Steiner, 1974: 16). This emphasis on the centrality of the relationship swung the historical pendulum away from diagnosis, which was seen to be contrary to and destructive of the creative, growthful encounter between two people in psychotherapy. Psychiatric diagnosis had often been used in a reductionistic, controlling manner to label people as incurable or abnormal – a way of creating a chasm between 'us who treat' and 'them who come for treatment' and a practitioner may feel more at ease discussing terms than relationships. When diagnostic procedures become a nefarious substitution for engagement in a healing relationship, it is destructive. Of course there is not a *real* polarity between diagnosis and relationship; it's just often used that way.

We can never find our real selves or any other person through diagnosis, evaluation, or analysis. These methods break up the self and attempt to objectify and make finite what is essentially personal, unified, and infinite. They are inevitably fixed in the past and fail to recognise the emerging powers of choice, promise, and the sudden new awarenesses and discoveries and creations of a unique growing person. Inevitably analysis is a destructive approach, looking as it does behind reality for causes and events instead of recognising that reality is contained in the immediate experiences of the person and in his unfolding life ... even the person with severe emotional problems does not need diagnosis and analysis. What he requires is genuine human experience, meetings with real persons.

(Moustakas, 1967: 131)

Many research studies have suggested that psychotherapist factors such as psychotherapist warmth, respect, empathy, acceptance and genuineness are associated with positive outcomes of psychotherapy (Lambert, 1986; Truax and Mitchell, 1971). Carl Rogers states it eloquently:

For many people in psychotherapy the establishment of a significant relationship with a client or patient is of the greatest importance. Indeed many practitioners believe that this relationship is not only the healing vehicle but the balm itself. It is clear, however, that the stress is upon a direct experiencing in the relationship. The process is not seen as primarily having to do with the client's memory of his past, nor with his exploration of the problems he is facing, nor with the perceptions he has of himself, nor the experiences he has been fearful of admitting into awareness. The process of therapy is, by these hypotheses, seen as being synonymous with the experiential relationship between client and therapist. Therapy consists in experiencing the self in a wide range of ways in an emotionally meaningful relationship with the therapist.

> (Rogers, 1986: 171–2)

An over-reliance on diagnosis can create false certainties if used in a restrictive, insensitive way leading to cookbook treatment planning, an emphasis on sameness, an avoidance of valuing cultural or temperamental idiosyncrasies and an adherence to techniques or labels. The pernicious effect of stereotypical psychiatric labelling in mental health systems is nowhere more chillingly documented than in reports of investigators (for example, Goffman, 1962) who voluntarily admitted themselves to mental hospitals in order to study such phenomena.

Gestalt therapy has also particularly emphasised the importance of the person-to-person relationship. Laura Perls was greatly influenced by Martin Buber and considered that the true essence of Gestalt therapy was the relationship formed between psychotherapist and client:

> A Gestalt therapist does not use techniques; he applies *himself in* and *to* a situation with whatever professional skill and life experience he has accumulated and integrated. There are as many styles as there are therapists and clients who discover themselves and each other and together invent their relationship.

> (Perls, 1977: 223)

This also true of the best work in transactional analysis.

Other existential psychotherapists such as Yalom state clearly, 'It is the relationship that heals. Every therapist observes over and over in clinical work that the encounter itself is healing for the patient in a way that transcends the therapist's theoretical orientation' (Yalom, 1980: 401).

Diagnosis can give a false and premature certainty, preventing experimentation, openness, and intellectual flexibility in terms of alternative frames of reference.

It is considered that transactional analysis is a humanistic, existential psychotherapy because of its emphasis on autonomy – intimacy, awareness, and spontaneity. Implicitly transactional analysis mandates against rote use of labels which reduce the individual and his or her unique human experience. However, Berne's facility with identifying and labelling such patterned wholes of human experience was probably one of his greatest contributions to modern psychotherapy. It is also probably one of the most frequently misunderstood and hence abused aspects of transactional analysis. Berne (1964) himself was sensitive to this in his cautions against the games of 'Psychiatry' and 'Transactional Analysis'.

The pioneers of the 1960s bequeathed this generation of clinicians a precious awareness of the uniqueness, possibilities and growthfulness of each individual human. It is important that the growing professionalisation of psychotherapy in the 1990s enhances this heritage.

USES OF DIAGNOSIS

Traditionally transactional analysis has placed great value on accurate diagnosis. Indeed one of the greatest gifts of Eric Berne (1980/1961) was the four diagnostic criteria (behavioural, social, phenomenological and historical) to be used in accurately identifying a person's current ego state. Such rigorous diagnostic criteria enable for example, the clinician to distinguish between treating the 5-year-old child which once existed in the client and the 5-year-old child in the client's father which was incorporated by the client at about the same time. In this way diagnosis provides a structure for treatment planning and decision making about the appropriateness of interventions as well as strategies for predicting outcomes and assessing changes.

Eric Berne was proud of being a 'real doctor' (1971: 6) and encouraged his students to practise psychotherapy in the same way. At his last public lecture, he used the analogy of a man with a splinter in his toe which becomes infected causing the man to limp and his leg, back and neck muscles to tighten up, leading to headaches and a fever from the infection. Berne contrasted two approaches to this problem which so clearly involves the whole personality. In the first case the doctor lists all the symptoms, points out the difficulty of guaranteeing results and estimates that it would take about three or four years to cure with the patient's help. In the second approach the surgeon diagnoses that the man has an infected toe caused by the splinter, which he then pulls out with a pair of tweezers. All the symptoms disappear within 48 hours. Berne added:

> Running through this I think you will hear the dread medical model of psychotherapy, which scares the hell out of people – gives them nightmares. But I think it's a very good model. That's because it works for other conditions, and if you are going to cure people's heads I think you should use the medical model.
>
> (Berne, 1971: 12)

Clinical training in transactional analysis continues to expect familiarity and facility with psychiatric and TA diagnosis which must be demonstrated at the examinations if the candidate is to be certified as a competent clinical transactional analyst. This can be a source of justified or unjustified criticism. The problem with diagnosis is not that it gets used but how it gets used, by whom and in what spirit.

Regarding the use of diagnosis, Brill states:

> In spite of many deviations and retrogressions the record is one of cumulative observation, with gradual evolution of concepts and clarification of thinking over more than 4,000 years. Traces of the evolutionary process survive in current psychiatric terminology and the evolution has been in part a reflection of advances in knowledge.
>
> (Brill, 1967: 583)

Our current psychiatric diagnostic categories such as ICD-9 (WHO, 1978) and the DSM-III-R (American Psychiatric Association, 1987), also provide a common language (or technical shorthand) for professionals, which cuts across different disciplines and countries. As with any other language, it is open to misunderstandings of apparently common meanings and is profoundly influenced by ulterior transactions (process variables).

None the less, provided the terminology is adequately defined, diagnosis can be a useful tool to spread information, clarify and explain symptoms and build up banks of information for national and international research into the ills that plague the minds of men and women of our time.

For the beginning psychotherapist in particular, diagnosis can be useful in the initial stages to recognise patterns of behaviour or distress which exceed the limits of competence of the practitioner. In such cases recognition and appreciation of the accumulated wisdom of the psychotherapist's predecessors can provide protection for both the psychotherapist and the client. In a sense, the function of diagnosis can be seen as a commitment to an ever-refining process of acknowledging individual differences – differential diagnosis:

> Differential diagnosis ... of two apparently equally anxious and emotionally distraught individuals, diagnosis of an underlying schizophrenic process in the one and not in the other will lead to a different treatment plan for each. One could multiply such examples indefinitely; what is important is the fact that differential diagnosis never takes place in a vacuum and that it is relevant only in so far as the therapeutic fate of the patient depends on it.
>
> (Harrower, 1965: 381)

Any discipline needs to be grounded on a sound theoretical base which has been scientifically tested and validated to the best efforts of the time. The basis for hypotheses does not have to be rigid in order to present scientifically verifiable and testable measures of progress.

A common misconception is that a classification of mental disorders classifies individuals, when actually what are being classified are the disorders that individuals have. For this reason, the text of DSM-III-R avoids the use of such phrases as 'a schizophrenic' or 'an alcoholic' and instead uses the more accurate but admittedly more worthy 'an individual with schizophrenia' or 'an individual with alcohol dependence':

Another misconception is that all people described as having the same mental disorder are alike in all important ways. Although all the people described as having the same mental disorder have at least the defining features of the disorder, they may well differ in other important respects that may affect clinical management and outcome.

(American Psychiatric Association, 1987: xxiii)

Diagnosis *can* be used to open up thinking and clarification in the client–psychotherapist partnership. Once a diagnosis of paranoid schizophrenia has been released of its connotations of incurability and stereotype, it can become a fertile matrix for the psychotherapeutic journey towards health. One of the greatest benefits of becoming fluent in differential diagnosis (without getting married to one idea) is the sheer pleasure of increasing knowledge and expertise, the enhanced sensitivity to patterns of behaviour and the more effective use of supervision. The case against diagnosis is against bad diagnosis. Each argument against it can be turned into a guideline for its better use and a monitor against abuse.

METAPERSPECTIVES

Beginning clinicians often experience this debate between proponents for the use of diagnosis and those against. Sometimes it seems like an either/or choice: one either learns differential diagnosis and becomes indistinguishable from the worst kind of 'Psychiatry' player, or one eschews it altogether as dehumanising and focuses instead exclusively upon the uniqueness of the person in the therapeutic relationship. Both views are partly correct, and together they form a whole. It appears to be a false dualism based on a perceived conflict between certainty and complexity, as between Aristotelian and Galilean conceptual systems (Gellert, 1975).

Both orientations together could contribute to the evolution of a more adequate paradigm. There is a third option to what might be considered a false polarity: on the one hand the Scylla of an overprecious relationship and on the other hand the Charybdis of deterministic categorisation. This metaperspective utilises the work of investigators who have paid particular attention to the differential functions of the brain, viz. right-hemispheric and left-hemispheric functions:

Research over the past twenty years has shown consistently that the two hemispheres of the brain tend to be involved in opposite but complementary functions. The left hemisphere which controls the right side of the body, seems to be more specialised in analytical, linear thinking, which involves processing information sequentially; the right hemisphere, controlling the left side of the body, seems to function predominantly in a holistic mode that is appropriate for synthesis and tends to process information more diffusely and simultaneously.

(Capra, 1983: 318)

Studies have shown that the different specialisations of the two sides of the brain represent preferences, not absolute distinctions. The left hemisphere is associated with intellectual functioning, historical time, analytical processing, sequential thinking and linguistic functions; it operates on the principle of causality, like a digital computer. The right hemisphere is associated with sensuous and intuitive functioning, rhythms and patterns, eternity or timelessness, processing of experience in terms of Gestalten or wholes, simultaneous perception, symbolic functions; it operates acausally. In left-handed people these functions are usually reversed and are more like an analogue computer (Ornstein, 1972).

For the psychotherapist engaged in the therapeutic process an understanding and appreciation of both kinds of brain functioning is of paramount importance. With the left hemisphere we do differential diagnosis, make prognoses, anticipate and predict behaviour on the basis of past sequences, plan treatment in accordance with similarities to other clients in the same category and organise our information and interventions systematically, logically and analytically.

With the right hemisphere we experience this moment with the client as ever new. The emergent Gestalt of this I–thou dialogue appears unrelated to clock time and shared intimacy over 50 minutes can be experienced as a lifetime of mutuality. Jean Houston (1982: 151) refers to this kind of temporal time distortion as 'alternate temporal process' and it is of course a phenomenon very familiar in hypnotherapy. We know that the unconscious is timeless. A nightmare may feel as if it lasts forever and the fixated Child ego state of, for example, 1952 still has a potential life in this moment.

Working from the right side of the brain emphasises the melody of the relationship, the pattern of 'whole gestalten' as opposed to an analysis of frequently occurring linear sequences more characteristic of the left side of the brain. The rhythm of this relationship in this moment has never been played before; nor has the exquisite logic of accurate observation, past wisdom and current inference. Both modes of functioning can be used to foster a better future for the client.

But again the dilemma facing the psychotherapist is when to use one kind of functioning and when to use the other. Most of us feel more comfortable in one than the other and may specialise in or strengthen one mode of functioning at the expense of the other. However, in order to develop as skilful psychotherapists with the widest possible range of interventions it may become necessary to pay special attention to strengthening and nurturing our less-developed mode (methods have been developed for this purpose, for example, Zdenek, 1986).

According to Steiner (1974), psychiatry historically has been dominated by male members of the ruling classes. Left-hemispheric functioning is more highly valued in the traditional educational system than the more subtle, intuitive and relational aspects associated with the right hemisphere. One of the great contri-butions of humanistic and existential psychotherapists has been their reversal of this order. Specifically, people such as Virginia Axline (1964), David Cooper (1978), Laing and Esterson (1970), Thomas Szasz (1961) and other radical thinkers (Boyers and Orrill, 1972; Steiner, 1974) in the Anti-psychiatry Movement have argued most eloquently for an end to the abuses of psychiatric diagnosis. They challenged what they saw as the rigid reductionism of the psychiatric establishment and insisted on the primacy of subjective experience, intuitive awarenesses and the validity of immediate perceptions.

Gestalt therapy in particular made a major contribution to this *Zeitgeist* (which continues today) by emphasising the figure–ground nature of human perception and psychological processes. Many people are familiar with the diagram which sometimes appears as two vases and sometimes as two profiles even though it remains the same picture (see Figure 4.1).

One of the most significant findings of the Gestalt psychologists was that human beings cannot see both figure and ground at the same moment. At one moment you may be most aware of the words on this paper and the position of your body on the chair may be background. As the need to stretch comes into awareness, this emergent need replaces the previous figure and the words on the paper become the background of the experience. This analogy has been found to be useful for psychotherapists who have struggled in vain to see relationship *and* diagnostic patterning at the same moment. It becomes a tool for understanding and integration. At times the here-and-now authentic moment between us as two

Figure 4.1   Figure and ground diagram
Source: Perls *et al.*, 1969: 26

human beings engaged in a healing process which neither of us fully understands is the only all-encompassing reality. At other more reflective times (such as recording and supervision) analysing and systematic sequential treatment planning, in terms of diagnostic indicators and agreed contracts, takes precedence.

When watching master psychotherapists at work, novices often have the fantasy that they are consciously processing the mass of data at incredible speeds. If this is not the explanation, then it might be a kind of 'magic' attributable to their specific charismatic qualities. In the first case, the task seems overwhelmingly difficult, and in the second, unless you introject the master wholesale, it appears impossible. This apparent mystery can be explained in terms of right- and left-hemispheric functioning according to the Gestalt principles of figure and ground. Neither process becomes fixed in a rigid attitude, nor does the competent psychotherapist slip haphazardly between them in a fickle and arbitrary manner.

There may never be a truthful or final solution to the debate pro and con diagnosis. The concepts are also in a continuing process of evolution. The very process of the debate is, however, an interesting and worthwhile exercise. Psychotherapy trainees are encouraged to build their ability and evidence in order to argue equally passionately and intelligently on either side and to add to the considerations mentioned here. Obviously there are individual preferences but perhaps a metaperspective is a realisation that this may be a false polarity, a paradox and a non-question. The real goal of psychotherapy is an organismic flow between these two positions, using the best of both, at the expense of neither, in rhythm with the appropriateness of the task and the demands of authentic I–Thou encounter.

Modern physics also has a metaperspective on the dualistic paradigm which is exemplified in Sir William Bragg's comment that elementary particles 'seem to be waves on Mondays, Wednesdays and Fridays, and particles on Tuesdays, Thursdays and Saturdays' (in Koestler, 1972: 52). Neither is false; they only appear to be mutually exclusive. It all depends where the observer stands (Einstein *et al.*, 1935; Capra, 1978).

DIAGNOSIS USING BERNE'S EGO-STATE APPROACH

According to Eric Berne: 'Ego states manifest themselves clinically in two forms; either as completely cathected coherent states of mind experienced as "real self"; or as intrusions, usually covert or unconscious, into the activity of the current "real Self"' (Berne, 1980: 71). Because an ego state comprises the total behaviour and experience of an individual at any given moment, an active uncontaminated ego state of any particular type would characteristically influence each and every element of behaviour and experience. So any ego state can be differentiated from other ego states through actions, attitudes or ways of experiencing. The diagnostic criteria, therefore, can be found through involuntary behaviour, voluntary behaviour, social clues or by introspection of any experience. *Behavioural diagnosis* of types of ego states or individual ego states were the first examples which Berne used. Most superficially, a raised voice, a tilted head and a submissively coy body posture looks more like the behaviour of a chronological child than a chronological adult. A person behaving judgmentally by raising their fingers, shouting insults from a superior position and towering over a subordinate in an office, for example, is observed as acting more like an authoritative parental figure. Such an ego-state diagnosis is obviously provisional to further corroboration and is necessarily based on behavioural cues. As such it is subject to great misinterpretation in all but the most standardised social situations. This aspect of TA has been extensively used and occasionally abused, particularly in organisational development and communications training in industry. In many cases, due to its apparent simplicity and easy accessibility, such partial comprehension has led to Berne being misunderstood to mean that behavioural diagnosis is the only way to diagnose ego states.

Berne, postulated three psychic organs: exteropsyche, neopsyche and archaeopsyche. He saw the three types of ego states as residing in these organs or as manifestations of these organs. All ego states manifest in idiosyncratic patterns of organised behaviour which can be spontaneously activated in response to environmental stimuli, memories or intentional psychotherapeutic procedures: for example, age regression, Parent ego-state interviews or hypnotic induction (Watkins and Johnson, 1982).

An appreciation of the phenomenological realities of ego states in clinical practice and everyday life can provide enormous refinement in terms of understanding individuals more accurately and thereby providing improved treatment. For example, sometimes it seems particularly difficult to diagnose a patient in a way which will facilitate treatment because different whole or part ego states may be confusing or even contradictory. Here follows an exposition of a way of diagramming ego states for the purpose of more accurate diagnosis and therefore improved treatment planning (see Figure 4.2).

The upper circle represents a more detailed version of an individual's Parent ego states which takes into account that the individual's introjected Parent figures may have been internalised as complete persons each with three types of ego states. In this example Sally carries within her Parent ego state the Parent, Adult and Child ego states of her mother. Thus, Sally may carry within her her mother's caretaking and valuing capacities (Parent in the Parent), her cool and efficient way of problem solving (Adult in the Parent) and the pain and confusion mother experienced during her orphaned childhood (the Child in the Parent).

People may also introject part-persons where only one or two ego-state categories were available. Sally's father's psychopathic personality structure excludes, for example, a valuing Parent ego state and the introjection of a psychopathic paternal introject would involve an excluded Parent ego state. Therefore Sally may have internalised only her father's Adult and Child, and may have a subsequent lack of ethical consciousness, since antisocial personalities usually have a defective or absent Parent ego state. So, when Sally's paternal Parent is active and in the executive, she may behave in an unethical or antisocial manner.

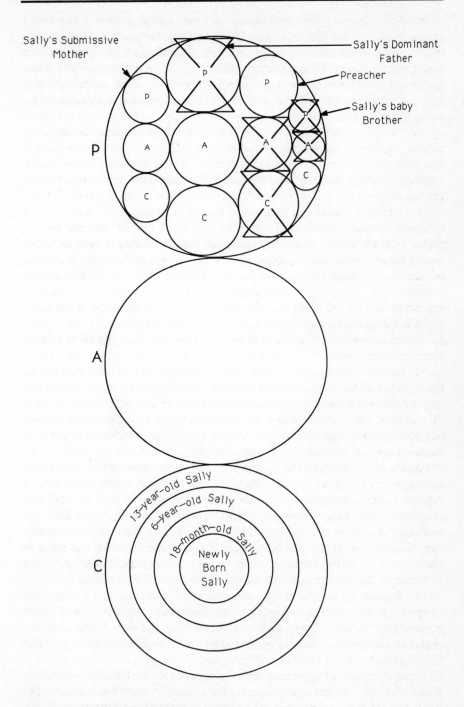

Figure 4.2 Diagnostic ego-state diagram

Equally, Sally may have introjected only one ego state from a significant person from her past. This may be, for example, an extremely righteous, judgmental and condemnatory preacher from the church which she attended as a young girl. However, she may not have included his sense of fair play, proportion and compassion, since she was overimpressed with his moral certainties. This was exacerbated by her need for structure and control which was not provided by either of her parents.

She introjected only the confused lascivious Child ego state of her elder brother who abused her sexually before he had a fully developed Parent ego state. She may on occasion experience this attitude (if not the same behaviour) in relation to her own children when she makes jokes about their genitals in front of her friends.

So in Sally's Parent ego state there will be representations, more or less complete, of many significant figures who have influenced her past and may be active by involuntary (automatic) activation (active Parent) or may be influencing her behaviour by controlling, provoking, or caring for any one or more of her Child ego states (influencing Parent). Whether Sally habitually cathects mother, father, preacher, or brother and whether she 'inhabits' these borrowed ego states in her relationships with others or is influenced by them intrapsychically in her relationship to herself or as she responds or projects onto current relationships, will depend on the decisions she made as a child and her present circumstances.

The nature or patterns of her intrapsychic relationships with these internalised figures will also be internalised and forms the blueprint for all her future external object relations. Because of the introjects and their related patterns and because they are alive and can be *present* in the consulting room and relived as if currently real in the relationship with the psychotherapist, therapeutic change is possible. Berne used this phenomenon of the externalisation in interpersonal relationships of our internalised object relationships, fears and wishes as the framework for the development of his game theory, which has been so widely disseminated in both popular culture and psychotherapy. For anyone who is not familiar with this part of transactional analysis they are referred to *Games People Play* which was published in 1964 by Grove Press in New York. Suffice it to remind the reader here that the task of the psychotherapist is to become aware of and assist in changing the repetitive, negative, interpersonal patterns (games) which the client will enact or attempt to enact with the psychotherapist. This is of course another way of referring to transference phenomena which will be further discussed in Chapter 7. In his approach to group psychotherapy and the observation of lateral transferences to other group members, Berne found a most fertile field for analysing and resolving limiting or destructive games which form the day-by-day building blocks for the unfolding of life script.

Social diagnosis of ego states refers technically to the use of countertransferential evidence – how other people (or the psychotherapist) feel in response to the person. Thus it may be more or less accurate to the extent that 'the others' or the psychotherapist are not transferring their own past reactions and interpersonal reactions onto the present situation.

A diagnostic examination of the integrated Adult ego state, represented by the middle circle in Figure 4.2, would consist in establishing its capacities for remaining in the executive, assessing reality, responding with appropriate emotions to the here-and-now circumstances, firming appropriately permeable boundaries and its general lack of contamination by interference from the ego states of others (Parent) or historical 'Child' ego states (from childhood or the more recent past).

The Child ego state representation in Figure 4.2 is based on English's diagram (in Barnes, 1977: 305). English's diagram offers a most useful contribution to understanding the complexity of Child ego states, their simultaneous phenomenological reality, and their potentially conflicting or confusing manifestations in terms of diagnosis and treatment planning. It represents a second-order structure of the Child which more closely resembles the experience of clinicians than the usual representation of the Child ego state. It can also take into account the developmental nature of the formation of separate Child ego states with greater precision.

Berne's understanding of child development took for granted Freudian developmental stages as embodied in his admonition to 'think sphincter' when doing psychotherapy. The whole psychosocial emphasis of his work also reflects the developmental stages of Erikson who was his analyst for a time. We have already shown the importance of Klein, but particularly Fairbairn for whom the infant as attachment-seeking organism took priority over predetermined expectable sequences of development. Berne saw children as pro-active decision makers, shaping the impact, nature and meaning of the influences on their lives in the light of their own temperament, preferences and biological predispositions. Each of the Child ego states are, however, formed against the background of commonly observed and well-known developmental patterns. All ego-state diagnoses, particularly Child ego states, are made using this information. Pam Levin (1988) has made a particularly fetching TA translation of Erikson which again serves comparison with the developmental schema of Freud and others. Every clinician naturally uses the version(s) which are most suitable to their particular approach. All working alliances, relationships and treatment of Child ego states are influenced by the developmental stages or tasks of the individual Child within the person. Essentially though, Berne, Fairbairn and the more modern child development theorist/clinicians such as Pine (1985) and Stern (1985) emphasise that the quality of parent/child relations is of at least equal if not of greater influence than the traditional stages of anticipated biological growth or socioemotional development. Berne's TA theory is a personality theory not an impersonal energy-controlled theory.

In the example in Figure 4.2, the newly born Sally representing very early ego states, may have experienced a particularly traumatic birth process with doctors panicking, doors slamming, and mother going from being anaesthetised to shocked to depressed. In Erikson's terms this could seriously undermine her ability to develop basic trust. Of course it is very likely, and clinically not at all uncommon, to find organised segments of psychophysiological complexes relived in psychotherapy which appear to recapitulate intra-uterine experiences. Most clinicians who have done regressive work with patients, whose mothers historically tried to abort them, can attest to the organismic, if pre-verbal proto-decisional, psychophysiological effect of such experience. Sally, whose mother tried to abort her, for example, lives her life as if she can be destroyed at any minute. The atmosphere of her internal psychic world is precarious, dangerous and fraught, even though her adult circumstances are substantially safe and beneficial.

Sally's child subsystem at 18 months may be a rather shy and schizoid child reacting anxiously to her mother's hospitalisation. This may be the Child ego state who made a decision that she should never share her feelings in case people leave her again, which could be activated or brought to the fore by Sally's psychotherapist going away on holiday. In contrast to this is her 6-year-old Child ego state, which flourished under the encouraging care of her favourite teacher, is confident, outgoing, creative, and quite extrovert.

At other times her 13-year-old self – who survived by submerging her budding sexuality into endless obsessive–compulsive rituals, anorexia, and studying for 10 hours a day memorising school work – may be active. Which of these Child ego-state subsystems the psychotherapist discovers, forms relationships with and treats, and in what order, can substantially influence the effectiveness, direction and success of treatment.

Of course, these Child ego state subsystems may not represent a calendar year and there are naturally many more, but they are experienced by both client and psychotherapist as phenomenologically real relivings of prior chunks of psychological time as explained in Chapter 3. This is a perspective of what amounts to a group of ego states or a collection of organised states of consciousness of different ages (or events) and differing original sources. These may of course overlap in time, and survival decisions or conclusions about self, others and the nature of the world may correspond with or contradict each other. All of these decisions represented in all of the different ego states will of course comprise physiological, affective, behavioural and cognitive dimensions in the person because ego states are whole, organised patterns of experience.

Historical Diagnosis of ego states refers to the actual prior existence of the individual's present whole or part 'borrowed' (Federn's term) objects in the individual's Parent or the historical veracity of the segments of experience laid down as Child ego states. Often, historical diagnosis of ego states is made quite easily, for example: 'Did one of your caretakers ever behave in such a way?' or 'Can you recall the scene in which this first happened?' By investigation, enquiry and clinical reconstruction it is usually possible to verify the truth of the individual client's experiences. Sam experienced an internal mother who hated him. He often felt disgusted with himself and alienated from his bodily functions.

His mother was, however, to all of his knowledge and family reports a fine parent, affirming, supportive and liberally welcoming his appetite for life. It had begun to seem as if (an inexperienced psychotherapist may have been misled to believe that) he had created this disguised, physically rejecting parent out of his own fantasy. Several years into psychotherapy he happened to meet an aunt who told him the family secret – just after his birth his mother had had a 'nervous breakdown', with complicated symptomatology including suicidal depression and cleaning rituals of the extent that she had had to be stopped from washing baby Sam so much that his skin became raw.

As pointed out by Alice Miller (1985) in *Thou Shalt Not Be Aware*, children are often abused, hurt, neglected, or frightened and then persuaded, hypnotised, (Conway and Clarkson, 1987) or seduced out of awareness for these events (conscious memory). Then it becomes convenient for parents and psychotherapists to attribute to the child the seductive, destructive, or chaotically uncontrolled intentions as result. Furthermore, often the greater the abuse, the more likely the child is to be loyal and internalise the aggressor (Bloch, 1979; Ferenczi, 1980). This is further discussed in Chapter 10 in the section on ego-state dilemmas of abused children. Suffice it to point out here the weight of evidence accumulating that any psychological or psychotherapeutic approach which attributes greater formative power or 'truth' to the child's destructive or seductive fantasies rather than to the actual reality of the caretaker's behaviour of the child, may in this view be guilty of further abuse. The child's fantasies are shaped on the actual material of their relationships with their caretakers in the real world.

Berne, by stating that the *phenomonological diagnosis* is the ultimate criterion for ego-state diagnosis, validates the subjective truth of a person's childhood experience whether or not historical evidence is available. The 'evidence' for the phenomenological truth of Sam's Parent ego-state representation may never have been uncovered if Sam had not as a grown-up attended the funeral of a distant relative and 'accidentally' met an aunt who (without him even asking or consciously wanting to know) corroborated his internal truth. For Berne the child is not on trial. The person contains their history in their ego states which is most truly verified by the psychophysiological completeness of reproduction of borrowed egos or developmentally earlier ego states. These can be present in the consulting room and are more likely to appear and to be healed if psychotherapists believe them rather than doubt them – perhaps in an attempt to protect themselves from the phenomenological truth of the beloved parent's persecution which the psychotherapist cannot yet face (believe?) in themselves.

Latent psychosis may therefore, for example, be conceptualised in terms of an individual containing a parent's Child ego state which is actively psychotic and hallucinating, but because the individual has developed a sound Adult and reasonably good adjustments in Child, they may not manifest the psychosis (as active Parent ego state) but they will of course experience the stress and tension of containing within them a 'mad Child'. The cornerstone of dealing with any client in a way consistent with classical Berne and the most modern information from child development and on child abuse is the respectful understanding that the subjective, phenomenological or experienced truth of the person is the essential verification of its accuracy. This original, clinical orientation of Berne's has been validated repeatedly over many years in clinical practice and by anecdotal investigation. Children may, of course, symbolise their experiences before they allow themselves to remember and well before they may be strong enough to relive the traumatic relationships or events (which they re-experience under certain stresses in their adult lives) in full consciousness.

A 12-year-old boy, Marvin, developed recurrent night terrors of being attacked by a killer bird vomiting in his mouth. This was affecting his school work. It only emerged in family therapy that Marvin's father had abused his infant son by masturbating into the baby's toothless mouth. The father was, several years after, a man of integrity and compassion to all intents and purposes. The son could not remember and the father had also 'needed' to forget. When a child experiences an internal wolf tearing them apart and mother is mild, kind and beyond reproach, that 'wolf' may only be more vicious as a result of its caged condition in mother's psyche. Our patients may lie, but the Child in our patients will usually tell the truth and be their truth with a therapeutic respectful adult who will listen with the assumption that the child is innocent.

DIAGNOSIS AND TREATMENT IMPLICATIONS OF SUICIDAL, HOMICIDAL, OR PSYCHOTIC RISK

The author's basic assumption is that people do not want to kill themselves, to kill others or to go crazy. These are not primary human needs but three hamartic or tragic script outcomes, as identified by Eric Berne. Whatever the philosophical, cultural, or social pressures, these behaviours are rather viewed as potential solutions to problems experienced as insurmountable, unsolvable or intolerable. Technically, people who fantasise suicide, want to kill themselves, or actually do so, are confused (i.e., their Adult ego state is contaminated), in conflict, ill or traumatised. Exceptions are possible when they are indeed choosing autonomously to kill or be killed, for example, against oppression, in wars or in self-defence.

By maintaining suicidal, homicidal, or psychotic notions clients are often protecting themselves from feeling the full psychophysiological impact of the pain locked in one or more of their ego states. Wanting to die is ultimately anti-organismic and against *Physis* unless the person is very old or very ill, in which case it is in harmony with nature.

In order for a psychotherapist to work at all, the establishment of a working alliance between the Adult of the psychotherapist and the Adult ego state of the patient needs to be negotiated. Such an *Adult–Adult contract* is necessary for out-patient treatment based on the obvious fact that 'I can't work with you unless you stay alive and you don't go/act crazy outside of my consulting room'. Hospitals and residential facilities are available and are more suitable for patients than out-patient treatment if they are serious suicidal, homicidal or psychotic risks. According to some TA authors (Boyd and Cowles-Boyd, 1980; Stewart, 1989) such contracts between the psychotherapist and the patient are not sufficient to ensure that it will be kept, since they believe that 'contracts' can be changed or renegotiated.

Usually the suicidal, homicidal or psychotic script decisions of a person encapsulate the script conclusion: 'I feel so awful that the only way out is to die, kill or "go mad".' Holloway (1973) suggested that these represent three 'escape hatches', one or more of which may be decided upon early in life, at the time of script decisions, to be exercised when life got too stressful. Drye, Goulding and Goulding (1978) developed a method of assessing the actual risk of suicide. They ask the patient to make the following statement: 'No matter what happens, I will not kill myself, accidentally or on purpose, at any time' (p. 128). Then they observe the reactions and attend to the reports of patients' internal responses. They do this procedure as soon as they:

> believe that patients are aware of their fantasies .... If the patient reports a feeling of confidence in this statement, with no direct or indirect qualifications, and with no incongruous voice tones or body motions, the evaluator may dismiss suicide as a management problem.
>
> (Drye *et al.*, 1978: 128)

Incongruity may signal that the client has shifted into a Child ego state and may be making a promise instead of a decision. When qualifications are detected, the highest priority becomes to get an unconditional and congruent *'no suicide' decision*. Interim short-term contracts, for a day or a week, can temporarily provide the necessary protection. It is vital in this case to ensure that adequate arrangements are made to extend the commitment before its expiration date and that protective measures such as hospitalisation be considered:

> There are two situations where its use requires considerable flexibility. One of these is long-term therapy, where the method itself becomes a major issue in the relationship and needs to be dealt with as such. The other situation is with patients who have made suicide the central theme of their lives .... Finally, this method is not safe with patients who use alcohol or other drugs heavily.
>
> (Drye *et al.*, 1978: 133)

For Drye, Goulding and Goulding suicidal or self-destructive fantasies (including fantasies of accidents, food or chemical abuse, or exhausting or dangerous work habits) immediately call for such careful investigation and action. Some authors such as Maggiora (1987) in treating severe depression do not always find it necessary, but Boyd and Cowles-Boyd (1980) recommend that therapists close all three escape hatches in a single session routinely with all patients as early as possible in the course of treatment. They see this procedure as resulting in social (Adult) control of the hamartic script, and not as a redecision. According to Stewart (1989) the Child in the person overhears this firm decision or unconditional Adult commitment and the Adult will honour a decision taken congruently. 'As time passes, the person adjusts in Child to the new situation' (p.83).

This is based on the assumption that the client's Adult is both decontaminated and will remain in the executive until further reconstructive psychotherapy can be done. It is of course possible that patients may interpret such a decision procedure to mean that they cannot explore their suicidal, homicidal or psychotic aspects and fantasies. This can rob them of an existential choice to take responsibility for their own lives (its irritations, griefs and beauty) of depth and poignancy. 'Social control' may be achieved, but experienced as a prohibition from the psychotherapist to plumb such depths of the human psyche even in long-term psychotherapy. In order for such commitments to have lasting value, it may be important to identify and diagnostically locate the borrowed or archaic ego states of the person where experienced events or periods of pain, frustration or despair, which led to such tragic decisions, are contained. It is by re-experiencing the original events and the making of the original decisions in the introjected or historical ego states that the psychological commitment to tragic outcomes can be 'turned around' or redecided.

Mellor has pointed out that 'no suicide' or 'no homicide' contracts and *redecisions* need to be made with all the ego states in the person which have a wish or commitment to dying. This may involve forming alliances with Parent or Child ego states or bargaining with them. It is only when each destructive or psychotic ego state has made a redecision (with full feeling re-experiencing the 'chunk of associated psychological time'), that the clinician can be sure that all the work is done. 'Any or all of these aspects may be found in the Parent or Child and may be invested with different levels of energy' (Mellor, 1979: 186). In discussing *Parent ego states* in this regard, Mellor mentions the example of a patient called Geraldine who had three homicidal people (objects) in her Parent: two were suicidal and one wanted to die, while her mother and father were homicidal towards each other. He recommends that psychotherapists who have experience in working with violent or severely disturbed patients conduct Parent interviews in order to safeguard the patient's life. The author has also found it clinically necessary to make 'no suicide' contracts and invite redecisions with the Parental introjects of patients. For example, Jack had introjected his mother's Child ego state (in his Parent). When he came into psychotherapy, his mother had already in fact committed suicide several years before. In psychotherapy it was necessary to make a 'no suicide' redecision with her. Jack's real mother may have acted out her hamartic script but within Jack's psyche there remained in existence (until the therapeutic intervention) the despairing Child of his parent who continued to threaten suicide. Sometimes a parent passes on to their child a script instruction to be killed or to go psychotic in an attempt to rid themselves of the lethal injunction (English, 1969).

Life- or sanity-threatening decisions can also have been taken by *different Child ego states* as indicated by the concentric circles in the Child illustrated in

Figure 4.2. For example, because of the still-birth of a deformed twin there may conceivably be a psychophysiological wish to be killed. Because of the mother's depression at the birth, the baby was separated from her and may have decided that she was going to die from the pain of the abandonment. In a 3-year-old ego state the Child may have made a decision that he deserved to die after the death of a baby sister following shortly on a fantasy of wishing the sibling dead. In a 16-year-old ego state a young man may make a negotiation against the 'don't exist' injunction: 'I don't want to kill, so I'll become a surgeon who saves people's lives.' A decision to die may be reconfirmed as a result of adult trauma at 40 years of age, such as interrogation under torture. So, one could find in any one patient an intra-uterine *injunction* not to exist as a result of an attempted abortion, a *script decision* not to live in a 3-year-old ego state as a result of magical thinking and guilt, a bartering or *negotiation agreement* in a 16-year-old ego state, and a *desire to die* rather than live under oppression as a 40-year-old.

The importance of this is that the clinician be alert to the fact that working with tragic outcomes is neither routine nor simple. The process of diagnosis and doing psychotherapy is enhanced by an accurate diagnosis of the nature, motivation and identity of the ego states involved. Furthermore, it is important to be alert to any potential disruption to the solidity and reliability of the Adult as well as the possibility of disassociative phenomena such as multiple personality. After a 4-year-old redecision to live the patient reported back the following week that 17-year-old Nancy (a fully developed other personality) was not at all comfortable with this and the psychotherapist had to promptly establish a new working relationship with this hitherto undiscovered part of his patient.

Clinically it has often been found that the person's Child can assist the psychotherapist in dealing with Parental resistance. The redecision to exist or to live needs to be made in every ego state involved and it is particularly important that significant Parental introjects contract not to kill, hurt or provoke the Child to kill while the psychotherapist is working with helping the Child to make a true *redecision to stay alive and to live in health and in fulfilment while supporting the same in other people*. Another phase in treatment would indeed concern integration work in which the different ego states of the person:

> discuss their reactions to each other after or during the decision making. It is also valuable at times to get them to discuss signals they will send to each other to warn each other of areas that create problems or, preferably, to signal what support they can give each other.
>
> (Mellor, 1979: 187)

At all times the psychotherapist, in working with suicidal, homicidal or psychotic risk, needs to be flexible in their use of theories and techniques, suiting them to the person, their characteristics and the nature of the psychotherapeutic relationship between them. Countertransferential grandiose fantasies of taking responsibility for the lives of others or saviour wishes need to be transformed in personal psychotherapy and in supervision. Finally, as Jung cautioned: 'learn your theories as well as you can, but put them aside when you touch the miracle of the living soul' (Jung, 1928: 361).

SUMMARY

The abuses of traditional psychodiagnosis in terms of psychiatric nomenclature such as ICD-9 or DSM-III-R is explored as well as the benefits of using such categorisation for professional communication, clinical understanding and the development of treatment hypotheses.

It is suggested that diagnosis can have a valid place in psychotherapy if it counterpoints a genuine appreciation of the unique individuality of each person. A metaperspective suggests that left-hemispheric classificatory clarity alternates usefully with right-hemispheric, intuitive holistic impressions in relationship. Neither necessarily excludes the other and both can benefit from using a non-dualistic neophysical metaphor based on wave/particle identity related to observer subjectivity.

Ego-state diagnosis based on a modified ego-state diagnosis is discussed, offering a visual and conceptual tool for differentiating different kinds of ego states, identifying or diagnosing them by means of behavioural, social, historical and phenomenological criteria and as such potentially facilitating treatment design at the same time as emphasising the uniqueness of each individual. Finally, there is a discussion of diagnosis and treatment of suicidal, homicidal or psychotic risk using ego-state theory.

Chapter 5

The psychotherapy of ego states[†]

> There was a child went forth every day,
> And the first object he looked upon and received with wonder or
>   pity or love or dread, that object he became,
> And that object became part of him for the day or a certain part of
>   the day ... or for many years or stretching cycles of years.
>
> (Whitman, 1976: 138)

This chapter is intended to describe one of the ways in which Berne's original phenomenological model of ego states, as discussed in Chapter 3, can be expanded to incorporate new concepts which can be applied in clinical practice. A summary diagram of the major methods of transactional-analysis treatment of ego states is presented, followed by a brief description of each. A fifth category of ego-state intervention is presented and the term 'rechilding' is introduced to describe the creation of ego states congruent with developmentally earlier psychophysiological levels in intact Adult personalities. This chapter then discusses how 'rechilding' can be employed in conjunction with other established theory and practice to achieve stability under stress. This material is illustrated by clinical examples and diagrams which enable the concepts to be accessible for clients in planning their therapy.

To recap, ego state is used here as Berne defined it: 'a consistent pattern of feeling and experience directly related to a corresponding consistent pattern of behaviour' (Berne, 1966: 364). This is understood to mean the recognisable ego states identified by Federn (1977/1953) which Berne himself equated with the natural way of experiencing and of recording experiences in their totality at neurophysiological levels in the brain as Penfield discovered in neurophysiology (Berne, 1966: 201).

Transactional-analysis treatment traditionally deals with three categories of ego states – Parent, Adult and Child. The majority of psychotherapeutic approaches that have been developed in TA can be conceptualised in terms of the

[†] Co-authored by Sue Fish with clinical contributions from Renee Walinets

changing or replacing of these ego states. These approaches have been divided (not necessarily in this order) into four major categories: (1) Decontamination in order to establish integrated Adult ego-state functioning, (2) Psychotherapy of Parent ego states, (3) Creating or providing new Parent ego-states and (4) Psychotherapy of Child ego states. It is proposed in this chapter that a *fifth* category – the creation and provision of new archaic Child ego-states – seems implicit and a corollary to all four of the above. However, this does not appear to have been formally conceptualised or represented in common TA terminology, although many transactional analysis psychotherapists implicitly include these ideas in their therapeutic work. This process is here termed *rechilding* to be congruent with the accepted process of reparenting.

Rechilding is meant as an adjunct to the other approaches and not as a substitute to any one of them. Although it can be used alone, it is also used in conjunction with the other four methods in an integrative framework. Rechilding is the creation of new ego states on developmentally earlier substrata.

Table 5.1 presents a summary of ego-state intervention categories with examples of some relevant techniques for each category.

Table 5.1 Summary categories of ego-state intervention with examples of some relevant techniques

Ego-state intervention categories	Examples of techniques
1 Decontaminating and establishing integrated Adult ego-state functioning	Therapeutic operations (Berne, 1966)
2 Psychotherapy for Parent ego states	Parent-resolution process (Dashiell, 1978) Reparenting the Parent (Mellor and Andrewartha, 1980a) Redecision in the Parent Parent-grafting (Mitchell, 1983) Parent interview (McNeel, 1976)
3 Creating/providing new Parent ego states	Spot-reparenting (Osnes, 1974) Reparenting (Schiff *et al.*, 1975) Parenting (Schiff *et al.*, 1975) Self-reparenting (James, 1974) Interpositioning (Berne, 1980/1961)
4 Psychotherapy of Child ego states	Deconfusion (Berne, 1966, 1980) Redecision (Goulding and Goulding, 1979) Disconnection of rubber bands (Erskine, 1974)
5 Creating/providing new Child ego states	Redecision reinforcement techniques (Goulding and Goulding, 1979) Reparenting correlates (Schiff *et al.*, 1975) Rechilding procedures

DECONTAMINATION

In in-depth psychotherapy (in conformity with Berne's original formulation), the aim is healthy functioning of the personality in the integrated Adult (i.e. with a physiological and biological maturity and the capacity for full spontaneous emotional responsiveness to current reality) in its objective (A_2), interpersonal (Pathos) and valuing (Ethos) aspects. The first step towards achieving such full integrated Adult functioning would be to remove *contaminations* (prejudicial or emotive historical distortions of current reality) as has been discussed before (see Figure 5.1).

This goal is complemented and amplified by using the redecision (Goulding and Goulding, 1979) and reparenting (Schiff *et al.*, 1975) models in an integrative way (Mellor and Andrewartha, 1980a, b) as well as with specific therapy of the Parent ego states. One of the major ways in which decontamination is achieved is by dealing with confusion between different ego states. The ultimate goal would still be to place the person's Adult in the executive so that he or she takes full responsibility and experiences autonomous choice between cathecting (investing with selfness or psychic energy) different ego states whilst recognising that these various ego segments are all part of the self. This means that no part of potentially active historical or internalised ego states is dissociated, denied or disowned.

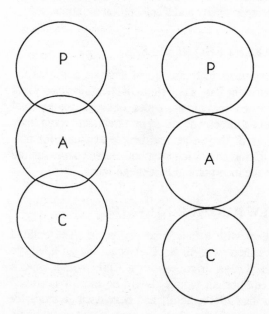

Figure 5.1 Ego states before and after decontamination

Certain ego states can be decathected or the involuntary activation of certain ego states can be psychotherapeutically prevented, by disconnecting 'the electrodes' or 'the rubberband'. For example, Janine used to flinch whenever someone touched her unexpectedly. In response to a sudden movement by another person, she reacted from a Child ego state by flinching in the same way as she did to escape surprise assaults by her bad-tempered father. Through cathartic work, she no longer reacts involuntarily in this way and has developed much greater trust in the basic goodwill of most human beings as she surrounds herself with people who are more trustworthy and relationships which are more nourishing. Except in cases where the particular historical or introjected ego-states are particularly toxic or traumatic, most people can benefit from getting to know the different ego states which constitute: '"the society of self" within a single individual' (Watkins and Johnson, 1982: 130) and learning how to reduce conflicts between ego states, how to utilise conflict and how to enrich themselves by experiencing and validating many different aspects of themselves.

Such inter-ego state psychotherapy can be effected by procedures which facilitate different ego states to dialogue, engage and find resolution with each other while the Adult remains in the executive or the centre of consciousness. So in a sense, individual psychotherapy is conceptualised as being a kind of family or group psychotherapy in so far as more-or-less complete ego states or different organisational patterns or ego state networks are brought into interaction. The object of such work is to facilitate greater cohesion of the self and appreciation for its multiplicity, and to develop the person's capacity for choosing freely from integrated Adult with awareness, spontaneity and a celebration of intimacy.

PSYCHOTHERAPY FOR PARENT EGO STATES

One of the most fruitful developments in transactional analysis concerns the discovery that clinicians can contact the Parent ego states of clients as vividly real phenomena. Since these incorporated 'psychic presences' of significant parental figures from a person's past can be directly accessed in a treatment room, they can be interviewed or treated 'as if' they were real people available for new information, permissions and resolutions. Such psychotherapy operations are intended to establish changes in the incorporated Parent ego states.

CREATING/PROVIDING NEW PARENT EGO STATES

In 1961 Berne wrote of a patient with a functional psychosis: 'The optimal prognosis was also clear; since there was no hope of acquiring an adequate Parent, the Adult would have always to cope with a Child without much exteropsychic help. Thus the equilibrium would always be more precarious' (Berne, 1980: 149). Yet by the late 1960s, Schiff had developed methods for providing adequate Parent ego states for psychotic patients which would help them in retaining their equilibrium even under stress. This involved, e.g., the decathexis of the original pathological Parent ego state and the voluntary contractual incorporation of a complete new Parent ego state (frequently that of the therapist) (see Figure 5.2).

Reparenting is not always a radical procedure, but can involve short-term regressive techniques to deal with quite specific issues (Mellor and Andrewartha, 1980a, b; Osnes, 1974) and the providing of new parental messages around those issues. None of these authors state as their goal the achievement of integrated Adult functioning without *interference* from historical introjects or archaic relics. Rather, their goal is to change or influence or provide a new 'introject' for the Child so that the person feels safe enough to implement the redecision and/or new behaviours. In the radical model of full reparenting (Schiff *et al.*, 1975) a new parenting experience is provided by allowing a complete regression which allows the patient's Child to move through the developmental cycle once again in a healthier way. This is not necessarily only in response to the original pathogenic stimulus but also in response to new stimuli provided by a 'good-enough' new parent along a developmentally appropriate continuum of responses. Further psychotherapy may be necessary to work through the newly replaced Parent ego structure for Adult integration.

With a non-psychotic client population, the new Parent ego state may be of value for survival under stress, or when automatic responses are speedily

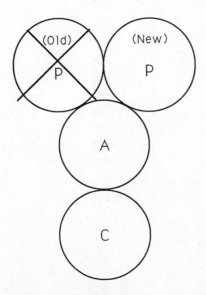

Figure 5.2 Decathexis of old Parent state and incorporation of new Parent ego state from psychotherapist

required for the patient to fall back on the old Parent introject. In such cases the therapist can provide new Parent experiences but can leave part of the old Parent intact so that the client can tap into her old resources and information which can still be valuable without having to incorporate the psychotherapist as Parent (see Figure 5.3). The person thus has options involving the old and the new Parent. In the self-reparenting process of James (1974) the person provides herself with new Parent messages without necessarily introjecting or incorporating from the therapist at all. This is possible with a non-psychotic population because of the relative integrity of the personality in contrast with the fragmentation and the destructiveness of the Parent ego states found in psychosis.

PSYCHOTHERAPY OF CHILD EGO STATES

As explained on p.42 in Chapter 3, Berne considered each ego state as a phenomenological entity representing natural psychobiological epochs of a person's life. Some ego states from earlier periods in a person's life may be fixated in response to early unmet needs or psychological trauma. Others of these like the 'unbent pennies' are 'potentially capable of contributing to his personality exactly what a happy actual child is capable of contributing to his family life' (Berne, 1977: 149) Methods which directly address the Child ego state are designed to change the originally fixated Child ego states. Redecision

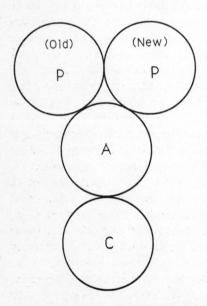

Figure 5.3 New and old Parent available to person

(Goulding and Goulding, 1979) therapy is aimed at the relevant re-experienced Child ego state which was fixated in response to the recreation of the original traumatic incident or series of incidents. The redecision is made in the archaic Child ego state in the context of a relationship with a potent permission-giving psychotherapist who will also provide protection. A new Child decision (redecision) is made specifically in response to the pathogenic stimulus which brought about the fixation of the original Child ego state.

CREATING/PROVIDING NEW CHILD EGO STATES

> The Child ego state is the part of people that thinks, feels and behaves as they did in the past ... particularly as children but sometimes as grown ups.... We see the Child as ever growing and ever developing, as the sum total of experience that he has had and is having in the present.
>
> (Goulding and Goulding, 1979: 12, 20)

This corresponds to Berne's idea that Child ego states are manifestations of the archaeopsyche which 'gives rise to its own idiosyncratic patterns of organised behaviour', is 'capable of adapting behaviour to the immediate social situation' and can 'mediate the phenomena of experience'. Most importantly in this context, is the property of 'biological fluidity, in the sense that responses are modified as a result of natural growth and previous experiences' (Berne, 1980: 75).

It is postulated that, particularly under stress, the healthy equilibrium of the integrated Adult depends on the health of the optional Parent repository (Berne, 1980: 149) (see Figure 5.4). Equally the equilibrium of the individual can be affected by the health of the optional Child ego state repository. The question that arises in certain circumstances is: are we creating a new archaic memory repository that can act as a supporting Child function to the here-and-now Adult reality of the client inserting some healthy new 'unbent or unwarped coins'? The goal would be for the client to have sufficient new healthy Child ego states which have been activated in therapy to act as a stable and reliable support system as well as memory bank for integrated Adult ego state functioning. For example, a client who, as a mature student at college, was extremely nervous at the thought of sitting a forthcoming examination, attended a rechilding workshop. She chose to regress to various ages at which she had had experiences of being examined. She did not revisit her previously gruelling examination experiences but set herself her own examinations and tasks at these ages, one of which entailed examining how many jokes she could tell in 10 minutes and how many jokes she could listen to in another 10 minutes. This gave her 11 year old an enjoyable experience of task-setting, thinking, remembering and formulating, i.e. aspects of examination procedure unfamiliar to her in connection with enjoyment. In the real examination situation she was able to access these enjoyable feelings rather than her nervousness in support of her Adult functioning which proved to be competent and creative.

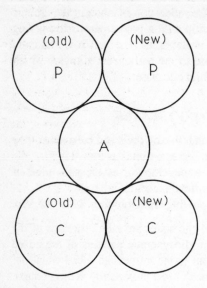

Figure 5.4   New Parent and new Child ego states available under stress

The difference between the Adult and the new Child ego states is that the Child repository is related to psychic timelessness: 'A peculiarity of the ego related to its needs for integration and continuity is its sense of immortality – of being without beginning or end in time' (Weiss, 1950: 15). Along with a sense of psychic timelessness of the Child ego state goes a heightened state of suggestibility, whereas the Adult ego state is predicated on consensually defined here-and-now reality in a dehypnotised state (Conway and Clarkson, 1987).

Just as it is not necessary for parents to be present for their children to have healthy experiences, it is not always necessary for rechilding to be accompanied by reparenting. A group of adults voluntarily regressed to puberty may find or create new Child (historical) ego states as they relate to each other, share sexual fantasies and experiment with peer relationships at that developmental stage without any specific Parental intervention. Some psychoanalysts describe such a paradoxical kind of 'regression' which does not mean re-experiencing feelings or events from the past but a child-like experience of something for the first time and hence 'a new beginning' (Balint, 1959). The process of rechilding also appears to have similarities with what Moreno (the originator of psychodrama) called the creation of 'surplus reality'. In this way, the protagonist gets the opportunity to experience a past event in new ways. Sb surplus reality is, for Moreno, 'an enrichment of reality by the investments and extensive use of the imagination' (Moreno, 1965: 213). Cure, which can also be defined as a permanent frame-of-reference change, is accomplished when the new Parent and new Child ego states are grafted onto the Adult and are stable under stress (SUS).

The end result should be that the previous pathogenic-Parent and injured-Child repositories become defunct or fade away through non-use since an integrated Adult would only prefer to draw upon the newly created experiences (see Figure 5.5). The old Parent and old Child still exist, but are practically never used. This approach to treatment conforms well with the behaviour-modification model for the extinction of affective, behavioural, physiological and/or cognitive response patterns. This approach is of particular importance when there is a lesion in the Child ego state that cannot be cured by redecision and selective reparenting alone. There may be so much hurt in a particular Child area that it may be necessary for the client to cathect Child and to make a neurological and physiological implacement of absent, positive Child experiences that will be durable over time. The Adult is, in this way, supplied with a supportive history to replace the pathogenic history in the Child ego state. The psychotherapeutic goal of the attainment of functioning of integrated Adult is viewed as complementary (not contradictory) to the therapeutic creation of new Child ego states. These can then be available as optional, supportive reservoirs to a mature person under stress.

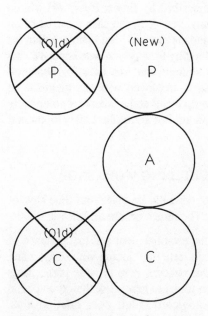

Figure 5.5 Pathogenic old Parent and old Child ego states defunct

In the 'rechilding'[†] process, clients contractually cathect to physiologically younger age levels at which there are experiential or developmental deficits and ultimately allow themselves to create new Child ego states with positive, healthy and resourceful responses to a variety of situations ranging from stressfully challenging to peaceably reparative. This approach affords an emotional, sensory and physiological corrective experience which is lodged in a newly created Child ego state but which is, nevertheless, an historical reality for tomorrow's integrated Adult. Thereby it becomes available as an optional historical resource. The new Child ego state is *both* archaic and new; it is new in its creation today and is the archaic relic of tomorrow. Furthermore, it is archaic because it is formed on an earlier developmental psychophysiological substratum. The creation of new healthy experiences for the historical/phenomenological inner Child is particularly important for those clients who 'rubberband' (Kupfer and Haimowitz, 1971) to an ego state lesion under stress of life experiences, illness and catastrophe. Here the force of the redecision may need additional support from a new psychoneurological experiential substratum. We believe that such new Child ego states are indeed created in most forms of psychotherapy, but frequently in an arbitrary and random fashion. This 'rechilding' approach provides for the systematic and highly accurate provision of developmentally required Child ego states, and falls into the category of what can be called 'replacement therapy'.

This approach has similarities to that described by Ernest Rossi and Milton Erickson (1980) in *Innovative Hypnotherapy*, vol. 4, in the case material of an hypnotic corrective emotional experience, and the story of 'The February Man' as he used it to create a self-consistent internal reality for a person who needed a new experientially real childhood to act as a strength and resource for her adult functioning. An essentially similar process is employed with the inclusion of emotional, physiological and behavioural components at the exact chronologically accessed neurophysiological organisation of the individual developmental lacunae.

TREATMENT STRUCTURE IN A RECHILDING WORKSHOP

Such a paradoxically 'regressive workshop' typically involves four time slots of 90–120 minutes per day over several days. The time slots are as follows.

1 The *group-process* slot has as a focus the establishment and maintenance of 'pro-activity' from autonomous Adult ego state functioning with support and confrontation within the community. Our concern is to provide participants with ample and potentially stressful opportunity to generalise their therapeutic and regressive experiences to chronologically adult peer relationships.

[†] The term self rechilding is used by Muriel James (1977: 143) in reference to self-therapy with the Child ego state using the functional model (adapted child/natural child). What we clearly are dealing with in this section is rechilding according to the structural (phenomenological) model of ego states.

Problems here are usually diagnostic of potential difficulties in generalising their personal changes to the 'outside world', and frequently form the basis for the therapeutic contracts which are the cornerstones of the work during the psychotherapy slot.

2 During the *psychotherapy* slot, the psychotherapists work in small groups doing contractual decontamination; Child ego state therapy (e.g. redecision or cathartic work); or Parent ego state therapy (e.g. reparenting the Parent). The goal is to resolve script issues to make affective, cognitive, and physiological changes in the archaic or introjected ego states (Erskine, 1980).

3 During the *regressive* (or better-called *rechilding*) slot, clients create, access and programme new Child ego states by allowing regression to earlier psycho-physiological levels of development (chosen contractually and in consultation with the therapists), with or without specific new parenting by time-limited contractual 'parents'. The effect is not unlike that of being in a large family with children of different ages (although they are physically fully grown). Schiff in Schiff and Day (1970) describes her reparenting approach with schizophrenic patients. It is important to note, however, that our client population, unlike Schiff's, are mostly *not* 'schizophrenics' but well-functioning mental health professionals who find this form of regression both therapeutic and preventative of 'burn-out'. We are also using a different theoretical model of ego states, aiming for stable Adult ego state cathexis while allowing that under stress, temporary replenishment from Child or Parent ego states can enhance/support mature intellectual and emotional functioning.

4 A time slot is also set aside for *cognitive integration* which provides specific opportunity for clients, trainees and assistants to question, comment and receive supervision on aspects of their own or others' experience and to relate their experience to different theories of child development and to applications to clinical practice and parenting in general.

CLINICAL EXAMPLE

In the following clinical example, one of the author's clients gives an account which focuses on the therapy and the rechilding (regressive) slots in order to illustrate how she understood and utilised them in the particular workshop which she attended. Other items of worth, e.g. Parent ego state therapy, have been omitted for the sake of brevity in order to focus on Child ego state work:

I had been in therapy with the author for nearly five years – the last three in training. I had worked through most of the unresolved issues that I had previously used a lot of energy to block. I slowly relinquished my 'Never' script (my life decision that I would never be contented or achieve my goals) and the passivity that advanced it. My functioning had been spontaneous, aware and capable of intimacy. And yet I still felt that under stress I could revert to not thinking, withdrawal and feeling the despair and hopelessness with the same intense pain as I did at the beginning of my therapy. I needed a regressive experience which would have the same *psychic intensity* but with a *positive outcome*.

During one training weekend, the psychotherapist talked of her new model and I saw immediately how I could use it. I had booked in for three days' regression (rechilding workshop) which would provide me with the opportunity to do the necessary therapy on the archaic Child and exteropsyche (old Parent) and then to create the New Child experience with a New Parent introject. I knew that I had a tendency to be passive about thinking and was still obeying a 'don't think injunction'. I sometimes felt a sense of not belonging and envied others who would bounce up and down to the therapist's office (which I had designated as 'out of bounds') without fear.

I knew that I had cried once when my therapist was telling a myth and that I longed to allow myself access to understanding classical and ancient worlds; to have permission to reach for a world that I defined as beyond me but for educated middle-class people. I needed to claim my right to think my own thoughts.

I also knew of three specific childhood incidents where these injunctions were reinforced and in order to give myself maximum chance of using the time well, I decided to deal firstly with my earlier experiences of not belonging.

As a child, between the ages of 3 and 10, I stayed with eight different families – partly because of the war. In between I returned to my mother or grandmother but my mother had never had a home of her own – she and my father were constantly evicted.

A. Old Child Experience

I remembered arriving at the fourth family – quite excited because I would be seeing two children I'd met at another house. I went straight into the garden and was delighted to see apple and pear trees. The pears were large and ripe. I reached up to pick one when I heard a voice behind and above me, coming somewhere from upstairs in the house I was to stay in, shouting with deep and terrifying command, 'STOP'. I froze and decided I must be still and quiet, not take anything and remember I did not belong in this house.

Psychotherapy

I re-enacted this scene by cathecting 'little'! As I reached for the fruit, one therapist shouted STOP. Another therapist encouraged me to shout back, be angry; I did this successfully. She then suggested that I allow myself to get excited and that the point when the voice said STOP, to continue my excitement to a crescendo, through the shouted injunctions 'don't get excited' and 'don't get what you want'.

New Child Experience

In the regression slot, I asked that the door should be opened to me after I had rung and banged and made a lot of noise and that then someone would take me all over the house and answer all my questions. I would play as well like the friendly 7 year old I'm sure I had been. I did bang and ring and nearly stopped when the dogs barked, but I decided to keep going and rang long and hard. My therapist opened the door and said 'Hello, I'm so pleased to see you' and opened the door wide. She assured me I was expected and wanted. Later, I wandered around the house. I discovered I was particularly interested in the rooms that had lots of items to do things with – paper, glue, string, typewriter. I now have an *internalised childhood memory* of arrival, welcome, interest and curiosity satisfied on the inside of a house where I was wanted – I had previously barely any memories of pleasant indoor scenes from my actual childhood. I now feel accepted and I can use this memory if I ever feel fearful of going to a new place, or feel that I don't belong. I feel a different sense of confidence in being where I am most of the time.

B. Old Child Experience

When I first left home at 3 years old my memory was of hiding my face from what was happening, of my parents not being there and of shutting down my feelings and thoughts and pretending a pleasing happiness. My decisions were 'I won't think' and 'I won't show you my feelings' and 'I won't know what I feel'. 'Be happy for others' was the counterscript message in my family.

Psychotherapy

I re-enacted this scene with the 'regression parents' there. I had already done the anger work – anger at my mother for not being there, decontaminating my belief that it was because she didn't care and I was bad or lacking something; this was partly doing some of that again and partly creating a NEW CHILD EXPERI- ENCE. This time my new parents allowed me to be with them, to cry and support me through this, to say Goodbye to as many people as I wanted to, and no more, and then when I was ready, to let me go off on my own even though I was crying deeply. I shall not forget the pain of waving goodbye and yet that was so real and my pain was manageable and it was mine and I was allowed to have it. I could trust my feelings and express them.

New Child Experience

In the following regression slot I planned to be three-and-a-half and to make sure I let grown-ups (the therapists) know how I felt and what I wanted. The part I most remember is when I went into a room where some were being teenagers; they told me rudely and roughly to go away. I went and found my 'Mum' and told her how frightened and unhappy I was and she listened and sympathised. I asked her if there was something wrong with me and she explained that sometimes teenagers behaved like that. There was nothing wrong with me or them. The important 'New Child Experience' enables mc to believe, at a level beyond being given permission, that I can tell people my feelings, they can be heard, they are important, and they will be understood – given that I choose the right people and make myself clear! I don't have to pretend I 'don't mind' things happening around me.

C. Old Child Experience

When I was 11 or 12, and living with my stepfather, who was a fiercely rigid political party member, and my mother who was also very active in the same party but more prepared to consider other people's views, I went to a conference which was proposing certain revolutionary ideas, some of which clashed with my parents' beliefs. I was very excited and enthusiastic and returned home to tell my mother and stepfather of this exciting development, as I then saw it. My stepfather was furious. I argued with them until 3.00 in the morning (that they stayed up so long was a reflection of the gravity of my deviation). Eventually I gave up and decided I would probably leave their party when I was older, but I wouldn't tell them and I wouldn't ever again tell people what I really thought. I was a traitor and the biggest disappointment of their lives.

Psychotherapy

I asked two of the therapists to be my parents whilst I told them I was leaving their political party and was going to think my own thoughts and have my own ideas. I did this firmly, fluently and briefly and felt pleased that I kept the real respect and compassion I have for both of my parents; they did achieve good things in their lives and had childhoods at least as difficult as mine to survive, without the benefits of therapy.

New Child Experience

I returned to 10 and asked my 'new mother' to read me a Greek myth. She read me the story of Echo and I asked as many questions as I needed to until I could understand every aspect of the story I wanted to. Some questions she didn't know the answers to and that was all right, she said what she thought could be an answer but said we could probably find out more or other answers. This is how I have answered my children but I wanted this experience for myself. Later I asked one of the male therapists lots of questions and he said I was very clever and he couldn't answer everything. This astonished me because I always thought that a man educated enough to be a doctor would know more than me. He said he hadn't even thought about the interesting things I had been asking and that I could think some answers for myself if I wanted to. I did think through some of the answers and he was genuinely delighted at my cleverness! So I know now that I am clever enough to answer and find out about the things I am clever enough to ask. This way, how I think and what I think has validity and people can be delighted, not dismayed, if I think new things and tell them.

Much of my recent work has been about thinking and I am very grateful that this model was developed as it has enabled me to plan what I needed and how to get it. I have in addition some solidly integrated NEW CHILD experiences to which I turn whenever I feel that I don't belong, don't think, don't feel, don't think my own thoughts, and don't show I'm clever. From my own experience, I am certain my script changes are now stable under stress and I want to create more NEW CHILD experiences to let this part of me flourish and grow.

In conclusion:

The ultimate aim of transactional analysis is structural readjustment and reintegration. This requires first, restructuring, and secondly, reorganisation. The 'anatomical' phase of restructuring consists of clarification and definition of ego boundaries by such processes as diagnostic refinement and decontamination. The 'physiological' phase is concerned with redistribution of cathexis through selective planned activation of specific ego states in specific ways with the goal of establishing the hegemony of the Adult through social control. Reorganisation generally features reclamation of the Child, with emendation or replacement of the Parent. Following this dynamic phase of reorganisation, there is a secondary analytic phase which is an attempt to deconfuse the Child.
(Berne, 1980: 224)

There is an optional next phase – the replacement of archaic Child ego states with new Child ego states which are correlated with early developmental neurophysiological stages.

SUMMARY

This chapter has developed Berne's original structural model of ego states to incorporate therapeutic methods that can be employed to help individuals develop such that they can become 'stable under stress'. Faced with stress the person may move to her/his greatest area of defence and may lose her/his 'equilibrium' (Berne, 1980: 149). In terms of Berne's original model of ego states, a person with here-and-now life stress may be triggered into seeking assistance from the reservoirs of experience (i.e. from his/her archaic fixated Child ego states or from one of his/her introjected Parent ego states). If these reservoirs hold little which is supportive or much that is destructive, the person will be unable to remain stable under stress and may revert to script. It has been found that providing new parenting and new 'rechilding' experiences enables the integrated Adult ego state to draw on these positive experiences under stress and so achieve greater stability, as is illustrated by the material generously provided by the client.

Chapter 6

Treatment planning[†]

'And yet what a dear little puppy it was!' said Alice, as she leant against a buttercup to rest herself, and fanned herself with one of the leaves, 'I should have liked teaching it tricks very much, if – if I'd only been the right size to do it! Oh dear! I'd nearly forgotten that I've got to grow up again! Let me see – how *is* it to be managed? I suppose I ought to eat or drink something or other; but the great question is, "What?"'

(Carroll, 1987/1865: 52)

ASPECTS OF TREATMENT

The psychotherapeutic treatment of clients involves both microscopic and macroscopic perspectives. These will be looked at in turn.

A microscopic perspective

Using a short transcript of a session with a client, a microscopic lens will be put on the first few minutes of an initial consultation. Berne said that the psycho-therapist should start each meeting in a fresh frame of mind and focus on the microscopic observation of expressions, gestures, movements, voice tones, choice of words and so on. 'Any well-read student or properly-programmed computer can make correct interpretations, given properly weighted findings; the real skill lies in collecting and evaluating data' (Berne, 1966: 66). The first few minutes of any session are usually the most important; and the first few minutes of the first session contain in many cases, in embryo form, most of the major themes which will subsequently emerge over a period of months or years within the psychotherapy. Some of the preliminary thinking and treatment-design impressions and hypotheses will be indicated, but this is not to promote the idea that this is the way to do it nor to suggest that these initial ideas were necessarily 'correct', but rather to encourage trainee and experienced clinicians to begin to

[†] In collaboration with Phil Lapworth, Fran Lacey and Elana Leigh

articulate and to share some of the thinking and parameters they use, perhaps out of awareness, on a second-by-second basis, to encounter, assess and begin to draw up treatment directions from the very first moments of meeting a new client. Where sequencing suggestions are mentioned, please consider these indicative, not definitive. The full-scale rationale for each of these fleeting directional notions would take many more pages. Hopefully, for our purposes of understanding microscopic perspectives of treatment design, these samples of psychotherapist process are sufficient to indicate the nature of this kind of thinking, not its clinical exactitude.

In the following example, the client has contacted the psychotherapist on the recommendation of a colleague, as his current psychotherapist is retiring due to ill health. Both have agreed that the client would benefit now from working with a woman psychotherapist.

The client, whose name is Peter, arrives exactly on time for his appointment. The receptionist opens the door to him. He asks to see Penelope. This is a slip of the tongue, Penelope being the name of a friend of his, not the name of the psychotherapist. (Later attention to this slip reveals that it was in fact Penelope who referred Peter to the now-ill psychotherapist, necessitating Peter's search for another. Thus the very first word contains a theme – illness and the search for 'the other', for 'completion' – which, it later transpires, has been repeated throughout his life.) The receptionist informs him that there is no-one of that name in the Institute but that she is willing to introduce him to the psychotherapist (who enters the hall at that moment). Aware of some atmosphere of nervousness and unease, she comes to join the client. The client tightens his mouth in a smile while his eyes remain large, the pupils dilated, and eyebrows raised in an expression resembling fear. His shoulders are bowed and his body appears disproportionate and too frail to support such a large and potentially attractive man. He says, 'Hello' in an indistinct voice, breathing shallowly. The psychotherapist notes that he is dressed in rather drab autumnal colours and that there is a smell of cigarette smoke about him. (From this brief encounter at the door, the psychotherapist has already begun to form some intuitive, tentative hypotheses, based upon her years of clinical experience, to help shape these first impressions.) If carefulness reflects a rigidity of thinking and compulsiveness in other areas, attention will have to be paid to obsessive–compulsive adaptations. On the other hand, if it is based on responsibility towards others, it may be that he is 'on time' for others but feels resentful and put-upon if they are less conscientious than he. What would it be like for him to autonomously choose to be late? If he were caught in an unavoidable traffic jam, would he blame himself or others?

She has already eliminated as highly unlikely his being 'narcissistic' or 'anti-social' – he has presented as too shy, nervous, withdrawn in his manner and eager to please. In terms of her countertransference she may need to be careful not to rescue him or feel responsible for his welfare. She posits as being more likely adaptations such as schizoid, passive–aggressive or avoidant. Certainly the client's passivity seems to be a central feature of his personality organisation.

Whatever behavioural contract the client should ask for, it is highly likely that work would not be successful unless an autonomy contract is also achieved. The client may very well adapt easily to what he perceives as the psychotherapist's expectations, therefore she will need to be very careful to articulate and demonstrate congruently that he can differ from her and disagree with her. Since script decisions are also reflected in body armour (characteristic muscular-tension patterns), the psychotherapist observes the restricted breathing pattern and passive, benign posture which indicates to her a somatic Child decision not to experience feelings. Extensive bodyscript work and emotional catharsis appear to be indicated, but it would be extremely unwise to attempt this before he has built up sufficient cognitive and behavioural supports. She questions, therefore, what could have happened to this Child that led to such a decision to limit its capacity for breath and life, and plans to take opportunities to build insight and understanding as well as to provide information about the naturalness of emotional expression and the nature and function of feelings to support a healthy, responsible and ethical life. The therapist will be sensitised to this apparently health-impairing character-armour solution in her contact with the client and her further treatment planning. The ego image is that of a lonely child breathing carefully so as not to upset people in his environment. In order to establish a genuine working alliance it will probably be necessary for him to experience the psychotherapist as robust and healthy enough to stand up to a challenge without disintegrating or punishing him. She sees the client's smoking as another way of deadening his sensations and a way of protecting his loneliness. Furthermore, this represents a suicidal decision; at a core level this client is not seriously enough invested in his life to be engaged in actions which will preserve and prolong his healthy life. It is essential that he makes a no-suicide contract as soon as possible and that his commitment to his life be explored and redecided as soon as he allows himself to experience the extent of his childhood despair and the cost of physical and psychical pain which its suppression has caused him so far. She sees a lack of Adult under stress, grasping for an adult who originally failed him. Predictably this client will have unrealistically high expectations from her at a social level but his psychological-level expectation (based upon his childhood experience) is that she will fail him. Sometime during his psychotherapy the psychotherapist would have to fail him again, or be experienced as failing him again, in a similar manner to the way his parents failed him. Hopefully in psychotherapy though, this failure would be done in full conscious- ness this time and with a better outcome than that of the original failure. (Creating an ideal world where the psychotherapist is all-providing and nurturing has short-term appeal but little long-term generalisability.)

His nervousness could either be a Child ego state based on a historical reliving or maybe an enactment of an inadequate introjected Parent ego state (or states). This would entail structural ego-state analysis, perhaps deconfusion of the Child and, if the symptoms persisted, also decontamination and deconfusion work, or reparenting work with one or more of the Parent ego states. In terms of a social diagnosis, the psychotherapist is aware of the protective posture, and nurturing, reassuring voice of the receptionist which she knows from past experience indicates an automatic nurturing response to the distressed Child. The symbiotic pattern is clearly one of taking care of and being taken care of. It would be vital to establish a relationship where both parties are conceived of as OK, healthy and capable of looking after themselves, in addition to being available to others. Any sign of stress, weakness or disease on the part of the psychotherapist will need to be handled with extreme caution. Even when the psychotherapist is hypervigilant about this potential in the relationship, the client may still fantasise about her vulnerability and his possible role in taking care of her. This would most likely exacerbate the more he began to experience himself as benefiting from treatment. It will be essential to check out for mistakes, fantasies and particularly dreams which indicate a symbolic or unconscious reconstruction of the initial dysfunctional Parent–Child couple. It is quite possible that he has difficulty in maintaining intimate friendly or loving relationships with peers where there is an absence of Victim–Rescuer dynamic; this indicates the importance of group psychotherapy as a modality in his future treatment planning.

In spite of all these hypotheses, observations and impressions, the psychotherapist is keeping herself as open as possible, allowing each impression to focus for a moment and then to pass so as to allow the space for others to emerge. It is only as an impression is repeatedly etched that it takes on the force of even a tentative diagnostic or working hypothesis.

She introduces herself to the client, saying 'Hello, welcome. I am the person you have come to see. This is the consulting room.'

The psychotherapist is careful not to be overly warm – which might replicate the Rescuing stance of the receptionist – but takes up a friendly, businesslike manner particularly to establish how quickly the client can recathect Adult. It is possible that his thinking disintegrates under stress and it would be important to establish whether this is a problem of capacity (intelligence), skill or vulnerability under stress. Each of these can be worked with in turn, but if it is the latter, it would be important in the relearning phase of treatment to help him perform and practise thinking clearly and efficiently under stress.

The wording of the psychotherapist's first comment is very carefully chosen to emphasise both the particularity of the psychotherapist and the responsibility of the arrangement being with the client's initiating actions. At the same time, the simplicity of language and instruction is providing the Child with clear parameters in the new environment. The extent of impairment and resilience of his Child can begin to be assessed by his use of these instructions.

The client follows her into the psychotherapy room, waits for the psychotherapist to sit, then positions himself at a right-angle to her, crossing his legs and arms.

The psychotherapist notes how his body posture restricts his breathing capacity even further which, on the one hand, probably feels more protected and reassured, but at the same time cuts off the possibility of receiving nurturance or support from the environment. This indicates at least two reinforced treatment emphases – emotional bodywork and the importance of physical and unconditional stroking.

The psychotherapist remains silent in a relaxed and expectantly open body position while looking at him intently but not intrusively.

If he has decided to barricade himself in this way, the psychotherapist is not going to 'rush' his defences but allow him ample time to find his bearings, look around the room if he needs to, become acclimatized and initiate contact if and when he is ready. She is also demonstrating that it is permissible for him to 'look her over' without engaging in the usual social 'chit-chat' which often gets between people and what they experience in the time of 'first impressions'. She is assessing in a preliminary way his pacing of himself in interpersonal situations and beginning to calibrate the timing of her interventions and expectations of response to his rhythms.

The client is silent for some time before saying, 'I want to be in psychotherapy with you because I've heard that you're an experienced psychotherapist and my psychotherapist's ill.'

The client is not afraid of silence and would rather risk the interpersonal emptiness than fill it with words or attachment behaviour the way a person with a more borderline personality structure may do. He will need to take his own time, his introversion will need to be respected in the course of psychotherapy (a strength and a limitation) and given patience he will most likely respond to subtle, not too demanding opportunities for self-disclosure, change and growth. He is capable of enough self-generated motivation to make use of psychotherapeutic openings if he is not rescued. The psychotherapist hears in his voice a plaintive Child note in response to a threatened abandonment contained within the social level transaction. Later, the client said he actually felt like nobody wanted him and he was all alone as he was when he was a young child. So the behavioural and social diagnosis was supported by historical and phenomenological agreement. In terms of treatment direction the cautions against assuming the carer or cared-for role either in reality or in fantasy is reinforced. It would become a treatment priority to attempt to establish a working relationship of warmth, understanding and empathy without unequal sharing of responsibility for the work of his psychotherapy. Would he be willing to experiment with this?

The psychotherapist asks, 'Have you discussed this with him?' Here she is ensuring that her colleague has been informed of this consultation in order to maintain good colleagial relationships and to test if he may already be involved in a game of 'Let's You and Him Fight', for example. She is testing a potential for certain kinds of games or sabotage in treatment. A questionable or suspect answer here may lead to different diagnoses and a different direction in thinking about treatment altogether.

The client replies, 'Yes, he's supporting me in finding another, suitable psychotherapist.'

As Steere's studies (1982) show, people's bodies frequently mismatch between the psychological- and social-level messages. Here the psychotherapist, seeing no incongruence, has some supportive evidence that Peter has a pattern of conscientiousness, reliability and trustworthiness in interpersonal relationships even though he may be somewhat disappointed in that relationship. However, the psychotherapist notes the flatness of affect and the rather resigned, passive demeanour as he speaks. She wonders if he has repressed his natural (if irrational) feelings of resentment at being let down, or if he genuinely does not even experience it. In other words, is this a schizoid inability to register an organismic affront? Or a more passive–aggressive reluctance to confront which results in a nice fat stamp-collecting album! Treatment direction in the former case would involve the psychotherapist possibly in a much more active capacity than has so far been indicated. An intervention which tests the way he manages his distance from his feelings may be of value.

She says, 'What do you feel about that?' The psychotherapist probes for affective expression of how it is for him to have accessibility to his feelings and share them. If he redefines the question, it will need to be approached again, perhaps in a more indirect manner.

The client replies in a very polite way, 'Well, it's unfortunate that it's happened like this, particularly at a time when my ex-wife is moving away with my children and I won't see them so much, and feeling lonely and having financial difficulties. But I do understand that my psychotherapist needs to retire.' He again smiles resignedly.

He did not respond with affect or a statement about his emotions to a question designed to elicit affective responsiveness. There may be many reasons for this, not least the fact that he is not yet feeling safe enough in his relationship with the psychotherapist. She notes the way in which the client rationalises himself away from any recognition or expression of affect. At the same time the presence of an ex-wife and children reduce the likelihood of a severe schizoid disorder on Axis II. He has the capacity to get involved with people and to hurt when these attachment bonds are threatened. Phrases like, 'It's unfortunate' and 'I do understand' within such a list of painful events indicate use of the Adult to avoid feelings rather than assist them; in other words, a contamination in the area of feelings most likely from the Parent ego state.

He has, however, disclosed 'feeling lonely' which fits with the psychotherapist's earlier impression of the abandoned Child. However this psychotherapy ends, the termination phase will have to be handled with extreme care in order to avoid a script replay. His apparently prevalent psychological preoccupation is reflected in the theme of 'abandoned children', potentially a vicarious identification with his own children. She is already forming a Child ego-state history of loss, loneliness and, perhaps, lovelessness. If this is borne out by further observations and experience, this Child will need considerable protection in order to feel his feelings and mourn his losses, including the loss of the spontaneity and carefreeness of childhood. He will also need to regain or develop and maintain friendship-making and intimacy-maintaining skills and capacities in order to counteract the potential lovelessness in close relationships with significant others. It is possible that his restriction on his breathing, his gaunt body, and his overdeveloped sense of responsibility may get in the way of his sexuality. If this is so, it would need attention later in psychotherapy, certainly before termination.

The psychotherapist says, 'It sounds like a very painful time for you. It must be particularly distressing that the psychotherapist you've been seeing for such a long time appears to be abandoning you even though you realise that it's not his fault.'

The psychotherapist is still creating space for an emotional response by reflective, empathetic listening while stroking his rationalisation, understanding and compassionate motivation not to blame the original psychotherapist. She is saying that there can be a difference between Adult facts and a feeling-full response to these facts and makes a mental note that he will need to learn emotional literacy/fluency in order to begin to communicate effectively about his emotional life. This corroborates her earlier impressions that it will be necessary for him to develop emotionally in order to become available for intimacy in friendship and love relationships.

The client replies, 'Well, it wasn't that bad. He's been ill for some time so I've been helping him run his group for quite a while. It wasn't a shock.'

Here it is immediately apparent that Peter does not experience the psychotherapy group, for which he pays, as a facility which is there for him. Although he went to the group for his own needs, again, due to forces of illness beyond his control and his apparent air of competence and responsibility, he has been put in a position where he is shouldering responsibility for an ill parent at the expense of his own needs. The use of the phrase 'It wasn't a shock' alerts an ear attuned to script to a script expectation of the recurrence of early symbiotic failures. So this all has an air of familiarity to him. It is not a shock because his Child expects (out of awareness perhaps) this to happen over and over again in his significant relationships and is already defended against an emotional response. In terms of treatment planning the psychotherapist sees the necessity for not allowing him to take positions of responsibility or caretaking in the transference, even though it may be harder for him to establish a relationship of trust if this proof of his functionality is withheld. He will need to learn that he can be useful to others and others useful to him, but from a position of mutual benefit where both persons' needs get met.

The psychotherapist registers a repetition of the themes for treatment concern – of abandonment, incompetent parenting and the assumption of the role of caretaking person in the psychotherapy group and other relationships – hypothesising that this is a replay of a childhood situation. She then checks this out in her next question to both get more explicit information and to see if the client can make the connection. This will also give her some insight into the degree of self-understanding established in the previous psychotherapy.

She then asks: 'Did you help either of your parents when you were little?'This is obvious to the psychologically minded, perhaps, but none the less important to test.

The client, with a grin, says, 'Funny you should say that. When I was a child my mother used to have "nervous breakdowns".' At this point he leans back, uncrosses his legs and appears to relax a little.

The 'obvious' question from the psychotherapist has reached several destinations. The grin of the client indicates both an understanding of the question and the meaning of it in terms of his own script, and establishes a beginning of trust in the psychotherapist's competence or potency. He appears to relax somewhat, perhaps as a result of feeling more understood. Although the information that he was a helping child is old, the realisation that he had inadvertently repeated the pattern with his previous psychotherapist is new and surprising. He has begun the story of his life.

The psychotherapist asks, 'What do you mean when you say that?' She is careful not to attach her own meanings to the phrase 'nervous breakdown' but is wishing to understand his phenomenological language. She is also demonstrating her willingness to be educated into his frame of reference in order to understand his experience better.

The client replies, 'Well, I remember her being very depressed and having lots of nose bleeds and I would sit and look after her for hours with a bowl to catch the blood.'

He responds immediately and with a very vivid, simple image capturing the essence of his relationship with his mother and the experienced nature of her illness. In terms of future treatment the psychotherapist has reason to believe that if she sincerely shows that she understands and is willing to enter into his phenomenological world, he would use the interventions well. In this way she is also beginning to have a sense of what works more-or-less better or worse for this particular patient. Observing his reactions when she makes a helpful intervention, the psychotherapist begins to develop a baseline for judging errors of content, timing or process.

The psychotherapist asks, 'What was that like for you?' To which the client replies, 'In the silence I used to to make up stories about fantastic lands and people. I created nicer places to be in my head – places I hoped I'd be one day and share with a very special friend.'

The psychotherapist has an ego-state image of a Child desperate to find purpose and meaning in a life that so far seems to be merely to look after others. She has a fantasy of the young Child needing to 'go away' to feel his feelings 'in his head' or even physically. Withdrawal either through sulking, silence, emotional withholding or actual absence from sessions are distinct possibilities. Before this initial consultation is out, they will have to discuss how the client would terminate if and when he wanted to do this, and the psychotherapist will need to obtain a commitment from him not to leave psychotherapy either emotionally or physically when the 'going gets rough'. Later in their work together, the early ego-state image is confirmed. As a boy, Peter used to build small 'shrines' in the garden where he would go to feel his feelings. He would light candles and make crosses and often become tearful for a while, though he was not sure what about. It was as if he needed to create a space in which to make some meaning – and, by necessity, this was an isolated, lonely place. The 'very special friend' who would 'one day' appear enabled him to deal with his present distress by creating a hopeful future. The psychotherapist is aware of the 'waiting for Santa Claus' element here and knows that she must disillusion him as part of their work together. However, if this disillusionment comes too early it might be experienced as a destruction of hope and an undermining of one of his psychological strengths, which could also be a creative talent.

The psychotherapist reflects, 'So you learned early on to use your imagination as a comfort.'

This intervention is meant to specify imagination as a potential solution as well as a potential problem. A vivid imagination is very useful in developing treatment possibilities. Visualisation, dreamwork, guided fantasy and multiple chair-work or voice dialogues would potentially all be possible and most likely beneficial for his psychotherapeutic journey.

Misty-eyed, the client nods and breathes a deep sigh, perhaps of relief. Later, he referred to this moment as an experience of being 'seen' both in his pain and in his capacity to deal with it. Compassion conveyed increases his physical and probably psychological comfort.

The psychotherapist enquires, 'And where was your father?' The client replies, 'Well, he looked after her too. So much so that he didn't have much time for me. He died of lung cancer when I was in my twenties.'

The absence of father as a competent protective figure in the tale so far is telling itself. The psychotherapist initiates the question since Dad had not spontaneously been mentioned. The client will need to find or develop male role models who take care of themselves as well as of others, and particularly find men with whom to identify who are neither weak nor self-destructive. Father's death of lung cancer proves both a possible genetic predisposition to cancer as well as lifelong modelling of suicidal behaviour leading to a self-induced cause of premature death. This signifies a priority in terms of investigating and preventing a hamartic script payoff, and certainly also a tendency to discount at the level of existence and significance of a problem. The fact that the client is still smoking despite the experience of having watched a relative die slowly of a smoking-related disease is a very grave signal. There may be a level of despair far exceeding his conscious awareness. Although an early no-suicide contract is called for, it is doubtful whether psychotherapy will really get through to his deepest levels unless he experiences the pain of his early deprivation and the profound self-destructive anguish which must have been modelled by father as well as the cruel, apparently other-inflicted pain of his mother's psychological and physical illness.

At this stage, although none of the observations and speculations has the status of more than a hypothesis, several provisional maps can be drawn. In script-matrix terms the message from the father's Parent appears to be 'Be strong and be pleasing.' Father's programming shows Peter how to smoke and how to care for ill mothers, and from his Child there is most likely a lethal 'Don't exist' injunction as well as a 'Don't feel' injunction which may indeed be similar to what father experienced in his own childhood. It is hypothesised that from mother's Parent Peter has clearly taken and enacted the instructions to be pleasing and care for others, particularly those who are too ill to take care of themselves. Her programming offers a model of 'nervous breakdowns' and physical illness where others look after one. At this stage we do not have the information yet of what Peter's physical incapacitation is likely to have taken. Later we find it is back problems 'which lay him up' and during which others have to tend to him. The metaphor of 'breaking his back' caring for others is never far from mind. It would be important to guard against accidental injuries as well as self-inflicted harm through smoking. His loneliness as a child indicates a decision (probably wisely taken to ensure survival and some distance from what could have been an emotionally overclose relationship with his sick mother) not to be close to people. His behaviour and symptoms signify decisions not to exist, to live for others, to deny himself feelings and a full, sensually rich life, difficulties with close relationships (divorce), and a questionable sense of competence (financial difficulties). These may stem from having tried so hard to help as a young child and yet probably repeatedly failing to cure his mother. His loving nature took flight into imagination, dreams and wishes. This represents the thrust of *Physis* in his life and a potential strength of creative talent which could help support his work of breaking out of his script, putting a new show on the road and perhaps using his imagination not only to free himself from the deterministic constraints of his background but also to actualise himself as an artist, perhaps a writer. He is a seeker after meaning – and as such it is likely that he will respond well to psychotherapy. His history of passivity and fantasising as a means of escaping may, however, impede him taking the responsibility for his outcomes in life and encourage a pattern of sullen resentment when other people do not care for him in the way he cares for them, or in the way he used to care for his parents.

In phenomenological ego-state terms we can anticipate a paternal introject with some nurturing, but little structure, and a suicidal Child. His maternal introject is incompetent, depressed and ill. His Adult functioning is impaired under stress, but he has insight and fortunately also a sense of humour, which will make future confrontations easier and psychotherapy more fun. There are at least four identifiable earlier ego states which are strained or traumatised: the pseudo-competent caretaking child, the lonely fantasising child (perhaps a guilty child?), certainly a child who decided real life wasn't worth living and a 20-year-old historical (Child) ego state which most likely had not allowed himself to mourn the death of his father. Being as cut off from his feelings as he has been since an early age, contra-indicates that he has allowed himself to experience a thorough emotional grieving for his father. When he died Peter was 20. However, one would also expect that there were other child ego states for whom father, and even mother, had 'died' much earlier – when the child had to come to terms with their emotional abandonment of him, engrossed as they were in their symptoms, addictions and self-absorption.

In the course of the person's psychotherapy most of these issues were corroborated and some not; some aspects of treatment were achieved and some not achieved. This has been more an exercise in demonstrating how the psychotherapist works with a combination of intuitive, right-hemispheric awareness as well as diagnostically informed clinical knowledge. It must be apparent how one can divergently generate many possibilities in the very first few minutes of a psychotherapeutic encounter which provide, not definitive categories or labels, but provisional hypotheses and potential treatment directions. It is important to remember that Berne considered transactional analysis to be a systematic phenomenology. In this sense it is truly phenomenological, applying the rule of 'horizontality'; i.e. the awareness of phenomena while considering them all to be equal (Spinelli, 1989), approaching them without prejudice, premature interpretation or being wedded to any particular possibility more than another. Therefore, based on further experience, there will be a selection and prioritisation as a more informed overview or macroscopic perspective develops.

A macroscopic perspective

Here we look at the macroscopic aspect which is required for effective treatment planning.

Berne's classical sequence of treatment planning was: establishing a working alliance, decontamination, deconfusion and relearning. A model of treatment planning which expands on this is presented here in terms of stages.

Stages of psychotherapy

Establishing a working relationship
Contracting
Decontamination
Deconfusion
Establishing an internal Nurturing Parent
Emotional fluency
Redecision work
Parent ego-state work
Rechilding
Reorientation
Relearning
Termination

Any experienced clinician will know that no psychotherapeutic journey progresses in an absolutely logical, step-by-step fashion. It is the unfolding of a journey into an interior for which the psychotherapist indeed does not have a map but brings map-making skills. The stages that are being discussed here are not discrete. Thinking about treatment planning is designed to be more of an aid to clarity than a specific prescription as to how clinicians should work.

Instead of elaborating on the various stages at this point, it may be more useful to identify the observable criteria by which the clinician can judge that certain phases of treatment have been satisfactorily established, or at least sufficiently grounded, in order for subsequent work to grow to greatest value from fertile soil. It appears that each phase is necessary in order for the next phase to progress.

In order for a client to make a good workable contract, a significant working relationship needs to have been established. Decontamination can be done most satisfactorily when there are sound and mutually agreed contracts. Deconfusion, particularly expressing unmet needs and feelings, can be dangerous or harmful in the absence of stable, preceding decontamination. Decontamination also facilitates the establishment of the internal Nurturing Parent and is a necessary requirement for emotional fluency and redecisions. Parent ego-state work may not be structurally of a lasting nature if thorough deconfusion has not taken place. In turn, Parent ego-state restructuring needs to precede reorientation which again becomes a necessary precondition for relearning.

This sequence is intended to facilitate clinical acumen and intellectual questioning of the treatment approach to the client. There may be many instances where these phases do not apply. Exceptions could and should be made where the exigencies of the psychotherapeutic relationship or the vicissitudes of life require.

The establishment of a working relationship

A working relationship requires the development of mutual trust between psychotherapist and client. The clinician can often assume that trust has been established when his or her interest has been engaged and when respect for the relationship is explicitly demonstrated by the client honouring the boundaries of paying their fee as agreed, of attending regularly and on time and informing about possible delays or alterations to the agreed parameters of the relationship. There is an accepted mutuality inasmuch as the client and psychotherapist have agreed how they will work together. They develop a shared language and honour each other's conventions. There is often explicit acknowledgement from the client that the relationship has become important to them. This frequently occurs after a break when the response to the therapist's absence can indicate that it has made a difference to the client's life. This may not always be positive and indeed may even be an overtly stated indifference. Essentially, the development of trust within the relationship has to do with the establishment and management of the boundaries and taking care that the norms are agreed ones within which disagreement or boundary leakages can be managed. Such care is also necessary in the management of boundary errors made by the psychotherapist. For example, ending the session early due to a faulty watch may cause a vehement response from the client. This may be an important crisis in the psychotherapeutic relationship but may be used constructively to establish ways of negotiating, taking risks within the relationship, expressing negative feelings and exploring options that satisfy both parties and enhance their working alliance.

Clients may report that they feel from their Child ego states an irrational rage or a desire never to come again in response to such an error. It is the development of an available Adult-to-Adult communication channel in such circumstances and the willingness to identify and work through the archaic feelings that indicate that a working relationship has been established.

Clearly, this is a two-way process. It is not only the client's trust in relation to the psychotherapist but also the psychotherapist's trust in relation to the client that constitutes a working relationship. The human-to-human quality experienced by the therapist may range from a simple lack of fear of the client entering the consulting room, to a trust that even if the client were to lie, he or she would tell them about it as soon as they could. Negative trust does not mean that the person has not bonded in the relationship. In fact, the very strength of a negative transference may be an indication that the person is accepting the relationship enough to risk experimenting with their negativity, rejection and fear. On the other hand, hassling, negotiating and staying away may be an indication that the person is engaging in a transferential acting-out or 'game' instead of establishing a genuine relationship which can contain the psychotherapist both as transferential object and working partner. It is only through the established working relationship that the symbolic enactment of the game or transferential, interpersonal pattern can be understood, worked through, transformed or cured. Non-establishment of trust and a working alliance may lead to the client remaining stuck within the transferential relationship (as opposed to moving through it as a means of transformation).

The working alliance is very simple in TA terms: it means that there is the possibility of Adult–Adult understanding even if the Child is in transference with the psychotherapist. The client may transfer negative or positive feelings, may believe the psychotherapist to be bad or good, may fantasise being abandoned or rescued by this ogre or saviour – but whatever happens in Child (even if it is acted out), it is possible to return to the working alliance.

It is not that the client is constantly in Adult but that, at times of difficulty, that channel is open. Even a client involved in a very bad game to the extent of feeling like killing the therapist can be trusted to hear the therapist's reminder that such feelings are OK to express but not to act upon once a working alliance has been established. When this Adult–Adult communication is not possible, there is no working alliance and in the example here concerning a threat upon the psychotherapist's life, the psychotherapist should not be working with this person in any minimum-security situation.

The length of time needed to establish this working relationship clearly will vary from client to client: it may be that one relationship is established within weeks of the first meeting; another may take months, or even years. For some clients, threatened by the idea of a relationship and scared of the potential for intimacy, the very establishment of a healthy relationship with the psychotherapist may indeed be the psychotherapy and, in itself, the end goal. As the working relationship is a developing process over time, it is not useful to say, as happens too frequently in TA training, that clients should be doing 50 per cent of the work. In the early stages of psychotherapy, many clients do not know what the work is and may need the psychotherapist to be doing 90 per cent of the work for a time. Conversely, there are those clients who come into psychotherapy to treat themselves. They plan it, rehearse it, do 'the piece' (and psychotherapy becomes almost a masturbatory activity and the psychotherapist a receptacle against which to do it). Gradually, as the work becomes more equally shared, the working relationship becomes more established for both the overly dependent and the overly self-reliant client. With the former, the sign of a working relationship being achieved may be the day the client says, 'I remember the work we did last time and I think what would be really useful for me to do now is this.' With the latter, the sign may be when the client says, 'I don't know what to do. Will you help me?' The general point here is that it is the changing and developing pattern of the relationship, each unique in itself, towards a sense of mutual trust and respons- ibility that indicates the establishment of a working alliance.

Contracting

Contracting in TA is used to emphasise mutuality and respect between psychotherapist and client. The client, in true existential fashion, has to take responsibility for what he or she wants and learn how to use the psychotherapist to best advantage for his or her own goals. This maximises the likelihood of ownership, agency, and success. Concomitantly, every 'contract' achieved is another stepping stone towards self-esteem which creates further expectations of personal effectiveness and goal achievement. Modern infant and child psychology is increasingly drawing attention to the pre-eminence of the human motivation for competence or effectance (Pine, 1985; Stern, 1984). Clinical experience also bears out the folk observation that 'nothing succeeds like success'. Moreover, however small the achievement, accomplishment often generates and maintains hope for larger, longer-term goals.

In contrast to orthodox psychoanalysis, where the focus on change (rather than understanding or insight) in psychotherapy is often ignored and sometimes deplored (Freud, 1973/1917), transactional analysts consider that psychotherapy is for change or growth in certain directions. Therefore psychotherapy has both a practical and academic research interest in whether it actually accomplishes what it sets out to achieve.

Finally, a major advantage of establishing workable contracts early in psychotherapy is their efficacy in flushing out manifestations of 'bad faith' (games, cons and gimmicks) before manipulative habitual avoidances become entrenched in the therapeutic matrix.

The contracting stage of treatment is achieved when the psychotherapist and client have used the working relationship to establish clear, well-defined goals that set the focus for treatment. Research on the effectiveness of psychotherapy repeatedly associates successful outcome with 'high focus' that is the clarity of the goals or aims of the psychotheapy (Frank, 1982; Malan, 1979; Parloff *et al.*, 1978). In the course of developing the working relationship, general contracts concerning time of appointments, frequency and duration, fees, and holiday arrangements will have been agreed.

Now the emphasis is placed on specific changes the client is wanting to make in terms of beliefs, emotions, thoughts and behaviours in order to reach his or her goals. There is a commitment between both parties to the client's achievement of these goals and to assessing the feasibility, legality and desirability of such goals. Acknowledgement is also made that the contracts may be changed or adapted in the course of psychotherapy to suit the client's current needs as well as their long-term aims. Both Steiner (1975) and the Gouldings (1979) provide excellent guidelines for making contracts. James (James and Jongeward, 1971) further provides a set of useful questions to assist in the contract-making process.

Contracts may be long term or short term. Often, in the initial stages, a client will be more willing to make a clear, behavioural, short-term contract, the success of which encourages further, perhaps deeper contracts. Sometimes a sessional contract will be made as a first step to change. It must be remembered that contracts are an aid to psychotherapy and not laws or tasks set to test the client. In some cases, making contracts may be contra-indicated. One client who had spent much of her life writing lists of things to do and setting herself perpetual goals which she would 'Try Hard' to achieve was relieved that her psychotherapy did not collude with this by similar goal setting. For her, psychotherapy was 'time and space just to be'.

What is most apparent at this stage is that the work of psychotherapy has really begun, often accompanied by appropriate feelings of excitement and enthusiasm as well as fear in deciding to make changes. The making of 'No Suicide', 'No Homicide' and 'No Go Crazy' contracts will be dealt with in a separate section.

Decontamination

Decontamination is occuring during the establishment of the working-relationship stage and the contracting stage. Both involve the client's agreement and willingness to behave in accordance with an Adult reality even when the Child feels scared, wobbly or crazy. At this next stage, the decontamination becomes more specific and defined. The client experiences a greater sense of choice in terms of which ego states they may cathect. They may also become aware of experiencing archaic or other historic feelings (introjects) at the same time as knowing that this is not 'here and now' and experience their behaviour as ego-dystonic as it is out of proportion to any real (or significant) deprivation in the present. Such decontamination then leads to a widening of options for the client in terms of getting their current needs met in ways more appropriate to a grown-up person while at the same time identifying areas of work within archaic-Child or introjected-Parent ego states which may need to be dealt with in later stages of psychotherapy.

The client at this stage is taking social control of their ego states and, as in most learning situations, will proceed through the stages of hindsight, midsight and foresight on the way to decontamination. Clients often experience a shift in their 'frame of reference' at this stage of psychotherapy as they recognise that which was previously seen as 'just me as I am' with parts perhaps not liked nor understood (and unchangeable!) is seen in terms of past experiences and a developed intrapsychic structure for which they are responsible and over which they can develop control. It is important to ensure that this is a frame of reference which involves responsibility as opposed to one which uses the concepts of ego states as a disclaimer of responsibility. An irresponsible frame of reference is one where shouting abuse at the therapist (or anyone else for that matter) is excused by 'that was my mother talking from my Parent ego state' or accusations of 'you're in your Child ego state' as if such knowledge is in itself useful.

Berne compared decontamination to 'scraping barnacles off a ship' (1980) and provided the diagram of contaminations whereby the Adult circle diminished. Decontamination involves the separating out of these historic ego states and freeing up energy in the Adult (like a smooth, clean-sided ship moving through the water divested of its barnacles). It is often this shift in energy of a client that indicates that a satisfactory level of decontamination has been established (accepting that decontamination is never completed but remains an ongoing process). The client's energy increases in the here and now as it is withdrawn from involvement with the 'there and then'; away from adaptive script fixations and towards the service of the biological organism in its present environment with its present wants and needs. When this energy shift has occurred, decontamination is usually stable. Other signs that decontamination has been satisfactorily achieved are when the client has a sense of being in charge of their life (i.e. not just their ego states!) and makes a shift in language. There is more accounting for what is happening and what they are making happen in their lives, and a concomitant shift away from negative and self-limiting language. Taking note of different ego states and their restrictive influence, the client differentiates past from present needs, the historical Parent from parent values, the voice of encouragement to change from the voice of script reinforcement and appropriate responses from conditioned ones. It is at this stage that belongs a common paraphrasing of Berne, 'If you can hear the voices in your head, you are probably sane' (1980). It is a stage of heightened awareness and often change in thinking and behaviour, but not necessarily of change in feeling. Clients may say, 'I know this about myself but I don't feel any different.' Awareness of the source of fear in destructive script messages does not necessarily help the client feel any less scared. Equally, understanding an explanation or interpretation does not necessarily lead to the client feeling differently in response to what is being explained. These are signs that decontamination has taken place but deconfusion has not yet been established.

Deconfusion

This stage of psychotherapy gives attention (mainly) to the Child ego state and the client's needs and feelings that have been repressed from early years. The suggestion that the Child ego state is 'confused' for me engenders an empathy-inducing picture of thoughts, feelings and beliefs from many and various stages of development (verbal and pre-verbal) needing expression in order to be understood, clarified and given their rightful place: in other words, deconfused. In this way, it can be seen that sometimes deconfusion precedes decontamination. Approaches in treatment planning will need to be differentiated according to each client's personality adaptation, i.e. it is likely that a client of an 'hysterical adaptation' may need to work at the deconfusion level before decontamination can be established. In these situations, it is a kind of treatment loop that needs to be followed whereby the client may need to recycle to the decontamination phase from the deconfusion stage and vice versa. Cathartic work or deconfusion work will not necessarily hold unless decontamination has been established. Contrarily, sometimes the discharge of emotional energy needs to be facilitated in order for decontamination to take place, following which there is a different quality to the expression of feelings in the subsequent deconfusion stage. In attempting to separate out her archaic and current experience, a client says, 'Tears are getting in my brain, so I'll cry first and then I'll think about it.'

Sometimes people need to do a great deal of the emotional work in order to achieve decontamination. It seems as if the Child ego state needs to discharge emotion in order to disengage from its contamination of the Adult. This is still the decontamination phase of treatment. It may look like deconfusion but it is likely to be a cathartic discharge where the person is not owning that this is their hurt Child. Until this is acknowledged and experienced, further decontamination will need to be done. This is a phase where the person might be expressing racket (learnt substitute) feelings (English, 1971).

These may need stroking by the psychotherapist, at this stage, if the psychotherapy is to go anywhere. People are not willing to let go of their racket feelings and adaptations unless they are being understood. Being heard and known and understood by another person is such a profoundly healing force for the client. This means being known not only for one's genuine feelings but also for one's substitute feelings, which include one's badness, manipulations, doubts and terrors as well as gifts, generosity and humanity. Being known and accepted for who one is, then one may change. I think it is important to get away from what has become all too common in TA, that of only accepting what is 'real' and labelling experiences as 'genuine' or 'not genuine', as if anyone can know these things anyway. Racket feelings may be a very useful concept but only in the context of an accepting and understanding relationship. Carl Rogers' basic idea that people need to be fully accepted in order for them to move on is clearly relevant here. For many clients, the most important aspect of psychotherapy is being known by the psychotherapist better than by anyone else.

Establishing an internal Nurturing Parent

Though there may be some theoretical confusion as to which ego state is addressed when developing an internal Nurturing Parent, there is general agreement that the establishment of such self-parenting skills are important prior to any redecision work on the part of the client if new decisions are to be taken safely, securely and with the maximum internal permission, protection and potency. These self-nurturing behaviours are accessible, observable and believable in two-chair work, for example, where the client talks to his or her hurt Child with a quality of love, care and understanding that feels congruent and contains appropriate Adult information relevant to the Child. This is not to imply that a self-nurturing Parent is always gentle, sweet and permissive. Many clients feel the need for a strong internal Parent to help provide necessary boundaries and restrictions for their Child, brought up as they were in limited or inconsistent family structures where controls were lacking. They may require such a Parent to prohibit them from driving when feeling tired or overworking when feeling stressed. They may need controlling when about to lose their temper in an inappropriate situation.

It is important that, prior to redecision work, this internal Nurturing Parent be properly informed about the different needs of children at different developmental stages and understands the characteristics and tendencies of their own particular and unique Child – especially of the needs of their Child at the specific age at which the redecision is to be made. A sound internal Nurturing Parent takes the individuality of the Child into account both in their limitations as well as in their gifts. A caring Parent asks for help and support when they cannot manage alone and knows when this is appropriate. It is clear that an internal Nurturing Parent is established when, if they are asked, 'How would you treat this child in this particular situation?' they respond with useful, reliable answers or thinking structures to solve the problem.

In the following clinical example, the client, with the psychotherapist's assistance (simultaneously modelling good Parent behaviour), is establishing a nurturing Parent and giving permission to her Child to express her feelings when appropriate. Two-chair work is being used to facilitate this process of self-parenting.

(*P* = Psychotherapist; *C* = Client)

P: Tell her, 'When you were really little ...'
C: Gill, when you were really little, you used to feel all sorts of feelings but you used to stop yourself feeling them because you were told off if you did. So you kept them inside. Whenever you allowed your emotion to come to the surface you were told you were bad. If you were angry or even very happy, you

had to keep it all down. And I feel really sad that you did that.

P: Tell her ... she wants to hear.

C: I feel really sad that you did that and that you kept all those feelings inside you for all those years. (cries)

P: Speak your feelings to her.

C: I just ... you really missed out. For fourteen years, from birth to when you were a teenager.

P: A bit louder – 'When you were a teenager ...'

C: When you were a teenager it was even more difficult because you had even stronger emotions, so you started to be scared of them because they were so difficult to keep in. And when you didn't, at home or school, you got into trouble. So that just reinforced the fact that you shouldn't show them.

P: So for all those years ...

C: You thought it was really bad and wrong to show your feelings and so you just kept them inside.

P: So what do you want to tell her now?

C: I want to tell you that it's OK to have those feelings. It's OK to let them out.

P: When it's safe for you and other people.

C: Yes, when it's safe for you and others, it can be good to let your feelings out.

P: And what I'm going to do for you is ...

C: What I'm going to do for you is ... something like ... when you have a feeling, I'll tell you what to do with it.

P: That's fine. 'You can have your feelings and I'll decide what you can do with them.' OK? Give that to your Child again, give her permission to have her feelings.

C: I want you to know that it's OK for you to have your feelings and that I will protect you by deciding when it's OK to express them.

P: I think she needs to hear that things are different now. When she was little, she couldn't express those feelings and when she was a teenager, she got into trouble for expressing them. What she needs to know now is that there's a grown-up on her side who really has a lot more information than the parents and teachers of those days. Will you tell her that?

C: Yeah: it's OK for you to do this now. As your Adult, I know what to do with feelings. You don't need to feel overwhelmed because I can use my knowledge and control to make you safe. So you don't have to worry that it's dangerous anymore.

P: Do you think she's listening to you any more?

C: Yeah, and I think she's saying, 'Thanks, and about time too! I feel much safer.'

Emotional fluency

At this stage it is established that formerly unmet needs are now being met and formerly unexpressed feelings are being expressed. The latter is evidenced by the client showing less sluggish cathexis in the area of expression and vocalisation of needs, when energy is unbound and when expression is spontaneous. It is when the psychotherapist feels real trust in what the client is describing of their experience knowing that the client has an understanding of their own emotionality and is secure enough to both feel and report the feelings. It is at the point when they are moving freely between thinking and feeling and regularly demonstrating all four of the primary feelings in healthy and appropriate ways that this stage is accomplished. This takes into account the ancient Chinese acupuncture prescription for an emotionally healthy life, which suggests that a person should feel all four of the primary feelings at least once a day. Indicative phrases and remarks at this stage of psychotherapy are:

'Now I can cry and think about my sadness.'
'I can feel angry and know that I'm not going to hurt my Child.'
'I was frightened last night and I phoned my friend.'
'I got angry and tore up some papers and then I felt better.'

Thus, emotional expression becomes normalised and healthy. Feelings are neither stored to dangerous capacities (which lead to explosions or illness) nor are they treated like something precious that has to be admired and marvelled at.

The psychotherapist can assess that this structural level is in place when the client can naturally and spontaneously express their feelings, know what they need to do and move on. The expression of feelings is a natural process to be moved through: the feeling of fear leads to protection; the feeling of sadness leads to relief; anger leads to change, while joy leads to pleasure or relaxation. There is a sense of naturalness and the absence of stereotype. Emotionally fluent people have many ways of behaving and in the therapy room express their feelings in wide-ranging ways – certainly, they do not beat the cushion in the same way nor cry in the same way *ad infinitum*. Anger may be expressed in short bursts, long tirades, by shouting, stamping and tearing. Sadness, too, becomes expressed in more subtle, nuanced ways.

Clearly, at each of these stages of treatment, the experience and expression of feelings is important. However, we are suggesting here that at each stage the expression may be at different levels, from different ego states, for different outcomes (catharsis or redecision) and in different ways. Under each heading, the various aspects of expressive psychotherapy have been described. In this section we have referred to the emotional literacy material of Steiner (1984) who has made a valuable contribution to improving human communication and understanding.

In the 1960s (in a swing away from repression and the outlawing of feelings) emotions almost became compulsory! A client reported, 'In order to be seen as a healthy person, I thought I had to express my sexual desires or my aggressive impulses (as well as have so many orgasms per week). These were seen as marks of authenticity.' The cost of 'doing your thing' to others was disregarded as well in this period of psychotherapy, which had its reflection in a world where everything seemed free – water, air, minerals, etc., with no cost to the environment.

At this point in the century, we are at a very different place in psychotherapy where the question has become more focused on how to live intelligently with our feelings. Our intelligence is here to serve our feelings, not the opposite way around. We have brains in order to understand our feelings and to get our needs met. Meeting our own needs is explicitly connected with meeting the needs of others as we are forced to realise how the ecology of the planet demands its dues.

Redecision work

At this stage of treatment, the client may have made several redecisions without formal 'redecision work'. Some clients may make redecisions without any such formal approaches to redecision. The Gouldings tell of a man who, after attending one of their lectures, complained to his psychotherapist that she had never done 'any of that redecision work' with him.

> The psychotherapist reminded the client that he was no longer suicidal, was making friends instead of staying alone, and was functioning with increased effectiveness at work. To do all this, he must have made redecisions. 'Oh,' he said, disappointed. 'Somehow I thought redecisions would be fancier.'
>
> (Goulding and Goulding, 1979: 8)

With or without formal redecision work, there are several indications that help the client and psychotherapist know when redecision has taken place. One is that the client's behaviour has changed outside of the psychotherapy situation. It may be, for example, that a client makes observable changes in relation to the psychotherapist or the group, asking for what they want and getting their needs met in appropriate ways. These may be important steps for the client but only when they are doing the same with their partner, their boss or others in situations away from the psychotherapy room is it likely that redecision has been made. Even then, this new behaviour may be partly in adaptation to the psychotherapist or group; the client may be responding to some newly acquired introject that says they 'should' behave like this in order to be acceptable. Duration and staying out of script on a solid and predictable level, even in stressful situations, then becomes the best criterion for redecision having been made.

There is also with many clients a marked physiological change accompanying psychological redecision. A client who formerly adapted to a 'Don't be important' script message and who presented as hunched and retiring may now appear taller, straight-shouldered and solidly grounded (a similar example is of a client who even increased his shoe size!). A woman with a 'Don't be the sex you are' adaptation may now lose weight, have definable hips and even experience the growth of her breasts. Many clients change their style and colour of clothing; others make changes in their career or their relationships or their lifestyle. Again, the lasting quality of these changes is important as an indicator of secure redecisions having been made.

Redecisions, however, need not be dramatic. An agoraphobic client who makes it to the psychotherapy room has made a redecision; so has the client who visits the dentist for the first time without fear; or another who sorts out a cupboard untouched since her husband's death. True redecisions are changes in each person's Child ego state, not in adaptation to parental figures, nor even to a better-informed Adult, but from a new Child ego state that has been rid of pathology.

Parent ego-state work

Sometimes Parent ego-state work may need to be done at earlier stages of psychotherapy: for example, if a client has a very violent Parent introject, the psychotherapist may decide to do Parent ego-state work before the redecision or decontamination period. If it is clear that the Parent is going to sabotage the psychotherapy, then it may be *necessary* to do the Parent ego-state work even earlier. Usually clinicians proceed through the stages as discussed. When something appears to remain undone, or the client seems to persist in reverting to original behaviours despite apparently good deconfusion, decontamination and redecision, Parent ego-state work is indicated.

When relevant Parent ego-state work has been accomplished, the client has for all practical purposes decathected the toxic power and influence of the Parent ego state. No matter what happens, the formerly cruel, violent or 'crazy' Parent ego state will not be cathected even under provocation. This is tested out through provocation within the group and through life stresses outside the group. The client no longer fears showing anger as they now know that it is their anger, not their mother's or father's, that they will be expressing. There is no fear of their Parent's anger taking over or 'possessing' them. Any fear that remains is an indication that further Parent ego-state work needs to be done. It may be, for example, that the Child ego state of a Parent introject may need to be reparented or may need to do cathartic work or make a redecision that will reduce the fear. The same process may need to be done in turn with the decontamination and deconfusion of their Parent ego state – in other words, direct work with the Grandparent ego states of the client.

In doing psychotherapy with the Parent ego state, it may be necessary to repeat the whole process of psychotherapeutic stages. It is as if the Parent now becomes the 'new client', needing the establishment of a relationship with the psychotherapist, a clear contract of aims, decontamination, etc., before any further work can take place.

Parent ego-state work means that a client is now freed to be healthy. They no longer need to be the Parent's confidante, protector or competitor. A jealous mother or father in the client's Parent ego state may not let a client form a relationship with the psychotherapist until work with them has been done. One particular client reported to her psychotherapist, 'I heard my mother's voice talking to you like she was talking to a teacher, telling you not to encourage a child (me) like that. She hated the cure you were showing me.' This was the vivid experience of the internal influencing mother really protesting that the psychotherapist would encourage the client to do things she would not approve of, such as taking a vacation from work; the mother's jealous Child needed her own attention. Once given, the client was able to take a vacation 'without guilt'.

In the following example of Parent ego-state work, the client has agreed to 'become' his father while the client's Child ego state is represented by a cushion.

(*P* = Psychotherapist; *C* = Client)

P: Your son still remembers you like you were when he was small. He doesn't remember you the way you are.

C: No he wouldn't. He's keeping the old image of me alive.

P: What could you do to change that image?

C: I could tell him how I changed.

P: Mm. He's very invested in that old image, so what can you tell him that will be useful for him?

C: I don't know, I'm not used to this.

P: No, you're not used to this. On the other hand, you did change ...

C: Yeah, that's right. But I'm not sure that he wants to hear.

P: I suspect he'll hear if you're genuine in what you say: not the old dad but the dad that changed.

C: I don't know if I can do that.

P: I understand that it's very hard for you to talk to your son. But it's very important ... it's very important.

C: (cries quietly) I ...

P: It's fine to let him see you cry.

C: (sobbing) I'm sad I left it so late to talk to him.

P: Tell him, he's right here, he wants to hear, he's listening.

C: I'm sad it took me so long to realise how what you had to offer was valuable and important – so long that by then you weren't around for me to share that with you, by then, you weren't prepared to be around.

P: And that hurt.

C: What really hurt was that I didn't know how to contact you and you rarely contacted me. So I never got a chance to tell you so many things.

P: Will you tell him now?

C: Well, I think I want you to know that I realise it's more important to look for feelings and caring in people than to look for competence and capabilities. I ignored the feelings between us and I lost you.

P: Tell him some more about that.

C: It wasn't worth it to be so invested in my need to appear strong and capable and outgoing to the extent that I would lose you. It wasn't worth it and I realised that too late.

P: Do you know he behaves like you sometimes?

C: Yes. But you can change. You don't have to do what I did. You don't
have to wait till it's too late. You don't have to kill yourself.

P: Tell him again.

C: You don't have to kill yourself.

P: Because ...

C: Because you are important and valuable without having to be strong and
competent and respected. I just didn't know how to show you that I cared. I
wanted so much to have a son to be close to. I didn't know how to make that
work.

P: Tell him now. He needs to hear that so much.

C: You are important to me. You are more important to me than your
competence or your capabilities in your work. You are important as you
(embraces the cushion representing his son, and weeps). You are very
important to me.

There may be rare occasions when the actual parent is brought into the psychotherapy situation. This can be very hard for the parent. Ideally, the parent's
psychotherapist would also be present. A female client who, at 14 years of age,
had felt responsible for her parent's break-up heard in a combined session from
her mother's mouth that this was not so. In this particular case, this was both
possible and desirable, and a very healing experience for both. As was another
example of a reconciliation between an abusing mother and her abused child (the
client) 17 years later. Clearly it is important to reassure the parent that they are
not there to be 'bashed'. Parents easily feel blamed and need to be protected from
this eventuality.

It is frequently inappropriate to include the real parent in psychotherapy with
the client since the developmental task might be precisely to separate emotionally
from the parent – a separation which is sometimes avoided by continuing the
hostile–dependent relationship (and often colluded with by overenthusiastic and
inexperienced family psychotherapists) (Salters and Clarkson, 1988).

Reorientation

At this stage of treatment, having made the intrapsychic adjustments necessary
for change and putting those changes into effect, clients often report the need to
reorientate themselves in the world. They experience themselves as 'not knowing
what to do', 'walking around in a daze', being surprised by their own and other
people's actions, not in a phoney 'Here I go again' sort of way but with a new
way of seeing things. It seems like there is a shift in the client's whole frame of
reference which they will need time to adjust to. Bridges (1980) mentions
disengagement, disenchantment, disidentification, and disorientation as components of this stage of treatment. The old patterns of thinking, feeling and behaving
can no longer be relied upon. This results in some clients losing a sense of who
they really are – 'If I'm not what I used to be and thought I was, who am I now?'

Or, on a more basic level, 'I used to be the kind of person who never wore yellow but now, I'm not so sure.'

One client put it this way, 'When I'm walking along, it's as if I look around and discover I've grown two wings that I never knew I had. It's just so peculiar. I might slowly learn to fly!'

At this stage, the psychotherapist needs to be willing to suspend the plan in order to be where the client is, trusting that even if you let go of it you will be able to find it again. So reorientation involves the willingness to let go of the previous adaptations and identifications in order to discover new possibilities and ways of being. This can be a frightening experience. It is a leap into the abyss, into the unknown. It is an act of faith on the part of the client that if they let go of their old familiar self, they will survive.

A new self is not possible without letting go of the old self. The client needs to be willing to risk a state of uncertainty, unsureness and suspense from which a new life can emerge. The psychotherapist needs to allow this process to happen and resist the temptation to create structures (certainty) on the client's behalf.

Relearning

As much as reorientation is about experiencing 'not knowing', relearning is about 'knowing'; about learning what to do and how to do it within the new frame of reference. Once knowledge about their own patterns and changes has become a part of the client's information pack, energy can be used for life-enhancing purposes rather than for tail chasing. This stage of psychotherapy entails learning about learning; about knowing in a new way.

Clients at this stage have sorted through their old messages and introjects and have made decisions about what to throw away and what to keep. Sometimes relearning involves recapturing or retrieving the original ways in which a person functioned before taking on script restrictions. For example, as a child, Fred wrote very good essays and came top in English at school but as his parents put on more and more pressure for him to achieve better and better results, his enjoyment of writing lessened. At university he began smoking and while writing for his degree often doubled the number of cigarettes. In psychotherapy, not having written for years, Fred began to reclaim those early skills and work from a decontaminated place (without using his internal Parent to put pressure on himself). He has recognised the useful way in which he used to write as a child and how, later, smoking used to relieve the internal pressure he would put upon himself. Now he is relearning how to write. 'I have to learn not only that it is possible to write without smoking but *how* to write without smoking.' The skills are in place, retrieved from the past and recreated in the present, with a new level of confidence. What used formerly to be pseudocompetency now becomes true competence.

At this stage, too, there is a new questioning energy from the Child. Unfortunately, this stage is often skipped over by the psychotherapist perhaps too keen to move through to the termination phase and, seeing the client well and competent, not allowing for the client's very real need of asking and answering questions in a re-educative way following, for example, redecision. It may be important for the client to get well first but remain in psychotherapy so they can learn the skills or acquire the information that was missing in their original situations. In our culture, we are desperately undereducated in emotional and problem-solving skills. It may be very reparative to emphasise this stage of therapy with clients. Time management or assertiveness courses may be useful at this stage; more so than earlier in the therapy when clients make short-term behavioural changes without a firm structure to maintain those changes. Now, in a healthier position, clients are more successful in making use of the relearning. Most people need to have cleared out the old in order to make way for the new.

In a similar way, clients earlier in therapy often ask for, but do not use, advice or information given by the psychotherapist. A very good test of the achievement of this stage of psychotherapy, is the client's ability to make use of the learning provided. They are thinking on behalf of themselves and request information and advice with the intent of making it work for themselves.

Termination

It is difficult to establish hard-and-fast criteria for what is 'good enough' for termination of psychotherapy. Psychotherapists as part of their professional practice often remain in therapy throughout their working lives in order to keep their own issues out of their work with clients. A client who is not a psychotherapist may reach a point where termination is achieved within a few months. One of the guidelines, therefore, is to see termination as appropriate when the person has met their contract. A psychotherapist's contract as client is therefore likely to be met only when no countertransference issues are interfering with their work with clients (i.e. when they cease to work as psychotherapists!). Another client's contract is met, for example, when the client says, 'I wanted to ejaculate inside my wife. I am now doing this, thank you very much, and so I want to finish psychotherapy.' In other words when people get what they came for, it is appropriate to terminate. In many cases it is possible to make a fair assessment of how long someone will be in therapy according to the issues being presented and it is important that the psychotherapist share their thinking about this in as honest a way as possible at the beginning of therapy.

It is also important to differentiate between psychotherapy, psychotherapy needs and psychotherapy clients. The emphasis should remain with the client. It is unfair to burden the client with idealistic 'psychotherapy' expectations. It is oppressive to see people as having 'psychotherapy needs' rather than as people, as individuals. This abuse can most easily occur when humanistic psychotherapists generalise from their own experience of psychotherapy without respecting differences in capacities, preferences and goals which may be very different in their clients.

Other signs and symptoms appropriate to the termination stage are the recycling of earlier issues, apparent regression, the expression of all the classic stages of grief, sadness, anger, rejection, fear of the future, checking up on the possibility of returning, personal questions about the therapist and an acknowledgement of how special the therapist has been to the client. This is often the stage where envy, in the Kleinian sense, has been transformed into appropriate gratitude.

One client reported that her therapist wasn't large enough for her at the beginning of psychotherapy. Later, she began to experience the therapist as being so large she almost filled the room. In the termination phase she realised that she was responsible for making the therapist bigger or smaller in accordance with her own psychological needs and expressed her gratitude that her therapist was the kind of person with whom she could do this. Any attribution of potency at this stage is neither idealised nor diminished by the client.

There is a lot of reviewing, summing up and reminiscing. There are many questions like, 'Do I exist for you?' and 'Do you exist for me when we don't see each other?' The psychotherapist has to learn to discriminate between needed information, avoided information and problems with getting information. If the psychotherapist genuinely has information useful to the client, it may be sadistic to withhold it and be an avoidance of the educative task of psychotherapy. Masterson (1985) stresses this educative task, particularly for borderline and narcissistic patients, when he writes that the therapist deals with this immaturity by providing a learning experience. Therefore, as it begins to emerge in treatment, all of these relatively obvious and almost common-sense notions about the reality of life and interactions between people have to be not relearned, but learned for the first time.

Treatment planning can, if approached in the wrong spirit, seem antithetical to the nature of the evolving relationship (which is always the priority) between therapist and clients; and sometimes it is, when it has become a 'cookbook' approach or when it is used to avoid the vicissitudes of the interpersonal encounter, when it's become mechanical and predetermined, rather than the creative use of previously developed maps in order to rediscover new territory as if for the first time. In a psychotherapeutic approach such as TA, flexibility and range is highly valued. Different therapists may have different natural gifts and preferences (such as exquisite left-hemispheric logic and planning capacity or an acute right-hemispheric, intuitive grasp of the very core of a person's being). These therapists may celebrate their strengths or even wish to extend and to develop their capacities in areas in which they are less familiar, less practised, and which are less 'natural' to them. The assumption is that intuition is better informed as a result of knowledge and prediction skills, whereas planning and goal-setting is improvised by intuitive images, rhythms and leaps. It is also possible that clients may require these different capacities from their therapist at different developmental stages of their psychotherapeutic journey. Having discussed a rather formal framework, within which, of course, psychotherapists are allowed to play as much as they please, what follows now is an attempt at communicating the flavour of a supervision session which evolved from imagination, intuition and play towards structure which served the function of enhancing creativity rather than diminishing it.

Macroscopic sequencing strategies to encourage intuition and right-hemispheric functioning:

The trainee on whom the following account is based was well versed and experienced in classical treatment planning. However, she had lost confidence in her treatment approach having become somewhat mechanistic and 'dry' thus losing contact with her intuition, spontaneity and serendipity which should be as integral a part of treatment design as observation, hypothesising and intellection.

The supervision session provided the psychotherapist with the opportunity to experiment with right-brain creativity as an approach to treatment planning.

She gives the following account:

I felt stuck with a client in terms of where I was heading with her, and if I was clear about what she needed. I had up to this point been using my left brain in diagnosing the treatment planning and my intuition was that what was missing was my heart.

I asked to use my supervision session in an experiential way. We established the firm contract that this was the way I wanted to use my session, and my outcome was to have a clearer understanding of where I was with this client and were I was heading.

My first instruction from my supervisor was to walk in the way of my client. I felt slightly inhibited at first but finally did it. It was a real breakthrough for me from being rigid in my thinking into allowing myself to be more loose and flexible. The next instruction was to sing like her, dance like her, talk like her, put my jacket on and off like her. From really experiencing my client I felt very much in touch with my true experience of her as opposed to a clinical diagnosis. I was also aware by now that I was extremely similar to her and therefore my countertransferential issues were clouding my ability to see her clearly. This was already an exciting and illuminating experience.

The next instruction was to draw her as I saw her. I drew a sun radiating many bright and optimistic colours. In the centre of the sun was a broken heart. This symbolised how broken she really felt even though she masked this with her outer shine. This was also a pictorial way of showing her false self covering her true self. I was now clear about my creative and intuitive diagnosis which at this stage was backing my logical and clinical diagnosis (narcissistic disorder).

My next invitation was to go out into the garden and around the house and find five articles that illustrated what my client needed. I felt nervous and excited at this point as I was really going to continue trusting my intuition. I felt childlike and free and off I went. I came back with a heater, a sheepskin rug, a set of Russian dolls, a bottle of milk, a handful of soil and stones with a shrub growing out of it and a heart-shaped box. I was asked to lay these items out on a large sheet of white paper and then number the articles in terms of priority. I felt very excited by now as I knew I was creating a story but at this stage did not know what – I was excited by myself and my hunger to learn in a new and creative way. I felt stroked and supported by my supervisor who was right there reinforcing my wanting to learn. For me this was a developmental gap. I had not had teachers or parents who would teach me in a way that matched my energy level and style of learning. The next task to number the articles was done as follows: (1) milk , (2a) heater, (2b) fur rug, (3) heart-shaped box, (4) the Russian dolls, (5) the soil and plant. I was asked to write up next to each number and article what that meant in terms of treatment planning. This was so exciting as for me it felt like an integration of my right and left brain and I was experiencing how they were equally reliable, interchangeable and could benefit from each other.

I did the task as follows:

1 Milk	Providing nurturing and a knowledge she could get 'fed' here. Providing security	Relationship building Theraputic alliance
2 (a) Heater (b) Fur rug	Providing warmth	Security
3 Heart-shaped box	Being there, having empathy, mirroring, reflection	Testing phase ensuring I am here for her not her for me (as with mother)
4 Russian dolls	Discovering parts of her, layers of her, i.e. working with introjects, her available Adult and Child	Decontamination, deconfusion with Child and Parent ego states
5 Mud, stones with plant growing out	Working with the grit of her true self and getting to a place where her new self can grow and flourish as opposed to adapting for others	Redecision and then relearning, affirming her real self in her freshness

My supervisor asked me to look at all that I had constructed and created, and said 'Go next door and be alone, reflecting on what you have let yourself do. When you are doing this ask yourself, what has this client come to teach me?'

I went next door feeling very emotionally churned as I had had such an affirming experience of using what I intuitively knew in a concrete way. I felt validated, that is I felt my natural self. When sitting alone I realised that this client had come to me to teach me that to love was healing and therapeutic. To be myself and to allow her to be herself was the lesson we were to learn. I burst into tears, ran next door and told my supervisor what I had discovered and connected with her that this in fact was what I had received in my psychotherapy and I had truly found my real self and was so grateful. Because of my personal experience, I realised that it was fine to do the same for my client, when in fact this is what she needed as she had never been loved for 'being'. We had therefore identified my countertransference issues and having done this I was able to move through in my treatment planning, and no longer felt stuck, we had therefore fulfilled our contract.

We ended the session with me playing a music tape which was a Hebrew song written about identity and that each one of us deserves a name and a true identity. For me having the music played very loudly helped me immerse one of the most powerful learning experiences into my very being. The song was powerful for me as it was in Hebrew, and as I am Jewish, this truly symbolised my identity and my tasks, thus reinforcing my new knowledge that what we do is so much to do with who we are, and that we need to own all of ourselves and access all of us to work in a comprehensive, congruent way. Now when I am stuck with a client, I know I have many more ways and options to choose from.

AN EXAMPLE OF DIAGNOSIS, STAGES OF TREATMENT AND TREATMENT DESIGN

At the time of referral, Pauline, aged 23, was in the final year of a 3-year teacher-training course at the local college of higher education. She was living in a shared flat with other students but later moved with her partner to a new flat which they share with one other friend. This is the first relationship with a woman that Pauline has had.

Pauline's presenting problems related to her having been raped 9 months previously by her ex-boyfriend. She had sought very little help for herself, and the two agencies and individuals she had spoken to, she had not wanted to maintain contact with. She had, however, partially told her GP what had happened and had been prescribed antidepressants and tranquillisers which she was still taking. However, she had not had a full medical examination despite knowing that she was in pain from internal injuries, nor had she told the police. The man was at college with her so she continued to see him when she attended college. Her final exams were approaching so this had serious implications for her. He also continued to harass her with letters and phone calls.

Pauline was not sleeping at night, except occasionally, and she then had violent nightmares. She had had asthma for some years, and this was considerably worse. She also had panic attacks. She had severe back pain. She had broken off most of her social contacts and had become withdrawn and remote.

My initial impression of her was that she was like a rabbit, frozen with fear in the headlights of an oncoming car, unable to move to protect herself. She was clearly in a state of shock and traumatisation, aggravated by a deterioration in her physical health. She had an almost total absence of affect which was compounded by her medication.

The stated reason for the referral was Pauline's state of physical and mental health, as a result of having been raped some 9 months previously by her ex-boyfriend. Using the DSM-III, my initial diagnosis of Pauline was of Post-traumatic Stress Disorder (Axis I), as she had experienced a brutal rape 9 months previously, consequent to which she had phases when she can think of nothing else. When sleeping, she has nightmares and screams out. She reported sitting huddled up, petrified for hours at a time, waiting for her abuser to appear. In a couples session, when my male colleague confronted her, she became rigid with fear and felt unable to speak to him or look at him. She had also stopped all involvement in social life and activities. On coming into psychotherapy, she reported having felt numb for months. She told of 'jumping' when the telephone rang, experienced insomnia for most nights and also reported difficulty in study-ing due to poor concentration. She experienced terror when attending hospital for an internal examination regarding her injuries. For a fuller clinical diagnosis, I have used the DSM-III multiaxial system. This is the system I use in addition to a TA diagnosis in my practice. I particularly value the multiaxial system as a structure for building a more complete picture of my client, not just in terms of her mental disorders, but also her physical condition, who she is in her life, the stresses she may be experiencing and her ego strength or potential. This provides a realistic diagnostic structure from which to develop a treatment plan and to make a prognosis.

Again on Axis I, I diagnosed Dysthymias present in her Child ego state as Pauline reports significant times in her childhood when she experienced a depressed mood for more days than not for at least one year as a child, during which time she overate, had very low self-esteem, and feelings of hopelessness.

Pauline has two diagnoses on Axis II – Avoidant Personality Disorder and Dependent Personality Disorder. Both these are from Cluster C. As for Avoidant Personality Disorder, Pauline fitted most of the criteria. For example, she is easily hurt by criticism or disapproval, is unwilling to get involved with people unless she is certain of being liked, is reticent in social situations because of a fear of saying something inappropriate or foolish, or of being unable to answer a question. She also fears being embarrassed by blushing, crying or showing signs of anxiety in front of other people. She exaggerates the potential difficulties, physical dangers or risks involved in doing something ordinary but outside her usual routine. As for Dependent Personality Disorder, Pauline fitted the following criteria: she agrees with people even when she believes they are wrong, because of fear of being rejected; she volunteers to do things that are unpleasant or demanding in order to get other people to like her; she feels uncomfortable or helpless when alone, or goes to great lengths to avoid being alone; she feels devastated or helpless when close relationships end; she is frequently pre-occupied with fears of being abandoned and is easily hurt by criticism or disapproval.

On Axis III Pauline was diagnosed as having asthma, insomnia, bowel prolapse, vaginal injuries and back injuries. On Axis IV, which measures the current life stress of a person, Pauline scored in the 'extreme' range, having had the experience of being raped; continued harassment from the abuser; involvement with the police and court procedures; starting a new job; starting a new relationship with a woman, which is vehemently disapproved of by her family and about which she feels the need to keep secret at work. On Axis V, I assessed her level of functioning to be 'good'.

Discussion of diagnosis

On Axis I, I retained my initial diagnosis of Post-traumatic Stress Disorder.

At the time of writing, 18 months into Pauline's psychotherapy, she no longer manifests the majority of the symptoms of her Post-traumatic Stress Disorder. She is, however, still on a low dosage of antidepressants and tranquillisers.

At this stage, I am of the opinion that she is not experiencing Dysthymia in her Adult life. However, I hypothesise that as a child she was considerably depressed. She reports that she overate and consequently was overweight, believed that she was bad and felt helpless about her life. Dysthymia is still present, therefore, in her archaic Child ego states and, when working with her Child, I have observed and experienced these characteristics. The work that Pauline has done in her psychotherapy I think has been significant in her no longer suffering from Dysthymia in her Adult.

On Axis II, Pauline manifested an Avoidant Personality Disorder. This was particularly apparent in her fear of getting involved with people unless certain of being liked. Her behaviour in social settings superficially appears competent and I therefore questioned this diagnosis. However, when Pauline joined the group, her avoidant behaviour became very obvious as the social banalities she learnt to deal with her family's expectations became inconsequential and non-effective. Pauline, therefore, has a superficial social persona which disguises her avoidant personality. As a result her social relationships are often one-sided and in her words 'I know them, but they don't know me.'

These one-sided relationships have often included a significant level of dependence on Pauline. As Pauline has become less scared of allowing herself to be in contact, the extent of her own dependence has become evident. The creation of dependence on her, seems, therefore, to have been a way of avoiding and yet satisfying her own dependent personality. In contrast, in the last six months, the extent of her dependence has become very clear. There have been times when she has felt unable to decide whether or not to have a cup of coffee and has asked Julia (her partner) to decide. Her 'fits' have resulted in her being banned from driving so her partner now chauffeurs her about. She has expressed fear when other group members leave the group as she anticipates the day 'she has to leave'.

For these reasons, I have made a diagnosis of more than one personality disorder as Pauline meets the criteria for both, rather than a differential diagnosis.

Contracting

Pauline's initial contract, in her own words, was: 'To come and see my psychotherapist because I recognise that I need to do something about having been raped because of my deteriorating physical and emotional health.'

Establishing a working relationship

My understanding of this contract was that Pauline would come and see me regularly on a weekly basis, which would be evidence of her reaching out for help and therefore accounting for the existence and significance of her problems. I was willing to work with this initial contract although it was 'soft', as Pauline's level of scare about reaching out for help was so great. I considered, therefore, that the action of coming and establishing a contract and beginning to build a relationship was, in itself, a significant behavioural change.

However, as part of my conditions for working with Pauline, I required her to agree to seek medical help and to inform the police about being raped. I specifically said I would not put a time limit on these requirements, as I did not want to parallel the process of forcing her. My requirement for her to contract to seek medical help reflects my ethical standing as a psychotherapist, in that I would require any client who had physical injuries to be medically examined. However, because in Pauline's case this was a particularly sensitive issue, I was not willing to make it immediate; rather to respect Pauline's need to be in charge of this process as she took back control over her own body. Similarly, with her reporting the rape to the police, I thought it was vital for her to take charge of when and how she reported her situation to the police. As she was continuing to see the man who had raped her, and he continued to harass her with phone calls, I decided that this condition was a necessary part of my confronting her 'helpless' belief and her Victim role. In so doing, I was providing her Child with the protection of positive Controlling Parent behaviours. I was also supporting her in getting the protection she needed in her life.

Pauline agreed to these conditions and made a further contract to use her psychotherapy to enable herself to seek full medical help, and to support her in taking effective action with regards to informing the police.

History

Pauline is the second of two children, the elder sibling being her brother, Phil. She was born in the Yorkshire Dales, in a rural area, where she spent all her childhood, and where her parents continue to live. Grandfather lived with Pauline's family until she was 15, when he died.

Immediately after her birth, Pauline's mother had a 'nervous breakdown' and for 8 months she stayed in bed. Pauline's father mostly looked after Pauline. Her mother had a further 'breakdown' when Pauline was 8 years old and has been on valium 'all of her life'. The family's energy is largely put into protecting Pauline's mother from anything that might 'upset her nerves', and into dealing with her illnesses and irrational behaviour.

The family story relating to Pauline's babyhood is, 'She was such a good baby, you could put her down between meals and never know she was there.' As a child, Pauline's experience of her mother was of a highly unpredictable and dangerous woman who often hit Pauline for doing something wrong like walking in at the front door from school when her mother had just cleaned the floor. Pauline can remember her father saying, 'Don't upset your mother, she takes weeks to re-settle.'

Pauline remembers her father as a quiet, calm man whom other children saw as a wonderful father because he ran the local youth club and football team, but who had little time for her unless she was actively involved in these activities. She believes he loved her and loves her – and that his priority is a quiet life with his wife, even if that means betraying Pauline's needs. As a small-town family businessman he upholds a strong moral and dutiful family set. When Pauline was 11 years old, her father broke his neck and spent one year on his back in the sitting room downstairs. During this time Pauline was only allowed to see him if she was 'quiet' and 'good'.

Pauline's maternal grandfather lived with them until Pauline was 15 years old. She was deeply fond of her grandfather and he represents for her the parental figure who was consistent and accessible to her, and for whom, as a child, she felt and showed trust and affection. When he died, she was sent out of the house and was not allowed to go to the funeral. Her experience was of an absolute denial of the significance of her attachment to her grandfather, and, therefore of what his death would mean to her.

Pauline was very close to her brother Phil and although there is 4 years difference in age, they spent a lot of time together as children, share a sense of humour, and a love and excitement for the outdoors and sports activities. Phil's robustness and strength were very important to Pauline as a child, and contrasted with her experience of her parents as fragile both physically and mentally.

Pauline first left home at 18 to train as a secretary. However, she failed to complete the training and returned home. She then came up to London to do the teacher-training course in which she was involved when she came to see me.

Her first sexual involvement was with Jim, the man who subsequently raped her. This relationship lasted for about 15 months, during which time there were several breaks as a result of his having a relationship with another woman.

Social relationships at time of referral

Pauline has a personable presentation developed in response to her family's expectations that she will be a polite and pleasant young woman, and socially adept within their rural community's defined ways. Pauline describes herself, when like this, as 'social, witty and a good listener – so there are lots of people who think of me as a friend but from whom I feel distant and untrusting'.

Pauline presents like this: polite and pleasing at work and is therefore liked and respected. This adaptation, however, covers her deep-seated lack of self-confidence and fear in genuinely relating to other people from her core self, which is reflected in her subsequent diagnosis of Avoidant Personality Disorder.

Her primary friendships dated back to her childhood and she has, in her family home town, two or three long-standing close women friends. She is deeply attached to her elder brother whom she describes with relief and admiration as 'big and strong'. This sense of her brother as a physical, protective figure has always been important for Pauline and while, in the course of psychotherapy, she has come to understand some of the reasons for this importance, she remains closely bonded to him and, tangentially, to his wife.

Outside of her childhood and family relationships, Pauline's social relationships seem to have been limited. She has had one-sided social contacts at work and through her personal interests of choral singing and women's football. Otherwise she has had very intense, dependent relationships with her sexual partners – her ex-boyfriend and her current lover (see Figure 6.1).

In his award-winning article on egograms, Dusay (1972) discusses the concept in terms of ego states. His emphasis on the approach as 'physiological' and dealing with 'pressure, frequency and intensity' is related to a functional model of ego states. In drawing Pauline's egogram, therefore, I have adhered to my analysis of her observable behaviour, its 'pressure, frequency and intensity'. Using the structural model of ego states, I believe that her high Nurturing Parent behaviour is a manifestation of her Child ego-state decision to look after others rather than herself. Similarly, her low Critical Parent behaviour is a manifestation of her Child ego-state decision that she was bad and to blame, and she directed her aggression inward on herself rather than out into the world. Her Critical Parent behaviour was often therefore, not observable.

I initially worked with Pauline to enable her to understand her script with particular reference to her experience of having been raped. This was important in understanding what she needed to change in order to fulfil her initial contract to seek appropriate medical and police help, and her final contract, to 'recontact the human race'.

The script matrix (Figure 6.3) is based on work Pauline did when she was exploring her fear of seeking help and anticipating that others would not take her seriously or believe her story. I think this particularised script matrix is interesting as a construct for looking at how a particular crisis in a client's life fits into her overall life script; how she is primed, at best, not to prevent such an experience and at worst, to invite it. This crisis, which in this case was Pauline's experience of being raped, became a focus for diagnosing her script and therefore her self-limiting behaviours, rather than a discrete, one-off experience to be 'got over'.

The statement, 'If you are hurt by someone ...' was the stimulus to which Pauline responded in compiling the script matrix. The model for the script matrix is from Berne's (1972: 128) *What Do You Say After You Say Hello?*

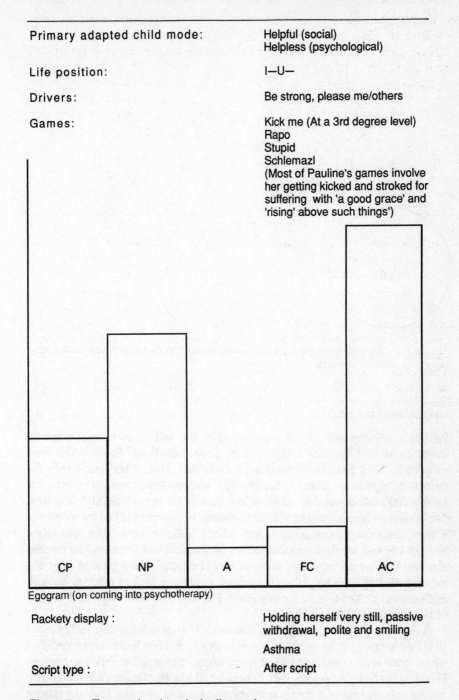

Primary adapted child mode:	Helpful (social)
	Helpless (psychological)
Life position:	I—U—
Drivers:	Be strong, please me/others
Games:	Kick me (At a 3rd degree level)
	Rapo
	Stupid
	Schlemazl
	(Most of Pauline's games involve her getting kicked and stroked for suffering with 'a good grace' and 'rising' above such things')

| CP | NP | A | FC | AC |

Egogram (on coming into psychotherapy)

Rackety display :	Holding herself very still, passive withdrawal, polite and smiling
	Asthma
Script type :	After script

Figure 6.1 Transactional analysis diagnosis

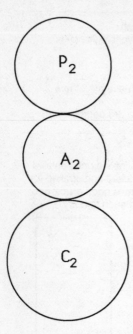

Figure 6.2   An ego-state portrait of Pauline when she came into psychotherapy, using the structural model

Definition of the problem

Pauline's development of her sense of self, and self-identity, was seriously impaired by her childhood experiences. From babyhood, Pauline had been scripted to be a passive, well-behaved child and adult. This was within the context of significant threat to her physical and emotional wellbeing from her family. Her mother was dependent on medication 'for her nerves' and on at least two occasions became sufficiently ill to require her to retire to bed for months at a time, including once immediately after Pauline's birth. She was often emotionally and physically unable to care for Pauline, and frequently hit Pauline and behaved quite irrationally towards her. Her father was a passive man and avoided dealing with his wife's behaviour, preferring both to practise himself, and train his children, to suffer in silence. Pauline, therefore, never told anyone of her mother's violence to her.

As a result, Pauline's survival decision was 'It's not safe to think, feel or move so if I do nothing, I may survive.' In her adult life, Pauline lived out this decision when faced with emotional and physical threat. Having thus failed to prevent herself from being raped, she then continued to live by this decision rather than ask for help and support. She was therefore unable to move on from the trauma

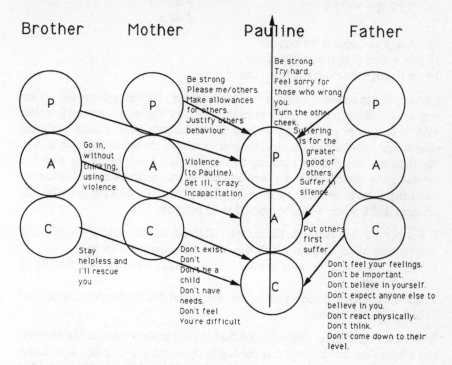

Figure 6.3   Script matrix: 'If you are hurt by someone ...'
Source: Berne, 1972: 281

of the rape, which also triggered her childhood traumas of violence. Instead, she repressed her feelings, felt ashamed and guilty about what had happened and attempted to continue her life by denying what had happened. At the point when Pauline came into psychotherapy, she had begun to experience both physically and emotionally the high cost of these adaptations and to know, in her Adult, that she could not continue to lead her life for much longer in this way. She was therefore, available to look at her options and to find alternative Adult ways of dealing with her life experiences.

Final contract

Contracting

Pauline's final contract which she made some six weeks into psychotherapy, was:

'I will recontact the human race and will survive and complete my exams.'

After discussion, Pauline broke down this contract into various parts:

To ask for and get help: Medical
                                            Police

To ask and get support for myself
To start seeing people socially again
To get through the exams as best I can

Her decision to continue with her exams meant her continuing to see the person who had raped her, therefore considerably compounding her trauma and fear. Her wish to use her psychotherapy to help her to fulfil the aim of completing her exams, was a contract which I had some reservations about working with at first. My thinking was that by agreeing to the contract, I was colluding with her continuing to abuse herself, by regularly seeing this person without her having taken any steps to protect herself. When I discussed this with Pauline, she was adamant that this was what she wanted to do because:

1 For her to fail to complete her exams, and therefore not to qualify, would be a repetition of her 'failing' which was a familiar experience for her.
2 Having continued for nine months, she wanted to make this worthwhile by completing.
3 She did not want to delay leaving the college and thereby begin to put that part of her life behind her.

It was also clear that for Pauline to ask for help and support through this time was a new behaviour and to know that she had options, and was choosing to continue at college for her reasons, was also a significant change. Pauline also agreed to visit the college GP and to get a medical statement of support which she could use if she needed her marks to be compensated.

Pauline has subsequently made further psychotherapy contracts which reveal her motivation to change other aspects of her self and her life. In Holloway's terms (1973), these are contracts for autonomy and are indicative of a significant shift in Pauline's psychotherapy from short-term psychotherapy with a contract for social control, to longer-term psychotherapy with contracts for autonomy.

Psychotherapy planning

In treatment planning for Pauline, I looked at a number of factors:

1 Her diagnosis on Axis I, namely that she was suffering from a Post-traumatic Stress Disorder. I also remained alert to the possibility of an underlying Dysthymic Disorder.
2 Her initial contract.
3 Her presenting personality type as named on Axis II, Avoidant Personality Disorder.

(At this early stage of treatment planning I had not been significantly aware of her Dependent Personality Disorder to account for it in the treatment plan.)

On the basis of this information, I planned to work with Pauline individually. My thinking was that her contract was at this stage essentially a social-control contract (Holloway, 1973), and therefore my expectation of psychotherapy was that it could be relatively short term.

Furthermore, and importantly, given her diagnosis on Axis II as manifesting an Avoidant Personality Disorder, I wanted to work in a way which was commensurate with, and informed by this diagnosis.

Deficit model

One of the primary unmet needs of someone who has this particular personality type, is the need for attachment, contact and intimacy. The individual sessions, therefore, would provide Pauline with the opportunity to make a significant attachment, and to use the security of this relationship to work through her Post-traumatic Stress Disorder.

When, at a later stage in her psychotherapy, Pauline renegotiated her psychotherapy contract away from the original trauma to a more fundamental change in her personality, my second treatment plan had a continuity of approach with my original formulation. Some of the basic ground work of relationship building had been completed and some of the decontamination and awareness stage had also been completed.

Contracting

As shown earlier, the TA concept of contract is central to my treatment planning strategy. The formation and content of Pauline's psychotherapy contract informs my conceptualisation of a treatment plan for her psychotherapy.

Working relationship

Part of this process is the development of a working relationship at both the administrative and professional levels (Berne, 1966), and I account for this in my strategical consideration.

Decontamination

Commensurate with this process is the concept of decontamination which I see as beginning almost as soon as the client begins negotiating our relationship and her contracts, as this will include looking at and developing an understanding of here-and-now reality, options and responsibility for self. I use decontamination as a guiding concept to know when the client's Child is available for deconfusion, and am also aware that these two processes are often mutually facilitating.

Using the concept of decontamination as a guide during the initial phases of psychotherapy, I have in the foreground some of the TA methods which I have found most effective, such as ego-state dialogues using two-chair Gestalt techniques, multiple-chair techniques (Stuntz, 1973), game and script analyses, and transactional analysis. I also teach Steiner's Emotional Literacy (Steiner, 1984) and use Crossman's Permission Transaction (1966).

Confusion model

I will also confront discounts and passive behaviours. The centrality of the concept and process of decontaminating the client's Adult is important for me. From experience, the client's Child is not willing to disobey her injunctions and to redecide that she can safely be different in the world, unless this time, she is very certain that there is a clear and competent Adult on her side. This requires for the client to live her life at least for the most part, from an Adult awareness. This means not setting up games or reinforcing rackets so the Child can genuinely experience that life is now different from the past.

Deconfusion

The deconfusion of the Child stage is the way I conceptualise the phase of treatment when I anticipate working more consistently with the client's Child ego state to allow 'expression of unmet needs and feelings' (Woollams and Brown, 1978) and to facilitate redecision.

Redecision

Redecision work using methods developed by the Gouldings (Goulding and Goulding, 1979).

Parent ego state work

During this stage I also use techniques such as Child interviews and Parent interviews (McNeel, 1976). It is also important during this stage of psychotherapy that I maintain my potency and protection for the client as she challenges her script in profound and life-changing ways.

Relearning

Following the redecision, the client then needs to be supported as she relearns how to be in the world according to her new decision and this is the relearning and re-orientation phase.

Reorientation

During this time, I often return to the basic constructs of the stroke economy (Steiner, 1971), time structuring, methods of confronting games (Dusay, 1966), and options (Karpman, 1971), as tools to facilitate the client's reorganisation of healthy life structures.

Deficit Model

Throughout treatment, I also think in terms of child development and use appropriate developmental concepts in my treatment planning. I had diagnosed that Pauline's main developmental trauma was in the 6–18-month period.

According to Levin: 'when we work through problems from the ages of around 6 months to 18 months, we are beginning to bridge the gap between the symbiosis with parents and doing things on our own' (1974: 28). If the child is unable to complete this developmental task because the environment is not supportive, or dangerous, then she will learn not to do and become passive.

In treatment planning for Pauline, I am aware of the significance of her contracts to be pro-active and of her need for encouragement and permission to do on her own behalf, to explore options and to be supported at the same time. I am sensitive to her possible dulling of her little Professor (A_1), and I therefore know to stroke her intuition. I am also looking for opportunities to encourage and support Pauline in making demands on others, to bother them, rather than remain passive.

While I hold the developmental issues of the 6–18-month period as foreground initially, I also anticipate that Pauline may manifest developmental gaps from other ages and that I need to respond accordingly.

Therapeutic process

For me, an important aspect of cure is that I and the patient agree on what *we* are talking about. So, for example, in relation to Pauline, cure could mean:

1 That she had achieved any one of her contracts, including the initial 'social control' contract.
2 That she no longer suffered from a Post-traumatic Stress Disorder.
3 That she had achieved autonomy in Berne's sense of awareness, spontaneity and intimacy (1966).

I think it is appropriate to apply the concept of cure to any one of these three possible outcomes of psychotherapy. I also think it is important to differentiate explicitly between what the client has achieved in these different outcomes. For example:

1 The client curing herself of specific pathological behaviours – in Pauline's case, doing nothing, cutting herself off from the world and neglecting to seek appropriate help.
2 The client being cured of a specific clinical syndrome as recorded on Axis I – in Pauline's case, a Post-traumatic Stress Disorder or Dysthymic Disorder. While clearly the client will have made considerable intrapsychic changes and experience significant release from distress, cure in this category is particular to this presenting syndrome. Pauline, for example, may have worked through the traumatic experience of being raped; however, given a similar set of circumstances she may not prevent a repeat of the experience.
3 Script cure, or autonomy, requires that the individual has made new decisions about how she will be in the world. 'Real and lasting script cure is achieved when the new decision is stable under both ordinary and extreme stresses' (Clarkson, 1988b). As Berne says, 'Such a script cure, which changes his character and his destiny, is also clinical cure, since most of his symptoms will be relieved by his redecision' (1972: 362). For Pauline, this will mean she has

developed the capacity to avoid repetitive, destructive patterns in her life, and to be actively in the world, in touch with and valuing her own feelings and thoughts.

The process and stages of Pauline's psychotherapy have been a fascinating, if at times a painful and complex journey for Pauline and myself. The dimension of this journey which has been particularly intriguing to me has been the inter-connecting of Pauline's contracts, my treatment plan for her based on her mani-festation of Avoidant and Dependent Personality Disorders, and the significant events in her life, particularly those relating to the legal and other events consequent to her being raped.

The first stage of treatment

Dealing with Pauline's Post-traumatic Stress Disorder

Working relationship

The first few sessions of Pauline's psychotherapy were focused very much on establishing a relationship between her and myself. This was in line with her making her initial contract to come and see me each week, and her second contract, 'to re-contact the human race'. The style in which I worked took into account my initial diagnosis on Axis II of Avoidant Personality Disorder. In the first two or three sessions with Pauline, I used the psychotherapeutic operations referred to by Berne as interrogation and specification (Berne, 1966). I used these to build Pauline's Adult awareness of her own Child process as a way of her feeling more in charge of her own physical and emotional boundaries. She gradually began both to be aware of her options and to exercise her choice. For example (from Pauline's second session):

P: I'm noticing that you are sitting with your knees bunched up under your chin and clutching your legs. How do you feel?
C: I feel scared and like I want to back into the corner away from you.
P: Do you want to do that and see how you feel?
C: No, I want to feel safe enough to do the opposite.
P: What is the opposite for you?
C: To let go with my arms and put my legs down. (she begins to do this)
P: How do you feel now?
C: Terrified – completely exposed (shaking and flushed)
P: Is there a position somewhere between the two which you could experiment with?
C: (Pulling her legs up slightly and folding her arms across her stomach) This feels OK today.
P: And now you have more information about how you feel in different positions of openness, you can choose which you feel comfortable with.

While these transactions were at the social level from my Adult to her Adult, the ulterior message to her Child was 'I accept you as you are, and you can choose how and when you open up to me.' Given her experience of being raped, in response to which she had developed the Post-traumatic Stress Disorder, it was important that she took charge of herself. Her fear of being in contact and intimate, which is symptomatic of the Avoidant Personality Disorder, I also addressed in this ulterior giving her unconditional acceptance and acknowledging her fear. Furthermore, in the transactions described previously, and others like them during the first few sessions, I made clear that I did not *need* her to be close to me which is important for someone with a Dependent Personality Disorder.

Contracting

During this period we were also involved in the contracting process. This in itself challenged Pauline's script as she decided what she wanted to do for herself and enlisted my energy to help her, rather than enlisting her own energy to do what I, as a transferential Parent, wanted her to do. Furthermore, I confronted her passive behaviours and the underlying discounting by setting the conditions for her coming into psychotherapy with me, i.e. her contacting the police and seeking appropriate medical help.

At this time Pauline discounted at the level of T_2 (Schiff *et al.*, 1975): the existence of problems, and options, and at the level of significance of stimuli, problems and options. The importance and effectiveness of my interventions were evident in the relief she expressed and the profound level of emotional and physiological discomfort she experienced. Since I did not discount the existence or significance of what was going on for her (stimuli), her problems and her options, she could then begin to unfreeze and account for her trauma herself.

I had been aware from early in Pauline's psychotherapy of her potential for self-destructive behaviour given her 'Don't Exist' injunction and her self-blaming script beliefs. I did not initially (i.e. during the first six weeks) require Pauline to make a 'No Suicide' contract or 'No Hurt' contract. My reason was that I did not judge Pauline to be at risk from herself at this stage. The numbing of response and constricted affect symptomatic of both her underlying depression, further compounded by her anti-depressant medication, meant she had not had energy prior to this to be actively suicidal. Pauline also had a clear contract to come to see me each week and to ring me between sessions if she needed to. Initially, I judged this to be sufficient protection. However, after her first few weeks of coming to psychotherapy, Pauline began to be in touch with herself and her feelings, and therefore with her despair and pain. At this stage I did require her to close her 'escape hatches' (Holloway, 1973) and make a 'No Hurt' and 'No Suicide' contract. At first Pauline was only willing to contract from one session to the next. She still had open access to me by phone and agreed to ask for extra sessions if she needed them. As Pauline experienced her own

Adult strength in keeping her contracts, she became less dependent on her partner and me and was willing and able to make an Adult contract that she would not kill or hurt herself, no matter what happened in her life. She also made a 'No Homicide' and 'No Hurt To Others' contract.

In making these decisions with regard to when it was necessary and appropriate for Pauline to make 'No Hurt' and 'No Suicide' contracts, I referred to two authorities on working with depressed clients: Kapur (1987) and Maggiora (1987).

Kapur, in his article, registers the importance of closing the escape hatches. He then goes on to say:

> However contract agreement is often pragmatically dictated by the intensity of the depression, severely depressed clients will be very passive in the case of any commitment. As with all aspects of treatment planning, evaluation is required on an individual level.

> (Kapur, 1987: 30)

Maggiora suggests that where a 'No Suicide' contract is not appropriate, she prefers to 'stress his [the client's] positive resources' and to encourage her client 'both to recognise his own resources and those available to him from the environment' (Maggiora, 1987: 40–1). Similarly, when Pauline was most passive, I focused on Pauline's positive action in using me as a resource, and only after five weeks of therapy, judged that it was appropriate and necessary for her to make 'No Hurt' and 'No Suicide' contracts.

Six weeks after first coming into psychotherapy, Pauline stated, 'I want to come to therapy because I don't want to go on being like this i.e. switched off, ill and hurting'. She then asked me if I thought she could change, to which I replied that I thought she could, if she wanted to. Maggiora (1987), in her article 'A case of severe depression', refers to the importance of the instillation of hope and optimism in the process of curing depression. Pauline concluded the session by saying that she did want to change and she knew she needed to. Following this, Pauline made her contract to recontact the human race.

In the subsequent three months Pauline worked on meeting her contract in a variety of ways. She now went ahead and talked to me about the experience of being raped and in so doing allowed herself to unfreeze some of her feelings. She made and kept appointments with the hospital; she began her relationship with Julia.

Confusion model

Prior to talking to me about her rape experience, Pauline did some important decontamination work. She asked me how I thought I would react to her sharing with me what had happened. Although this was presented as an Adult question, I heard the ulterior from her Child as ... (see Figure 6.4).

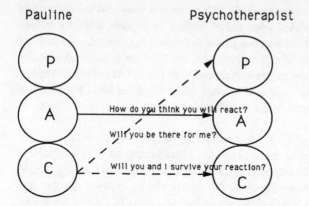

Figure 6.4   Transactional analysis of Pauline's question

Decontamination

I experience Pauline dramatising the telling of her experience in a grandiose way, while (I hypothesised) she was discounting the reality of her experience. She was transacting, therefore, on the basis of her Child and Parent contamination of her Adult, as shown in Figure 6.5.

My first response was at a social level, to her Adult: that I could not specify my reaction in advance, but I imagined I would feel sad and/or angry and that it was OK for me to feel that. I also added that whatever I felt, I would also stay thinking and be present for her. This was to reassure her Child. In this way, I also confronted Pauline's Child and Parent contaminations.

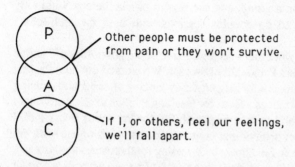

Figure 6.5   Decontamination

Pauline breathed a huge sigh of relief and went on to describe how her parents had reacted. Her mother's response was – 'You should have told me; you don't know how hurt I am; don't tell your dad or brother, or anyone, it'll look bad on the family.' Pauline had then become ill and increased her valium. She had not told her father and anticipated that his response would be not to respond with any emotions, but rather be very matter-of-fact and urge her not to tell her mother.

In this and other similar pieces of work, Pauline began to build her Adult in relation to feeling and expressing emotion and therefore to increase her internal sense of safety.

Pauline took responsibility for contacting doctors to have appropriate examinations. On the first occasion, she asked that I came as well. I agreed in order to fulfil two psychotherapeutic tasks: to support Pauline in learning how to be assertive, particularly in relation to her body; and to be there for her and provide a strong presence, particularly given the sensitivity of the examination.

Deficit model

I was also aware, at this stage, of Pauline's developmental needs to initiate and to do, and to be supported at the same time (see discussion on developmental aspects of treatment and treatment planning). In the event, this was an extremely important therapeutic intervention. I was able to teach and model for Pauline how to ask for what you want and take charge of the process. Pauline was also extremely scared and, because I was there, allowed herself to express this fear, much of which she had held in her body since being raped. My thinking at this stage was also supported by Miller's work (1985) on the psychotherapist as advocate for the client, which is discussed in more detail below.

At this time, Pauline began her sexual relationship with Julia and increasingly began to bring her thoughts and feelings about their relationship into psychotherapy. This was clearly important in the process of her 'recontacting the human race'. Furthermore, it meant that her contact with me was about more than her experience of being raped and this was, I think, an important stage in her letting go of the all-embracing quality of her Post-traumatic Stress Disorder. As I had briefly worked with Julia in a group, and she was in psychotherapy within my joint practice, we agreed to do couples sessions with both me and Julia's psychotherapist.

It was as a result of this work that I became aware of the possibility of Pauline also manifesting a Dependent Personality Disorder. We worked out how Pauline recreated her internal symbiosis with her partner by looking after her and denying herself. This was also important as a focus for teaching Pauline to ask in a straight way for what she wanted and to take responsibility for her needs being met. I stroked her thinking and set behavioural contracts for her to complete with her partner, such as: I will not ask Julia how she is feeling for three days and, instead, when I want to ask her, I will ask myself what I am feeling and act appropriately; I will not smile when saying something I think Julia may not like; I will tell Julia if I want to be on my own and for how long. In this important work, I assisted

Pauline in changing dependent patterns of relating. Pauline's successful achievement of the behavioural contracts was also an important way in which she began to regain her self-confidence and sense of hope, a vital stage in the cure of depression (Maggiora, 1987).

Six months after coming into psychotherapy, Pauline had successfully completed her first social-control contract: 'I will recontact the human race and will survive and complete my exams.' She had been active in seeking and receiving medical and emotional help; she had asked and received support from friends and had begun going out socially. She had completed her exams and got a job. She had not, at this stage, contacted the police.

In terms of the second type of cure, Pauline no longer suffered the symptoms of a Post-traumatic Stress Disorder. She was still on a low level of antidepressant medication but was no longer incapacitated by fear, numbness and withdrawal, or obsessed by memories of the event and fear of a repetition.

In their monograph on contracts, Holloway and Holloway (1973) comment: 'Our experience in group treatment is that those persons who initially set social control contracts will discover in the group that changes of a more extensive kind are possible.' Although Pauline was not in a group, this very much sums up my experience of Pauline's process. She had moved into a new flat with Julia, started a new job and in psychotherapy made a new contract: 'I will feel my feelings.' This, for Pauline, was an autonomy contract that required significant intrapsychic change and redecisions from her Child. I experienced her as some- one who had decided to get on with her life and the contract would have been pertinent to her, whether or not she had been raped. Through her psychotherapy to date, she had built a sound Adult awareness of the ways in which she limited herself, and her real options in life.

The second stage of treatment

Working on Pauline's contract, 'I will feel my feelings', we expanded this contract to mean the following: to identify, to experience and express feelings appropriately.

The second stage of treatment for Pauline, as someone who has developed an Avoidant Personality Disorder, involved my working with her to help her refind her inner sense of self and security. This involved my providing a strong experience of support and backing, so Pauline could begin to build her internal sense of safety, and feel and express her sadness.

Deconfusion

This stage I also conceptualised in terms of deconfusing the Child. During this stage, the work that needs to be done is twofold:

1 Expression of unmet needs and feelings
2 Development of internal sense of safety

Confusion model

During the first three months of this stage, I particularly used TA techniques such as ego-state dialogues and Child interviews as a way for Pauline to be in touch with her Child. For example, in one session, Pauline's contract for the session was 'to do something so I have something to feed on – I feel empty'. I asked her where she felt emptiness and she replied that she felt it in her eyes. Using a Gestalt method of working, I invited her to be her empty eyes.

C: I'm empty because I keep everything in so no one sees me, I'm scared to let anything out.

P: Say some of the things you might let out.

C: Me – my feelings and thoughts – and I won't let you see in because then you'll still see – my rawness and fear and vulnerability.

P: Who's the 'you' that you're speaking to now?

C: My mother.

P: (moving Pauline into an ego-state dialogue) Tell her what's going on for you now.

C: I want to show you what I'm feeling but you won't love me if I do – you'll leave me – so instead I won't let you see in and I won't show you me because that way I'll be good and you'll love me.

C: (as mother) – I'm scared – there's some things you don't talk about – there's nothing wrong with you. Where did you get these ideas from?

Following this work, Pauline said she 'felt sad all through'. When I asked her how she lived out her decision in her Adult life, she replied that when people asked her how she was feeling, she did not say, and she did not share herself even with people whom she knew she could trust. She then went on to decide, in her Adult, that she would share herself with some people and she acknowledged that she had already begun to share herself with me.

Over the following weeks, Pauline began to share her Adult and her Child self with me in a number of ways. I did a Child interview with her 12-year-old Child ego state. She spoke of her sadness about her older brother Phil going away to college, but also about how sad she felt that her mother and father were so sad, and they seemed to live for Phil's phone calls, as if they had no other children and she did not count. As her 12-year-old self, Pauline was profoundly in touch with her Child decision (probably made earlier and confirmed at this age) that she would be like Phil so she could be loved by her mother and fill in her mother's life as he did.

As Pauline began to allow herself to experience herself more fully, she also began to experience her Pig Parent (Steiner, 1974). In the Gouldings' redecision theory, this process is described as moving from a first-type impasse to a second-type impasse (Goulding and Goulding, 1979).

Deconfusion/redecision

The first-degree impasse is between the client's P_2 and her A_1 in her C_2, and for Pauline's work described previously is illustrated as shown in Figure 6.6.

As Pauline began to express her feelings and share herself, she also became more acutely aware of her 'Don't Exist' injunction and her decision either to live as if she didn't exist or be like her brother instead. This is illustrated in Figure 6.7. As Pauline became more in touch with this tension between her A_1 and her P_1, I facilitated her in exploring this, and invited her to speak as her tension in her body. Pauline, as her tension, described herself as a cage which was saying to Pauline 'I'm not going to let you out – if you push against me and try to get out, I'll hold you tighter, even if that hurts – you're not OK to be in the world'.

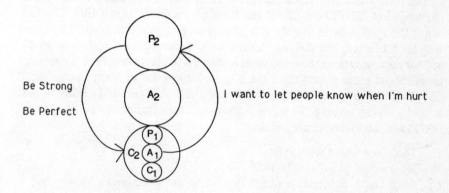

Figure 6.6 Type I impasse

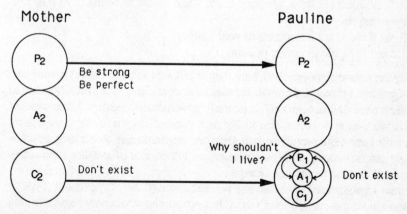

Figure 6.7 Type II impasse

Redecision

Pauline did not, during this session, make a redecision to exist in the world. However, as a result of the work we had done, she understood so much more about her Child's process and experience, and contracted, from her Adult, to be vigilant about the ways she encaged herself and to stop doing this. In so doing, Pauline again increased her sense of internal safety, and in the following weeks, I did more work with her Child in which she cried for the first time for many years. On another occasion, I set up a piece of work in which she experimented with pushing back at me by pushing against a large cushion we had between our backs. Whenever Pauline got scared, I told her to stop, breathe deeply, check out her fantasies and, if necessary, affirm for herself that she was OK and what she was thinking. Although Pauline found doing this work difficult, afterwards she expressed she was glad to have done it and to know both she and I could survive, and knowing this, she then made a redecision to survive and to live.

The effectiveness of this redecision was evident in that Pauline went on to challenge her 'Don't be a Child' and 'Don't have needs' injunctions. She had begun the session by saying she felt grumpy and worried that I would be cross with her for feeling like this. As I helped her to unravel her projections on to me and her contaminations she understood further the implications of her 'Be strong' counterscript message and this time, a related injunction of 'Don't be a Child' and 'Don't have needs'. She summed up the self-extinguishing quality of her script by saying 'so long as I was good, strong, a nondescript suet pudding I was OK'. Then she looked at me and said:

C: That's not what I want to be.
P: What would you like to be like?
C: What I am – rich, needy, varied, interesting and sometimes a bit crabby.
P: You sound like a lobster thermidor.
C: (laughing) And heaven knows lobster thermidor would be far too rich for mother's stomach but it sounds good to me – and I want to be me from now on, whatever 'me' is.
P: Even if me is not acceptable to your mother?
C: I'd rather be me than suet pudding.

During the period just described, I also began talking to Pauline about joining one of my groups. I thought she now had sufficient confidence in our relationship to feel secure enough in a group, particularly a women-only group. I also thought that as she was now committed to her own personal psychotherapy on a more long-term basis, she would benefit from the opportunities that group psycho-therapy offers: support, confrontation and an experience of a wider community committed to good health and change.

I also hypothesised that, having worked through her Type I and Type II impasses in relation to her 'Don't exist' injunction, she would now begin working with a Type III impasse (Goulding and Goulding, 1979). I thought that this exploration of self and affirming of her new self-identity could be done very effectively in a group which she subsequently joined.

The third stage of treatment

Relearning and reorientation

Pauline joins the group and works on her contract 'I will come to the group, say what I am thinking, feeling, and needing.' Pauline reports having been raped to the police and is involved in the ensuing legal process, including the consequent court case.

This contract seemed to me to be an expression of Pauline's core self and her need to relate to others from this core.

Redecision (conflict model)

Pauline making this contract also confirmed my hypothesis that she had moved on to working with a Type III impasse in relation to her 'Don't exist' injunction. Goulding and Goulding (1975) conceptualised the Type III in terms of the Child's struggle with herself; between her adapted self whose identity is bound up with her Child survival decision, and her free Child who wants to be free of the adaptation. This is illustrated in Figure 6.8.

The adaptation is often so early that the client may not recognise it as an adaptation but rather as 'the way I've *always* been'. Pauline would express that 'I–I' struggle in many ways. For example, she would come to the group and hardly speak. She would then come to an individual psychotherapy session and say, 'I don't know why I don't say anything – I know I can and I want to – but I feel like I don't know how – I never have – I've always acted as if I wasn't there.'

Pauline also decided to inform the police that she had been raped. Although the rape had happened some eighteen months previously, there was sufficient evidence for the police to go ahead with their enquiries and to take statements.

This involved Pauline in many tasks which were not only of themselves painful and difficult, but in doing them Pauline was challenging and disobeying her script messages and script beliefs. For example, telling the police was no

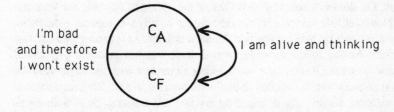

I'm bad and therefore I won't exist C_A C_F I am alive and thinking

Figure 6.8   Type III impasse: redecision (conflict model)
Source: Goulding and Goulding, 1979

longer suffering in silence and her experience of the police taking her very seriously counteracted the injunction 'Don't expect anyone to believe you.' At the time she gave permission to the police to arrest Jim, the man concerned, she felt right up against her script belief 'If people attack me, it must be because I am bad.' I worked through the impasse with her to the point where she was able to know that she did not deserve to be violated and Jim needed to account for his actions.

According to the policy of the Special Unit at the police station, Pauline had the right to stop the legal process up until the time when Jim was arrested. Part of my psychotherapeutic task with Pauline was to ensure that she stayed in charge of what was going on and made the demands she needed to on the police, solicitors, myself and the group.

Deficit model

In this context, at Pauline's request, I accompanied her to the police station when she was going to make her statement and stayed while she made her statement concerning the actual rape. In agreeing to this request, and when I accompanied Pauline to the hospital and later at court, I had, as part of my theoretical framework, Miller's work on the need for the psychotherapist to act as advocate on the Child's behalf and to bear witness to his or her pain and feelings.

> He [the client] finds out, often for the first time in his life, what it means to have someone on his side, as an advocate. A person who has never known this support is unlikely to be able to appraise his earlier situation, because he doesn't realise life can be any other way.
>
> (Miller, 1985)

Establishing internal Nurturing Parent

These interventions were also in line with my overall treatment plan for Pauline, which was to facilitiate her building her own Positive Parent. As well as modelling a strong validating Parent, I also used other techniques such as dialogues between Pauline's A_2 and her Child. During this time Pauline also had her first asthma attack in the group. I had discussed previously with Pauline what she normally did when she had an asthma attack. She had said she withdrew from company as she was scared, and used her Ventolin inhaler to help her to retrieve her breath. On this occasion, I offered Pauline the option of fetching her Ventolin inhaler. However, she said that if I would hold her tightly she wanted to deal with her asthma differently and not use her Ventolin inhaler. At this stage, I was clear that Pauline, having made her redecision to live, was not going to put herself unnecessarily at risk. Rather, she was making a contract with me to provide the protection and support she needed to deal with her fear, regain her breathing and feel her sadness. I also judged, based on my first-aid training, that Pauline was sufficiently in control of the situation to be able to do this. She was successful in achieving what she wanted.

This is also an example of my thinking developmentally when planning treatment interventions. Asthma is one of the symptoms some children develop when, during the first year of life, they have been neglected and have experienced considerable stress. My intervention was, therefore, also intended to provide Pauline with an experience of being strongly supported and held as an antidote to her previous neglect.

In May the court case regarding Pauline's rape was brought foward to June. At this stage, as I described earlier, Pauline could no longer affect the timing of the legal process. However, Pauline was not ready psychologically to deal with the court case, and regressed. She experienced several 'black outs' and was hospitalised with suspected epilepsy. My hypothesis is that in anticipating attesting in court to the 'violence done to her', she threatened her internal symbiosis, the core of which was not making public the physical and emotional abuse she received from her mother.

The earlier date of the court case meant that she had not yet developed the necessary new Parent and Adult to support her Child; hence the concept of a 'fault line' or structural weakness. In terms of her treatment plan, I think it was significant that she had not moved into Stage 3, expressing her anger, and learning how to defend herself psychologically.

My treatment plan following the period in hospital, was to continue to build Pauline's Adult, including Nurturing Parent behaviour, with particular reference to the court case. To this end, I worked with her in four main ways:

1 Accounting for the level of support she needed and to ask for it.
2 To use the time in hospital to feel 'held and safe' and Pauline contracted to set up a similar experience later without getting ill. Also, to experience 'bothering' the nurses and making demands on them, rather than being passive as she had needed to be as a child.
3 To understand her own psychological process; to stay in touch with what she was thinking and feeling, writing it down and to make sense of it.
4 To develop strategies to build Pauline's sense of herself as a *woman*, who would champion her own Child.

This work was successful and Pauline attested in court and stayed Adult and functioned extremely well. At the beginning of the court case the police and barristers had been dubious about Jim being found guilty. However, because of his weak defence, Pauline's strong evidence, and the way the court case had gone, they changed their minds and towards the end were 99 per cent confident he would be found guilty. Pauline also became extremely optimistic and she therefore experienced a real shock when the jury found him not guilty.

For two or three weeks Pauline experienced the syptoms of shock: numbness, 'spacey feelings' and disbelief. As she came out of the state of shock, she regressed and felt terrified of being 'out in the world'. In my opinion this was a re-enactment of what she had felt when she had first been raped. However, then she had still been living according to her full script pattern and had therefore denied and discounted her feelings, and 'been strong' and suffered in silence.

Now, however, she told people what had happened, she asked for support and help, and took the time off work to work through her feelings. She knew that many people, including the senior police officers, her barrister, the journalists and, she thought, the judge *had* believed her. She did not blame herself and although at times over the next few weeks she felt so despairing she thought of killing herself, she also said she knew she would not do this.

The fourth stage of treatment

Working with Pauline through her regression and on. Over the summer, while I was away on holiday, Pauline went home to her parents – both to avoid being in the same town as Jim and also because she felt very safe in familiar childhood surroundings. Within this context, she maintained her Adult responsibility for herself.

When she returned to London, she still said she felt very small. She was not going to work and would sit at home doing nothing for hours, as she felt unable to decide what to do. Under the severe stress of the court case and the court's decision of not guilty on the man she accused of raping her, Pauline regressed and had to work through some of her stages of psychotherapy again. This time, she had considerably more Adult and her Child had already previously made significant redecisions, and her process was therefore both deeper and quicker.

The process that Pauline went through in response to the jury's decision was, I think, intensified because when she had originally been raped, she had not been able to work through her feelings. I think Pauline regressed to a Child ego state where she felt terrified, believed the world was not a safe place, that others were out to attack her. In this psychological place, she had no internal sense of self and therefore of internal security. However, she would also, on occasions, tell herself she must snap out of this and would force herself to go out and travel on public transport despite her fear. She also avoided me by not talking in group and not making individual sessions. When I confronted Pauline about this, the extent to which she had regressed to a fixated ego state became clear. She felt she was unacceptable to me because I would think 'she ought to be over it all by now and getting on with life'. By avoiding me, she could maintain the negative transference and reinforce her Child beliefs and counterscripted injunctions of 'Be strong', 'Please me', 'Don't be a child', 'Don't have needs'. Moiso (1985) would illustrate this as shown in Figure 6.9.

My confrontation of Pauline was to the effect that she needed to see me twice a week and, she was not to force herself to do things she was terrified of. I also said that if she needed to be young and regressed and felt unable to take care of herself, then together we could make appropriate arrangements. My purpose was to challenge Pauline's racket response to her feeling young and vulnerable, so I could work in a reparative way with the developmental trauma.

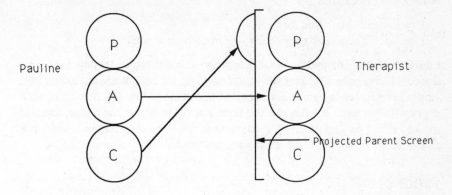

Figure 6.9 Projected Parent

My challenge was sufficient for Pauline to recathect Adult, to contract about her Child needs, and to reaffirm that she had options, and that *I* was who *I* was and not her mother. Having done this, I was able to re-establish my relationship with her and to facilitate her building, at an even deeper level, a secure sense of herself. Her contract for therapy was 'to relate "cleanly" to others' which she broke down as asking for her needs to be met and to be close, without playing Rescuer or Victim games.

The evidence that Pauline's psychotherapeutic change is now stable under pressure is that recently, a member of staff for whom she has managerial responsibility was abducted, attacked and abused. The woman eventually was released and made her way back to the work premises. Pauline, as her line manager, was responsible for dealing with the situation, calling the police and managing the proceedings. She had clearly managed the situation well, had kept appropriate boundaries including saying she would not go to the police station herself as she wanted to come to her own psychotherapy group and arranged for someone else to go in her place.

Emotional fluency

She came and allowed herself to experience and express in a profound way her fear and pain about her own trauma. She rang me the next day to say she felt very good and very angry. She made considerable space for herself during the week to do aggressive sports and came the following week to her session. In this session she began by decontaminating the ways in which she gives away her energy or herself so she ends up feeling deprived. She then moved into an ego-state dialogue with her mother and eventually expressed her anger and fury at her mother for terrifying her and hurting her when she was a child. When she had completed her expression of anger she said, 'I feel frightened to think I can be that angry, but it's more frightening not to know I'm that angry so, this week my mother, next week, Jim ...'

Psychotherapist: And then ...?
Pauline: The world's my oyster – or my lobster thermidor.

I think in identifying and expressing appropriately her anger, Pauline knew that she could, and redecided that she *would* stand up for herself and no longer be a victim. The following week she reported that she had, for the first time, been angry with her mother when she had been abusive to her on the phone, and that she had asked for and received, repayment of the loans she had made to friends as a result of which she had been in financial trouble.

PROGNOSIS

My prognosis for Pauline is good. I think that I will now be able to go on to work with her to express her feelings further, including her anger and rage, both about her Adult abuse and her abuse as a child. In doing so, I hypothesise that she will no longer feel depressed or anxious and will therefore be able to stop taking her medication. Pauline will in this way significantly separate from her mother because: (a) the medication is an external manifestation of her mother's demand not to feel, but rather to suppress any strong feelings; (b) her mother's programming of Pauline included a dependence on medication. Pauline will, therefore, be actively choosing a different way of managing her feelings and not following her mother's 'dependent' patterns.

Pauline still has significant aspects of her journey to do. I think she needs to continue to work through her Type III impasse referred to earlier. To do so, she needs to build her own Parental value system and set of nurturing Parent behaviour. She will then become a reliable and consistent Parent to her own Child. This, I hypothesise, will allow her to separate further from her internalised Parent and therefore to achieve greater autonomy as her real, free self. She will then be taking responsibility for who she is in the world and will therefore have let go of her Dependent Personality structure.

As Pauline achieves this sense of separation, I plan to work with her to experience intimacy both with whoever she has as a partner, and to develop friendships, confident in her own OKness. She will then be free of her Avoidant Personality Disorder.

CONCLUSION

I have enjoyed working with Pauline and have felt challenged by the parallel of her adult trauma which brought her into psychotherapy, and her childhood trauma. One way in which I have conceptualised my work in order to keep a sense of perspective, is to see it as 'doing psychotherapy in the deep end'. The analogy is with learning to swim: that whether you learn to swim in the shallow end which

is very safe, in the middle of the pool, or in the deep end, the task
swim is the same. The process of learning may, however, feel a littl
and dramatic in the deep end than in the shallow end. So, Pauli
therapeutic tasks were what they were; the context in which she wa doing them
could, in human terms, be likened to the deep end. Similarly, there is a difference
between choosing to walk into the shallow end of a swimming pool and learn to
swim – and being pushed into the deep end so you have to learn to survive.
However, as Pauline's script decisions are evidence of, we are also responsible,
in some way, for deciding to let ourselves be pushed in to the deep end.

The other profoundly important experience I have had while working with
Pauline, is the validation of my belief, reinforced by Miller's work (1983, 1985,
1987) of the importance of me, as a psychotherapist, acting as an advocate for the
Child, and believing that my client's truth is my client's truth. Based on my work
with Pauline and the evidence I heard in court, I have no doubt that the man she
accused of raping and brutalising her did, in fact, do just that. However, in many
ways this is not important: that my role is not to play 'court room' any more than
it is to blame the parents for the Child's suffering. What is important is for me to
be a witness to the Child's suffering so she can achieve 'the emotional discovery
and emotional acceptance of the truth in the individual and unique history of our
childhood' (Miller, 1983: 17). For only then can the Child release herself from
her scriptbound behaviours and achieve her aspirational growth to 'autonomy'
(Berne, 1966).

Transference and countertransference in TA

If that you were the good Sir Rowland's son,
As you have whispered faithfully you were,
And as mine eye doth his effigies witness
Most truly limn'd and living in your face,
Be truly welcome hither. I am the duke
that lov'd your father.

(Shakespeare, *As You Like It* II. vii. 191–6)

INTRODUCTION

From both Greek and Latin the word *transference* has the meaning of 'to carry across'. The phenomenon of carrying across qualities from what is known (based on past experience) to what is analogued in the present has probably been a feature of human psychology since the dawn of time. Shakespeare shows familiarity with the phenomenon in many plays. For example, the Duke in *As You Like It* is 'transferring' his affectionate feeling for the father to the son whom in fact he has not yet had occasion to get to know. He has no evidence that the son is a good man, yet he uses his past experience with the father to assume this. This is very similar to the 'shared transference' which clients experience when a trusted colleague makes a referral to another. It is important to realise or to remember that transference and countertransference in the general sense of conveying across are ubiquitous phenomena and necessary components of any learning process. It occurs between husband and wife, teacher and pupil, citizen and state functionary. It occurs whenever emotions, perceptions or reactions are based on past experiences rather than freshly minted in the here-and-now.

Transference as a specialised technical topic of study and vehicle for use in psychoanalysis and psychotherapy usually constrains the meaning to the feelings of the patient for the psychotherapist. As a subject it has filled several volumes and a great many entries in textbooks with an astonishing variety of contradictions, ambiguities and connotational disputes. The number of 'types' also decreases or increases depending on the author and the method of classification used.

In this chapter the author presents a map for psychotherapists which they can use, *not* as an analytic disturbance to the delicate flowering of the psychotherapeutic relationship, but as a tool which is more likely to be useful in supervision (from self or supervisor). It has been found to be an effective compass for planning or anticipating directions in treatment or helping the psychotherapist understand the situation better when there are intractable difficulties, unmoving plateaux or unrelenting confusion. Of course the map is not the psychotherapy and the goal is certainly not to memorise the whole map but to use it as a guide to find one's way around.

TRANSFERENCE PHENOMENA IN TA – DEFINITIONS AND TYPES

In Freudian psychoanalysis transference was originally regarded as an unfortunate phenomenon which interfered with the process of psychoanalysis. Later however, Freud (1973/1917) saw it as an essential part of the psychotherapeutic process and indeed one of the cornerstones of psychoanalytic practice. Fairbairn (1952), Klein (1984/1957) and Winnicott (1958, 1975) assumed that patients' responses in the transference relationship were valid evidence on which to base their theories about the origin of object relations in infancy. It is as well to be clear as to a generally acceptable, technically accurate psychoanalytic definition of transference.

> TRANSFERENCE 1. The process by which a patient displaces on to his analyst feelings, ideas, etc., which derive from previous figures in his life; by which he relates to his analyst as though he were some former object in his life; by which he projects on to his analyst object-representations acquired by earlier introjections; by which he endows the analyst with the significance of another, usually prior, object. 2. The state of mind produced by 1 in the patient. 3. Loosely, the patient's emotional attitude towards his analyst.
>
> (Rycroft, 1972: 168)

According to Racker (1982) Freud denominated as transference all the patient's psychological phenomena and processes which referred to the analyst and were derived from other previous object relations. Therefore in loose usage it refers to all feelings of the client towards the psychotherapist which are transferred from past relationships. The phenomenological time of transference is thus the past replayed in the present as if it were the present. The phenomenological shape of transference is the fantasised externalisation of an internal relationship between the individual and one or more others. These 'others' represent significant relationships of the individual's past (e.g. the mother/infant dyad, the child/parental couple triad, the child/family group, or the child/teacher/peer relationships). Transference is thus that anticipatory pattern of relationship which the individual seeks to replicate with significant others, regardless of their individual, unique qualities.

Steven expects women to disappoint him and will anticipate this even with women for whom this is not a pattern at all. He may also seek out women who need to disappoint men. Furthermore, he may even find women whose patterns are to fulfil men and find, interpret or fantasise ways in which they are disappointing him, irrespective of their personal qualities. Transference is that relational pattern people carry with them from situation to situation. It may be singular (Berne 1980), split (Moiso, 1985) or plural as in group psychotherapy (Berne, 1966). It may also involve first- or second-order, structural, ego-state phenomena. The other person is not freely met for the first time, the other is more often met through a screen on which the person is projecting their own particular movie. In this chapter I will be concentrating on dyadic transferential relationship patterns, leaving the triadic and group transferential phenomena for later discussion. However, the same analytic map presented here can be easily extrapolated to fit these uses.

In a certain sense transference is future-oriented. It is one of the primary mechanisms by which human beings learn from their past relationships how to behave in present relationships. For many people past object relationships have been traumatic or strained (Pine, 1985) and they carry the pattern of these learned relationships into their present lives as well as into the psychotherapeutic relationship. Therefore, until the transference is resolved, the 'anticipated other' remains psychologically unchanged as the script process unfolds outside of Adult awareness.

Quoting Freud directly:

> The decisive part of the work is achieved by creating in the patient's relation to the doctor – in the 'transference' – new editions of the old conflicts; in these the patient would like to behave in the same way as he did in the past, while we, by summoning up every available mental force in the patient compel him to come to a fresh decision.
>
> (Freud quoted in Racker, 1982: 46)

Some measure of transference may even be operative in an individual reading this book in the sense of transferring learning experiences from the past in anticipating the quality of satisfaction in the contents which follow. The reader is invited to consider the possibility that they might be bringing some past experience into the relationship even with this written word, for example, a fear of not being able to understand, delight in finding other professionals questing in the same dark arena of human endeavour or an anticipation of finding 'blemishes'.

Transference of this anticipatory kind is often identified by clients before they even meet the psychotherapist. A client reports, for example, that from the time she decided to enter psychotherapy, she already anticipated that the psychotherapist would not *really* be able to help her. This was based on her past experiences of parents or professional adults failing to notice or intervene in her abuse at the hands of her mother. This anticipation (pro-active transference) would tend to manifest whoever the psychotherapist was, since it is a product of the client's own past as it is repeated in the present. This may apply not only in psychotherapy but also towards other significant figures in the client's life. It used to be held that the less information that is available, the greater the possibilities for transference. This is the basis for the neutral attitude or 'blank screen' so often recommended for the psychoanalyst who primarily, if not exclusively, works through the transference. However, the driving tendency of human beings to complete the unclosed present Gestalt with fantasies based on the past seems remarkably unimpaired by the presence of a 'real' person. Several decades of psychotherapy in the humanistic/existential tradition have borne out that the inveterate tenacity of the transferential fantasy/expectation is usually quite impervious to information (a therapist's self-disclosure or otherwise) which would create cognitive dissonance with past expectations. If Yasmin's need is to experience a care giver as judgemental and persecutory, she will believe her fantasy ('In my Child I feel you're out to get me') whereas she knows ('In my Adult') on the basis of extensive adult experience and the corroboration of other group members, that this is not the case. Until the transference is resolved, however, the fantasy will have formative power and she will probably shape her relationships with significant others in similar, repetitive, unsatisfactory ways. This observation is based on many years of practice and supervision within and outside mainstream psychoanalysis and is reported to be true for a great many of my colleagues. Regardless of whether the psychotherapist attempts to present a blank screen or not, workable transference phenomena occur with sufficient duration and intensity necessary for effective psychotherapy.

Although the terms complementary and concordant are used by Freud (1973/1917) and Racker (1982) to describe not transference but countertransference types, the author is here also using them to describe several other kinds of transferential phenomena. Novellino (1984) in his discussion of countertransference, appears to use the term 'conforming countertransference' in the same way as Racker's (1982) 'concordant countertransference', but retains the use of 'complementary countertransference'. The terms abnormal and normal were used by Winnicott (1958, 1975) also in relation to countertransference. This author prefers the terms facilitative and destructive for the same purposes, and extrapolates their use to the other categories of transference phenomena in the psychotherapeutic and supervisory relationship.

The author has also introduced Lewin's (1963) terms, 'pro-active' and 'reactive', in this context, to designate whether the subject of the discussion originates the stimulus (pro-acts) or responds (reacts to) a stimulus from the other. Since the psychotherapeutic space belongs essentially to the client, the psycho- therapist's pro-activity usually, though not always, detracts from the primary task which is the enhancement of the client's pro-activity.

Categories of transference

Complementary transference

In this category, the patient seeks completion of the symbiotic relationship. In a complementary transference towards the psychotherapist's Parent, the client projects the actual or fantasised past historical parent onto the psychotherapist. For example, the client expects the psychotherapist to humiliate them in the same way as their historical parent humiliated them. Alternatively, the client may hope for an idealised fantasy parent based on their childhood wishes. In another variation of complementary transference, the client projects the actual or fantasised past Child ego state(s) of the parent onto the psychotherapist. For example, the client takes care of the psychotherapist's Child by protecting them from the client's own rage, or behaves in a way similar to the punitive parenting which the client introjected from their own abusive parent(s).

By the nature of the psychotherapeutic relationship, projections onto the psychotherapist's Child will tend to be of second-order structural symbiotic kind. That is, since it is not the patient's function to take care of the psychotherapist, but vice versa, it is usually based on fantasy (the psychotherapist needs to be taken care of because they are frightened) or an impaired psychotherapeutic relationship (where the psychotherapist is inappropriately showing vulnerability or making demands on the client for such caretaking). To avoid the despair of realising and reliving the failure of the original parents, the client may move into the complementary Child-to-Parent transference.

Concordant transference

This occurs when the client projects his/her own past Child onto the psycho-therapist in an attempt to find identification. For example, the client imagines that the psychotherapist feels sad and lonely whereas the client's historic Child is grieving for an early parental abandonment. In this form of transference, the client may experience both self and psychotherapist as equally helpless. People with a narcissistic personality disorder often use this form of transference, particularly in the beginning of psychotherapy. 'I see in you, my psychotherapist, the ways you are like me.' So in a sense, this has similarities to the mirror or the twin transferences (Kohut, 1977). Either complementary or concordant trans-ference may contain potentials or elements of destructive or facilitative forces.

Destructive transference

This describes the client's acted-out or fantasised destructive past as manifested in the psychotherapeutic relationship. It specifically refers to behaviour which has exceeded the boundaries of the psychotherapeutic contract and which cannot be dealt with within the psychotherapeutic arena any more. Such acting out of second- or third-degree games – e.g. homicide, suicide or transference psychosis – effectively destroys the psychotherapeutic contract and often represents a script payoff or conclusion. Such destructive acting out makes management procedures (e.g. hospital admission or daily supervision) extraneous to the psychotherapeutic relationship necessary.

Facilitative transference

I consider it very important to differentiate normal or healthy transference phenomena from other types of transference. The client in this case may transfer (carry over) a temperamental preference or style on the basis of what has been effective for them in the past onto the current psychotherapeutic relationship. An easy-going phlegmatic client, who has a temperamentally slower pace (Eysenck and Rachman, 1965) may prefer a psychotherapist of a similar temperament. This is not necessarily pathological. This category of transference would not fit the definition of script. It may represent productive learned patterns from the past which are transferred into the present with a successful outcome. These patterns are not self-limiting (as scripts are), but rather, self-actualising or aspirational (Clarkson, 1989). Therefore, they should not be pathologised but seen as the possible basis for choosing a compatible partner in the psychotherapeutic journey. However, they are technically transferential in the sense that they are transferred from past affective relationships.

Table 7.1 summarises this discussion for the sake of comparison, clarity and overview. Diagonal arrows are used in relation to complementary transferences to indicate the psychological inequality of the complementary relationships: the horizontal arrow visually demonstrates concordance or identification; the downward arrow alludes to the destructiveness of unhealthy transference and its possible relationship to the force of Destrudo (Weiss, 1950: Berne, 1981); the upward-pointing arrow represents the aspirational arrow which Berne (1981: 128) postulated as an essential part of the script matrix, possibly related to *Physis* (Berne, 1972: 140), the generalised creative urge which reaches upward out of the individual's past experiences towards the transformative potential inherent in human nature.

Table 7.1   Client transference – pro-active type

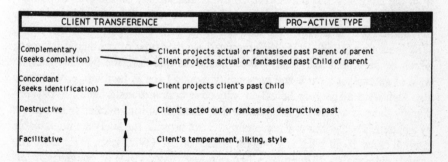

CLIENT TRANSFERENCE	PRO-ACTIVE TYPE
Complementary (seeks completion)	→ Client projects actual or fantasised past Parent of parent → Client projects actual or fantasised past Child of parent
Concordant (seeks identification)	→ Client projects client's past Child
Destructive	↓ Client's acted out or fantasised destructive past
Facilitative	↑ Client's temperament, liking, style

Most psychotherapists are familiar with manifestations of client transference as described on p.153. Traditionally, if the psychotherapist brought their own transference (displaced from their own past) into the psychotherapy, this was referred to as 'countertransference' and considered undermining of the psychotherapy. Such psychotherapist-induced distortions will be discussed later; first, the definitions will be explored again. This will be followed by the less familiar countertransference reactions which are not conceived of as originating from the psychotherapist's own issues but arise as reactions to the client's issues when the psychotherapist is free enough of the pressure of the past to be empathically available to the client and willing to resonate and use their responses as valuable allies in entering and understanding the client's phenomenological world.

COUNTERTRANSFERENCE PHENOMENA IN TA – DEFINITIONS AND TYPES

COUNTER-TRANSFERENCE 1. The analyst's transference on his patient. In this, the correct, sense, counter-transference is a disturbing, distorting element in treat- ment. 2. By extension, the analyst's emotional attitude towards his patient, including his response to specific items of the patient's behaviour. According to Heimann (1950), Little (1951), Gitelson (1952) and others, the analyst can use this latter kind of counter-transference as clinical evidence, i.e. he can assume that his own emotional reponse is based on a correct interpretation of the patient's true intentions or meaning.

(Rycroft, 1972: 25)

In the loose usage of the term, countertransference refers, therefore, to all psychotherapist responses in the psychotherapeutic relationship. Originally all countertransference reactions were seen as possibly impeding psychotherapeutic progress and probably related to the psychotherapist's inability to keep their own material ('issues') out of the psychotherapeutic arena.

Winnicott defined as abnormal countertransference 'those areas that arise from the analyst's past unresolved conflicts that intrude on the present patient' (Winnicott, 1975: 175). In a sense these are the psychotherapist transferences – the psychotherapist is transferring material from their own past onto the client. Winnicott also (1958, 1975) differentiated another type of countertransference which he described as normal – those reactions that describe the idiosyncratic style of an analyst's work and personality, which I see as facilitative. Winnicott also identified a category he called 'objective countertransference'. In psychotherapy there is a growing recognition that 'those reactions evoked in an analyst by a patient's behaviour and personality ... can provide the analyst with valuable internal clues about what is going on in the patient' (Winnicott, 1975: 195). The present author also differentiates between two major kinds of countertransference depending on whether the psychotherapist is *reacting* to a client or whether the psychotherapist is pro-actively *introducing their own transference* into the psychotherapeutic relationship. The type called by Winnicott 'objective counter-transference' (1975) is here referred to as reactive countertransference to empha-sise that the psychotherapist is reacting accurately or objectively to the client's projections, personality, and behaviour in the psychotherapeutic relationship. The type called by Winnicott 'abnormal countertransference' will be discussed here under the heading 'Pro-active countertransference' (psychotherapist transference), after an exploration of the kind of reactive countertransference which has enormous potential for diagnostic information and psychotherapeutic leverage. Its efficacy depends on the ability of the psychotherapist to separate out their own issues from their reactions to the client's issues.

Categories of reactive psychotherapist countertransference

Complementary reactive countertransference

The psychotherapist complements the client's real or fantasised projection as Parent or Child of the client's parent by responding with the feeling probably experienced by the original parent (see Table 7.2). For example, the psycho-therapist responds to the client's projection of their overnurturing mother by feeling the urge to rescue.

Concordant reactive countertransference

This occurs when the psychotherapist experiences the client's avoided experi-ence or resonates empathically with the client's experience. For example, after a session the psychotherapist feels unaccountably and uncharacteristically despairing; although the client talked about her brother's death, she did not let herself experience the emotion and the psychotherapist is left with the weight of the unexpressed feeling.

Destructive reactive countertransference

When the psychotherapist accepts the projected identification and acts on it in an unhealthy way, this is termed as destructive countertransference. For example, the client sees the psychotherapist as her neglectful mother: the psychotherapist responds by 'forgetting' appointments and going on holiday without giving the client due notice; the client's expectation acts as a subliminal, hypnotic induction to the psychotherapist, who responds outside of their awareness.

Facilitative reactive countertransference

It is again important, along with Winnicott (1958, 1975) to differentiate a category of countertransference which can be normal, healthy and even possibly facilitative for the client. It is natural to feel affection for a lovable patient, appreciative of a creative client and respect for a humble person. Withholding any emotional response to the healthy self-expressions of one's clients can make psychotherapy very barren and neglect many opportunities for the enhancement

Table 7.2 Psychotherapist countertransference – reactive type

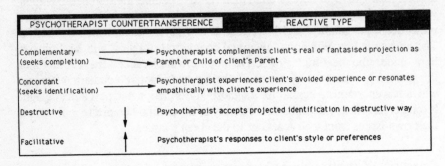

of creative capacities and the reinforcement of healthy behaviour patterns. This kind of countertransference can be seen as the heart of the person-to-person psychotherapeutic relationship which is discussed more fully in Chapter 12.

Categories of pro-active countertransference

Complementary pro-active countertransference

This occurs when the psychotherapist complements (or completes the Gestalt of) the client's real or fantasised projection as Parent or Child based on the psychotherapist's own past, or projects the actual or fantasised past Parent or Child (see Table 7.3). For example, the psychotherapist may behave in a withholding, passive and coldly analytical way in response to the client's neediness, not because this is psychotherapeutically appropriate but because this is the way the psychotherapist has been treated by their parents. Another example concerns a situation where the psychotherapist re-enacts their own experience of being intimidated or bullied and elicits from the patient the protective, parental response which they had not experienced in the original situation. This may occur where the psychotherapist works in an agency setting and 'management' or the NHS are introduced into the psychotherapeutic arena in a way which is ultimately unhelpful to the client – such as a therapist's implied helpless complaining about lack of resources to a client who refuses to take any responsible initiative in their own life.

Concordant pro-active countertransference

This is when the psychotherapist experiences the client's experience based on their own past. For example, the psychotherapist assumes that the client feels guilty about injuring a schoolfriend in the same way as they did when younger. The client may or may not have a similar experience and such identification needs from the psychotherapist may be unhelpful or actively hindering the process of psychotherapy.

Table 7.3 Psychotherapist countertransference – pro-active type

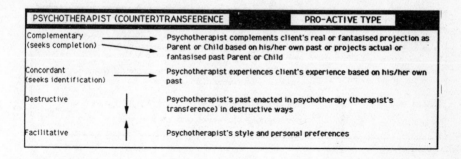

PSYCHOTHERAPIST (COUNTER)TRANSFERENCE	PRO-ACTIVE TYPE
Complementary (seeks completion)	Psychotherapist complements client's real or fantasised projection as Parent or Child based on his/her own past or projects actual or fantasised past Parent or Child
Concordant (seeks identification)	Psychotherapist experiences client's experience based on his/her own past
Destructive	Psychotherapist's past enacted in psychotherapy (therapist's transference) in destructive ways
Facilitative	Psychotherapist's style and personal preferences

Destructive pro-active countertransference

When the psychotherapist enacts his or her own past in the psychotherapy in ways which are destructive or limiting to the client's welfare, it is said that the countertransference is destructively pro-active. This of course is identical to what would be understood as the psychotherapist's transference as long as it is taken in the wide sense (i.e. of transferring relationship patterns from the past into current relationships) or transference in the narrow sense (i.e. the feelings engendered towards the analyst based on transferring relationship patterns or expectations from the psychotherapist [client's] past). A young psychotherapist may expect that an older client will find fault with them in the same way as the psychotherapist's father did; he may then reject the client at the first sign of negativity. Alternatively the psychotherapist may transfer his or her own suicidal tendencies on to the patient and if the patient is obliging and, for example, needs a parent for whom sacrifice is necessary, the client may commit suicide in a sense 'for the psychotherapist/parent'.

Facilitative pro-active countertransference

This is based on the unavoidable and probably necessary existence of the psychotherapist's individual style and personal preferences. For example, the psychotherapist may enjoy working with people with creativity problems rather than control issues.

CLIENT COUNTERTRANSFERENCE REACTIVE TYPES

Every psychotherapist will no doubt occasionally introduce pro-active counter-transference elements into the psychotherapeutic relationship, i.e. the psycho-therapist's self-generated issues may affect the psychotherapy (see Table 7.4). For example, as in the case of the psychotherapist who comes to the session late as result of a traffic snarl-up and resulting accident. (Issues do not always need to

Table 7.4 Client countertransference – reactive type

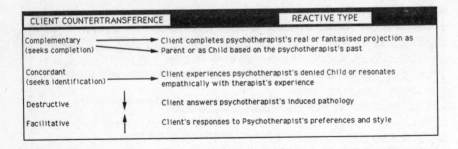

CLIENT COUNTERTRANSFERENCE	REACTIVE TYPE
Complementary (seeks completion)	Client completes psychotherapist's real or fantasised projection as Parent or as Child based on the psychotherapist's past
Concordant (seeks identification)	Client experiences psychotherapist's denied Child or resonates empathically with therapist's experience
Destructive	Client answers psychotherapist's induced pathology
Facilitative	Client's responses to Psychotherapist's preferences and style

come from a pathological past, but may be ordinary humans responses, such as aggravation at traffic jams or grief in times of bereavement.) Naturally, patients will respond to such events or the psychotherapist's characteristics: they may of course respond in archaically determined ways, e.g. through transference; or in ways which are more reactive to the psychotherapist's past than to their own.

In addition to the types discussed so far, the author identifies another type of countertransference: that of the client's reactive countertransference to the psychotherapist's introduction of their own material. Technically this is not the client's transference, since it is not based on the client's past material, but is elicited from the client by the (abnormal or pro-active) countertransferences of the psychotherapist. The choice of the word countertransference is to indicate that it is 'counter' to a transference, and to recognise and allow for the fact that the client may be responding to material based on the psychotherapist's past in the psychotherapeutic relationship. (If countertransference as a technical term is restricted to psychotherapists' feelings and reactions, another word will have to be found. Until then this author considers it very useful in that it draws attention to oft-neglected aspects of the psychotherapeutic relationship.)

Complementary client countertransference

As to any transference, the client will of course respond to this in a variety of ways. They may react complementarily by completing the psychotherapist's real or fantasised projection as Parent or as Child based on the psychotherapist's history or recent past. For example, a client who does not have issues about taking care of parents may find that they are invited or 'induced' to take care of the psychotherapist when the psychotherapist is experienced as tired, burnt-out or fragile. The importance of differentiating this form of response to psycho-therapist-induced reaction lies in *not* attributing projection to the patient, whereas in fact the patient is correctly perceiving the psychotherapist's emotional states as they impinge upon the process of the psychotherapy.

The management lies in identifying what the psychotherapist brings into the psychotherapy room and listening to what the patient brings to bear upon these problems, without blaming, or attributing causality to the pathology or projection of the patient. It is the psychotherapist's responsibility to separate out such elements from the psychotherapeutic relationship and take preventive or corrective action through, for example, further analysis and/or additional supervision.

Langs (1985) and Casement (1985) have repeatedly addressed themselves to such issues – the many ways in which the patient provides the psychotherapist with feedback, supervision and active attempts to heal the psychotherapist. When neither of the partners are aware of this collusion, psychotherapeutic progress may be undermined or destroyed. Searles (1975) is another theorist who developed the notion that the patient needs to heal their psychotherapist. Alternatively, the patient may try very hard to be a good patient for the psychotherapist because they need children who work hard but never achieve success.

Concordant client countertransference

This happens when, for example, the client experiences the psychotherapist's denied Child or resonates empathically with the psychotherapist's experience. In other words, the client identifies or seeks to identify with the psychotherapist's denied Child, whether or not those feelings or experiences are valid for them. The client may sense the psychotherapist's fear of violence, based on the psychotherapist's unresolved issues about a violent childhood home and, in resonating with them, prohibit sharing with the psychotherapist their feelings of violence or murderous rage towards the psychotherapist since they may be afraid that the psychotherapist could not cope with it. There are certainly numerous clinical examples of patients who with the second or third psychotherapist begin to talk about issues which they could not share with the first. Some also, according to Alice Miller (1983), are based on the patient continuing to protect the parent/ psychotherapist from dealing with their own feelings of abandonment or abuse.

Destructive client countertransference

Here the term is used to refer to particularly damaging acted-out patterns between psychotherapist and client which are primarily based on the psychotherapist's pathology. In such a case the psychotherapist's transference may induce pathological responses of an extreme nature, such as 'going mad for the psychotherapist'; therefore the psychotherapist can continue to avoid dealing with their own madness whilst dealing with the madness 'out there' in the patient.

Facilitative client countertransference

This term connotes the client's natural responses to the psychotherapist's style and way of being. After a long and intimate relationship such as psychotherapy, which leads to productive changes in a client's life, they may naturally enough feel fondness and affection for certain qualities of the psychotherapist. An example would be a particularly apt use of metaphor or a clarity of thinking and expression which is not countertherapeutic but based on an appreciation of the particular attributes of the helper.

In summary (see Table 7.5), there are thus two perspectives in which transference and countertransference can be viewed: that which the client brings to the relationship and that which the psychotherapist brings. These can be either pro-active (originating) or reactive (responding). Pro-active transferential/ countertransferential issues exist *in potentia* prior to any form of psychotherapeutic interaction. They are based on previous experiences and will probably be re-enacted or repeated in most significant interpersonal relationships. As such, their repetitive compulsivity is relatively independent of the respective personalities and histories of the client and psychotherapist involved. Reactive transference/countertransference issues are directly related to reactions within the relationship and are thus usually unique to it.

MANAGEMENT AND USE OF TRANSFERENCE PHENOMENA IN TRANSACTIONAL ANALYSIS

Berne saw scripts as belonging in the realm of transference phenomena:

> They are derivatives, or more precisely, adaptations of infantile reactions and experiences. But a script does not deal with a mere transference reaction or a transference situation; it is an attempt to repeat in derivative form a whole transference drama, often split up into acts, exactly like the theatrical scripts which are intuitive artistic derivatives of these primal dramas of childhood.
>
> (Berne, 1980/1961: 116)

In transactional analysis, transference may be allowed, invited, resolved, temporarily interrupted, avoided or minimised, depending on the diagnosis of the client, their needs, and the nature of the psychotherapeutic contract. The extent to which transactional analysts recognise and utilise transference phenomena depends very much on their training and personal experience of psychotherapy. In the above sense, however, it is clear that the transactional analyst is always essentially dealing with the transferential encodement of the individual's life drama as they work with the script (Novellino, 1984; Moiso, 1985).

In classical psychoanalysis, the analyst was conceived of as a mirror for the client – this detachment gave the client the space to externalise the internal conflicts and the psychotherapist's work was the analysis and interpretation of the transference. Kernberg (1982) uses the term genetic interpretations, which we understand to relate to the historic origins of transferential phenomena. He distinguishes between such interpretations and dealing with the transference as it affects the ongoing psychotherapeutic relationship. Therefore, the transference manifestation is dealt with but not necessarily accompanied by a genetic interpretation. Instead of saying 'You're angry with me the way you used to be angry with your mother when you experienced her as withholding', the analyst would acknowledge the client's anger in the here-and-now context and reflect

Table 7.5 Summary diagram

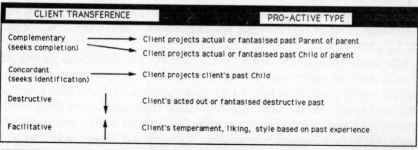

CLIENT TRANSFERENCE   PRO-ACTIVE TYPE

Complementary
(seeks completion)   Client projects actual or fantasised past Parent of parent
                           Client projects actual or fantasised past Child of parent

Concordant
(seeks identification)   Client projects client's past Child

Destructive   Client's acted out or fantasised destructive past

Facilitative   Client's temperament, liking, style based on past experience

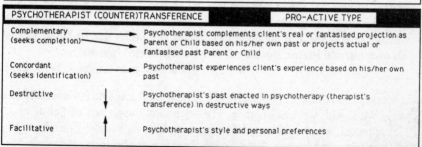

PSYCHOTHERAPIST COUNTERTRANSFERENCE   REACTIVE TYPE

Complementary   Psychotherapist complements client's real or fantasised projection as
(seeks completion)   Parent or Child of client's Parent

Concordant   Psychotherapist experiences client's avoided experience or resonates
(seeks identification)   empathically with client's experience

Destructive   Psychotherapist accepts projected identification in destructive way

Facilitative   Psychotherapist's responses to client's style or preferences

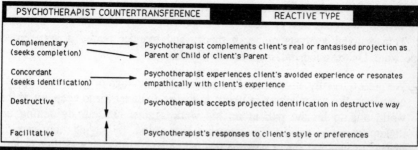

PSYCHOTHERAPIST (COUNTER)TRANSFERENCE   PRO-ACTIVE TYPE

Complementary   Psychotherapist complements client's real or fantasised projection as
(seeks completion)   Parent or Child based on his/her own past or projects actual or
                           fantasised past Parent or Child

Concordant   Psychotherapist experiences client's experience based on his/her own
(seeks identification)   past

Destructive   Psychotherapist's past enacted in psychotherapy (therapist's
                           transference) in destructive ways

Facilitative   Psychotherapist's style and personal preferences

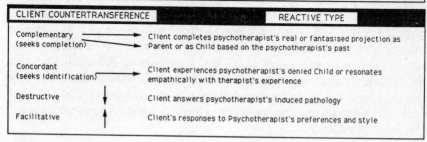

CLIENT COUNTERTRANSFERENCE   REACTIVE TYPE

Complementary   Client completes psychotherapist's real or fantasised projection as
(seeks completion)   Parent or as Child based on the psychotherapist's past

Concordant   Client experiences psychotherapist's denied Child or resonates
(seeks identification)   empathically with therapist's experience

Destructive   Client answers psychotherapist's induced pathology

Facilitative   Client's responses to Psychotherapist's preferences and style

back that they thought it was exaggerated. The danger is of interpretations being experienced as persecutory. Moiso (1985) uses a similar example to illustrate his approach to the transference which he calls psychodynamic TA therapy. 'Therapist: "Maximillion, you are not only discounting me professionally but you are destroying the image of me that you carry within yourself. Don't do that and ask for what you want"' (Moiso, 1985: 200).

Masterson (1985) and Kernberg (1982) claim that it is essential for the analyst to focus on the external circumstances of the client and do some life-management skills to enable the client to be available for psychotherapy. Many Kleinians and Freudians would consider such interventions anti-therapeutic, as anything which focuses on reality and not on the relationship between analyst and patient is considered an interference to the analysis. Kernberg and Masterson believe as I do, that the client's present circumstances are legitimate, indeed an essential field for investigation and intervention.

Transactional analysts range in theory and practice across a very broad spectrum. On the one hand, there are the Gouldings:

> We prefer, usually, not to invite a transference, although of course we do use ourselves. We are much more likely, however, to endeavor to keep out of the work, and to let the patient do his work against himself, by setting up dialogues, by keeping I–Thou transactions going, by saying 'any more?' instead of 'tell me'. Thus we hope that the patient, instead of resisting us, will resist himself, recognize the impasse when he gets to it, and either break through or stay stuck at the point of impasse. We prefer that he battle against his own internal Parent, instead of with his transferred 'parent', us.
>
> (Goulding and Goulding, 1979: 210)

On the other hand there are Moiso, Novellino and Clarkson who intentionally and actively work with the transference. The reparenting approach of Schiff *et al*. (1975) approach which uses a replacement model is a radical departure from any other form of psychotherapy. Even though there is talk of entering the symbiosis, it is indubitably *not* transferential since it is specifically different from what has happened before and is therefore not transferring from the past. It is neither undoing nor understanding; neither insight nor redecision: it is replacement. One may find that replacement work of this kind is inadvisable, potentially damaging and probably not genuinely possible until the transferential space has been cleared. Moiso (1985) writes that redecision work, reparenting, and two-chair work can be damaging at the beginning of therapy, when the transference is still very much in evidence.

Allowing the transference

If the client's development was arrested at an unresolved symbiotic stage, they will project those issues and expectations into the psychotherapeutic relationship and there will inevitably be a transferential relationship within the overall psychotherapeutic relationship. This cannot be different because of the nature of the contradictions. If the client has failed to successfully separate the self from the mother, how can they possibly see the psychotherapist as separate? The arrested or sedimentary self requires a symbiotic partner and will create one according to its expectations, whatever the psychotherapist does or does not do. The psychotherapist cannot but allow this and needs to concentrate on how to work with the phenomena creatively and towards an eventual resolution.

There is sometimes a misunderstanding that the game must be stopped at all costs even at the first con (invitation to the game). This is deleterious because the client learns superficial adaptation or obedience to the psychotherapist's rules rather than engaging in a psychotherapeutic relationship. According to Berne, it is often more important to allow the 'game' or transferential projection to unfold so that there is sufficient evidence for both parties to recognise the pattern and provide material for analysis; thus denial is made more difficult and a common language can be developed for referring to the characteristic phenomenon. If the client had a homicidal parent, or a very judgmental critical parent, or a weak or ill parent, the client probably fears that the psychotherapist will use, abuse or neglect them. One possible strategy which is particularly useful in the earlier stages of psychotherapy is for the psychotherapist to temporarily accept this sort of transference. The psychotherapist can then invite the client to explore and experience it in its minutest detail including physical, emotional, behavioural and cognitive manifestations. In the safe place of the psychotherapeutic relationship the client can do this without the response that would usually occur in the outside world where people respond to the game invitations and thus reinforce the experienced 'truth' of the transferred expectation. Once the unfinished business or transferential situation has become fully alive and clear, the client, supported by the psychotherapist, can embark upon the work of comparison, by checking present evidence against the client's archaic expectation learning, developing skills in self-analysis and generalising that can eventually lead to resolution of the transference as described on p.166ff.

Inviting the transference

Usually the psychotherapist does not have to be a mirror in order for the client to enter into a transference relationship. Existing in the transferential space is usually sufficient to evoke transferential reactions. This is borne out by the ubiquitousness of transferential phenomena in everyday relationships including marital partners, who are usually the least 'mirror'-like to each other. However, the difference in the psychotherapeutic situation is not the difficulty of eliciting the transference, but the opportunity to understand it and work through it. However, some people do not enter the transference. This may be either because there is no need to enter the transference or because they 'resist' entering the transference due to an inability or unwillingness to engage.

In the first case the client sees the psychotherapist clearly and is able to get on with the task. For example, this occurs in some forms of short-term psychotherapy or specific contracts where a mild benign transference may operate with no harm and endless beneficial results – the kind of warmth which is potentially transferred to teachers and doctors who have been helpful to us in the past. Without this type of positive transference, there can be little hope for a successful human relationship at all. It is a moot point whether this should technically be defined as transference if it is not based on earlier positive experiences wrongly transferred from past people onto the present person without any evidence. It can be more accurately described as a realistic expectation based on knowledge of the reliability of the person's own judgement and intuition. In TA terms we are here talking about Integrated Adult functioning and reality-testing skills. If someone consults a psychotherapist, they expect that the psychotherapist will be able to help them; this is based on a reasonable expectation that specially trained people will have the skills they claim. So, in such instances it may *not* be necessary to 'enter' the transference. This may be because the person did not have particular difficulty with the parent in the past or because the person had already resolved the tendency to project transferentially.

In the second case there are people who may not enter the transference; possibly they resist doing so because they are unable or unwilling to engage, and avoid doing so through the use of intellectualising or rationalising defences. An example is a patient in a group-psychotherapy situation who, in a throw-away manner, makes the comment that 'Of course I should be jealous because Joe is getting the attention, and I probably felt that way about my younger brother.' However, there is no emotional involvement or genuineness to the remark; it is devoid of emotional fibre. This could be resistance to the sibling transference which is then even more secure because it is so thoroughly denied or repressed out of awareness. The psychotherapist may choose to confront such a rationalisation and invite the client to slow down and allow sensation to enter into the communications, to breathe and re-own the emotion, and thus relive the earlier ego states through regression, hypnosis or 'spontaneous combustion' in the psychotherapy.

Some examples of transference-inviting questions are: How do you feel as you say that? How do you feel about me? What do you think when I say that? How am I like your mother? What do you imagine I might do next? I imagine you think I will reject you? Inviting the transference can be done: passively (by being the mirror); actively, by displaying emotion or behaviour similar to that which the patient is projecting, e.g. being late for a patient who fears abandonment: 'This is what you were frightened to happen, and now it has happened.' Sometimes there is so little uncontaminated Adult that almost whatever the psychotherapist may do, say, or be (or not) is used by the client to confirm the projections.

Another kind of resistance to the transference is displayed by people who have a more schizoid adaptation. Of course, for such people it is technically transferential *not* to have a genuine interpersonal relationship, since this is probably what happened to them as children: people did not relate to them in ways which were beneficial to their growth, or sometimes did not relate to them at all; parents may have been over-invasive, neglectful, abusive of siblings. They are, perhaps, transferring a fear that the psychotherapist may be as invasive as the original parent, and their withdrawal is part of the transferential relationship. The psychotherapist respects their withdrawal – as soon as one goes closer, they experience it as intrusive, but it is necessary to do this, not just neglect them for years and years on the couch or in the group. It is sometimes necessary and humane to enter into the relationship and to risk the approbation or fear in order to make the beginnings of a human relationship. Such patients can then begin to learn when and how to trust and how to protect themselves appropriately without cutting off from nourishing human contact. For example, a psychotherapist said to a client, 'What happened just then, I'm very sorry that I missed you in that way', which is clearly what mum would never have done. The client's eyes filled with tears.

Temporarily interrupting the transference

Sometimes it is necessary and desirable to interrupt a fully developed transferential situation. For example, when a client is totally taken up with rage or grief towards the end of a session, the psychotherapist might remind the client that he has only has 10 minutes left and ask him what he needs before he leaves. In doing this the psychotherapist is calling upon the client's Integrated Adult function and strenthening the working alliance with the client. If the client is insistent upon seeing the psychotherapist in an unrealistically negative way (based on past expectations of neglect or abuse), the psychotherapist may decide to refuse to play the game any longer and invite the patient to cathect the Adult. The psychotherapist may, for example, remind the patient of their real relationship or working alliance by saying:

> You are not trapped by me or with me. You are paying for a service and you are free to stop paying me for this service, if it is not to your satisfaction. This is different from when you were a child and you couldn't leave the parental home.

If the client is so completely gripped by rage (due to the transferred expectation that the psychotherapist cannot help them) that they threaten to leave, the psychotherapist may talk to the client's Adult self by reminding him:

> You have an opportunity now to work this through with me. The chances are that if you don't, you will continue to find or make other similar situations again and again. You can walk out on me now but you will walk with the same problem in the future.

Avoiding or minimising the transference

It is not really possible to avoid transference completely but it can be minimalised by: ignoring the game; analysing the game; commissioning the Adult; establishing Adult-to-Adult contracts; reality testing; and so on.

Examples of minimalising the transference in these ways include the following: a client is overwhelmed by feeling in a transferential way and the psychotherapist chooses to work with someone else and let them continue to cry until they are more in a position to think. The psychotherapist may or may not make this explicit by saying what they are doing and why.

In another case a client was angry with her psychotherapist because she had such a late appointment. By going through their diaries and rediscovering some restrictions on the client's as well as her own time, the psychotherapist went over the facts, and appealed to common sense, their working alliance and the client's mutual responsibility for making arrangements for appointments.

Humorous exaggeration of the client's transferential moan: 'Oh no one loves you, not even your psychotherapist!' Or humorous confrontation, 'Of all my clients, your success is the one most likely to really damage me, is that it?' (Humour obviously needs to be used with care and where a relationship is already established and some evidence of the client's tolerance of teasing has been ascertained.)

Refusing the parental role is another option. A client asks the psychotherapist's permission in a child-like way and the psychotherapist responds 'What would stop you?', i.e. refuses to be the granter of permission. The psychotherapist could also use a method of working that demonstrates that clients are a resource, as well as the psychotherapist referring clients to other clients for their support and by using other group members to attract transference.

It is important that trainers and supervisors minimise the transference in their relationships with trainees and supervisees as they do not, in these instances, have the contract to go in there and work with the transference to resolve it.

It is essential that the transference be effectively minimised or resolved before moving into doing developmentally needed replacement work. If it is not resolved, the attempted replacement work could be damaging or, more likely, ineffective because it will not get through the sort of shell of fixed expectation in which the client is still caught. The Gouldings (Goulding and Goulding, 1975, 1979) minimise the transference by externalising the internal dialogue (rather than inviting dialogue with the psychotherapist), use of Gestalt techniques, A–A contract, and analysing the game.

Resolving the transference

To resolve the transference, the psychotherapist must allow the transferential situation to develop sufficiently to become fully alive and yet be experienced as something alien to here-and-now reality. At that point the psychotherapist may invite the client into reality testing through the use of the client's senses.

> When you were little it is true that no one listened to you or paid you attention. Is that still true now? Look around the room, what do you see? People, yes. Are they looking at you? Do they seem to be listening? Are they paying attention to you? How can you tell?

In the work of resolution the psychotherapist uses experiencing, collecting evidence, analysing, confronting, putting the transference where it belongs, cognitive understanding, emotional catharsis and moving from reliving to remembering with the affective charge removed. The psychotherapist also fosters skills in spotting the transference in future relationships, and either avoiding situations which will echo the original unmet need or being skilful in them. The psychotherapist helps the client develop reality testing – identifying the kind of people to whom the client is repetitively attracted, helping the client change their attractiveness for the psychotherapist, as well as the psychotherapist changing their own reactions to the client. The psychotherapist encourages the client to have new experiences with real relationships and real people, to get used to this, account for this, begin to trust and expect this, and know what to do when something goes wrong. Living without the transference is replacement – a radical departure from any other form of psychotherapy. Any resolution of the transference is inevitably healing since past damage usually occurred because there was an absence of a true and genuine relationship.

There follows an example where a transferential situation is resolved towards the end of the client's psychotherapy. The client, who had a history of somatising, and a tendency to hypochondriasis and feeling the Victim, used to get most of her strokes or recognition for ways in which she was incompetent, incapacitated or inadequate. Although she had made great gains in psychotherapy, some of the old patterns lingered and it was difficult for her to relate to new people as a healthy person without inviting them to see her in the first instance as 'an individual who suffers'. In her own words:

> In a psychotherapy group one member asks about how I got paralysed when I was twenty. Pleased to have the opportunity to tell my story again, I commence with tears in my eyes. The psychotherapist intervenes by stopping this. I protest: 'I am only telling what happened.' The psychotherapist reiterates that I should not continue with this tale of drudgery and misery, which had been told many times before. I scream at the psychotherapist, 'I hate you!' glaring at her with all the rage I can muster. The psychotherapist then stops an interaction with someone else on the far side of the room and comes over slowly to sit cross-legged, about a yard in front of me, in a receptive, open posture. I say, 'I feel very, very angry with you.' The psychotherapist says, 'What would your mother do now?' I reply, 'What a stupid question. My mother would hit me and then send me to my room. She would never let me speak to her like this.' The psychotherapist continues

looking steadily at me with what I can only describe as compassionate concern. Then she reached out her hands to me, palms upwards, without touching me, and I dissolved into tears as I realised that I can show my anger at her without being punished or rejected the way I had been in the past.

The client has done that herself. She chose to respond in a self-reparative way.

Another example is Georgina, who continued to believe that her own needs could not be met without detriment to others, just as her archaic baby needs had not been met. In a group situation the psychotherapist therefore chose to hold Georgina while she experienced her feelings of needs unmet and howled her pain. At the same time the psychotherapist allowed her to experience a contradictory here-and-now reality in that she made it clear with both her body and her words that she was perfectly able to take care of herself, of Georgina's needs, and of the needs of the other group members for the duration of the group. In assessing the capacity of such a psychotherapeutic intervention, the psychotherapist needs to ask: 'does Georgina still believe that her needs cannot be met or how attached is Georgina still to the transferential distortion?' Only when the psychotherapist has ascertained that the client has indeed resolved the pervasive transferential expectation is it advisable to move on to do repair work, which needs to be firmly based in here-and-now reality with the client taking fully aware adult responsibility for requesting the repair work.

MANAGEMENT AND USE OF COUNTERTRANSFERENCE PHENOMENA IN TRANSACTIONAL ANALYSIS

Hopefully, the psychotherapist who is using transactional analysis will have done a thoroughgoing psychotherapy themselves so that they will have resolved most of the major ways in which their own pathology (or scripts) may interefere with the psychotherapy which they do with clients. Realising that this is often an unattainable counsel of perfection it is important that they have understood themselves enough that they have become skilled in identifying and counteracting their own pathological patterns especially their countertransferential responses which are based on unresolved issues from their past.

However, Berne himself saw transference and countertransference reactions in the form of stimulus–response transactional patterns (see Figure 7.1).

Indeed, Berne saw interpretation as one of the eight major categories of psychotherapeutic operations which he listed among the basic techniques of psychotherapy as the prototype of a crossed transaction. The patient responds to an interpretation of a question from the psychotherapist which is directed to their Adult by Child or Parental reaction. On the other hand, the client expects a Parent Child to respond to their request for help or assistance, instead the psychotherapist invites them into Adult thinking about the historical roots of their manner of request – for example, 'Did you have to suffer more than your sisters and wait for someone to notice you in your family?' The psychotherapist's

THERAPIST   CLIENT

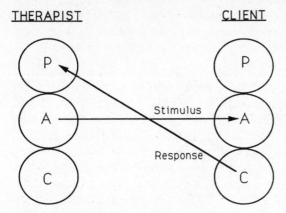

Figure 7.1   Crossed transaction, Type I
Source: Berne, 1972: 16
Note: Representing the common form of transference reaction as it occurs in psychotherapy

question or interpretation is experienced as a crossed transaction because the response is unexpected and contrary to the historical expectation of responses. Traditional psychoanalysis concentrates primarily on this particular form of transaction.

Countertransference, Berne represented by crossed transaction Type II where an Adult-to-Adult stimulus such as a question from the patient, for example, receives a patronising or pompous Parent or Child response not appropriate to the situation, but influenced by the psychotherapist's own past agendas (see Figure 7.2).

In both these drawings (Figures 7.1 and 7.2) Berne is showing an intuitive understanding of the interdependent phenomena of transference and counter-transference phenomena. As such they constitute an interactional field created by recurrent stimulus–response pairs within the relationship. As was shown earlier he also recognised the value of the psychotherapist (or the person diagnosing ego states) paying attention to their own emotional responses when he underlined the value of *social* diagnosis of ego states. That is, for example,

> How do I feel towards Joan when she offers to help me? If I feel slightly scared that she may not be able to keep her promise, but so grateful that she is offering that I do not want to offend her, my emotional Parental reaction to her Child ego state may help confirm a diagnostic hypothesis that she is relating to me from a Child ego state.

(This also needs to be corroborated by a behavioural, historical and subjectively or phenomenologically reported fit.) Thus already in 1957 Berne was

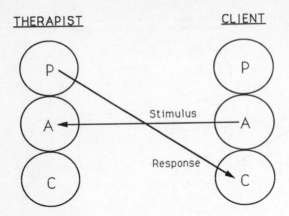

Figure 7.2   Crossed transaction, Type II

encouraging psychotherapists to use their own intuition to sense and diagnose Child ego states, and in 1961 (Berne, 1980/1961) he elaborates on this to include subjective social responses in order to diagnose any one of the ego-state categories.

This sense, that the meaning of the transaction lies in the communicative space between dialoguing partners has been developed by first analysing with examples of four categories of transference (for, respectively, the client as well as the psychotherapist), and four categories of countertransference (for, respectively, the client and the psychotherapist). In the next section the author posits a circular interaction as the dynamic field for the so-called parallel process.

It seems to be a well-known phenomenon that psychotherapists often behave in supervision in the same way the patient behaves in psychotherapy. Thus if a patient is experiencing a sense of helplessness and leans on the psychotherapist, the same sense of helplessness may be reflected in the psychotherapist as he leans on the supervisor (see Figure 7.3). This is a transient identification with the patient and it is acted out in the supervisory situation. This has also been called 'parallel process' in supervision (Moldawsky in Hess, 1980: 131).

Doehrman in Hess (1980) investigated the parallel process by clinical interviews of patients, psychotherapists and supervisors over a period of time. She concluded that the usual understanding (mentioned above as reflection of patient–psychotherapist behaviour in psychotherapist–supervisor interaction) goes only half the way. Rather, the supervisor stirs the psychotherapist, who then acts out with his patients. Thus, parallel process is not reflective alone – it works in both directions. This discovery has just begun to find its way into supervisors' work. It speaks to the complexity of the patient–psychotherapist–supervisor interactions and encourages a humbleness in supervisors (Hess, 1980: 131).

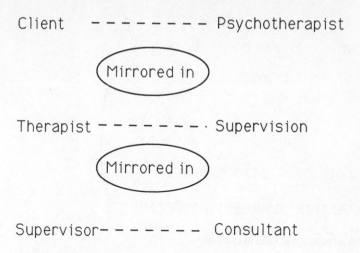

Client – – – – – – – – Psychotherapist

Mirrored in

Therapist – – – – – – – · Supervision

Mirrored in

Supervisor– – – – – – – Consultant

Figure 7.3 Parallel process
Source: Berne, 1972: 16

The author proposes that parallel process can be conceptualised as a way of describing the pattern of the client–psychotherapist relationship or the inter-personal pattern of the dyadic psychotherapeutic relationship.

Thus the categories and types so far discussed can be seen as the raw material for identifying parallel processes in terms of the interdependent field between client and psychotherapist. It is the author's proposal that what is understood by the notion of parallel process is the interactional field of the psychotherapist/client field replicated in the psychotherapist/supervisor field (see Figure 7.4). Any combination of client and psychotherapist reactions to each other thus forms a dynamic field and we propose that it is this dynamic field which is manifested in the supervisory relationship and variously referred to as parallel process.

Understanding the shape and nature of the parallel process is not only useful when it gets in the way of supervision, but also for prevention, understanding, learning, relief.

It seems to be more accurately representative of the complexity of the client/psychotherapist field to represent the different forces in a circular dynamic relationship to one another. As we know from physics, the idea that the observer can somehow not influence the observational field is now quite redundant (Zohar, 1990). Similarly, it seems obvious that we cannot unequivocally lay the responsibility on the client for transferring 'onto the psychotherapist' as if this transference could happen with any psychotherapist. Equally it appears to be clinically correct that for many psychotherapists patients present problems as if they are acutely aware of the vulnerable points or developmental tasks of the psychotherapist and sometimes seem to even work in some strange kind of

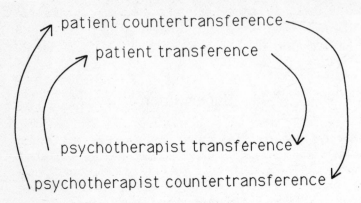

Figure 7.4 The interactional field in context

tandem. As the trainee becomes more in touch with their negative transference in psychotherapy, so the trainee's clients become more willing to express anger and disappointment to the trainee. To seek first causes in such a complex dynamically interactive situation seems to be futile. It is perhaps far more fruitful to recognise the co-occurrence of such phenomena and their ubiquitous prevalence in many clinical teaching situations or perhaps even to bringing the notion of synchronicity (the Jungian acausal connecting principle) to bear upon the situation so that the models may serve our ends instead of being forced on a Procrustean bed to fit our perceptual prejudices or existing cognitive categories.

Since most of these processes are also at the same time unconscious (or out of awareness) and the order of complexity approaches chaos, it may be useful to think about the parallel process as being a fractal of the field – representing (even though in minute form) the structure of the larger whole (Gleick, 1987). No matter how small the size to which it is reduced, the essential features of the field will remain present and available to inspection in roughly the same shape as on the larger maps. Following these analogies of fractals or even holograms, it becomes more possible to subject the dynamic interactional transference/countertransference field to investigation. However, it is important to avoid assigning first causes to either client or psychotherapist. Neither does it follow that one can prioritise a particular transference reaction before a particular countertransference reaction in a sequence. Might it not be possible that the psychotherapist draws to him or herself the kind of clients who are most useful for the psychotherapist's development?

In the absence of proof of causality and particularly directionality, it may be more useful and more congruent with the present state of our knowledge to assume that these phenomena are interconnected in ways which we do not yet understand. Mutual hypnotic inductions or projective identifications (see Chapter 1) from either or both the client and psychotherapist deserve intensive and long-term research, yet the clinical field is probably one of the very last which will open itself to rigorous scientific analysis, even supposing that we had the tools with which to do the studies.

It is certainly more pragmatic to place the emphasis on those categories where it is possible to achieve the maximum leverage or most efficient resolution. For this a simple figure–ground Gestalt model may be useful. When the psychotherapist is actively engaging in the therapeutic relationship with the client, they can assume that most of the dynamics are contributed by the client and develop the interventions from such a frame of reference. In other words, at the moment of therapeutic engagement in the relationship it is most useful to consider that client transference and the psychotherapist's reactive countertransference are most likely to provide the richest and most accurate options for intervention.

On the other hand, when the psychotherapist is doing supervision of him- or herself, the field most available for intervention is that of the psychotherapist – therefore it may be most fruitful to consider that most of the phenomena in the field are being caused by the psychotherapist's pro-active transference and the client's reactive countertransference to what the psychotherapist introduces. Let us then assume that the psychotherapist's unresolved conflicts, confusions and deficits are completely at cause in the psychotherapy. Of course, it cannot be proved that either of these positions is accurate, or even likely. Clinical supervisory evidence, however, bears out that frequent alternations between these two viewpoints, with the emphasis on where the smallest intervention is likely to lead to the largest degree of shift in the problem, are exceptionally useful and empowering for both the client and psychotherapist.

SUMMARY

This chapter is intended to offer the trainee psychotherapist, as well as the experienced clinician and supervisor, one possible map by means of which to understand parallel process in psychotherapy, counselling and the supervision of both. This is a way of discriminating between different types of transferential and countertransferential phenomena in order to facilitate teaching and supervision. A map is suggested for the analysis of the concepts of transference, countertransferences, client countertransference and understanding the notion parallel process. It is not intended to be a comprehensive review of the literature on transference, countertransference or parallel process, but a practical guide which may stimulate readers to investigate this fascinating area further.

An understanding of parallel process is invited which is achieved by analysing the constituent parts of the interactional field of the therapeutic relationship. Although these ultimately are conceived of as interacting as an inseparable systemic whole (or fractal) for the sake of discussion four categories of transferential phenomena have been separated out. These are: what the client brings to the relationship (pro-active transference), what the psychotherapist brings (pro-active countertransference or therapist transference), what the psychotherapist reacts to in the client (reactive countertransference), and what the client reacts to as a result of what the therapist brings (client countertransference or reactive transference). Any of these may form the basis for facilitative or destructive psychotherapeutic outcomes.

Chapter 8

The psychology of the self in transactional analysis[†]

Given by a client to her psychotherapist:

> losing through you what seemed
> myself,
> i find selves unimaginably mine;
> beyond sorrow's own joys
> and hoping's very fears

(e.e. cummings, 1987)

INTRODUCTION

The earliest Socratic dialogues contain instructions to strive for self-knowledge and Aristotle (pre-dating the humanistic psychology movement by several centuries) coined the term 'self-actualisation'. Likewise, the average twentieth-century clinician is quite familiar with people who come to psychotherapy to discover 'themselves'. The terms 'real self', 'self-actualise', 'self-esteem' and 'self-image' abound in psychotherapeutic jargon, while in a more ordinary parlance self-referent phrases like 'my old self', 'speak for yourself', 'she doesn't feel herself today', are commonly heard. Ordinary people are far more likely to use the word 'self' and other self-referent words than they would 'ego states' or 'object relations'. It is clear that when a loved one dies, it is that person's self that is mourned, not their ego states. Similarly, in an argument with a friend, it is the relationship between 'selves' which is concerned, not an object relationship. Yet there appears to be a conceptual chasm between ego-state talk and self talk. Much of the confusion may be due to the fact that psychological theorists have tried to relate these two universes of discourse as if they were similar, as if apples can be translated into symphonic notation.

Berne was aware of this when he wrote, 'The feeling of Self is independent of all other properties of ego states and of what an ego state is doing or experiencing' (Berne 1972: 249), thus implying that phenomenalistic ego-state

[†]Co-authored by Phil Lapworth

discourse is different from discourse referring to the 'self'. These are two different kinds of talk and it is easy for the novice clinician or trainee to be baffled by the many ways in which their mentors confuse these meanings and confound their practice.

Theoreticians show enormous variation, and often contradict each other when referring to notions of the self, thus making their operation in practice very difficult.

Fine (1986) points out that the psychology of the self in psychoanalysis can be seen as the fourth great wave, following object relations theory which succeeded ego psychology, which in turn replaced the original Freudian 'drive theory'. The so-called 'psychology of the self' has in recent years become more focal in psychotherapy, and indeed fashionable, as the increasing numbers of publications, definitions and authorities on the 'self' multiply. However, many fail to acknowledge the Jungian and analytic psychologists, for example Adler (1979), who have been centrally concerned with the problems of the self since the early years of this century. (Several excellent summaries of the various theoretical positions exist and readers are referred to these primary sources wherever possible in order to consult them for verification, comparison and development of their own theory.) Arguably, this growing body of work is accompanied by escalating confusion. It is not the authors' intention to make definitive statements about the theoretical and ideological disputes which are accumulating. Suffice it to point out that one of the foremost modern authorities in the field, Kohut, states:

> My investigation contains hundreds of pages dealing with the psychology of the self – yet it never assigns an inflexible meaning to the term self, it never explains how the essence of the self should be defined ....The self, whether conceived within the framework of the psychology of the self in the narrow sense of the term, as a specific structure in the mental apparatus, or within the framework of the psychology of the self in the broad sense of the term, as the centre of the individual's psychological universe ... is not knowable in its essence ... only its introspectively or empathically perceived psychological manifestations are open to us.
>
> (Kohut, 1977: 310–11)

It is our intention to clarify the uses of the notion 'self' in transactional analysis theory and clinical practice, drawing some parallels with other theories where these can amplify our understanding. Six different but interrelated concepts of the self in TA are identified and differentiated, thus clarifying the different emphases and different clinical manifestations of disorder described by each.

It here suggested that experiences of self, the development of the self and the healing of, or connectedness with, the self (however this may be described) are epiphenomena of other structural changes in the personality; for example, the direct psychotherapeutic work with ego states. However, one of the reasons for the fact that the self is so hard to define may be because it is not referred to as a structural entity but as a quality of experience that can range from terrified fragmentation to luminous transcendence. The idea is therefore offered for consideration, not as a truth, that reparative work on the self is usually done indirectly and as a concomitant effect of psychotherapy – for it seems that the self occurs in most effective psychotherapy whether or not the psychotherapist has ever specifically addressed the issue of self, indeed some may not even be aware of the theoretical debates on this matter!

Clients who have benefited from psychotherapy or psychoanalysis frequently report their experience of healing in terms of a new or rediscovered 'self'. This is similar to the descriptions people give of experiences resulting from religious conversion, falling in love and other life changes and experiences (Clarkson, 1989).

Here then are the six interrelated concepts of the self that have been identified in transactional analysis and which are compared with other theoretical conceptualisations.

WHOLENESS

Towards the termination of her psychotherapy, the client, Lisa, reported that she felt an increased sense of wholeness, of completion, of the richness of her total self. She associated this with feeling existent as 'a whole being' in the world, of 'being boundaried and contained in my body, but including my spirit', of 'no longer feeling fragmented'. We see this sense of boundary, containment and wholeness as being represented in TA by the three stacked circles of the three types of ego state enclosed within a 'skin' of body and sensory awareness (see Figure 8.1). This may be the sense in which Freud referred to the self as 'ego, id and super ego', which seems to correspond quite closely with the idea of wholeness or total self. Masterson (1985) and Kernberg's (1982) concept also appears to emphasise the self more in the sense of wholeness: 'the sum total of self representations in intimate connection with the sum total of object relations' (Masterson, 1985: 15).

According to Ryce-Menuhin, the self is rarely glimpsed in the work of the neo-Freudians except in its relative absence of ego awareness or by a clinical breakdown if the ego splinters. He writes that the self is:

a required unity if the psyche is to make experience coherently conceivable in a single consciousness. The ego develops out of its self and becomes the self's agent of consciousness. A self concept is needed to explain the pathology of the fragmented self (autism and personality disorder) and of the depleted self (depression), as well as the self as centre of initiative.

(Ryce-Menuhin, 1988: 17)

Jung (1971) seems to have had three senses of the use of the term 'self'. One of these is the idea of the self as totality. For him, this sense of self equals the ego

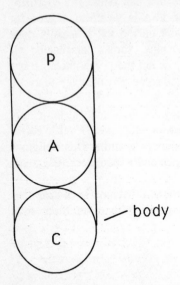

Figure 8.1   The whole self in transactional analysis
Source: Berne, 1964: 25

and the archetypes. That is, he views the self as a combination of consciousness (ego) and the collective and personal unconscious (archetypes and personal repressed material).

For Adler (1979), the self operates as an image of potential wholeness behind the psychic processes and bends them towards realisation of this wholeness, which appears as the synthesis of ego and non-ego, of conscious and unconscious, of the inner and outer worlds.

Neo-Jungians such as Ryce-Menuhin (1988) espouse the following view: 'A Gestalt of wholeness, of self-image while unattainable consciously except in peak experience or in symbolic image (e.g. the mandala) is nevertheless the a priori goal of the psyche and crucial to its dimension' (p.63).

Returning to the client at the beginning of this section, Lisa's former disorder of the self could be construed in terms of the fragmentation of wholeness. She described her experience of her self as being broken into a thousand pieces which could never be put together again. Her phenomenological experience was that of fragmentation, disintegration or nothingness. Indeed, there was often not a 'self' to complain of the disintegrative terror which had become her normal state after spending several years in a mental institution for schizophrenia. Lisa felt that the more important factor in her recovery was her psychotherapist's lack of fear or distaste in exploring her inner world, which encouraged her integration into wholeness.

Laing writes of the fragmented self:

> In many schizophrenics, the self–body split remains the basic one. However, when the 'centre' fails to hold, neither self-experience nor body-experience can retain identity, integrity, cohesiveness or vitality, and the individual becomes precipitated into a condition, the end result of which we suggest, could best be described as a state of 'chaotic nonentity'. In its final form, such complete disintegration is a hypothetical state which has no verbal equivalent.
>
> (Laing, 1965: 162)

If disorders of the self in terms of wholeness are conceptualised along a continuum, fragmentation or disintegration would be placed at the extreme polarity to wholeness. A less severe form of disturbance, the insulating self, would be placed at a lesser extreme. This is where the person denies their wholeness, insulating themselves against the possibility of growth and change by a restricting self-perception, identifying only with some of their capacities. In ego-state terms, the containment of the body-awareness 'skin' may be dissolved and certain ego states and their potentialities denied or disowned. In psychotherapy, a client who is suffering from this kind of limitation would benefit from affirmation and validation of their wholeness.

All disorders of this latter group usually respond to cohesion-inducing responses to the total self or whole self of the kind which Kohut (1978) and Masterson (1985) recommend. It seems unfortunately symptomatic of the ideologically solipsistic world 'schools of psychotherapy' that Rogers (1986) the great originator of empathy and communicative matching is seldom, if ever, credited with discovering, describing and researching this first condition of effective psychotherapeutic change.

In TA, the psychotherapist, by acceptance, by coming from an 'I'm OK – You're OK' position and by having a non-judgemental attitude, often gives the client a first experience of 'being known' as a whole person and validates the whole self contained within the body-awareness skin: physicality and sensations, thoughts and feelings, facts and fantasies, the past and the future, the realised and the potential, the 'good' bits and 'not-so-good' bits, and helps the client to be accepting of their 'self' in its wholeness and its multiplicity, to which this next section refers (see Figure 8.1).

MULTIPLICITY

Disowning or disassociating from parts of the self can be construed as pathological in the sense that the person is disowning or remaining unconscious of significant chunks of their own experience or behaviour. TA and its concept of three types of ego states provides a useful model for the exploration of the multifarious aspects of our self-experience. The structural model assists in differentiating between ego states which are repressed (bound cathexis), ego states which are temporarily out of awareness (unbound cathexis) and ego states which are currently active and in awareness (free cathexis), while the functional model usefully describes the various roles we may choose to express ourselves and our needs. In other words, there is an implicit assumption in TA that we have a multiplicity of 'selves' or self-experiences (see Figure 8.2). This is further elaborated on in the following section.

We know that through hypnosis, or certain surgical procedures, as well as ordinary life experiences, disassociated states (or repressed ego states) may become available. In such cases the individual still may or may not own the 'selves' which these ego states represent and may or may not take responsibility for their behaviour at such times. There is some fascinating literature (e.g. Watkins, 1976) on the questions of whether people are responsible for their behaviour when in a disassociated state, under the influence of drugs or experiencing some strong emotion. The French legal system once sympathised with offenders by allowing a disassociated state under the term *crime passionel* which practically absolved the person of responsibility for their actions. This gave credence to those times of human experience when passions are aroused and people make the claim 'I wasn't myself then'. In psychotherapy, particularly in the realm of the schizophrenias, multiple personalities and other disassociated states, the term 'ego dystonic states' is used. Perhaps a better term would be 'self-dystonic states' since it is not with the ego that they are dissonant, but with the self.

Being drunk, being 'in a blind rage', having a 'panic attack', or being very tired are reasons people sometimes give in their day-to-day lives for behaving in ways which are 'not myself'. Here, too, is the implication that there are parts of

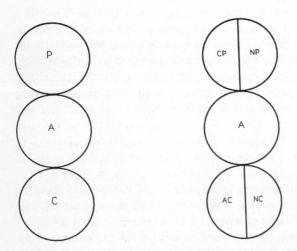

Figure 8.2 A multiplicity of selves: the self in structural and functional terms (states and roles)

the person which can act independently of the real self – some other self or selves. These breakouts can be experienced sometimes as 'possession' in the way that Fairbairn (1952) and others describe. Indeed, Berne (1972) describes the parent in the child ego state 'acting like a positive electrode, giving an automatic response' and continues, 'When the parent in his head (PC) pushes the button, Jeder jumps to it, whether the rest of him wants to or not.' This seems very like a description of possession.

A parent may 'fly into a rage', physically assault their beloved child (even though they fervently oppose corporal punishment) and afterwards experience themselves shocked, shamed and surprised at such behaviour. The most likely explanation, often corroborated clinically is that this behaviour is the uncensored and undiluted reproduction of an ego state of someone else (usually a significant parent figure as Berne implies in the above) which the person introjected at some earlier stage of their lives. The enactment of this behaviour, *apparently involuntarily*, is often experienced as evidence of the existence of the incorporated ego states of others in the individual person, giving rise to a multiplicity of 'selves', many of which we disown.

Another category of 'not-self' that we encounter clinically is that of the outbreak of old or regressive behaviours described by people as 'my old self' or 'the child I once was'. This can be described as 'rubberbanding' back to previous experiences. They are reported as behaviours that are 'no longer myself', indicating that at one time the person did identify with them and did experience them as behaviours belonging to 'myself'. This is often a manifestation of historic (archaic) Child ego states; a re-experiencing of the self not based in the here-and-now reality.

Since the here-and-now reality is always changing, the here-and-now experience of the Adult ego state is phenomenologically empty of the past (see Figure 8.2) since it is fully engaged in the present, even though, of course, memories are being recorded. The experience of the self, therefore, in the Adult ego state is a constantly changing one from moment to moment. The multiplicity of selves then in this sense, is innumerable. This said, it is little wonder that people report in their everyday language their awareness of having multiple 'selves'.

In psychotherapy literature, the notion of sub-personalities is increasingly being used to refer to the kind of experience where a person can own and identify with a multiplicity of selves (Assagioli, 1965). These can be conceptualised as capacities, potentials or role possibilities which are available to the person and under voluntary control. These may or may not be Parent or Child ego states but share the characteristic that the person can cathect them at will, that is imbue them with psychological energy. They may be destructive and limiting or growthful and healthy. They do not have to be fixated ego states. Even though the person may not intentionally plan to energise this subpersonality or subself, the person owns and identifies with this 'state of mind'. The ownership of subselves is implied in the Gestalt emphasis in dream work on encouraging the dreamer to 'become' the various aspects of their dreams: the other people in the dream, the scenery or setting, the 'props', etc., all of which reflect a multiplicity of selves or aspects of the self.

As an example of multiplicity, a woman may identify with her professional self, the competent executive in her 'power suit', but also have available to her the playful joker and the sportswoman. At other times she may be fully identified with herself as the 'earth mother' or the sexy seductress. She may engage in any number of age-appropriate behaviours from balancing accounts to regressing to an Archaic Child ego state in psychotherapy. These different selves or subpersonalities may have different wardrobes, different costumes, different vocabularies and styles of speaking and certainly different modes of relating to other people. Each is a coherent whole. Even though they may be sometimes in conflict with each other, they co-exist as potentials of the same person. She can cathect any one of these without losing her sense of self or a sense of continuity over time or a sense of coherence in terms of individual possibilities.

The task of psychotherapy is to facilitate awareness, understanding, owner-ship and responsibility for the self in its various manifestations and possibilities. For example, Elizabeth, when she first came to psychotherapy, experienced her self at times as inappropriately euphoric and manic and was clearly puzzled and distressed by her behaviour. The psychotherapist (working within a 'no go crazy' contract and sure of Elizabeth's ability to cathect her Adult on demand thus reinforcing the fact that she has other parts of self) invited her to experience the manic part of herself for a contracted period of time within the session. In this state of her self, she reported her feelings and thoughts and allowed herself to act in the way that this state 'seemed to require'. It was soon clear to her that she was phenomenologically experiencing her introjected mother. No longer puzzled, she then became aware of her option to enter that ego state or not. In other words, she owned it as a part of her self but realised her choice in the manifestations of it. The psychotherapist invited Elizabeth to look in a large mirror whereupon she said that she was seeing herself and all her parts for the first time. She felt shame, embarrassment and immense relief. She now had a sense of her multiplicity of selves and the possibility of exercising her options concerning them. This is the TA sense of functional behaviour – the notion of self where voluntary choice and autonomy seem to be emphasised. It implies the self as executive, equivalent to the integrative Adult functioning of Berne (1972: 254) and Federn (1977/1953). This leads to consideration of Berne's major contribution to self theory – that of the moving self.

THE MOVING SELF

Along with the biological principle of the 'Plastic Face' (Berne, 1972: 245–8) the psychological principle of the 'moving self' is equally important in keeping the script going, based as it often is, on a similar defect of awareness. The feeling of self, like the plasticity of the face is a mobile one. It can reside in any of the three types of ego states at any given moment, and can jump from one to another as the occasion arises (see Figure 8.3). Whenever one of the ego states is fully active, that ego state is experienced at that moment as the real self. When Tom comes on with his angry Parent, he feels that that is he, himself. A few minutes later, in his Adult ego state, when he wonders why he did it, he experiences the Adult as his real self. Still later, if he is feeling ashamed in his Child ego state because he was so mean, his Child is felt as his real self. All this of course, assumes that the incident is part of his real living, and that he is not merely playing the role of an

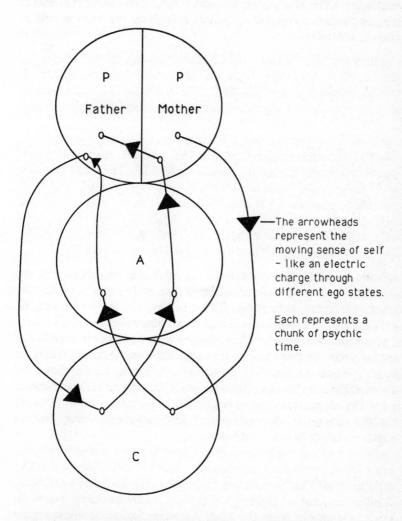

Figure 8.3 **The moving self: a PAC trip through the psyche**
Source: Berne, 1972: 252

angry Parent or of a contrite Child, in which case, his experiences of self may be in Adult, though there is the further possibility that he is playing an angry-parent role from a Child ego state or a contrite child (as his father used to do) from a Parent ego state.

Berne uses the terms the 'moving self', the 'real Self' and 'feeling of self' interchangeably, referring to what could be called the 'sense of self', i.e. that ego state in which free energy resides at a given time (Berne, 1966: 307). The person experiences this ego state as 'this is really me' even though this self may reside in a borrowed or historical ego state. This is what is understood as her phenomenological reality at any given moment in time. Berne quotes the case of Mrs Tettar, an obsessive–compulsive patient to explain the moving self as follows (Berne, 1961: 41):

1   In her healthy state, her 'old self', the Child contains only bound cathexis and is therefore latent, while the Adult is charged with free cathexis and is therefore experienced as her 'real Self'. The Adult also has the executive power, since it contains the greatest sum of active cathexis (unbound plus free).
2   In her neurotic hand-washing state, the free cathexis still resides in the Adult, while the Child contains unbound cathexis. This unbound cathexis predominates quantitatively over the active cathexis of the Adult. The Child therefore has the executive power, while the Adult is still experienced as her 'real Self'.
3   In her psychotic state, the Child contains unbound cathexis and also the free cathexis which has been drained from the Adult. This leaves the Adult relatively depleted of active cathexis. Therefore the Child both has the executive power and is experienced as the 'real Self' (see Figure 8.4).

If a patient's sense of self is in Adult and the Adult is in the executive of the personality, exercising volition and choice, then they are likely to be healthy, in good contact with reality, yet not disassociated from other parts or aspects of themselves (as shown in the previous section concerning multiplicity).

If the person partly experiences him- or herself in one ego state while the Adult remains aware of this cathexis (but apparently unable or unwilling to intervene) they would be described as neurotic. A person with a phobia of spiders, for example, may act afraid from Child whilst at the same time knowing in Adult that there is no reason to be scared. Such 'partial intrusions' (Berne, 1966) into the activity of the current real Self can also be described as contaminations as has been discussed before.

With reference to contaminations, Berne also includes latent psychosis, writing that a latent psychosis is said to exist when it can be inferred that the binding capacity of the Child is defective. Depending upon boundary conditions, there will either be areas of pathological activity where the Adult is heavily contaminated, or outbursts when the Adult is temporarily decommissioned, or both (Berne, 1980/1961).

If a person's experience of self or sense of self is not in Adult, this is

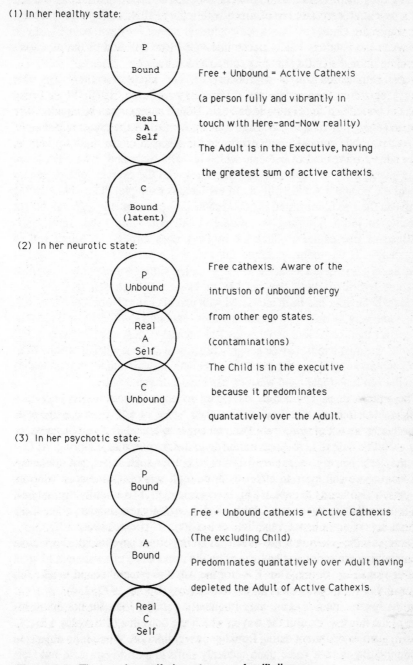

(1) In her healthy state:

P
Bound

Real
A
Self

C
Bound
(latent)

Free + Unbound = Active Cathexis
(a person fully and vibrantly in
touch with Here-and-Now reality)
The Adult is in the Executive, having
the greatest sum of active cathexis.

(2) In her neurotic state:

P
Unbound

Real
A
Self

C
Unbound

Free cathexis. Aware of the
intrusion of unbound energy
from other ego states.
(contaminations)
The Child is in the executive
because it predominates
quantatively over the Adult.

(3) In her psychotic state:

P
Bound

A
Bound

Real
C
Self

Free + Unbound cathexis = Active Cathexis
(The excluding Child)
Predominates quantatively over Adult having
depleted the Adult of Active Cathexis.

Figure 8.4   The moving self: three 'sense of self' diagrams

equivalent to a psychotic state. If a client really feels and experiences themselves as being truly the Messiah, their Adult is excluded and the experience of the self is in a psychotic ego state out of touch with reality. This could be a Parent ego state where the client cathects a schizophrenic parent introject, or a Child ego state when the Adult is totally decommissioned (the duration of the psychosis depending upon the Child retaining cathectic dominance).

Berne emphasises that in psychoanalysis, two kinds of cathexis (psychic energy) or *Besetzungsenergie* are differentiated (Berne, 1980/1961). Freud speaks of bound and freely mobile cathexis. Bound cathexis can be equated with repressed energy or fixated Child ego states governed by the pleasure principle, and freely mobile cathexis, with energy at the disposal of the reality principle. Berne adds a third kind of cathexis which he calls 'unbound' where the latent bound energy becomes unbound and interferes with the exercise of free energy without the person's Adult volition. In his famous example, the monkey sitting inactive in the tree is construed as bound cathexis – potential energy available for choosing to jump (jumping intentionally) but not being used. Jumping is construed as free cathexis which the monkey does through an act of will or intentionally. If the monkey should fall off, this represents unbound cathexis where energy is released in such a way that neither sitting nor jumping is possible but some hybrid of both occurs. The monkey hasn't chosen to jump. His volitional behaviour has been interfered with and his natural mobility hampered. In the same way, people with contaminations (unbound cathexis) lose a sense of choice over their behaviour and thereby lack natural elegance or congruence. For example, washing hands may be a highly functional act, but when it is done from a contamination spilling over from bound beliefs, now unbound, that the hands are evil, even functional hand washing can have a driven quality.

The patient in psychotherapy can learn to control their free energy to a considerable extent, so that they can shift their 'sense of self' from one ego state to another by an act of will: from Parental anger to attend to Adult business, or from a Child's sulk to give Adult nurturing to a sick spouse or offspring. At first they may rely heavily on external stimuli to bolster such shifts, but gradually, they learn more and more to effect them through acts of autonomous volition. The person also learns to appraise his own authenticity: 'is it really his real Self who is being Parentally tender, Adultly candid, or freely imaginative, or are these spurious acts of compliance, rebellion, or hypocrisy?' (Berne, 1966: 307).

Berne saw the 'moving sense of self' as an important psychological principle in maintaining the script and he focuses on the importance of awareness of what other ego states are doing. Thus it is 'for the Adult to remember and to take full responsibility for the actions of all the real Selves' (Berne, 1972: 254).

In the home situation, Jane may frequently criticise John for not doing his share of the housework. But the way in which she does this is to replay a highly punitive introjected Parent dating from her own childhood. When John objects to her humiliating tone of voice, Jane suddenly shifts to a Child ego state and feels very hurt that John is angry with her. John is then puzzled because the punitive harridan who berated him has so quickly has been replaced by a sensitive 4 year old deeply distressed at his anger. Jane now experiences her Child as her real self. She has 'forgotten' or disassociated from her former real self in her Parent ego state. She is not aware that she or her behaviour is changing from moment to moment because her feeling 'this is really me' has stayed the same throughout. 'Thus when we say that "she" moved from one ego state to another, we mean her free cathexis did, carrying with it a continuous sense of real Self' (Berne, 1972: 152)

To Jane herself, she seems the same consistent person all along but to someone else it may appear that there are several people or subselves in existence from moment to moment. When this happens the Adult may not know the behaviours which are causing the problems because the Adult may have been out of commission at the time, flooded by unbound cathexis from the other ego states. In the clinical situation, the transactional analyst encourages awareness and control of the moving self and utilises this ability in treatment of the client. Inviting a client whose energies are becoming more and more invested in the sulking racket of their Child ego state to 'cathect Adult' is inviting them to experience their self in an Adult ego state. Similarly, in order to work with parental introjects in, for example, a Parent interview, inviting the client to 'become your father' is asking them to experience their sense of self in a Parent ego state. Reparenting and rechilding call upon the client's ability to experience the self in a Child ego state.

In rechilding (Clarkson and Fish, 1988), a person uses some of their free cathexis to enter a specific Child ego state. While in this ego state, unbound energy, formerly bound or fixated around the specific issue being dealt with, is released and worked with in the situation. For example, as a child, Sheila repressed her natural curiosity about her body in response to her parents' messages that such interest was sinful and dirty. In the 'regression' part of the rechilding process, she uses her free cathexis to regress to the age at which she felt her decision to repress her curiosity was made. Initially, she experiences some of the shame she had felt as a child (i.e. she experiences this as her 'real self'). But as she continues to explore her body (with the encouragement of new 'parents' and 'siblings') her natural childish curiosity becomes unbound and with delight and excitement she explores every nook and cranny of her body, experiencing her 'real self' in a Child ego state that previously only existed as a possibility. Towards the end of the 'regression' she is requested to recathect her Adult which she does by her own free cathexis. This leaves a new Child ego state containing healthy bound energy which she can now cathect at will, should she need to, in order to experience her natural curiosity. We believe it is possible to cathect a healthy Child ego state whilst the Adult retains the executive; an important resource when a person is having difficulty remaining stable under stress.

The inherent paradox that 'the Patient' can control his 'Self' is so far no more resolvable in transactional terms than in philosophical or existential ones. What transactional analysis offers is a method for exploiting this paradox to increase autonomy and authenticity. The 'Self' and 'free energy' are left open-ended as an experience and as a construct, respectively, whose ultimate reduction and definition belong outside the province of psychiatry. This is an invitation to philosophers, theologians, poets, and creative and interpretive artists of all kinds to participate with psychotherapists in giving meaning to ultimate values.

(Berne, 1966: 307)

THE INTERPERSONALLY DEVELOPED SELF

Masterson conceived of the self as an intrapsychic entity with a separate development and its own capacities. 'In keeping with ego psychology and object relations theory, the term "real self" is used ... not as the total self but in the intrapsychic sense of the sum of self and object representations with their related affects' (Masterson, 1985: 21).

In the last section we dealt with the sense of self and the moving self; a self which exists by its own experience of, and relation to, differing ego states. But what of these differing ego states and what is their relation to the self? What part do they play in the development of our self-identity or self-awareness?

In terms of ego, Jung writes:

The ego stands to the self as the moved to the mover, or as object to subject, because the determining factors which radiate out from the self surround the ego on all sides and are therefore supraordinate to it. The self, like the unconscious, is an a priori existent out of which the ego evolves.

(Jung, 1969: 259)

Neumann (1954) introduces the term 'ego–self axis' to suggest the implied mutuality between self and ego. It may be along this axis that the interpersonally developed self, the self in relation to others, and the self in relation to resultant ego states belongs. So when does the self begin?

We suggest that the sense of self is already in existence at birth (and before) and is active as an entity within the environment which it may include as part of its self (i.e. to the baby, the mother is experienced as part of the self). This concurs with Fordham (1957b) who postulates that some time after conception and while still *in utero*, we are dealing with an original, mainly undifferentiated self composed mainly of archetypal potential. As interaction with the environment takes place, beginning with intra-uterine life and onwards, the original self progressively deintegrates, that is to say, the archetypes become differentiated from the undifferentiated whole and enable the self to experience objects as not-self. For instance, in connection with the mother archetype, the deintegrations are of predispositions to experience, in feeling terms, parts of the mother in the first place as nipple, skin, warmth, teeth, eyes, etc., and then later the mother herself as a whole person. These experiences are then reintegrated as part of the primary self integrate's rhythmic cycle of deintegration and reintegration.

The third-order structural diagram of transactional analysis provides us with an excellent model wherein which to place this deintegration and reintegration process (even though we may exclude reference to archetypes at this stage in developing the theory). The diagram shows (see Figure 8.5) not only the reintegration of objects and part-objects (or persons and part-persons) but the incorporation of the qualities of the relationship itself – in other words, the internalised object relation. If we postulate the self at birth as contained within C_1 (the somatic Child), the newborn baby may initially experience the nipple, for example, as part of her Self (P_o, A_o and C_o representing an as yet undifferentitated self), but through the process of deintegration and reintegration over time is able to differentiate self from object or part-object. We would suggest that this process may be modelled as the primitive differentiations of P_o (the nipple or part-object), A_o (the differentiating process) and C_o (the organismic experience of self). Though now differentiated, self-experience, part-object, process *and* relationship (between P_o and C_o) are now part of an ego state in C_1 and may be cathected, restimulated, projected or 'rubberbanded' back to in certain circumstances. If this process of differentiation does not occur (due perhaps to a deficit of enough healthy transactions – strokes – to allow for differentiation), such a state may give rise to such conditions as autism and schizophrenia in children and later problems of the borderline personality, depression and separation anxiety in adults. If self and 'object' are not differentiated, the sense of self is seriously distorted (James, 1981).

Thus, the early transactions between mother and child enable the self to be differentiated at the same time as being internalised. Here we agree with Pine that the developmental formulations regarding progressive differentiation of self from other and the varying affective tones of the experience also stem ultimately from an object relations view – *Self and other developing in counterpoint* (Pine, 1985).

Fairbairn (1952) supports this view maintaining that the baby is a whole psychic self from the beginning; a whole dynamic being with ego potential, and that the mother, who is a whole ego, enables the baby to perceive his or her own whole ego through the relationship. If this relationship is badly lacking, psychotherapy may repair this lack. Contrary to Klein, Fairbairn saw the baby as internalising a bad mother only if she is *actually* not good enough. Reality is more important than fantasy in shaping lives. Mothers are usually not wholly bad, so the baby splits his or her internalisation into a 'good mother' and a 'bad mother' which in its later manifestations we may in transactional-analysis terms refer to as the Fairy Godmother/Wicked Witch split in P_1 or a critical/nurturing split in P_2 according to the stage of development reached at the time of incorporation.

It is the authors' suggestion that this process is a continuing one, that the sense of self is perpetually affected by interpersonal transactions and that the differentiation that takes place (or is reinforced by the transaction) involves also an incorporation of that transaction. For example, an infant, now at a later stage of development (say 3 years) on being punished by the mother for 'interfering' with other children at play, feels angry in response to this restriction but is now punished by the mother by being isolated from the group.

Here we are dealing with the experience of self in C_2 (see Figure 8.5) and suggest that the internal manifestations of the external transactions (the object–relation incorporation) may now be modelled as: P_1 – Don't be close, don't show anger (projective identification with the punishing mother); A_1 – I am bad to be

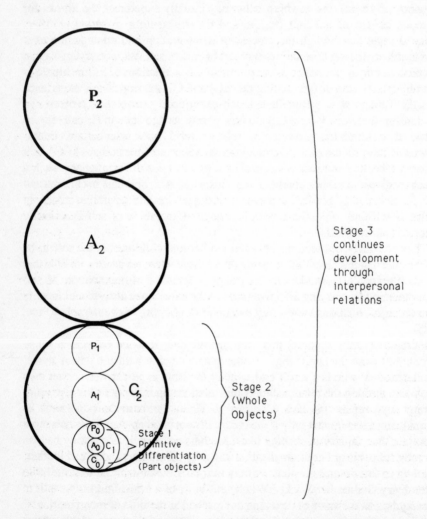

Figure 8.5 The interpersonally developed self: the incorporation of object relations into internal structure

close, to be angry, therefore I will not be close or be angry (the decisional process of how to be a good self); C_1 – I want to be close, to be angry. I feel punished (the repressed needs and feelings). Thus, in later life, it is probable that this person on getting close to another may experience their self as 'bad' as the internalised transactions are rerun and the relationship with the mother is replayed either internally or externally by the projection of that same relationship onto another. Conversely, the relationship may be replayed from the other side, as the person experiences his or her self as punishing while projecting his or her punished 'bad' self onto another.

In the psychotherapeutic situation, structural analysis of ego states is used to bring into awareness the internalised object relations that gave rise to particular senses of self at various stages of development. Henry said he was ready to leave psychotherapy because he could feel himself as having a duration in time even if his moods or ego states changed. He felt his self as having continuity and an identity over time. Further to structural analysis which helped to illuminate this developing self over time, he had been able to replay some of the internalised object relations with the therapist to a reparative and healing end. In other words, his sense of self (often negative) in relation to his mother was projected into the therapist/client relationship and reworked. He now both understood his self in relation to the past and could trace his self-development through to his present, more positive sense of self through a new incorporation of a healthy object and object relationship.

It may be that the healthy interpersonally developed (and still developing) self will manifest in the integrated Adult ego state which has an individually personal and historical sense of self enduring over time – from past to present and on into the future. This, we believe, concerns, too, the potential inclusion in the here and now of healthy senses of self previously developed and incorporated into the introjected Parent ego states and the archaic Child ego states and the inclusion of a 'Conceivable Self' which we write more of in the last section of this chapter.

TRUE SELF AND FALSE SELF

There is also the sense of self where people experience a split between 'who they *really* are' and the selves which they have constructed as a way of surviving or getting approval or reinforcement from their early environments. Much of psychotherapy is concerned with people discovering that they have identified with a self that is not truly him/herself but an adaptation.

Frequently, particularly towards the end of psychotherapy, people discover that they can no longer identify with the 'self' they once were. This shift in the sense of what is 'my true self' can be quite dramatic or gradual over time. It is often accompanied by some change in body sense, a change in habitual 'postures' or a change in their relationships with others. There is often a marked physiological change. For example, a person's circulation can improve, somatic symptoms may disappear, clothes may no longer fit, facial appearance and physical build may change.

These adaptations can be seen as 'decisions' within the Child ego state where the natural, spontaneous child thwarted of its needs being met appropriately experiences the necessity of developing another identity which is more likely to be responded to. A child deprived of love and attention when it cries may decide that quiet passivity will get more attention even if it occurs only sporadically or at the whim of the parent. Similarly, a child has to decide that it has to grow up quickly and look after the parent if it is to get any nurturing itself, thus ignoring the self that needs nurturing, developing instead a 'false' self that later in life may appear caring and highly attuned to the needs of others at the expense of its own needs.

In psychotherapy there is often a turning point (metanoia) or existential crisis which evolves as the client becomes increasingly in touch with the needs and wants repressed in childhood in order to create another identity that would survive better in his or her particular family environment. Gradually awareness and experience of these needs leads to a conflict between the true self and the false self, a stuck point, an impasse. The client's natural Child energy is directed towards growth and change of the status quo; the adapted Child energy towards maintaining it or, more likely, towards reaffirming dominance. This is not surprising as the Adapted Child has been the assumed identity that has ostensibly ensured the child's survival so far. Giving up what seems the key to survival often seems understandably frightening and threatening to many clients. (It is for this reason that not only attention, but also recognition and gratitude needs to be shown in the course of psychotherapy to the Child that, in his or her wisdom, created another self in order to survive.)

This stuck point is recognised in TA by the concept of a Type III impasse. While Type I and Type II impasses involve conflict between the self and an internalised other (the Parent introjected at later and earlier stages of development, respectively), the Type III involves conflict between the two 'selves'. Goulding and Goulding (1979) use the functional model of ego states to conceptualise the impasse as the Free Child energised enough to come into conflict with the Adapted Child. Mellor (1980) conceptualises the conflict as between P_0 and C_0 in the third-order structural diagram giving focus to the early, preverbal timing of the adaptation. Clarkson (1989) views this conflict within the framework of the second order structural model as between C_1 and A_1 giving emphasis to C_1 as the biologically and temperamentally earliest self and the A_1 as the self constructed in terms of adaptations to the early environment (see Figure 8.6). Jani provides an example of such adaptation. She is one of two sets of twins. Her twin sister is retarded, the other twins both handicapped. Her mother is diagnosed 'manic depressive', while her father is described as 'slow'. Thus she grew up with a sense of 'I'm OK – You're not OK' shadowed by a belief that she was bad because her OKness caused others problems. Her mother accused her of draining all the nourishment from the family as if she were to

(1) The Gouldings
(1979/82:15)

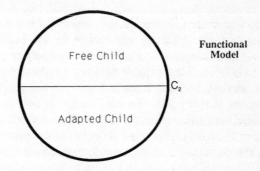

Functional Model

(2) From Ken Mellor
(T A J, July 1980:216)

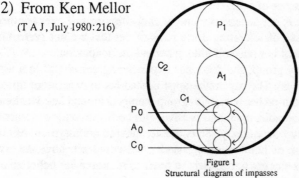

Structural Model

Figure 1
Structural diagram of impasses

(3) Petrūska Clarkson

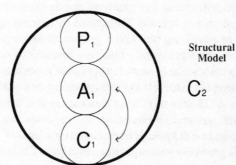

Structural Model

C_2

Figure 8.6 The split self: good and bad splits, true and false self, Type III impasse

blame for their difficulties. Jani made a decision that she would take care of them all and in her grandiose way, believed that she could fix their problems. She felt that she was there as an object for their pleasure and to heal them. In this way, she began to develop a false self as pleasure giver and healer within the family. Her true self was neither seen nor understood.

In psychotherapy, Jani described herself like a Hollywood film set. The outside that is seen is creative and wonderful but it is paper thin, there is no backing or depth. What she was stroked for was being happy, capable, perfect, dynamic, and energetic. So much so that this became part of her self-image. She came to believe, 'I am capable of doing anything, I am amazing, I am able to attract anyone because I am a happy, dynamic person.' However, she is discovering that her life, like the film set, is only an illuson of perfection. In particular, her current relationship is far from perfect, in fact it is all that she does not want. She feels embarrassed about this as it counters her experience of always being able to manage her life to perfection. She is experiencing herself as being 'not OK' in not being able to live up to her grandiose false self. – and this is proving to be very healing for her as she is learning humility, compassion and true empathy with others through this experience. Over time, she is integrating these aspects into her sense of self.

The resolution here is not necessarily one of choosing one self over another, but rather of integration, of tolerating those parts of her that are not perfect or manageable – the parts of her real self hidden behind the adaptation.

In her psychotherapy group, she describes experiencing herself 'as in a web tied in by all the spindles'. The psychotherapist invited her to experience this in group. She lay spread out on her back with group members around her. Her head was back. She felt vulnerable, open and passive. Her body hurt and in moments she felt numb. She saw how quickly she converted pain to nothingness. At one point she caressed one of her 'abusers'' hands, and could see how she was repeating a pattern of seducing her abusers in order to reinforce her belief about her self as the pleasure-giving healer.

She stayed feeling her passivity and helplessness in order to integrate this polarity as part of her self. This ended by her getting up, which she did without fighting or struggling but with a gentleness in her power that indicated that she knew what she wanted and could give instructions accordingly. She saw this as a very important piece of work for her in her process of integration. Sometimes she experienced her false self as more appealing and efficient ('Why should I change when I was OK like this?') but then moves into the experiencing of her true self as deeper and self-empowering. By experiencing both, she is beginning to integrate and work towards resolution. Her adapted Child functioning of 'I am for others' is gradually encompassing her natural Child functioning of 'I am self and complete with my feelings.'

In making this change she is experiencing hunger, pain and the need for sleep and is thus experiencing her basic somatic needs. At times she feels irritated by having to feel these and more and more, through them, she is experiencing being real. When she feels real, she is in touch with her drive and aspiration. Another client, at a time of deep despair, recounted the following dream to his psychotherapist:

> I am walking down a corridor at what seems to be a conference. The corridor is long and full of people walking both ways. I keep meeting people I know and am greeted warmly. Some of these friends are in rooms off the side of the corridor. They wave and smile at me as I continue walking. Now a woman comes out of one of the rooms and walks with me. She is a stranger to me but seems to know me. She says she is my 'surveyor' and moves off into the crowd. This happens with two or three other women none of whom I know. They each tell me they are my 'surveyor' and move away.
>
> I am now outside the building in a yard, preparing to leave. I put my bag on the ground in order to put on my jacket. I find it difficult to put on – it doesn't seem to fit and the arms are tangled. Another woman comes up and offers to help by untangling and holding the jacket for me. I get it half on but it still feels odd. I take it off, turn it inside out and put it on again. Now the jacket fits and I say, 'This is the right way round.'

This dream was very significant to the client. After dreaming it he no longer felt despairing but 'lighter' and the pain in his back of several days was much alleviated. He gave the following explanation:

> I had the dream following several days of feeling despairing and frightened having recognised that I presented a false self to the world. I was terrified to think, if I am not my adapation, who am I? I felt as if I was disintegrating, as if my Self was to be anhiliated and would explode into pieces in the void.
>
> The dream begins with lots of friends who know me as I am. I feel warm and safe being greeted by them. It would be easy for me to go on walking along this corridor just as I am. However, I am confronted by several 'unknown' women in the dream who claim to be my 'surveyor'. This is a link with the joke I once made about my psychotherapist being my 'site manager' following her analogy of psychotherapy to a building operation. These women are the different faces of my 'unknown' psychotherapist onto whom I project/reflect/deflect parts of myself.
>
> In psychotherapy, we had used the analogy of a 'coat' to describe my very early adaptation (which later became 'the nice guy'). I was terrified that if I took off this coat there would be nothing there. I have 'always' been like this – how can I exist if I don't wear this coat?
>
> The jacket in the dream assured me that I do not have to find other 'coats' outside myself. I do not have to totally discard the 'coat' (disintegrate). The qualities of my true self are already there in the lining! Thus my existential task is to turn the 'coat' around, to turn my self inside out. Though this task may not be so easy as in the dream, I feel reassured by the symbolism – I find my true self within myself.
>
> It is my psychotherapist who assists with the jacket once I am outside the

comfort and familiarity of the corridor (my life in a false self). Significantly, though she assists me and helps in the untangling of the coat, the dream ends with me discovering that the jacket fits inside-out *by my own efforts*.

While finding the true self by their 'own efforts', many clients have reported the value of a prototype image of their true self which might be named the 'conceivable self'. This image provides a vision of the possible and can be achieved over time by inviting clients to experience themselves 'as if' they were their 'conceivable self', including the associated kinaesthetic feelings. The more senses involved, the clearer their 'conceivable self' becomes and the more possible to actualise. Making change in a particular direction is made easier by prior conceptualisation.

Looking for models is one way in which a conceivable self can be created. A black person, training as a psychotherapist, had no significant cultural models for professional success. It was important for him to learn about the scientific and humanitarian achievements of other black people. He was particularly excited to find that Charles Drew, a black doctor, discovered the method of storing blood which saved thousands of lives during World War II.

There may be a female client who has never experimented with behaviour such as reading technical books for pleasure, as in her early world there were no examples of women participating in such an activity. Such a client may need to be encouraged into reading for pleasure in the psychotherapy session so that it becomes conceivable for her in terms of her physiology, her motivation and her behavioural repertoire.

One client reported that it was important for her to know that her psychotherapist had an image of a conceivable self for her. She was then able to confirm this for herself in her own kinaesthetic experience by recognising that she too could develop such an image:

I could begin to feel myself being different in previously painful situations. For example, I had found it very difficult to present my knowledge to my peers. I would suffer badly and actually present as not as competent as I am. My psychotherapist mentioned a conceivable self who might, in the same circumstances, be not only knowlegeable and relaxed, but also confident and competent; moreover that this would be exciting and interesting for myself and other people. I can only describe this experience for myself as physiological knowledge – I knew in my body that somewhere in me, I could be like that. I then began to practise with that image whenever I was presenting in a professional capacity with my peers. And I began to enjoy and relax.

Techniques such as visualisation can be used very effectively in actualising the potential of the conceivable self. Thus where causality was the major explanatory principle in script formation (the deterministic truth), teleology becomes the major explanatory principle for script transformation.

In many cases, this does not really concern new potentials, but more the removal of limitations of the original potential. People refer to automatic beliefs and behaviours as being 'second nature'. Implicit in this is the idea of there being a 'first nature' from which they have become alienated or estranged. Thus psychotherapy can be seen in many ways as a process of helping people back to their first natures – the original, spontaneous, creative, and natural Child self.

Often clients make adaptations which may even be temperamentally alien to them. Marianna, for example, who used to think of herself as being extroverted, sociable, hard-driving and fast, is discovering in therapy that she basically is slower, calmer and much more introverted than the self she has developed in response to the attributions of others. As she accepts this very different experience and understanding of her self, her personality becomes more elegant, unified and congruent – even though some of her friends complain that she is no longer the 'life and soul' of their parties.

In psychotherapy we discover over and over again that as the person gets closer and closer to their true, conceivable or 'first nature' self, which always involves a sense of somatic and organismic integrity, they connect more profoundly with an inner healing, and actualising drive. In this way, they discover *Physis* working within themselves at the most basic levels. At the same time, there is an accompanying, growing awareness and appreciation of universal meanings, a striving towards connectedness with spiritual, religious or transcendental values. Kant is one of the philosophers who differentiates this noumenal self; a concept further examined in the next section which considers the 'core Self' as the organising principle of *Physis*.

THE SELF AS ORGANISING PRINCIPLE OF *PHYSIS*

In *What Do You Say After You Say Hello?* (1972) Berne includes a script-matrix diagram showing an arrow rising through each of the three types of ego state as explained in Chapter 1. He calls this the aspiration arrow. Its placement implies the transcendence of scripting due, we suggest, to the aspiration arrow being the manifestation of *Physis*, 'the force of nature, which eternally strives to make things grow and to make growing things more perfect' (Berne, 1981/1969: 89).

Intrinsic to this conceptualisation is the notion of a healthy 'inner core' which James and Savary (1977) believe accounts for the changes in ego state which people self-induce. Our diagram (Figure 8.7) combines the aspiration arrow and the inner core both extending through Parent, Adult and Child ego states to represent the inner core. That is, a universal Self, independent of the three ego states (yet influencing the flow of cathexis in each) which is fuelled by *Physis*, the Self's natural aspiration for growth and development towards health, transcendent of ego states.

The healthy inner core is a concept shared by many writers and teachers whether spiritual, philosophical or psychological. Childs-Gowell and Kinnaman (1978), adapting the bioenergetic therapist Lowen's (1969) layered view of the

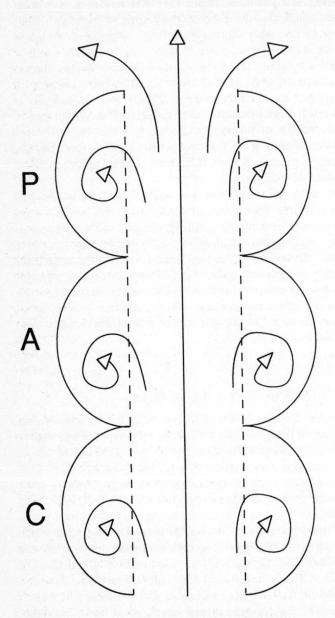

Figure 8.7　The self as organising principle of *Physis*

Source:　Berne, 1972: 128 and James and Savary, 1977: 33 combined
Note:　Ego states in the individual self being energised by inner core energy with the addition of the arrow of aspiration indicating the upward direction of *Physis*

personality, describe the centre of all the layers, the inner core, as potentially healthy, energetic and joyous.

In the interpersonal field of client and psychotherapist, where we know that psychotherapist expectation must interact with client progress, it makes an enormous difference to the outcome of psychotherapy whether this core is seen as healthy, homeostatic or primarily destructive. Studies have even suggested that experimentor expectation influences the maze-learning ability of rats. The speed of learning the maze was respectively slower for rats described as 'coming from a stupid strain' than for rats described as coming from a 'superior intelligence strain' despite the fact that there were rats from the same strain. There is research evidence that schoolchildren and students respond differentially to their teachers' unvoiced expectations of them (Rosenthal and Jacobson, 1968). When teachers believed children were unintelligent and could not learn, the children responded with lowered performance, no matter what their original gifts. In transactional analysis, the psychotherapist's expectation is that the person can become healthy, whole and actualising: that their inner core aspires in this direction.

James and Savary stress the importance of the inner core because it operates at the deepest personal levels with the urges to live, to love and be free. They see this inner core as equivalent to 'the universal Self' which 'continually searches for meanings that will help deal with the pressures that arise from external sources, or from internal ego states' (James and Savary, 1977: 29). They see the new Self developing 'because of changes made in the ego states through the power that can be released from the Inner Core' (ibid: 24). Their notion of the real Self thus appears to be an epiphenomenon or concomitant effect of ego-state changes. They appear to be saying that the Self will develop as the ego states change in psychotherapy and that this is motivated by the power within each human being which is both uniquely individual and universal.

The inner core provides energy for change within each ego state. As they change, a new self emerges which is connected at the same time with the individual's innermost centre and with the transpersonal or transcendent.

The inner core of the self in the Parent ego state manifests as the collective unconscious – the archetypal distillations of previous generations which, according to Jung, encapsulate the potentialities for creative meaning throughout all cultures and times.

The inner core in the Child ego state manifests as the biologically rooted needs (the organismic quest) for meaning and purpose in existence. The inner core of the Self in the Adult ego state manifests as similar to that as described by Duval and Wicklund (1972) as being unnameable and unspecifiable, 'when it relates to the internal or external world, it is the content of the relation and itself the process of relating' (Rowan, 1988: 210). For us this means relating in the here-and-now and connects with the phenomenologically empty Adult ego state described in the section on 'multiplicity'. In this way the ego becomes less and less important as the task of 'soul-making' (Hillman, 1975: ix) progresses.

If a person is alienated from this power source in the inner core in each or any of the three types of ego state or depleted in energy, the treatment focus would most likely be enhancement or recovery of their connection with a spiritual dimension both inside and outside of themselves. Ferrucci (1982), representing Assagioli, writes (along similar lines to James and Savary) that in psychosynthesis the Self is seen as the most elementary and distinctive part of our being – in other words, its core. Distinct from elements of the personality, it can act as a unifying centre, directing these elements and bringing them into the unity of an organic wholeness. Seen in this perspective, the Self not only differentiates us from other human beings, but it also differentiates us from our own ever-changing contents of consciousness. According to psychosynthesis, the Self can be defined as the only part of us which remains forever the same. Body sensations change, feelings fade, thoughts flow by, but someone remains to experience this flow. This 'someone' is the experiencer, the core Self. Thus the Self is consciousness in its essential state, undiluted, chemically pure. It is a state of psychological nudity in which we have taken off all our psychological clothes.

Jean Hardy further differentiates the Self from the 'I' (see Figure 8.8) again implying a transcendence of ego states or the personality. The 'I' is seen as the centre of the body, mind, and feelings, which can be assumed to make up the field of consciousness. The 'I' can be at different points in its relation to the self. Assagioli, in a discussion meeting, said that the self at the personality level:

is a reflection of the Higher Self or the Transpersonal Self and it reflects, however palely, the same qualities as its source. If you look at the reflection of the sun on a mirror, or on water, you see the light and quality of the sun, infinitesimal, but still the quality of the sun. So that explains why even at the personality's level the self is stable, sure and indestructible.

(Hardy, 1989: 30)

Implicit in all these various concepts of the core Self, the higher Self, or the transcendent Self – concepts which encompass both depth and upward direction – is the focus of the person's core Self seeking realisation. Jung (1986) uses two concepts of the Self in focusing on this aspect: the Self as archetype and the Self as mover of the ego. The latter is assumed to be *a priori* existent, a Self that is a central ordering system. This point was particularly developed by Fordham (1947) who separates the ego from the Self and reintegrates it as an operating centre of self-consciousness.

Even this formulation implies a 'ghost in the machine', a Self which can construct a false Self for survival or approval. This Self, we suggest, is seen as the organising principle of *Physis* in its quest to 'make things grow and to make growing things more perfect' (Berne, 1981: 89).

James and Savary (1977) emphasise the depth and upward direction of the Self when they write:

The deepest part of the self is traditionally described by words such as heart, soul, spirit, spiritual core, essence, substance, and so forth. Some simply add an adjective to the word 'self' and describe this inner essence as the 'real self', the 'undivided self', the 'integrated self', the 'transpersonal self', or the 'fully-human self'.

(James and Savary, 1977: 3)

The authors would suggest another description which we think is encapsulated in the combined diagrams of Berne and James and Savary (Figure 8.7): that of the 'aspirational core Self'. In this sense the Self is our life's goal and that equals the soul.

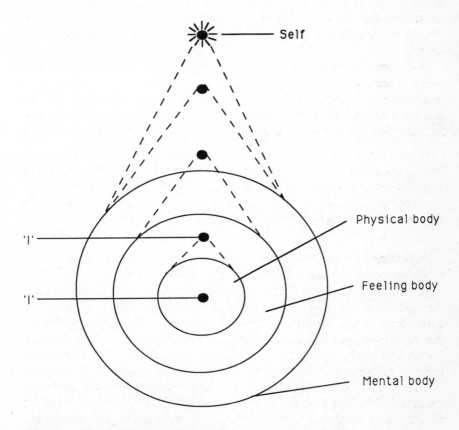

Figure 8.8 Higher self and personality

Source: From *A Psychology with a Soul: Psychosynthesis in Evolutionary Context* (Hardy, 1989: 30). © Jean Hardy, 1987

(1) Wholeness:

The body-awareness 'skin' of the whole Self.

(2) A Multiplicity of Selves:

The Self in structural and functional terms (states and roles).

(3) The Moving Self - Berne's phenomenology:

The Sense of Self in different ego states.

(4) The Interpersonally Developed Self:

The development of Self through the formation of ego states (internalised object-relations).

(5) True Self and False Self (Type 3 impasse):

(a)   (b)   (c)

Child ego states - the early splitting of the Self.

(6) The Self as Organising Principle of Physis:

The Self transcendent of ego states incorporating the aspiration arrow showing the thrust of Physis toward growth.

Figure 8.9 **The psychology of the self in transactional analysis – a diagrammatic summary**

CONCLUSION

In this chapter various questions have been raised and several possible explanations offered of what is meant by the 'self'. These possibilities have been explored under six headings with reference to transactional analysis and other approaches to psychology and psychotherapy in an attempt to weave a very complex, often confusing, sometimes contradictory mass of opinion into a framework that can draw the threads together in some meaningful way. Figure 8.9 is a diagrammatic summary for ease of reference.

What this offers you as readers is the challenge to take up these threads and continue weaving. The discussion presented here is by no means all-inclusive. Hopefully, we will one day end up with a tapestry that shows us how our various views and descriptions of the 'self' (like those of ants describing different parts of an elephant) make sense in relation to each other and create a whole picture.

As Berne pointed out, we will need the participation of others outside the field of psychotherapy to help us in this endeavour.

Chapter 9

Transactional analysis and group therapy

'That's right!' said the Tiger-lily. 'The daisies are worst of all. When one speaks, they all begin together, and it's enough to make one wither to hear the way they go on!'

(Carroll, 1986: 37)

INTRODUCTION

In the literature of group psychotherapy two streams dominate. On the one hand psychotherapies which focus on the group-as-a-whole of which Foulkes is a major representative, and on the other hand psychotherapies which focus on doing psychotherapy with *individuals* in the group. This latter approach is particularly well known through filmed versions of Fritz Perls doing individual 'hot seat' Gestalt therapy with individuals in groups. Although this book has primarily focused on using transactional analysis as an individual psychotherapy, it is also a method frequently used by group psychotherapists whose focus becomes a blend of group and individual. In the *Principles of Group Treatment* (1966), Berne differentiated between four kinds of group psychotherapy: supportive therapy, group analytic therapy, psychoanalytic therapy in a group and transactional analysis. Certainly TA offers a unique method of using a group to work with individuals' scripts.

The analysis of transactions, games and ego-state therapy usually conducted between the individual client and the psychotherapist, can be greatly aided, focused and enhanced by utilising the raw enacted relationships between the members of the group (as well as between members and psychotherapist). In the same way as the individual externalises his or her intrapsychic object relations in the client/psychotherapist dyad, each member externalises intrapsychic object relations in the matrix of other members of the group. In this way the live material of their interactions with each other can be directly used, interpreted, explained and confronted psychotherapeutically. This was certainly the fertile ground for most of Berne's popularised work, *Games People Play*. Berne's concept of the group imago's developing stages (1963) offers a framework which helps to understand this re-enactment of the early family and the subsequent corrective experience with its potential for healing.

This chapter compares this idea of group-imago adjustment with the stages of group development as conceptualised by Tuckman (1965) and Lacoursiere (1980). It utilises Berne's diagrams of group dynamics in order to explain the nature of the processes involved at different stages. It also considers some of the most relevant tasks of group leaders at the different stages – be they trainers, organisational consultants or group psychotherapists. Finally, it explores relevant constructive and destructive group-leader behaviours at different stages based on extensive surveys gleaned over more than a decade from hundreds of practitioners and trainees in the fields of group work, organisational consultancy and group psychotherapy. It is not intended to be definitive, but to encourage readers to co-operate in developing this area of transactional analysis theory and practice.

THE GROUP AS A WHOLE

Human beings are born into groups, live in groups and have their being through groups. As leaders of groups – as psychotherapist, trainer or manager – we are dealing with people who have already been shaped and affected by their previous group experiences. It can be very useful to understand this in relation to the process a group goes through as it forms and develops over time. The group psychotherapist in particular functions in this microcosm of human existence where there is the greatest potential for destruction or the greatest potential for healing.

Some of the most important changes in human history (for good or for ill) have come about through individuals combining their forces in groups, whether the group be a lynch-mob or a band of missionaries. Since the human being's first exposure to the human group is in his family (or children's home) this is the matrix for his most long-lasting and profound injuries or permissions. It is by virtue of these facts that the group is probably the most potent vehicle for individual and societal change.

> The need for social contact and the hunger for time-structure might be called the preventive motives for group formation. One purpose of forming, joining and adjusting to groups is to prevent biologic, psychological and also moral deterioration. Few people are able to 'recharge their own batteries', lift themselves up by their own psychological bootstraps, and keep their own morals trimmed without outside assistance.
>
> (Berne, 1963: 217)

Eric Berne's contribution to group psychotherapy was the development of the system of transactional analysis as a means for individual change in the group, but he was also interested in the theory of group process and the phenomenon of the group as a whole which Foulkes (1951) and others had also studied. He stressed that each group had its own distinctive culture, including the group etiquette, technical culture and the group character. These whole group descriptive categories correspond to Parent, Adult and Child aspects of the individual, therefore the whole group or whole organisation can be diagrammed as PAC, as Jongeward (1973) has already shown (see Figure 9.1). This distinctive personality configuration of the group as a whole is more than the totality of individual attributes. Any experienced group therapist can testify to the fact that different groups seem to have different personalites which send different shared psychological messages to the therapist. The group-as-a-whole forms a unique and distinctive entity which endures over time, goes through predictable stages of development or maturation, as will be shown. Groups can be more or less 'ailing' or healthy, energetic, thoughtful, worried or guilty. For example, in a group of mothers the psychotherapist is often subjected to a psychological-level message 'be guilty like us' whenever she plans to break for a holiday. (At a social level their questions are only concerned with the dates and number of missed sessions.)

A group can be defined as a collection of individuals who are in interaction with each other for an *apparently* common purpose. The notion of apparently common purpose refers to the fact that, although there may be a commonly agreed social-level definition of the task of a group, there may be very many conflicting, confluent or complementary ulterior-level agendas at the psychological level of the group. The particular Gestalt (whole) of all the separate members' psychological-level messages forms the collective psychological group entity. A *public structure* (Berne, 1963: 327) of any group may be identified and consensually agreed. The collective private structure of the whole group is much more complex and developmentally labile. Badly managed critical periods in a group's life may affect its future functioning just as certainly as ineffective parenting will affect an individual's subsequent social and psychological development. Later this will be explored in more detail.

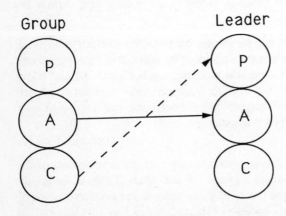

Figure 9.1 Social-level and psychological-level communication

Although many authors have considered the stages, phases or cycles in the formation of a well-functioning group, most emphasise that these stages must emphatically not be seen as discrete or distinctly separate.

Most groups and the individuals in them can be considered as going through a sequence of developmental stages during the group history or life cycle. These stages – like most psychological and social processes – blend into each other to some extent so that where one divides one stage from the others, and how many divisions are made, depends partly on one's purposes, on how one views the data and so on.

(Lacoursiere, 1980: 27)

In a group such as a training group or a task group brought together for a specific purpose with a membership which remains constant from its inception to its termination, the separate phases are, however, often quite recognisable.

Such predictable patterns in a maturing group can be perceived by a trained observer over the course of a 3-year training or over the duration of an hour-and-a-half committee meeting. Knowledge of these phases is therefore relevant and potentially useful to any person who is either a member or a leader of any group of individuals for almost any conceivable purpose, for example, from bringing up children to conducting an anti-nuclear demonstration, to running a self-help group.

In the closed psychotherapy group, the predictable stages can also be observed when the membership of the group remains reasonably stable and does not undergo major changes. However, if several new individuals are introduced into a group, the group will need to regress to earlier and less developed levels of functioning and the group leader or group therapist may need to help the group recycle the different phases again. This is not dissimilar to the process involved in combining two families into one 'stepfamily' which almost invariably necessitates a reworking of identity, conflict management, rules and values, before they can come to a well-functioning state of effectiveness and interaction.

A theoretical understanding of these stages can help the group psychotherapist conceptualise occasionally baffling group dynamic phenomena, and aid discriminating selection of techniques and interventions. He or she can also find support in drawing on the experiences of pioneers in the field who faced similar moments of anxiety, despair, pleasure or pain. Linking these stages to the concept of the 'group imago' can help to make sense of how the group's experience connects with that of the individual.

GROUP IMAGO

Berne defines group imago as 'any mental picture, conscious, preconscious or unconscious, of what a group is or should be like' (Berne, 1963: 321). The group imago exists in what Berne called the private structure of the group which is based on each individual's personal needs, experience, wishes and emotions.

Therefore, it is differently perceived by different members at different phases of the group. Imago adjustment is the process manifested in the observable stages in a group.

THE FIRST STAGE OF GROUP DEVELOPMENT

The provisional group imago (see Figure 9.2)

It should be clear now that each member first enters the group equipped with: (1) a biologic need for stimulation; (2) a psychological need for time-structuring; (3) a social need for intimacy; (4) a nostalgic need for patterning transactions; and (5) a provisional set of expectations based on past experience. His task is then to adjust these needs and expectations to the reality that confronts him.

(Berne, 1963: 221)

Before entering the group or before the group is activated, individuals form their own unique individual group imago (preconscious expectation) of what it is likely to be like, based on their fantasies and previous experiences with groups, including their families of origin.

The provisional group imago is suitable for structuring time through rituals. Rituals are interactions which we perform in a pre-programmed way, for example a greeting. At this stage individuals are concerned with the nature and boundaries

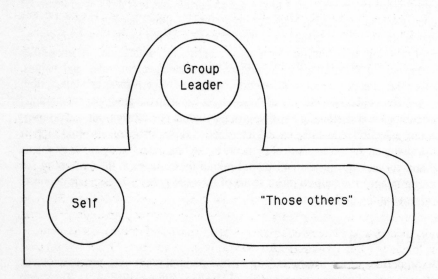

Figure 9.2 Provisional group-imago diagram
Source: Berne, 1966: 155

of the group task, they have fantasies about the ground rules and expectations of limits on behaviour based on past experiences of what is acceptable. According to Berne the primary focus is preoccupation with and dependence on the leader and how he/she stands in relation to the leader. This is the most frequent vector for psychotherapeutic understanding whether it be individual or the group-as-a-whole. This focus is illustrated in the group imago by the placement of the leader in the upper slot.

It is interesting how this placing of the leader corresponds with projection of the individual's image of the parent figure and how the slots as Berne indicates them symbolically represent the projective spaces in which the individuals can project their images of their own grandfathers, sisters, teachers and so forth.

> In a small group, the central transference is on to the monitor but there is also the lateral transference of participants on to one another. This is due to the fact that in a small group participants rapidly get to know one another. There is also a third type, much harder to discern, analyse and interpret: the transference of participants (and the counter-transference of the monitor) on to the small group as an object or entity.
>
> (Anzieu, 1984: 227)

In Tuckman's terminology the first stage, which apparently corresponds to the process of beginning to test the provisional groupings against reality, is that which he calls *forming*.

> Groups initially concern themselves with orientation accomplished primarily through testing. Such testing serves to identify the boundaries of both inter-personal and task behaviors. Coincident with testing in the interpersonal realm is the establishment of dependency relationships with leaders, other group members, or preexisting standards. It may be said that orientation, testing, and dependence constitute the group process of *forming*.
>
> (Tuckman, 1965: 396)

Example of Stewart: Stewart was the only son of a woman who worked in a children's home. His father had left home before Stewart's birth and he was brought up in the home with the other children – one of them and not one of them. His early experience was of being resented by the other children for having a parent, yet feeling that he never got enough from his mother. Before joining the psychotherapy group he knew the name of the female therapist whom he had met at a training course and with whom he had made a good connection. He knew no-one else in the group. In his awareness, his provisional group imago would have looked as in Figure 9.2. However, his scripted self (mostly unconscious) – his 'blend of Child fantasy and Adult expectation' (Berne, 1963: 223) – expected a reproduction of the early scene (see Figure 9.3). He had a history of leaving a group claiming that the therapist did not give him enough attention.

During the forming phase of the group, Stewart's transactions were clearly those of a person who was accustomed to having to get on with everybody. He

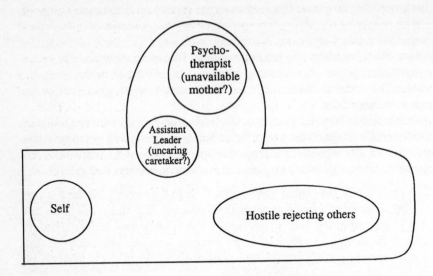

Figure 9.3   The script behind Stewart's provisional imago
Source: Berne, 1966: 155

was careful to make no 'special' demands on the group leader other than carefully to establish the rules. He expressed none of the fears and fantasies about what the group would be like but the other members did. In this way, he kept his behaviour unexceptional and was accepted easily by the group. By the end of the forming stage Stewart's imago was adapted as in Figure 9.6. (p.216)

Leadership tasks

The process by which the provisional group imago is changed, is influenced by member characteristics, but also by leadership tasks and behaviours.

In this stage the leader's most vital task is to deal with the external group process and define the major external and internal boundaries (see Figure 9.4). A physical and psychological external group boundary needs to be established which is secure and stable in order to ensure the survival of the group. Symbolically, the group therapist needs to create a *container* within which energy can be focused on the internal healing processes (safeguarded from external pressures).

There is an absolute necessity for clear contracts between the group members, the group leader, the group members with each other and the group leader with his or her supervisor, co-workers or agency. The external boundary includes the physical space in which the group has its life. The unexpected arrival of the police at a seance is one of Berne's most vivid examples of how pressure on the external boundary of the group can lead to disintegration of the group. In another setting an imposed fire drill may precipitate different relationships from the usual coming to the fore in the group dynamics.

Berne (1963) is describing an actual external boundary. However, it is important to remember that this boundary will have psychological implications for members. According to Gurowitz, the external boundary is largely a function of the internal boundary which he equates with the leader's potency. Therefore, a leadership task would be to create a strong and clear internal boundary which the group experiences as a barrier warding off external intrusions. 'In groups with a weak IB, the EB is seen as a fence confining members in an unsafe space' (Gurowitz, 1975: 184). One of the important factors in defining the major internal boundary is the psychological state of the leader or group psychotherapist.

Other essential tasks of the leader at this point are to clarify who's in and who's out and who's in charge. These considerations also define and safeguard the external boundary. Almost any group which meets regularly will, with seemingly relentless energy, focus on absent members until all are properly accounted for. Having established that George is in Switzerland, May has taken her husband to hospital, and Peter is late as usual, the group can settle down to its task, whether it is psychotherapy or a committee meeting.

It is equally vital for the group therapist to define the boundary between the leadership region and the membership region, that is which decisions and responsibilities are to be shared and which are the responsibility of the leader alone.

It is important for group therapists and group members to clarify confusions between leadership and power. Often people call a group undemocratic on the false understanding that democracies have no leaders.

Leadership needs to be balanced in such a way as to lead eventually to the empowerment of members. In a similar way to child development, leaders cannot responsibly avoid being leaders if that is the psychological need of the group at its initial phases, just as little as a parent can abdicate all structuring and decision making to an infant without endangering it. The task of the responsible leader at this stage involves, therefore, ensuring the establishment of rules, safety and boundaries. It is necessary to establish dependency before resisting it. The group leader, like a parent, has to have the courage to allow him- or herself to be loved, knowing all the time that the ultimate purpose is to lose this love.

Groups are often very anxious at the beginning of sessions or courses, so much so that experienced group leaders have learned that statements made in the first session will often not have been 'heard' by group members at this stage and may need to be repeated later when people are feeling less anxious and more relaxed. Excessive anxiety in the leader can be very disruptive and needs to be managed (in psychotherapy or supervision) both in terms of his or her archaic personal issues and in terms of concordant countertransference with the group process. The group psychotherapist often embodies the cohesive forces of the group and may have sufficient or excessive investment (through fear of loss of reputation or income) in the continued survival of the group.

The group leader's task is to find an optimal level of anxiety for the group. That is, a level of arousal or investment which is conducive to maximum risk taking and learning and yet not so extreme as to lead to incapacitation, retraumatisation or the reinforcement of a pathological system.

What may appear to be a lack of structure (overlong silences, undiscriminating refusal to explain) may in fact be the imposition of quite a violent covert process (leading to the appearance of psychosis, for example). Some of the casualities of the encounter group and T-group experiences of the sixties were no doubt results of the tyranny of structurelessness. Indeed, Berne defines structure-hunger as one of the basic hungers of the human being (Berne, 1963: 215, 327) and leadership hunger as rooted in the need for the leader to provide structure for the group within which their individuality and creativity can flourish (ibid, 216). In this way, as in many others, the role of group leader has similarities with that of a parent.

One of the most significant boundaries which affects the safety and trust of human beings is that of time. Carelessness around time is frequently reported as

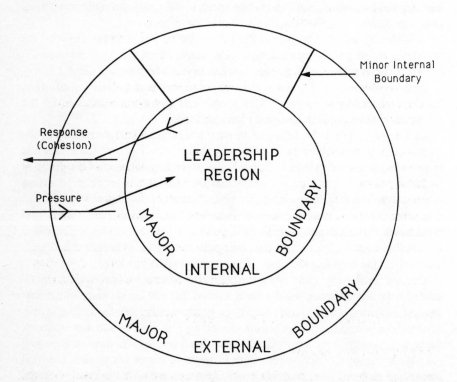

Figure 9.4 **The external group process: group cohesion vs. external disruptive forces**

Source: Berne, 1963: 38

one of the more destructive group-leader behaviours. Many psychotherapists who pay attention to the psychological-level communication of their clients (Langs, 1978; Casement, 1985) corroborate the severe repercussions of confusing time boundaries.

In terms of complementary countertransference, group leaders may need to monitor their tendencies towards overnurturing or overcontrol in the beginning stages of a group session or in the initial stages of forming a psychotherapy group.

On the evidence of feedback collected over several years with hundreds of practitioners in organisational, psychotherapeutic or social-work groups, the following behaviour has been most frequently identified as more destructive or more constructive in the experience of our respondents. Any or all of these behaviours may be relevant at all stages of group development. Also, most constructive behaviours could be destructive when used badly, inappropriately or mistimed in relation to different groups.

Equally many behaviours which are here listed as destructive may at times or in certain circumstances be useful, provocative or creative. Our results are summarised here to act as a spur to thinking, a supervisory aid and a tool for self-exploration, not a set of rules.

Destructive behaviours	*Constructive behaviours*
Excessive anxiety in leader	Clear contracts
The tyranny of structurelessness	Clear time structure
Hidden sadism	Building optimal anxiety
Confusion about roles	Clear assumption of responsible
Appears too aggressive or too	leadership
seductive	Clarity of boundaries and clarity of
Too task-orientated	group task
Too many rules – too	Facilitation of group members getting
authoritarian	to know one another
Focus on one person's	Early provision of practical/survival
pathology/acting-out behaviour at	information e.g. toilets, breaks, food
the expense of other members	limits
	Preparation of, e.g. the room in a
	manner which demonstrates that group
	members are expected and welcome

THE SECOND STAGE OF GROUP DEVELOPMENT

The adapted group imago

The adapted group imago is 'superficially modified in accordance with the member's estimate of the confronting reality' (Berne, 1980: 321). It is particularly suitable for structuring time by means of pastimes. When group members engage in pastimes or 'pastiming', they are usually engaged in relaxed, informal, general conversation that is not part of the group activity or task; they will take no action on their conversation. It is primarily characterised by agitation across the leadership boundary or the major internal group process (see Figure 9.5). The major internal group process results from conflicts between individual proclivities and the group cohesion as represented by the leadership and primarily takes place at the major internal boundary, that is between members and the leader.

In Tuckman's terminology this second stage corresponds to what he calls *storming*.

> The second point in the sequence is characterized by conflict and polarization around interpersonal issues, with concomitant emotional responding in the task sphere. These behaviors serve as resistance to group influence and task requirements and may be labelled as *storming*.
>
> (Tuckman, 1965: 396)

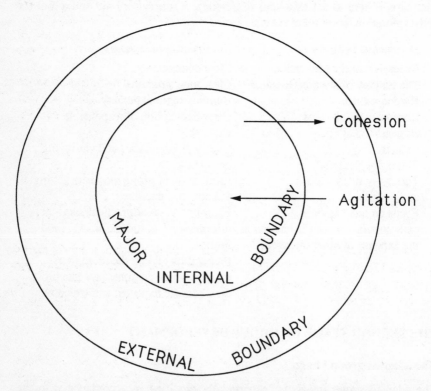

Figure 9.5 The major internal group process: individual proclivity vs. group cohesion (characterised by agitation across the leadership boundary)

Source: Berne, 1980: 38

This is probably one of the most important phases where conflict with, or rebellion against, the leader is a frequent occurrence. The stage is often thought of as the emotional response to task demands. Storming is not always obvious in overt or covert criticism but may sometimes be manifested in depression, passivity and lack of energy in the group members. In this case there has probably been insufficient forming.

The second phase in the development of the group imago is characterised by superficial modifications of the group imago in accordance with the members' estimate of the confronting reality.

Archetypally, the effective leader in this stage is represented by the 'firm and fair' teachers which some people experienced in their educational history. Experienced teachers often report that their relationship with the class can be made or marred in the first lesson. Group leaders can misguidedly avoid overt storming by exploiting their own fears and vulnerabilities. An education tutor told the group that 'I hear you don't like me'; Rescuers in her group told her what a nice woman she was but gossiped that they didn't really mean it.

The storming is frequently apparently about the nature of the task but psychologically about the ability of the group leader to be effective. Is he or she strong enough and safe enough to survive members taking power? The storming phase is a necessary pre-requirement to effective functioning later in the group life and probably as necessary as effective resolution of the 'terrible two's' rebellion in the young child. Storming is not to be seen as a distraction from the central task but a necessary stage in establishing the most efficient ways of conducting that task. This is a time when 'I'm OK – You're OK' as a life position really gets tested.

Example of Stewart (continued): During the storming stage of the group, Stewart's energies went into finding out where he stood in relation to the group leader. He continued to be superficially friendly with the other members, but did not make much good contact with them. On the contrary, he was unusually exclusive in his attention to the group leader (at a stage where preoccupation with the group leader is expected) and performed much of the group's storming task for them by challenging and testing. The therapist guessed that in the children's home he often took the challenging role on behalf of the children because of his perceived special status. In this stage, Stewart's internal work was on allocating the slots in his imago to the leader and members of the group (see Figure 9.6).

Leadership tasks

The leadership task is to keep the leadership boundaries and the group task intact at the same time as allowing individual members of the group maximum opportunity to test. At a psychological level the group therapist has to survive. The leader needs to withstand verbal attacks from the group without punishing or collapsing, neither becoming punitive nor apologetic (e.g. 'I'm only trying to

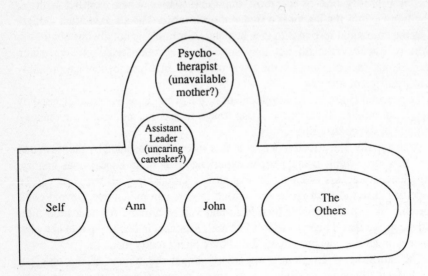

Figure 9.6   Stewart's adapted group imago
Source: Berne, 1966: 155

please you ...'). The feedback on leadership factors is less reliable at this stage than at later stages because of contaminated projections which colour their judgement. Later in the development of a group feedback can be enormously valuable but at this stage it is helpful for group psychotherapists to give themselves the benefit of the doubt, while seeking both support and confrontation in supervision. It is important not to seek inappropriate support from the group or group members, and perhaps thus reinforce second-order structural symbiotic patterns, that is, invite a relationship where the client inappropriately takes care of the psychotherapist in the same way that some children become 'caretakers' of their parents when their parents are not competent enough to appropriately take care of them.

Conflict and polarisation between members occur in response to adjusting their own needs to the task which does not fit the imago. Fight or flight might be predictable responses to anxiety and threat. In a psychotherapy group this conflict or withdrawal may appear as resistance to change, overadaptation or other passive behaviours.

In groups where the leader is perceived as too frightening or too fragile to test or question, premature conflicts and polarisation may erupt between group members. Especially vociferous and apparently irreconcilable differences between group members in the initial phases of a group often mask unsatisfactory management of the storming phase by the group leader. Although it is not unheard-of, it is more usual for groups at the beginning stages to be involved with ritual with each other and not serious games.

Similarly, in a psychotherapy group, an adaptable member will not begin to play his games until he thinks he knows how he stands with the leader. If he is arbitrary and not adaptable ... he may act prematurely and pay the penalty.

(Berne, 1963: 224–5)

The individual members of the group, unless seriously disturbed, will tend not actively to engage in second- or third-degree interpersonal games[†] before having established the group leader's boundaries *vis-à-vis* themselves. For example, a group of adolescents may test the group leader by means of coming late, verbal abuse or indulging in anti-social behaviour such as glue sniffing.

In the writer's experience how the group leaders or unit managers deal with these early testing situations will, to a large extent, determine the subsequent response from the group members in terms of how they use the therapy or the activity group.

Destructive behaviours	*Constructive behaviours*
Leader who defects or denies intergroup aggression and 'syrups over' conflicts	Taking people's feedback seriously without collapsing under the criticism
Leader interprets anger and rebellion as sign of individual pathology or of group sharing in a way which invalidates/patronises members	Not giving in to blackmail, threats Validating people's right to their feelings, thoughts, opinions and concerns without giving up rights
Group leader looking too fragile, sick or appearing hurt	I'm OK – You're OK Ability to negotiate issues – to be
Taking any of four *drama* roles (Victim, Rescuer, Persecutor or Bystander)[‡]	flexible about negotiation for group to form its own particular culture Discriminating between
Ignoring the conflict – pretends it doesn't exist	compromises/negotiations which would facilitate or handicap group task
Supporting polarisation or scapegoating	
No sanctions or unjust sanctions	
Abandoning group	

[†]On games, Berne says the following:

(a) A First Degree Game is one which is socially acceptable in the agent's circle.
(b) A Second Degree Game is one from which no permanent irremediable damage arises, but which the players would rather conceal from the public.
(c) A Third Degree Game is one which is played for keeps, and which ends in the surgery, the courtroom or the morgue.

(1964: 57)

[‡]The Victim is someone who inauthentically behaves as if they are being victimised in situations where they actually have reasonable opportunities to alter the situation. The Persecutor is someone who uses the position of authority in an inauthentic way exceeding the limits of control necessary for personal gratification. The Rescuer is someone who does things for other people non-contractually (and which they may later resent) out of sentimental, helpful or vicariously gratifying motivation. In all cases it is distinguished from the real victim, persecutor and rescuer who may display aspects of this behaviour, but who occupy these positions in good faith (Karpman, 1968). The role of Bystander is explained in Chapter 11 (p.257).

THE THIRD STAGE OF GROUP DEVELOPMENT

The operative group imago

Operative group imago is 'further modified in accordance with the member's perception of how he fits into the leader's imago' (Berne, 1963: 321). Time is structured by means of games.[†]

In Tuckman's terminology this corresponds to what he calls the stage of *norming*: 'Resistance is overcome in the third stage in which ingroup feeling and cohesiveness develop, new standards evolve, and new roles are adopted. In the task realm, intimate, personal opinions are expressed. Thus, we have the stage of *norming*' (Tuckman, 1965: 396).

This stage of the progression of the group imago is characterised by the development of group cohesion. This is where the games get played out and games and racket tolerance levels are established. Leadership difficulties with the leader have sucessfully been worked through and interpersonal conflict either based on script replays of archaic patterns or here-and-now social skills learning can be constructively dealt with. Thus the seemingly contradictory definition of 'operative image' and 'norming' can both be true. This *is* a time for maximum game playing and re-enactment of the family drama. Yet it is also a time when individuals are available for insight, are feeling safer in the group and invested in its future. There is a sharing of feelings and mutual support. A group in this stage has a clear sense of 'this is the way we do things around here'. Shared norms and values have been developed. The operative principle states that 'an adaptable member will not begin to play his games until he thinks he knows how he stands with the leader' (Berne, 1963: 225).

Example of Stewart (continued): During the norming stage, Ann, another group member, told Stewart that she had noticed that he talked only to the therapist. She said she felt sad about this and would have liked more of his attention. Stewart reacted by becoming withdrawn and depressed. He behaved in a pleasing, anxious way to other group members and did not speak to the leader. Two weeks later Stewart said that he felt furious with the leader for paying more attention to the others, and deeply bewildered by Ann's comment which he experienced as rejecting and persecutory. His own view was that he got less attention from the psychotherapist than the others did. The game was eventually exposed and Stewart's Adult was decontaminated as he brought into awareness, the way he had set up a repeat of his childhood. Stewart had been functioning from his operative group imago in which he had allocated slots for his mother, other caretakers (the assistant leader and a Parental group member – Ronald) and the rejecting children.

[†]A game is the process of doing something with an ulterior motive that (1) is outside the Adult awareness, (2) does not become explicit until the participants switch the way they are behaving and (3) results in everyone feeling confused, misunderstood and wanting to blame the other person (Stewart and Joines, 1987: 329–30)

Leadership tasks

The leadership tasks at this stage are more facilitation of interpersonal skills and modelling behaviours that will support constructive group norms. Effective leaders teach, for example, emotional literacy (Steiner, 1984) and provide information and resources. In a psychotherapy group, or any group where comment on personal process is appropriate, he or she can teach game theory and facilitiate the giving of feedback about how each member is playing out his/her games and script and to the whole group about how they encourage each other's games. The group imago is further modified in accordance with each member's perception of how they fit into the leader's imago. Other leadership tasks are encouragement, modelling and providing psychological-level messages which are congruent with the (genuine) values that they espouse.

Effective leadership can be said to be concerned with facilitating the healthiest forces within the individual or the group towards individuation and self-actualisation.

The leader may set rules or contracts for which there may be sanctions. Norms can be influenced by the leader(s) but primarily arise and are shaped by the group members themselves. The group norms comprise the most vital factors in establishing a healthy group culture. There is some indication that group norms are influenced not so much by what individual leaders say as by what they do. Often it is the throw-away comments or the peripheral management of boundary issues from which individual members draw conclusions about acceptable norms. In this way a group leader can challenge premature or oppressive norming to maintain flexibility and encourage members in informed and compassionate valuing processes, rather than norms based on rigidity, certainty and loudness.

Destructive behaviours	*Constructive behaviours*
Stroking rigidity	Members get stroked for making explicit queries around norming
Reluctance to let the group move to the stage where group members make more autonomous movement and the group leader often loses centrality	As a group leader, challenge norms to maintain flexibility and deny 'there is only one way to do it'
Rigidity concerning rules such as 'there are no exceptions', no allowance for individual differences and individual needs	Facilitate group developing own norms – norms are group's personality Flexibility around norms
Capriciously malevolent destructive members are allowed to stay and destroy group cohesion, tasks and process	Focuses on process of valuing and norm formation or culture building not as pure introjection of unconsidered rules or procedures
Carrying one's expectations of group norms based on past experience, thus perhaps interfering with the unique development of each individual group's norms	Referral/exclusion of destructive members after very careful consideration of cost/benefit effects on the rest of the group
Leader tries to set rules instead of norms	Explicit statements of leader's values, e.g. race, sexual orientation, where this is appropriate
Leader expresses own values excessively, allowing no freedom and causing possible repression of individuals' views	Respect for each particular group's uniqueness

THE FOURTH STAGE OF GROUP DEVELOPMENT

The secondarily adjusted group imago

The secondarily adjusted group imago is 'the final phase, in which the member relinquishes some of his own proclivities in favour of the group cohesion.... The minor group process results from conflicts between individual proclivities and takes place at the minor internal boundaries' (see Figure 9.7).

This corresponds in Tuckman's terminology, to what he calls the performing stage. The group attains the fourth, and Tuckman's final, stage in which inter-

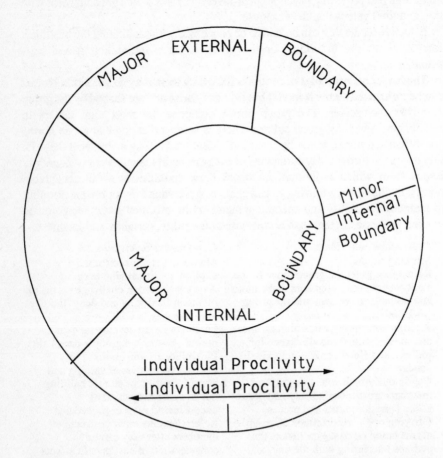

Figure 9.7 Minor internal group process: individual proclivity vs. individual proclivity

Source: Berne, 1963: 95

personal structure becomes the tool of task activities. Roles become flexible and functional, and group energy is channelled into the task. Structural issues have been resolved, and structure can now become supportive of task performance (Tuckman, 1965).

Here the group functions effectively in their task with minimal interference from distracting group process and the group can now deal adequately with what arises with a reality orientation. In the therapy group, members achieve insight and behaviour change, while the task group engages in effective problem solving. This is the phase where intimacy is more frequent between group members, and between the group members and the group leader; that is where feelings and wants can be expressed and heard without the need for censorship.

The performing stage of a group has been satisfactorily achieved if the leader or the psychotherapist ends up surrounded by individuals who take responsibility for their own psychotherapy.

Example of Stewart (continued): In the performing stage of the group, Stewart's imago was secondarily adjusted as at Figure 9.8. His relationships with his peers became warm and trusting as he accepted their support and affection. He

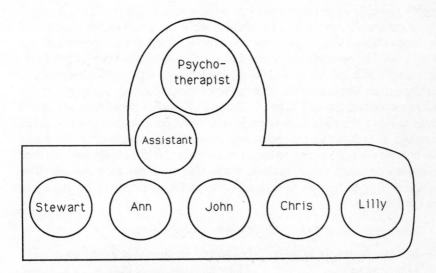

Figure 9.8   The differentiated group imago
Source: Berne, 1966: 155

developed a good relationship with the therapist in which he could make himself heard appropriately. His psychotherapy involved deconfusion of the Child ego state as he became in touch with, and worked through some of the painful experiences he had had.

Leadership tasks

The leader's task is to enjoy this phase having navigated the previous phases and really feel that he or she is doing psychotherapy: people are 'in treatment' (Berne, 1962). Group members have ways of using their interpersonal processes to each other's benefit and although everybody may not be happy all the time, everybody is learning all the time.

If a group psychotherapist has established this level of functioning in an ongoing group, it usually will, to a large extent, maintain the established culture even through temporary separations, such as summer holidays, or minor fluctuations in group membership. To some extent, though, recycling or reworking of previous phases will recur, perhaps in a less obvious way, but the working-through periods may tend to be shorter and the depth of discomfort/distress less intense.

It is important that the group leader let go of many leadership behaviours, allowing every member of the group to make leadership acts even as the group leader retains the responsibility. In successful and effective groups the leadership slot may be vacated and filled by one or more of the effective leaders in the group.

Leadership tasks involve offering praise, positive strokes and minimising control while maintaining some safety – though the group will usually do this for itself – and offering structures and resources, saying things like 'Let's try this.' He or she invites comment and evaluation while the group makes choices and decisions within a wide range of open boundaries regarding what is permitted and what is not. He or she relaxes, enjoys the group permission to have fun and work; encourages and validates: autonomy, immediacy, authenticity, spontaneity, feelings, skills and knowledge. Finally, he or she can be seen by the group as a whole person and so is able to be role fluent. Role fluency refers to the ability and skills to move elegantly from one role to another, for example, to allow group members to do things for the leader, support him/her or assist him/her. The group has become autonomous and no longer needs the leader in the same way as it used to and as a corollary, the group leader can receive more from the group and allow him/herself to be fully there without the need for such careful monitoring of earlier group needs.

Destructive behaviours	*Constructive behaviours*
Criticises destructively, says 'I know better'	Let people get on with it, letting go
	Allowing people to be leading
Puts people down	Becoming participant – joining group
Takes credit	Minimum control, maintains some
Deprives group of autonomy	safety boundaries – though group will
Too keen on schedule	usually do for self (time, refreshing, etc.)
Tells people what they're doing isn't good enough	Offers praise, positive strokes for being and for doing

Blemishing	Leadership slot vacated to appropriate
Holding too tight a rein	person, though ready to step in if necessary
Offers more punishment than reward	Says things like, 'Let's experiment with this'
Stresses task and ignores maintenance	Invites comment and evaluation, allows group to make choices
Is cool, impersonal and distant	Within a wide range of open boundaries
Refuses to listen to group members	says what's permitted and what's not
	Relaxes, enjoys group
Invalidates feeling	Permission to have fun and work
Invokes drivers	Encourages and validates: autonomy,
Invokes injunctions	immediacy, authenticity, spontaneity, feelings, skills and knowledge

THE FIFTH AND FINAL STAGE OF GROUP DEVELOPMENT

The clarified group imago

Although Berne only identified four phases as such, he says that 'The real aim of most dynamic psychotherapy groups is to clarify the group imagoes of the individual members' (Berne, 1963: 241). In so far as the group imago is a facsimile of an infantile group imago or a reproduction of a childhood group imago, its clarification and differentiation is part of the task of facilitating individuals and groups to live more of their individual lives in groups which are geared to their current here-and-now needs and to reduce or eliminate borrowed or anachronistic interferences with intimates, whether in the therapy group or in life. If a group experience has been successful for a member it will usually result in a higher level of functioning and integration.

Psychotherapy groups have as their major activity concerns with 'internal conflicts and concerts between forces, that is, in the internal group process, it may be called simply a process group' (Berne, 1963: 59). If this is the activity which operates across all stages of group development, withdrawal as a time structure becomes relevant and necessary at the termination of the group or the individual member's life in the group. 'Incidentally, a phantom is also left whenever a well-differentiated member leaves a group and persists until the mourning process is completed if it ever is' (Berne, 1963: 225). Withdrawal is the divestment of emotional energy or cathectic charge from group cohesion.

This last phase is that of *mourning* (Lacoursiere, 1980) or *adjourning* (Tuckman and Jensen, 1977). The collective group focus is on termination. Psychologically, the group has to say goodbye and negotiate all the relevant grief processes.

Example of Stewart (continued): In this stage, Stewart as well as mourning the end of the group, realised how much grief he was carrying for the father he never had. His leave taking of his fellow group members was warm and intimate. He said that he had never felt so close to his friends or peers before.

Leadership tasks

Probably the most important leadership task is to 'keep the group at it' and not allow individual members or the group 'to run away from' dealing with these issues at intrapsychic, interpersonal and group levels. It is expected that people may wish to avoid some of the pain of this period by making the group 'bad', blemishing the group leader, premature disengagement (physically by, for example, going sick, or psychologically by, for example, 'It wasn't really important').

According to Worden (1983) the four major tasks of mourning are the following: (1) to accept the reality of the loss; (2) to experience the pain of grief; (3) to adjust to a changed environment; and (4) to withdraw emotional energy and reinvest it in another relationship. As the group terminates the leader's task is to facilitate the working through of such similar processes as they are manifested in the collective consciousness and avoidances of the group dynamic.

Kubler-Ross (1969) identified a five-stage sequence in loss – denial, anger, bargaining, depression and acceptance. Such analogous phases of the grief process can be observed in some aspects or elements of the collective pre-occupation towards the termination phases of groups. For example, idealisation as part of denial prevents dealing with the sad feelings of separation by creating romantic ideas of reunions such as often happens on holidays with people to whom, if they did turn up on the doorstep back home, one would find that one had very little to say. Feelings that need to be dealt with at this stage include: anger, fear, sadness, appreciation. The leader can give information about the process of grieving but also needs to facilitate the group to grapple emotionally with its implications.

The leader has personally to participate with integrated-Adult emotions as well as intellectually in the process in order for the resolution to be effective in the same way as a parent needs to experience 'letting a child go' with the ambivalent feelings of sadness in the loss of a particular kind of closeness as well as pleasure in their independence. It is not infrequent for survival issues to emerge again at this stage. Prediction can be useful. Every time people say goodbye, or separate from meaningful connections with others, they have an opportunity to relive archaic separations in more healthy or creative ways, thus helping them to heal some wounds of the past, even if the short-term benefits are not immediately apparent. People have to say goodbye before they can say hello. Termination is often both deeper and more effective if the group has been successfully managed.

If therapy has been successful, people will have let go of their group imagoes in the movement from the third to the fourth stage, so that the mourning will be for real intimate relations not the fantasied one of their original imago.

It is to be hoped that their next provisional group imago is based to a greater degree on trust in their own capacities and in other people's rational goodwill.

The successful group leader will help individuals to handle grief in their own way. It is important not to go along with group denial (collusion) but to work out problems with endings vicariously through the group. It is also vital not to behave defensively at the blemishing stage but to listen and receive feedback; to support realistic plans for the future connected with endings; and to predict varied reactions and allow ambivalence to be expressed. Group leaders must let members know well in advance of a definite finishing time, and it can be their task to provide or facilitate leaving structures and rituals which are congruent with the group norms.

Destructive behaviours	*Constructive behaviours*
Being persecuting about mourning	Allowing individual to handle grief in own way
Going along with group denial (collusion)	Predicting varied reaction
Working out own problems with endings	Letting people know well in advance
Behaving defensively at blemishing stage	Very explicit and honest about what he or she is doing
Packing in the information	Realistic plans for future connected with ending
No time for process	Allowing ambivalence to be expressed
Sickly sentimental prescribed mourning e.g. all hug or all say something nice	Finishing at a definite time
Overly extends the mourning period	Knowledge of what leaving ritual is going to be
Too abrupt an ending, not allowing afterglow of satisfaction	Allows and encourages reminiscing
Overindulgent or allowing of idealisation or splitting	Graciously accepts appropriate recognition and appreciation from the group
	Focus on individuation, integration and generalisation
	Facilitates group to use this ending as a learning experience for future endings

BLENDING INDIVIDUAL AND GROUP PSYCHOTHERAPY

All the interventions and approaches discussed in this book are applicable to individual and group psychotherapy. The specific focus of this chapter has been to outline the group-as-a-whole dynamics which constitute the field of the psychotherapeutic activity. There are events and times which necessitate that the group-as-a-whole become the primary focus for intervention in order for the psychotherapy with individuals in the group to proceed in an optimal manner. These interventions will be geared towards maximising therapeutic conditions in

Table 9.1 Summary diagram of stages of group development

Tuckman	Berne	Time Structuring	Lacoursiere
Forming	Provisional group imago	Rituals	Orientation
Storming	Adapted group imago	Pastimes	Dissatisfaction
Norming	Operative group imago	Games	Resolution
Performing	Secondarily adjusted group imago	Intimacy	Production
(Mourning)	Clarified group imago	Withdrawal	Termination

the group. The smooth and efficient management of the stages of group development are considered the most important factors in creating optimal conditions for psychotherapeutic change: 'Encouraging processes such as cohesiveness and universality by varying therapeutic technique, decentralizing leadership, and promoting free interaction among group members should provide a positive overall group atmosphere with which to make more active, TA-based interventions' (Kapur and Miller, 1987: 299).

Other occasions when the group-as-a-whole process should take priority are at any of the transition points between the stages of group development which we discussed in the preceding sections. For example, attention should be paid to group rather than individual process when the group is beginning or ending or when the group has not moved on to the next stage of development.

Significant interruptions such as before and after breaks for holidays can cause interference in the performance level of the group, but when competently managed, can provide the basis for improved individual understanding and functioning. Changes in the psychotherapeutic 'frame' such as a change in fee, time, room, etc. need to take priority over individual change contracts. When members leave or when new members join, the collective response of the group will need attention as well as individual members' reactions. External causes of group anxiety, for example, a catastrophic news item, may gather the energies of the individuals together in a way which the psychotherapist can use with maximum leverage for change. The neglect of attention to such items, for example, a devastating hurricane or the death of a prominent person within the group's cultural milieu such as John F. Kennedy seems to lead to disruption or wastage. Similarly, with positive events such as the demolition of the Berlin Wall. If such neglect occurs, the group may become stuck in some way as signalled by poor attendance, the same issues being recycled, the same games being played, or group members being passive. Some group issue is being avoided and needs to be addressed if individual change is to be achieved. All the major existential issues including death, loss, loneliness and love may resonate for many members in a group or have meaning for the group collectively. Finally, although there may be more to be added to this list, one of the finest arbiters of identifying a disturbed group process or the impairment of performance is the leader's own informed intuition.

Figure 9.9 shows an example of headings on a recording sheet or card which is used effectively by many group and family therapists to keep track of every group session's group-as-a-whole vicissitudes.

SUMMARY

This chapter has drawn on similarities between Berne's concept of group-imago adjustment with the stages of group development as conceptualised by Tuckman (1965) and Lacoursiere (1980). It highlighted some of the most relevant tasks of group leaders at different stages of the maturation of the whole group. It collated feedback from practitioners and trainees identifying more or less useful group-leader behaviours at the different stages. Throughout the focus has been on considering how group-as-a-whole developmental phenomena can be understood and utilised as an adjunct to individual psychotherapy *in* the group, not as a substitution thereof. Particular factors in the blending of individual and group psychotherapy have also been discussed. Readers wanting to explore further the subject of psychotherapy group work and TA, may be interested to investigate other TA literature on the subject, including on *group dynamics* (Altorfer, 1977; Berne, 1963; Kapur and Miller, 1987), on *group-as-a-whole awareness* (Berne, 1966; Gurowitz, 1975) and on *stages of group development* (Berne, 1963; Misel, 1975; Peck, 1978).

```
┌─────────────────────────────────────────────────────────────────────────┐
│              Psychotherapy Group                                          │
│              Monday evenings/weekly                                       │
│ Group/Family ...........................   Session No ....15.........     │
├─────────────────────────────────────────────────────────────────────────┤
│ Theme :      Scarcity or Plenty?                                          │
├─────────────────────────────────────────────────────────────────────────┤
│ Content:      Group started with members discussing previous week.  Many │
│ had issues involving problems with family.  R's anger at his children not │
│ responding to him.  L - trouble with boss.  S - ignored by shop           │
│ assistants.  C's wife "doesn't make me happy".  A. had difficulty asking. │
│ Talked with S.  All gave feedback to each other - positive and negative.  │
├─────────────────────────────────────────────────────────────────────────┤
│ Group Structure:                    Stage of Group Development:           │
│                                                                           │
│ Location Diagram (Berne 1963)       Storming / Norming                    │
├─────────────────────────────────────────────────────────────────────────┤
│ Group Process:     For the first half of the evening, members addressed most │
│ comments to the therapist, talking about difficulties in relating to      │
│ families and friends.  They revealed a Child fear of scarcity.  There     │
│ seemed to be a belief that only the therapist could provide.  After       │
│ leader's intervention, members began to give feedback/strokes to each     │
│ other and sense of dependency decreased.                                  │
├─────────────────────────────────────────────────────────────────────────┤
│ Systemic Assessment/Manoeuvre:    Asked A. who did she have difficulty "getting │
│ things from" in this group.  Led to interchange between A. & S.  Then     │
│ between other members.                                                    │
├─────────────────────────────────────────────────────────────────────────┤
│ Major Interventions:    Helped C. to analyse Game of "Do me something".   │
│ Confronted A's agitation passivity.  Facilitated more group interchange.  │
│ Modelled empathising with R.  Kept quiet.                                 │
├─────────────────────────────────────────────────────────────────────────┤
│ Therapist's state of mind                                                 │
│ at entry:                           at end:                               │
│      OK                                  Relieved/warm towards group      │
├─────────────────────────────────────────────────────────────────────────┤
│ Incidents:   None significant                                             │
├─────────────────────────────────────────────────────────────────────────┤
│ Objective overall:    Increase of members' self-esteem, coping strategies.│
│ Facilitate individuals' movement towards autonomy.                        │
├─────────────────────────────────────────────────────────────────────────┤
│ Sessional:      Respond to group needs.  Facilitate sharing - establishment │
│ of group norms beginning.  Continue to resist demand for dependency.      │
├─────────────────────────────────────────────────────────────────────────┤
│ Other comments/supervisory insights:                                      │
│     N.B.  R. may be setting up "Kick me" game re: arrogant manner.        │
└─────────────────────────────────────────────────────────────────────────┘
```

Figure 9.9   Recording sheet

Chapter 10

Systemic assessment and
TA psychotherapy with children[†]

Your children are not your children.
They are the sons and daughters of Life's longing for itself.

(Gibran, 1926: 20)

TA CHILD PSYCHOTHERAPY

A number of TA authors have indicated that they have effectively worked with children in a variety of settings: Mannel *et al.*, (1968), James (1969), Piehl (1969), Boyce (1970), Freed (1971), Amundson (1978), Clarke (1978), Bendell and Fine (1979), Emerson (1979), Henry (1979), Berry (1981), Golub and Guerriero (1981), Campos (1986).

This chapter seeks to distil some methodological learnings from the authors' educational and psychotherapeutic work with children as well as their supervisory work with mental-health professionals working with disturbed and maladjusted children. It is intended to provide a framework which can guide the thinking of trainees and practitioners in selecting the most appropriate modalities for psychotherapeutic intervention in the very complicated area of helping troubled children. This is particularly important for psychotherapists working in agencies where treatment-planning decisions are based on their assessments of the most appropriate and economical intervention routes in these times of diminishing resources and escalating need. It is not intended to be comprehensive or exhaustive, but to give a flavour of how this model can be used to approach the extremely complex field of TA child psychotherapy. Children's difficulties can be manifested in disturbances of behaviour, emotion, physiologically or intellectually or any combination of these vectors. Any such difficulties must of course be viewed against the light of the child's appropriate developmental levels (Amundson, 1978, Babcock and Keepers, 1976). However, it is not the authors' intention specifically to discuss this aspect in this chapter.

[†] First section of this chapter co-authored with Sue Fish

Six major categories of difficulties that children of varying ages present will be discussed, using clinical vignettes to illustrate this material. These six major categories are seen as representing several subsystems within a larger system. The advantages and disadvantages of different psychotherapeutic formats for working with children will be considered. For further study, a selective resource list is provided for each of these formats. Some guidelines for maximising effectiveness in selection of treatment modalities are also offered. Differences and similarities in using TA psychotherapy when working with children as opposed to grown-ups are also briefly addressed.

In their experience the authors have most frequently encountered six categories of problem in child psychotherapy.

1 An impediment of normal developmental progress.
2 The effects of trauma, either chronic or acute.
3 Systemic pathology within the family.
4 Change in the constellation of the family system.
5 Socioculturally based problems, including school.
6 Adjustment to injuries or events not specifically related to any of the above ('acts of god' or 'fate').

These frequently occurring problem-categories can be usefully organised in a model of overlapping systems which can facilitate the choice, prioritising or sequencing of treatment formats (see Figure 10.1). The three subsystems are identified as (1) the individual child, (2) the family system and (3) the sociocultural system. All of these form subsets of the larger, more universal system of life. All three of these systems interlock and overlap. In addition, life, 'fate' or 'acts of God' contribute the unexpected and unpredictable events which impinge on human lives, such as death, disease and disasters. Any therapeutic focus on a subsystem is obviously a matter of emphasis for intervention, not to the exclusion of the influence of the other subsystems.

To compound the complexity, all three systems are also concurrently undergoing their respective developmental cycles. The *healthy child* is progressively moving through his developmental phases, which have been extensively studied in the literature (Levin-Landheer, 1982; Erikson, 1950; Mahler *et al.*, 1975). Magner (1985) provides a useful comparative chart of child-development theories.

The *family system* also undergoes developmentally progressive changes. In volume 2 of *Family Therapy*, Bentovim and co-workers (1982), organise their contributors' material within a context of the life cycle of the family. Friedman and Shmukler (1983) describe a model of family development and functioning from a TA framework.

The *society* in which we live, our sociocultural milieu, is also constantly changing and hopefully developing over time. The last recorded clitoridectomy was performed in the US in 1948 on a child of 5 years old as a cure for her masturbation (Ehrenreich and English, 1978: 111). This demonstrates how until very recently our society supported medical mutilation to children based on contaminated beliefs. Teilhard de Chardin (1959) suggests, however, that the human race is in the process of continuing evolution, increasing complexity and growing spiritual consciousness.

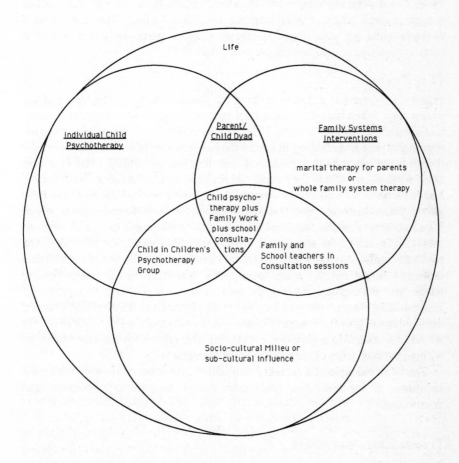

Figure 10.1 A model for overlapping subsystems in the assessment and planning of TA child psychotherapy

SIX PROBLEM-CATEGORIES WHICH FREQUENTLY OCCUR WITH CHILDREN

A blocked developmental process

Transactional analysis, as an existential humanistic psychotherapy, believes that any child is seeking to grow towards health and will move through predictable cycles of development towards autonomy, spontaneity and intimacy (James and Jongeward, 1971). Occasionally this developmental process is impeded through stress or detrimental environmental circumstances or inadequate parental support for his/her developing capacities. When this happens the child may stay stuck at the unresolved stage or may leapfrog over that section. This can cause a developmental lag with regard to certain abilities, particularly if it occurs at certain 'sensitive developmental periods' (Bee, 1985).

Clinical example

Felicity, a 4-year-old girl, was referred for psychotherapy by the leader of her play school. When brought to the school each morning she would weep copiously and cling to her mother's skirts. If her mother did not stay she would spend the morning crying and clinging to one of the play leaders. In an interview with the therapist Felicity's mother explained that they had previously lived in a very small rural village where the mother did not have much of a social life and there had been no other children of compatible age with whom Felicity could have played. From this description and observation of her behaviour at the play school it was obvious that she had missed out on the development of age-appropriate social skills due to the social impoverishment of her earlier environment. The psychotherapist started by seeing Felicity alone and with the use of toy children indirectly taught Felicity some social skills. She then started seeing Felicity within the play group playing predominantly with Felicity and gradually incorporating other children as they showed interest. Gradually Felicity's natural developmental processes were reasserted. After two months Felicity was able to attend play school in a normal way, relating enjoyably with the other children, without back-up from either mother or the therapist.

This is an example of a category of problem manifesting primarily within *the subsystem of the individual child* even though originating in sociocultural deprivation.

Trauma (chronic or acute)

In transactional analysis psychological difficulties are ascribed to decisions a child makes in response to the parental pressures on them during childhood. Any time a child takes on a destructive script message (curse) or an injunction such as 'Don't be a child', the organismically healthy child is traumatised because he/she has voluntarily to give up a part of his or her capacities in order to survive the family environment and maintain the love of parents (Berne, 1972). These traumas can be acute (e.g. sexual molestation) causing the fixation of a Child ego state which pathologically interferes with the child's future normal development. Trauma or fixation can also be the accumulation of many subclinical events, such as a parent consistently relating to the child with the ulterior message that they are a nuisance.

Clinical examples

Betsy, a 7-year-old girl, was referred for therapy by her mother for manic behaviour which often resulted in Betsy hurting herself. When the psychotherapist first met the child she ran around the therapy room and over the furniture, repeatedly stumbling and falling and then looking to the therapist to be picked up. Gradually, through the use of art and play therapy, it became obvious that the 'baby was surrounded by monsters and wild animals and that Mummy had disappeared altogether'. When asked how old the baby was, Betsy replied that she was only a few weeks old. Gradually from amongst the toys available Betsy selected a bottle. When the therapist suggested Betsy become that baby and be fed Betsy agreed and regressed with appropriate bodily changes. These feeding sessions lasted anything from a couple to a maximum of eleven minutes during which the therapist would hold Betsy firmly and safely, murmuring the unconditional strokes which Betsy needed. During this time the falling behaviour ceased both in and out of the sessions. Therapy still continues, though now Betsy seldom requests to 'play babies' and the manic and hurtful behaviour has ceased at home. In joint sessions with Betsy's Mum's therapist and Mum, it was learnt that when Betsy was a few weeks old Betsy's Mum had learnt by accident that her husband was having an affair and had been doing so throughout most of her pregnancy. Many nasty scenes had ensued and she had left the home and Betsy on several occasions. During the joint sessions it became obvious to both therapists that Betsy's redecision about how to receive care and strokes healthily had been successful in that she would regularly make physical contact with her mother and asked for attention straightforwardly.

Eleven-year-old Belinda, whilst spending a weekend with her uncle and his family, was sexually molested by him. This occurred when he was apparently 'comforting' her after she had called out during a nightmare. Some days later she developed a vaginal infection and the family doctor gently elicited the details of the assault. The general practitioner made a referral to an experienced social worker who worked with her on reliving the incident with the use of sexually explicit dolls, at the same time as working with the police and the rest of the family.

These are examples of chronic or acute trauma manifesting within *the sub-system of the individual child*, although obviously influenced by their respective family dynamics at the time.

Seeking help for the parent(s)

One of the most famous exponents of family therapy, Minuchin, experientially demonstrated the influence of the family on its members, i.e. how children respond with measurable, physiological responses to stresses affecting the family. He describes the children as functioning as 'conflict-detouring mechanisms', the repercussions of which involve a measurable increase in the levels of free fatty acid (FFA) in the child's bloodstream.

The interdependence between the individual and his family – the flow between 'inside' and 'outside' – is poignantly demonstrated in the experimental situation, in which behavioural events among family members can be measured in the bloodstream of other family members (Minuchin, 1974: 8, 9).

Clinical examples

The school educational psychologist referred 9-year-old Robin to the therapist as his academic attainment had deteriorated seriously and there seemed no physiological or basic learning difficulty involved. In his play-therapy sessions with animal puppets Robin repeatedly chose to enact stories of how a young animal saves its mother. It soon became clear to the therapist involved that Robin's deterioration at school was a call for help for his mother's depression. The therapist spent time building Robin's trust in her 'caretaking' abilities and then reassured him that he had done a 'good job' but that such work was not meant for children to have to do, and that she would now take over the looking after mum (this was done both straightforwardly in terms of verbal explanations and also in the animal enactments where the therapist had a wise owl fly into the scenes and help the cub 'hand over' the older animal to one of the grown-up caretakers in the pack). So the therapist started seeing his mother in individual therapy. Once Robin had perceived that a trustworthy adult was now looking after his mother, his school work regained his original high standard.

Seven-year-old Rita was admitted to hospital with recurrent severe stomach pain, unremitting lassitude, refusal to speak to anyone other than her father and a refusal to eat. Because of the gravity of Rita's physical condition through non-eating, her parents were requested to stop seeing her until she had voluntarily begun eating again otherwise intravenous feeding might have had to be used. The parents agreed and this was explained to Rita and she was also informed that her parents would, in the meantime, be seeing the doctor as well. The psychiatrist spent time on rebalancing the family system by strengthening the father's self-esteem and ego boundaries, rewarding and supporting Rita's age-appropriate behaviour and helping the parents to assesss openly their marital relationship i.e. a philandering non-involved mother and her passive husband. Father was dealing with his marital disappointment by his dependency on Rita in an emotionally incestuous fashion. He would not, however, consider leaving his wife. Once the symbiosis with father was broken Rita began eating almost immediately and was allowed home within a week although she continued to see the psychiatrist individually and with the family. Within six weeks all her symptoms had gone and she was functioning well at school. Often such symptoms in children are a cry for help from a parental or caretaking child (Winnicott, 1960) for whom the burden of looking after a parent has become too much to bear alone. Once this kind of child knows that the parent is being attended to by a more competent helper, premature parenting can be relinquished and the child concerned can continue the job of being a child mastering child skills.

Just as in an actual situation between a grown-up and a child, when the grown-up can demonstrate that he is able to take care of things better if he is left alone to do it in his own way, the relationship between them becomes better defined and perhaps more distant, but it is improved (Berne, 1980: 148).

An interesting sequel to Rita's story was that as her father dissolved his unhealthy symbiosis with his daughter, the wife became more interested in him again and ceased her extra-marital involvements.

Many family therapists (Minuchin, 1974; Lidz et al., 1965), contribute similar examples where apparent 'pathology in the child' is a *systemic enactment of marital relationship difficulties in the family system.*

Changes in the constellation of the family system

When, for example, parents divorce or leave home, baby siblings are born or elderly relatives join a household, the composition of the family system is greatly affected and the child has to readjust to a changed imago of his primary family group. Frequently, if supports for this change process are lacking, a child's distress becomes 'symptoms' and dysfunctional regression results. These symptoms then become the foreground problem instead of the difficulty in the family system.

Clinical example

After 8-year-old Frederic's father separated from his mother and moved out of the family home, Frederic would unpredictably soil his pants. Mother was scared of her own anger and would not allow him to 'raise his voice' at home, even in play. Initially, Frederic's compliance with this injunction was a real obstacle to effective therapy. The therapist gave Frederic information about feelings and options for expressing them. Eventually Frederic accepted the therapist's protection for his expression of his anger which he played out in the sandpit. This involved such scenes as Frederic burying the female adult doll under the sand, having her attacked by dinosaurs in his drawings and frequently reporting dreams during which the witch was killed in many gruesome ways. Much of his play and fantasy work involved the 'return of the hero'.

In one play session the therapist suggested Frederic build another home as well as the one he had just created and show how the hero now lived in this other place and how this affected the other people in his fantasy. This Frederic did and balanced a piece of string between the two structures. He explained this as Spiderman's magic thread which meant that he could zoom between the places at will. The therapist suggested that in the real world this would be like a telephonic connection. At this moment, Frederic beamed and obviously had an 'aha' experience. Soon after this the therapist decided to consolidate Frederic's progress by calling together a family session during which Frederic was invited to sculpt the family as he now experienced it. At first Frederic placed his parents and sister close together with himself a looker-on outside the group. After a short while he shook his head and rearranged them such that his mother and father were across the room from each other with his sister and himself first with one and then with the other. Again after a while he shook his head and rearranged them a final time such that both parents were close to both children yet on opposite sides from each other. This was obviously a painful exercise for him yet constituted a significant part of the working-through process of his mourning for the loss of the daily presence of his father.

This is an example where *a change in the family constellation* was most clearly the subsystem focalising the conflicts.

Sociocultural based problems, e.g. lack of information

The influence of the cultural milieu of human problems is both enormous in scope and profound in effect. 'Whereas this is changing, TA still seeks a wider perspective and needs to be taught with greater respect and awareness for culture and tradition' (James, 1983: 207). Sometimes children's difficulties are caused by differences of timing or adjustment to sociocultural context and this includes educational systems such as schools.

Clinical example

During a medical examination for an early childhood illness it was discovered that 3-year-old Homa had bruising to her back and buttocks not satisfactorily explained by her parents' claim that she was clumsy. The family was referred to the therapist by the social worker, called by the doctor. After many family-therapy sessions, having gained the parents' trust the therapist inquired of them if there was any reason why Homa needed punishment. Gradually it emerged that Homa's parents were extremely concerned about her tendency to talk to herself and within their Middle Eastern culture this was a sign that she was inhabited by devils which needed to be beaten out of her. 'We are not hitting our child but are saving her from the bad spirits which could harm her.' The changing of this belief system took many months and involved, amongst other things, showing Homa's parents films which demonstrated that young children quite naturally talk to themselves at times.

Homa did not need 'therapy' or 'treatment'. It would further 'pathologise' her. The *social milieu* in which she lived needed information on 'normal' developmental processes. There are many problems due to sociocultural differences which have hardly begun to be addressed, e.g. the cases of extremely gifted children born to economically and educationally disadvantaged parents, adolescent Indian girls resisting traditionally arranged marriages and other difficulties of second-generation immigrants. Such examples must be taken into account when considered as individual cases whether the cultural differences are obvious (colour) or not (religion).

Adjustment disorders

'The forces of human destiny are foursome and fearsome: demonic parental programming, abetted by the inner voice the ancients called the *Daemon*; constructive parental programming, aided by the thrust of life called *Phusis* long ago; external forces, still called fate; and independent aspirations, for which the ancients had no human name, since for them such were the privileges mainly of gods and kings' (Berne, 1972: 56). In TA we assume that every child can be a prince or princess in her own life story. Yet, fate can always play a joker.

The category of *adjustment disorders* is meant to make allowance for those difficulties in children due to injuries or events not specifically related to the other categories, such as non-psychogenic illnesses, intellectual or physical handicap and the effects of catastrophic events such as war or earthquakes.

Clinical example

Betty was a 9-year-old girl who had recently contracted diabetes and needed daily injections and a very controlled and careful diet. She was referred to the therapist because she had become depressed and withdrawn and became distraught prior to her daily injections. She had decided that she got sick because she was bad. In one of her early therapy sessions Betty chose from the toys available a bed, a girl doll and a large black spider. She acted out with these toys a scene involving the little girl being repeatedly attacked by this spider and when asked by the therapist if there was any way that the little girl could protect herself Betty replied that there was a silver sword that would protect the little girl and kill off the spider but it would also often stab the little girl and hurt her. The therapist introduced into the toy scene a knight plus tooth pick as a sword and had him help the toy girl plot the downfall of the spider. Betty became very animated and spoke from the position of the knight to the little girl explaining many of the things she herself must have heard from her doctor. After many weeks and many variations on this scene Betty's mother reported back that she was no longer distraught about the injections and after three months of therapy her adjustment to the diabetes was complete and she was re-energised and contactful. Her redecision was 'I am a healthy girl who has to take care of my body extra specially.'

This so-called 'adjustment disorder' is an example of a child's life touched by external forces, or as Berne said – fate. This can be conceptualised by a larger, more universal system within which the other three systems move as cogs on a wheel. It is well for the psychotherapist to avoid hubris and to remember with humility the limitations of our work and the exquisite vulnerability of the human being.

Table 10.1 Summary table: a model for overlapping subsystems in the assessment and planning of TA child psychotherapy

	Subsystem used for interventions	Most useful focal TA techniques
1 Blocked development Won't play 4-year-old Felicity	1st Individual therapy 2nd Individual with group therapy	Permission and teaching options
2 Trauma Betsy's self-destructive and manic behaviour	Individual therapy concurrent with therapy for child/mother dyad	Rechilding and Reparenting
3 Systemic pathology in the family system (the child seeks help for the parents) Robin's learning problems Rita's conversion symptoms	Robin in individual therapy; mother in individual therapy Rita in individual therapy; parents seen as a couple; and finally family therapy	Decontamination The undoing of a 2nd order structural symbiosis
4 Changes in the family system Frederic regresses to soiling when father leaves home	Frederic in individual psychotherapy concurrent with family therapy using family sculpt	Protection for expressing real feelings of anger. Permission to commence his natural mourning process instead of soiling behaviour (rackety display)
5 Socioculturally based problems such as lack of information Homa talks to herself	Family therapy and meeting with teachers at school Mother in psychotherapy group	Decontamination and Adult information
6 Adjustment disorder Betty develops diabetes	Betty in individual therapy	Redecision work

INTERVENTION FORMATS

Individual psychotherapy

There is a danger in my mind of an overemphasis now of the management of human difficulties in terms of family and other groups as an escape from the study of the individual, whether child, infant, adolescent or grown-up. Somewhere or other in the work involved in every case, a caseworker must meet an individual outside the grouping; it is here that the biggest difficulties lie and it is also here that there is the greatest potential for bringing about change. I start, therefore, with a plea: remember the individual child, and the child's developmental process, and the child's distress, and the child's need for personal help, while of course remembering the importance of the family and the various school groups and all the other groups that lead on to one that we call society.

(Winnicott, 1986: 129)

The *advantages* involved in seeing the child alone include:
In a very short time span the child can build a trusting relationship with the therapist and experience very focused attention from him/her. The child does not have to take anyone else into consideration, other than the therapist, and so may sooner and more easily start accepting help with his/her issues. The therapist can more easily work with the child's fantasies and beliefs without having to deal with contradictions about 'facts' from other 'witnesses'. Early unresolved issues involving the symbiotic relationship with mother can be replayed and more creatively resolved. Having the child 'go to the therapist' may be the only way in which really disturbed parent(s) can cope with beginning to face the realities of a disturbed family system.

The *disadvantages* involved in seeing the child alone include:
The one-to-one relationship may replay the closed system already in operation at home. Changing only one small part of the family system may not have as much impact on the system as could be achieved through involving more of the family. This manner of seeing the child may reinforce his/her and perhaps the family's belief that he/she is the problem. This could reinforce the child's experience that in his family he/she has to be responsible for evoking changes. The child may be afraid of 'grassing' on the family or being experienced back home as having done so.

Useful sources of information about individual psychotherapy are:
Axline (1964), Segal (1986/1964), Oaklander (1978), Moustakas (1966), Klein (1984), Schaefer *et al.*, (1986). Romanini (1982) describes transactional analysis treatment in some cases of infant autism.

Child and primary caretaker in therapy

The advantages involved in seeing the child with his primary caretaker include:
The therapist has the opportunity not only to treat the two individuals involved but also to pay much attention to the relationship between the two. Both the child and the parent can be witness to the other's changes and needs, and this can be experiential information of great use back out in the 'ordinary' world. Neither the child nor the parent needs to see themselves as the 'problem'. There is less secrecy involved so there need not be a fear of exposing the family as much as there might when the child is in individual work. The child may feel less isolated if he/she experiences the backup and 'partnership' involved in trying to solve 'the worries' together. The therapist, in responding to the child in the caretaker's presence, provides a valuable role model.

The disadvantages involved in seeing the child with his/her primary caretaker include:

What happens in the therapy sessions may be used 'at home' as evidence against the child. The child's worries may be compounded by him or her being made to feel that reluctantly the caretaker *has* to accompany the 'wretched' child. The child may be too afraid of the caretaker to confide in the therapist. There may be less opportunity for play therapy to work with the child's intrapsychic dynamics, through stories, fantasies, and enactment. The caretaker may experience their role and competence to be on display or 'at risk' – 'I want someone to be for the child, but not hostile to me!'

Useful sources of information:

Folkhart (1967), Lynch *et al.*, (1975), Main (1958) and Ounsted *et al.*, (1974). Winnicott (1960, 1986) worked for more than four decades as a paediatrician doing over twenty thousand consultations with the mother-and-child couple. His work is a rich education in the parent/child dyadic relationship. To the authors' knowledge this therapeutic format has not yet been explored to any depth in the published TA literature.

Family therapy

The advantages involved in seeing the child within her whole family include:

The whole system can be directly analysed and helped. The child has the backup of the entire group. There is no scapegoating in terms of only one or some members of the group being labelled as needing help. There is less paranoia about what was said to whom in secret. Any changes which occur have a stronger chance of holding when the family is out of the therapy framework. Change options may be maximised by maximising involvements of components of the system. Individual members of the system are managed whilst the interactive effects can be directly observed and dealt with.

The disadvantages involved in seeing the child within the whole family might include:

The child may not be getting the intense attention she deserves and needs. Some or all of the other members of the family may perceive this as further evidence of how the child disturbs the family's way of life. The family may withdraw from a treatment too threatening for a significant member. Influential/powerful members may resent/feel threatened by the therapist and withdraw or sabotage therapy.

Useful sources of information:

Minuchin (1974), Neill and Kniskern (1982), Bentovim *et al.*, (1982), Kempler (1974) and Satir (1976), Kempler (1981) and Haley and Hoffman (1967). TA authors who address family systems interventions are: Horewitz (1979), McClendon and Kadis (1983) and Massey (1983, 1985).

Psychotherapy groups for children:

The advantages involved in seeing the child within a children's group might include:
The child is presented with experience of how other peers operate and handle or fail to manage their lives. The therapist has opportunities to assess and assist the child directly in his peer relationships. Enactment and play therapy involving many characters becomes a real possibility. The group can be seen by the child and the family as a casual playgroup rather than a clinical and 'labelled' session. Support and encouragement given by peers maximises options not available in individual therapy. The group 'culture' provides a safe environment in which to both encourage and support change as well as to confront the child's behaviour when necessary.

The disadvantages involved in seeing the child within a children's therapy group might involve:
The child may use certain social skills as a defence to hide her underlying personal issues. Just as in her family, the child may find it difficult to compete for the one-to-one attention she needs. She may adopt other 'pathological' modes of coping modelled by other group members.

Useful sources of information:
Several articles on using transactional analysis in school settings are easily adapted to psychotherapy groups with children, for example, Pickett (1986), Golub and Guerriero (1981) and Henderson (1978). Examples of general writings on this topic are Ginott (1958), Symonds and Dawson (1974/5), Bellucci (1975) and Gerstein (1974).

Combinations of the above

The advantages involved in seeing a child individually and/or in a group and/or with some or all of their family might include:
The child has both the opportunity to get intense one-to-one attention without having to vie for it or to feel guilty about it, whilst also having the opportunity to work co-operatively within the group. The child would have the time to experiment with skills learnt in his/her individual sessions in the group whilst still alongside the trust and assistance of the therapist. The therapist can work easily with both fact and 'fiction', maximising change options by increased involvement of different subsystems.

The disadvantages involved in combining several formats of therapy or intervention, might include:
The child may play the one system against the other. Aspects of confidentiality may become unwieldy. Having to share the person with whom one-to-one sessions have been experienced may involve unnecessary complications. The number of individuals is increased (all with their own difficulties), and this may multiply the risk of breakdown in therapy. This arrangement of multiple-system

interventions can also be prohibitively expensive. It must be remembered that *any* intervention with any of the component parts of the child's socio-familial system is technically a 'family systems intervention'. Generally, the option of treating the parent alone, either individually or in a group-psychotherapy setting, should never be underestimated because, as the parents change, they can most powerfully reverse the script messages which they had been passing on to their children. 'As the participants learned to separate their 'self' from the self of others they became less intensely invested in the behaviour of their child and began to see her as a separate self with her own boundaries and her own personal power' Sinclair-Brown (1982). Berne also reported such therapeutic effects of treating a group of mothers of disturbed children: 'Concurrently there was social and symptomatic improvement among the patients' intimates, including the children who were their primary interest in first coming to the group' (Berne, 1980: 184).

The relative advantages and disadvantages of various combinations has not, to the authors' knowledge, been extensively discussed either in the literature of general psychotherapy or in the TA literature. This chapter is intended to be a contribution towards filling that gap and stimulating other practitioners and authors to mine this field theoretically and clinically.

Treatment guidelines (deciding when and how to intervene)

1 Identify the subsystem considered to have the most serious single pathology.
2 Identify which subsystems are most accessible/available for work.
3 Consider at least two or three possible interventions and make a balance sheet of potential advantages/disadvantages for each and for all before deciding. Remember that all interventions have advantages and disadvantages.
4 Decide a 'minimum crucial involvement' to engage in treatment. Avoid rescuing or involving a young child in an interminable 'treatment situation'.
5 Be flexible. Altering any single component of a system can lead to changes in other components and the system as a whole.
6 If the system (family/school) is too disturbed, allow for the possibility of a treatment outside the system in which the problem is presenting (i.e. residential care, boarding school, hospital, 'place of safety').
7 Also consider removing the offending parent, not necessarily the child.
8 Stroking is crucial to child growth/therapy. If the child has intense stroke requirements provide intense stroke therapy (individual or maximum agency involvement).
9 Start with the subsystem most likely to change. Judicious use of the forcefield analysis as developed by Lewin (1963) is a most useful aid in this kind of decision-making.
10 Maximise and support any healthy developmental 'thrust'.
11 Care for the carers – in situations involving children, the therapist's Child is likely to get involved and archaic issues may well be activated in the counter-transference. Adequate support and supervision are essential.

THE DIFFERENCES AND SIMILARITIES BETWEEN CHILD AND ADULT PSYCHOTHERAPY

We believe that there are not many fundamental differences between the therapy approaches for children and those used for adults. Much of adult psychotherapy involves work with the archaic Child as well as the introjected Parent and these are available in children from a very early age. However, the three differences we do perceive are in relation to – language, responsibilty and the incompletion of basic developmental tasks.

1 *The use of language.*
   Children have a more limited vocabulary than that used by most adults and the therapist has therefore to adjust her use of language to meet the child's needs. This is why there is a greater use of multiple media in child therapy, such as sandplay, puppetry, etc. This does not mean a linguistic condescension to the child. Comprehension of language always precedes verbal facility. There should not 'be a talking down to the child, but rather a utilization of language, concepts, ideas, and word pictures meaningful to children in terms of their own learnings' (Erickson, 1980: 176). Perhaps the demand on the personality, flexibility and creativity of the therapist is qualitatively different.

2 *Responsibility.*
   For the commencement or termination of therapy, children, unlike most adults (except those adults who are so deeply disturbed that they require the intervention of other adults), are usually 'taken' to therapy or made to cease therapy under the instigation of an adult caretaker and not, as with most adults, through their own instigation. Children are quite literally dependent on their caretakers, and this includes the therapist for the duration of the session.

3 *Developmental immaturity.*
   Children are more influenced by the natural process and it is more crucial for them to receive appropriate 'permissions' at crucial times, to prevent 'skewing of the pennies' (Berne, 1980), which is possibly more longstanding and difficult to change at a later stage (Campos, 1986).

Finally, the outcome of any therapeutic intervention is determined by the quality of the relationship between the therapist and the troubled child.

No matter how complicated, how discouraging or frightening, no matter how uncertain the therapeutic process, even during the most prolonged plateau, the possibility for encounter is present if the therapist's courage and strength and perceptiveness are available, if his resources for spontaneous engagement are present. The life of therapeutic encounter is a two-way process. It is a person-to-person meeting in which child and therapist collaborate in their search to unravel the hidden meanings; to clarify the distortions and confusion; to disclose real feelings and thoughts in a closed and fragmented self; to create a climate of learning, where conflicts, challenges and emerging insight and awareness integrate with sensitivity and compassion in restoring a child to mature and healthy self-hood (Moustakas, 1966: 6, 7).

EGO-STATE DILEMMAS OF ABUSED CHILDREN

In this section the author discusses the intrapsychic dynamics of the abused child. The theoretical basis is drawn from the correspondence between the theories of Alice Miller (1983, 1985, 1987) and Dorothy Bloch (1979) and those of Fairbairn (1952) and Berne (1966). The perpetuation of Parent ego states is discussed and Child ego-state responses to abuse as these are reflected in the existential life positions. It is suggested that the psychotherapist may take the role of the abusing or neglectful parent, supported by anti-child assumptions embedded in some psychological theories and a colluding sociocultural environment.

While working as a clinical psychologist in a clinic for child and family therapy in the sixties, Petrūska Clarkson had much experience of observing and working with children in play-therapy situations. The perennial question of working with the child rather than with the whole family system was frequently debated. Sometimes the original parents were simply not available when the children were referred, for example Andre at 7 years of age had been in seven foster homes. In play therapy he frequently related to a baby doll in a pram by shouting with a contorted face: 'You're always nagging me! I'll kill you if you don't shuddup!' This would be accompanied by beating and hitting the doll ferociously. His voice sounded quite different from his ordinary voice, a more pronounced accent was discernible and his gestures were apparently inconsistent with his age.

Although Andre's psychotherapist did not for some time meet the abusing parent whose psyche was thus incorporated, she could form a highly accurate picture of that parental person which provided the basis for her treatment of this unhappy child. This was the author's first conscious encounter with a phenomenological manifestation of a Parent ego state in a young child, i.e. the unedited and uncensored reproduction of the behaviour, attitudes and feelings of an actual parent figure.

The abusive Parent ego state:

Parent ego state as ego-dystonic   After Andre's angry outbursts he would claim that 'It wasn't me that did it' or 'It was an accident.' This led to Petrūska Clarkson's understanding that he was reproducing someone else's behaviour without editing and apparently against his conscious will. Subjectively, he was experiencing his aggressive attacks as manifestations of a 'naturalized alien, as it were, within the realm of the individual mind, an immigrant from outer reality. Its whole significance resides in the fact that it is essentially an internalized object' (Fairbairn 1952: 131).

Petrūska Clarkson was witnessing a Parent ego state as Berne described. Berne defined a Parent ego state as: 'a reproduction of nurturing, angry or critical behaviour on the part of one or both parents – or the parental influence – that is behaviour historically determined by borrowed parameters' (Berne, 1966: 222). Berne stresses that Parental ego states can be discussed psychoanalytically in terms of incorporation, internalization, introjection and identification, but that transactional analysis deals with it at a transactional or operational level (Berne, 1966: 296).

When the child is being *influenced* by an internal parental figure, he or she is experiencing a Child ego state. At this point the author wants to focus specifically on the direct Parent ego state manifestation.

Grown-ups frequently report this as an experience of being taken over by behaviours, attitudes and feelings 'foreign to them' and against their autonomous choice – as being 'possessed'. In 1944 when Fairbairn was already writing about the dynamics of endopsychic structures he was alert to this 'appearance of demonology. It remains true, nevertheless, that under certain conditions internalized objects may acquire a dynamic independence which cannot be ignored' (Fairbairn, 1952: 134).

For example, in explosive rages which are more typical of mother's behaviour with father, a client re-enacts such scenes with her husband whilst experiencing it as ego dystonic – 'not myself'. Transactional analysts often explain Parent ego states as collections of automaticisms incorporated from significant parent figures. The phenomenological truth of the child's Parent ego-state representation   Time after time in doing child psychotherapy the author found that parental behaviour (particularly violent and abusive behaviour) was re-enacted in an unedited manner which was far more true to the child's actual experience than the parents' version of their earlier behaviour at clinic interviews.

Berne (1980) and Steiner (1975) believe that the child takes in the complete Parent ego state as it manifests at a particular moment in time in an unexpurgated version of the phenomenological truth. This Parent ego state is experientially true whether the child enacts it or whether the child experiences it as an internally persecuting influence. The reality of Parent ego states challenges the psychoanalytic assumption that the child's envy and anger are inborn basic drives which inevitably manifest themselves as part of the death instinct.

Berne specifically refers to the case 'where one or other of the internal voices is heard as coming from outside the skull. This is usually the voice of the parent (actually the voice of his father or mother) and these are hallucinations' (Berne, 1972: 274.). Children's *hallucinations* in such cases are externalisations of parental ego states which are too intolerable to contain within the psychic structure. (It represents both escape and release from the persecuting internal object as well as maintenance of a libidinal cathexis with the persecuting parent.)

In the case of little Jenny who felt controlled by a red devil in the corner, the psychotherapist concluded that this was a symbolic representation of introjected parental material derived from parents who came from a very rigid Roman

Catholic tradition. The red devil is a representation at the concrete level of the child's intellectual functioning that is based on the child's intuitive awareness of the intentions of 'the crazy Child' ego states of the actual parents. What may *appear* as a distortion of the parents' facial expression or voice tone, represents the phenomenological and perceptual reality of a helpless and vulnerable child who is dependent for survival on the omnipotent parents.

In breaking away from the assumption of 'evil intentions' in the infant and her rightly placing these in the context of the unresolved conflicts of the parents, Alice Miller reads like a transactional analyst. Her concept of the phenomenological reality of these repetitive, pedagogical patterns resembles Berne's definition very closely. The analysand discovers the introjects within himself and that he has been their prisoner.

> For his anger, demands and avarice do not at first appear in a tamed adult form but in the childish-archaic one in which they were repressed. The patient is horrified when he realises that he is capable of screaming with rage in the same way that he so hated in his father.
>
> (Miller, 1983: 34)

This psychologically accurate internalisation of 'the crazy child in the parent' (Holloway, 1972) does not have to be based on the child's being the direct object of the violence.

As Dorothy Bloch says :

> With the children whom I have treated it was sufficient if the parents persistently committed violent acts of any kind, or were frequently violent, not toward the child, but toward each other or toward another child or even toward an animal, or if they repeatedly permitted one child to act violently toward a more defenseless one with impunity. In some instances, violent and habitually attacking older siblings were experienced as agents of the parents; where the parents did not intervene effectively to protect the child, he assumed they wanted him killed.
>
> (Bloch, 1979: 6, 7)

Whole introjection of parental conflicts   Berne specifically stated that the Parent ego states each have in turn their own Parent, Adult, and Child ego states and he called this second order structural analysis. The child not only takes in the abusive parent but also the Child ego states of the parent. Even if the parent is not being abusive or threatening at a social level, the child may accurately record intrapsychically the conflicts of the parent's Child at a psychological level. The child's incorporated Parent ego state representation is still an accurate reflection of the parent's conflicts whether overtly expressed or not.

Clinical example

Child: There is another part of me that wants to hurt me.
Therapist: So sit here and tell Mary what you're like.
Child: I am going to make you feel bad. I don't want you to feel human. I want you to worry about everything you do and say. I'll try to stop you for some reason.
Therapist: Tell her what the reasons are. I am going to stop you because you are .... . And then just imagine ... whatever words come into your head.
Child: I am just trying to stop you because, I've got .... You've got a lot of good qualities and I might even be jealous of you.
Therapist: Can you guess who it is who is jealous of you?
Child: My mother.
Therapist: Yes, it's not your mother as she is today but your mother as you saw her when you were little, that part of her that was jealous that you became those things and that you were so pretty. So inside of you is a bit of your mother that once was there, that was jealous of you and would like you to fail. Good thinking .... yes.
Child: Mm. Now I see this in a different way. It's quite frightening when you actually realise it. At the same time I feel relief that there's not actually a monster living inside of me. I can listen to that part or not.

Child ego-state responses to abuse: choice of existential life position

One of the most impressive characteristics of abused children is their need to deny the trauma, so much so that Miller (1983) comments on the fact that this material often only emerges in a person's second analysis. The force and embeddedness of these early experiences are notoriously difficult to surface. Conway and Clarkson (1987) describe how individuals are more susceptible to the hypnotic inductions of parental injunctions when such messages are combined with physical pain, discounting the independent thinking of the child and the extraordinary potency of a parent figure in relation to a child whose life is truly dependent on their goodwill:

> ... if the injunction is a demand made by a witch or giant whose features are distorted with rage, whose voice smashes through all the defenses of the child's mind, and whose hand is ever ready to strike humiliation and terror into his face and head, it requires enormous therapeutic power [to neutralise this programming].

> (Berne, 1980: 116, 117)

Such is the matrix from which children choose their existential life position depending on the various ways in which each reacts to abuse.

In his discussion of child development, Berne (1966: 265–80) has already adopted an object-relations approach albeit with existentialist intent. Berne takes from Klein (in Segal, 1986) the term 'position' to indicate an internal psychological condition, always potentially present in personality and formed in early childhood, which also has a defensive function. This is a different emphasis from subsequent behavioural elaborations of the four basic life positions (Ernst, 1971).

The three not-OK basic positions Berne identifies are paranoid, depressive and schizoid. These terms are taken directly from Klein (1949) whom we know he had read by 1966 since it is referenced in *Principles of Group Treatment*. Berne adds position one (I'm OK – You're OK), which Klein did not specifically address and calls it intrinsically constructive and existentially possible. He also emphasises the decisional nature of these positions predicated on the child's basic OKness.

Next the rescuing fantasy – I'm not OK, You are OK (It's all my fault). The child's desire to protect the abusing parent is well documented (Matthews, 1986; Armstrong, 1978; Bloch, 1979). The child is prone to take the blame and so exonerate the abusing parent. For example, from Matthews:

> Was that all my fault because I am so evil, because I know that sometimes when dad touches me he seems to make me feel as though it's pleasant for me even though I really hate it; that makes me feel even more guilty.
>
> (Matthews, 1986: 58)

The 'use of a vast range of "menacing figures" reveals the child's profound investment in camouflaging their [the parents] identity and hiding his perceptions' (Bloch 1979: 21). The *caretaker* decides that the way to rid the world of evil is to absorb the violence within themselves, psychically encapsulate it and to act symbolically as some benevolent container while they absorb the envy, negativity and rage directed at them. They often become helping professionals in later life often seeking to work with client groups who have suffered similar abuse. The overriding intrapsychic dynamic is a second-order structural symbiosis with the abusing parent (often in addition to a protecting racket with the other parent) based on guilt about the repressed anger.

Another mechanism of introjection is illustrated by the second-order structural symbiosis where the child at some unconscious level enters into a psychological-level bargain with the abusing parent in order to 'protect' one of the parents. The parent thus 'protected' often discounts at a high level the existence of the problem, for example, a 9 year old was sexually abused by her father for several years whilst the mother claimed, 'I did not know this was going on'. Social workers, however, established that she and her husband had not had sexual relations for all this period, and that the mother regularly went to sleep early in the evening before her husband came to bed. It was in this twilight time that he sought 'affection; from his daughter who experienced him as "a little boy who was lonely and needing to be held"'. The girl child chose temporarily to abrogate her own somatic child needs and took on a parent and adult role in relation to her putative caretaker.

Clinical example

Therapist: What's happening now?
Child: I am going back into the bathroom.
Therapist: Uh, uh … see your father's angry face?
Child: D'you know I don't want to call her. I don't want to ask her to help.
(cries)
Therapist: What might happen if you did ask her for help?
Child: I think she'd come.
Therapist: Uh, uh.
Child: I think she could control daddy as well, she could stop him.
Therapist: But you don't want to call her?
Child: If I called mummy and she came, she would get very upset and faint
and have to go to hospital, and perhaps she would die.

In another case the second-order symbiosis, or reverse dependency, was
effective in protecting the abusing mother from the negative impact of her own
cruelty on her social standing with friends and neighbours. If the child blames
itself, as it most often does, it is ashamed that other people may discover how bad
it really is that its 'good mother' or 'kind father' should have to beat him so.

A child conceals her bruised and battered body from the nuns while she prays
to God for forgivenness for her sins for not honouring her mother with
appropriate filial love. She is terrified not only by her own rage but also by the
potentially tragic consequences of confronting her parent with the cruel
behaviour.

With his concept of the magical nature of his thoughts, wishes and feelings, he
may also assume responsibility for an extraordinary range of unhappy events.
Is there a death in the family? – he is a murderer. An accident? – he is the
secret perpetrator. An illness? – he is the agent.

(Bloch, 1979: 5)

Essentially these children are stuck in a depressive life position (Klein, 1949;
Berne, 1966).

The victim's sanction: I'm not OK – You're not OK ('A dog that didn't
deserve to be a child' (Bloch, 1979)). Such a child seems permanently under the
influence of a vicious internal parent. This may show in symptomatology of
recurrent infections, addictions, somatic illness and third-degree outcomes, such
as accidents, schizophrenia, admission to mental hospital and consignment to
gaol. By retroflection, the child constantly punishes himself with the vicious
internal voices which keep up a stream of vituperative and humiliating internal
commentary on all aspects of the child's life. The hostile urges which threaten to
erupt against the external object (abusing parent) are turned against the self.

Defensive fantasies are designed, not only to provide an outlet for the child's
unbearable terror, but also, by projecting it onto imaginary creatures, to

conceal its source, thus enabling him to preserve the idealised and potentially loving image of his parents that appears so fundamental to his feeling of security.

(Bloch, 1979: 93)

For example, instead of hitting back at a hateful and hurtful parent figure, the child frequently hurts itself by deliberate self-mutilation, 'accidentally walking on glass' and seeking out situations of humiliation and danger. At the very least, they live life at odds with their bodies, since they have been trained to experience their physical selves as 'objects' of abuse. They may discount feelings, discomfort and pain at the level of existence of the stimulus to the extent where they may burn themselves at an electric heater without 'noticing'. This is the schizoid life position, a term which Klein (1984: ix) incorporated from Fairbairn. It is most vividly portrayed by Lowen in *The Betrayal of the Body* (1969).

In these cases the person may idealise some aspects of the parent figure as well as incorporating the abusive aspects of the parent. This may particularly happen where the parental behaviour is inconsistent, for example in alcoholic parents who are kind and sentimental when sober, and vicious and abusive when drunk (when their own crazy Child has the executive power over the ego display).

According to Bloch, the child's major need to maintain an idealised image of the parent is central, and abused children quickly convince themselves that their parents could love them but it was their own badness that provoked the parental violence. 'I cried a lot because of my sin and my wickedness.' Not only does the child introject the abusive internal object, but the child also introjects 'the guilt feeling of the adult ...' (Ferenczi (1932) in Masson, 1985: 298). This is the origin of the I'm not OK – You're not OK existential life position. Idealisation may be a defence against the realisation of the profundity of their betrayal.

The child's actual or psychological survival may depend on her finding within herself the cause of the parental injurious envy or murderous hatred. The author doubts whether it is possible for a child not to internalize any parent at all, particularly in view of the neurological and hypnotic studies which demonstrate time and again such perfect registration of past experiences.

Identification with the abuser – I'm OK – You're not OK ('Corporal punishment made me the man I am!'). 'As long as the introjects active within us remain unconscious, we will duplicate the same old pedagogical patterns, only in a different form' (Miller, 1985: 152). These are the children who pass on the injurious or lethal parenting, apparently compelled by their script 'to do unto others as had been done unto them'. The identification with the abuser is ego-syntonic. These are the battering parents who are the battered children of the battering parents which so frequently occur in the literature. These are the people who sexually abuse their children in a tragic repetition of the sexual abuse they suffered as children (Miller, 1987). Why does the child internalise an abusing parent? 'The answer to this question seemed to me to be that the child internalized bad objects partly with a view to controlling them (an aggressive motive) but chiefly because he experienced a libidinal need of them' (Fairbairn, 1952: 156).

Fairbairn stresses the positive libidinal attachments to internal bad objects. This corresponds so exactly to the frequently encountered clinical phenomenon of the battered child's pathetic loyalty to his or her oppressive parent(s). This phenomenon of abused and abuser developing a symbiotic attachment has been found in the literature of the strong affectional bond that can develop between the torturer and the tortured (Sargant, 1957).

This can be explained as 'identification with the aggressor'. Ferenczi, 1932 (in Masson, 1985), first described how the child responds to abuse by identification and introjection of the menacing person or aggressor, an identification based on fear.

The child who chooses *inhibition* as a primary defence against the pain of the parental betrayal of his love may inhibit his wish and his impulse to kill the threatening parent and, as a developmental stage, this corresponds to the paranoid position first identified by Klein (1949).

> In such cases the child responded by developing feelings of alienation and became consumed by a fear of losing control that caused him to inhibit all fantasy.... Inhibition may be his only solution. How ominous a development that may be is indicated by an investigation into the background of people who have actually committed murder.
>
> (Bloch, 1979: 108)

Bloch disagrees that aggression is a deep-seated universal drive and believes along with Miller (1987), Moustakas (1967) and Liedloff (1975) that it is a response to frustration and alienation. In the aforementioned cases this reaches an extreme. Bach and Goldberg (1975) quote several case studies where gentle, quiet and inhibited people eventually commit violent murder. Study after study establishes the brutal childhood experiences of individuals who subsequently, after many years of long-suffering suppression of feelings, erupt in apparently inexplicable outbursts of violence.

> Gradually the child is forced into a state where feelings and senses are muffled and subdued until eventually he is no longer aware that he is experiencing them. When people reject, humiliate, hurt, belittle, control, dominate, and brutalize others without being aware of what they are doing, there is extreme danger that man will cease to be man.
>
> (Moustakas, 1967)

The way out – experiential validation from self and others

Along with many transactional analysts Miller (1985) centralises the importance of reliving early childhood experiences with full emotional expression in the presence of a validating 'other' person.

In the opinion of the author structural ego-state analysis of the abused child is not used as effectively as it could be in the treatment of sexually and physically abused children. Often the Child ego states may be in treatment, but the introjected abusing Parental ego states are not. A child who is depressed and ignored may need protection from an introjected and encapsulated anti-social parent who is intent on infanticide. For the child this is a very real concern since they are actually sometimes destroyed by their caretakers, as witness the dreadful case of little Kimberley who was tortured and starved to death by her mother and stepfather.

Transactional analysis provides the conceptual and psychotherapeutic tools to intervene directly and powerfully to the relevant Child or Parent ego states. It also enables us to recognise different diagnoses for different ego states of the same person and helps us to design and implement differential treatment plans for Child and Parent ego states of each individual child (Clarkson and Gilbert, 1988).

As James and Jongeward (1971) reiterated, children also have Adult ego states. For the grown-up, as well as for the chronological child, the awareness and expression of their justifiable autonomous Adult feelings of anger and grief (Berne, 1980/1961: 158) can begin to free the young person within to a new level of integration and a potentially normal development for the 'Inner Child'. This process may, however, be hampered by covert collusion between the therapist and the wider society in which an anti-child assumption is embedded.

The psychotherapist's collusion with a culture which disbelieves and blames abused children and protects abusing parents

In psychotherapy, new historical ego states are created in a regressed psycho-physiological matrix under the influence of temporal distortion (Clarkson and Fish, 1988). Because of the client's regressive receptivity and heightened susceptibility to hypnotic instruction from figures in authority, healing can occur. Equally, new brutalisation can occur (Conway and Clarkson, 1987).

The loyalty and reluctance to 'point the finger of blame' at the cruel 'parent' is not confined only to children. It is also true that in psychotherapy people 'become as children' regressing to earlier neurophysiological layers of the psyche. This is when, by a process of 'rechilding', new historical ego states are formed which bypass autonomous adult functioning in the here-and-now. In such a heightened state of vulnerability the patient/client is often as susceptible to suggestion as a child.

The following example might be a case in point. Freud asked Fliess to conduct a nasal operation on a patient of his, Emma Eckstein. The two doctors considered this radical procedure necessary in order to treat her masturbatory practices which they believed to be at the root of her psychological disorder. She nearly died from haemorrhaging as a result of Fliess's error of leaving a length of blood-soaked gauze in her nose. Freud rationalised the aftermath of this operation. His letters concerning this case were omitted from his published letters. Freud wrote that her bleeding after the operation had nothing to do with the gauze Fliess had left in her wound but was hysterical in origin, 'occasioned by longing and probably occurred at the sexually relevant times. (The woman, out of resistance, has not yet supplied me with the dates.)' (Masson, 1985: 100). Emma Eckstein not only compliantly submitted to this procedure but also did not hold it against either of the negligent doctors, even after the cause of her frequent haemorrhaging became clear to everyone concerned.

According to Laing such blaming of the victim is still current in psychiatric institutions.

> Why does he hate his father and why had he even thought of killing him? We shall never know. The direct effect, and intention, of psychiatric intervention is to turn this young man into a 'young invalid': to *invalidate* his hatred of his father, under the name of treatment.
>
> (Laing, 1969: 73)

Feminist authors point out how the male medical establishment supports prejudices against women and children. As recently as in 1948 a clitoridectomy was performed in the US on a child of 5 years old as a cure for her masturbation. Ehrenreich and English (1978: 111) also demonstrate how until very recently our society supported medical mutilation to children based on contaminated beliefs about their intrinsic natures.

Because of the power ascribed to a psychotherapist by the client and as a result of the client's psychological 'regressiveness', introjection of the whole or part Parent ego states of the psychotherapist may occur. Several psychoanalytic writers subscribe to the view that internalisation of some aspect of the therapist occurs in psychotherapy (Bion, 1961; Horewitz, 1979). If such Parent ego states (of the treating psychotherapists) have attitudes which find the blame for parental sexual abuse in the 'seductiveness' or 'provocativeness' of the oedipal Child, this further traumatises the child in the patient who needs an advocate in order to absolve them from their 'victim's guilt'.

> Patients need therapists and analysts who will stand by them and support them as they suffer the pains of their powerlessness; they do not need people who, acting as spokesmen for prevailing societal norms, try to talk them out of their vague awareness of their early experience.
>
> (Miller, 1985: 155)

Bloch proposed in 1979 (the very same year that Alice Miller's *Drama of The Gifted Child* was first published in German) that Freud omitted a most significant part of the Oedipus legend – the murderous act of his parents. Freud's theory considers Oedipus's desire to murder his father and marry his mother as universal drives. However, he neglects to apply the same principle in establishing the universality of the parents' wish to kill their child. The ommission is crucial – it was that Oedipus's parents *in the first* place wished to harm or kill him! This significantly shifts the emphasis from a child 'driven by aggressive oedipal conflicts' to a realistic assessment of the dangers involved in being a vulnerable infant at the mercy of conflicted, often murderously envious parents.

Bloch also found the concept of the child's *fear* of infanticide, startling though it might be, more widely accepted than the likelihood that parents actually may wish to commit infanticide. Yet we are all familiar with the parental phrase 'there are times I could kill them'. Winnicott (1975) wrote a classic paper which listed fifteen good reasons for a mother to hate the arrival of her baby. Most parents in psychotherapy at one time or another admit to murderous thoughts and feelings towards their babies and children which may or may not have been accompanied by verbal or physical violence. Whether this fear of infanticide proves crippling for the child depends on the severity of the parents' intention and on other resources available in the child's network.

> In her descriptions of the early stages of the child's emotional life, Klein presents us with a portrait of a wicked infant in which she fails to show the connections between the infant's violent feelings (such as hate, envy or greed) and the unconscious of the parents, as well as the humiliation, mistreatment and narcissistic wounds the latter inflict on the child.
>
> (Miller, 1985: 60)

Miller repeatedly emphasises that the child's anger is *appropriate* to her situation. It is *not* transferential in the sense that it is actually directed correctly at the person who is hurting her or threatening to do so. Both Winnicott (1975) and Fairbairn (1952) also conceive the child as responsive and reactive to deficiencies or failures on the part of the maternal object, whereas Klein (1949) ascribes it to powerful primitive projective mechanisms fuelled by envy which is largely inherited!

Several recent authors have indicated their disagreement with Freud's basic assumptions about the nature of infant human beings. Bloch suspects that Freud might have had an investment in excluding the *initiatory* parental violence in his treatment of the Oedipus myth. Smail (1987) also suggests that the concern of Freud and his colleagues with 'repression' of sexuality served, however unintentionally, as a screen for the deeper and more pervasive repression of the inequalities and injustices of power to which the child often falls victim. He even suggests a renaming of the 'Oedipus complex' as the 'Jocasta complex' (after Oedipus's mother) on the basis that actual clinical experience more often produces evidence of mothers seducing their sons rather than the reverse. He sees the core of the pathology of family relationships as the misuse and the abuse of parental power over children. 'The basest of human motives lie not in our sexual affilliations but in our violence toward one another, and it is above all these motives which we repress most effectively' (Smail, 1987: 114).

At the same time as more psychotherapists and theoreticians are radically questioning 'parental motives', there is a significant and synchronous increase in the literature suggesting that 'therapist abuse' may be more frequent and more damaging than most traditional therapists have been willing to admit (Casement, 1985; Langs and Searles, 1980; Davidson 1981).

On a more subtle level there is even in humanistic psychotherapies a tendency to side against the victim. Fairly or unfairly, as Alice Miller perceives it: 'Unfortunately, all the new and creative attempts, be they transactional analysis or Gestalt therapy, insist on making reconciliation with the parents the ultimate goal of therapy' (Miller, 1985: 206). Religions and cultures which support the guilt of the child create particularly destructive situations where the child's distress may be difficult or impossible to treat. Five-year-old Melanie reports:

I prayed to God and I cried as I prayed. I confessed that I had driven thorns into the flesh of Jesus. I saw the blackness of my own heart and I was so ashamed I wanted to die. I confessed how I did not honour my mother, that I was rebelious when she burnt me with cigarettes and my thoughts and my tongue had been full of evil.

Bystanders (Clarkson, 1987) may witness parental abuse towards a child or be aware of mental or physical abuse of a psychotherapy client without taking action on behalf of the injured parties because of a misguided reluctance 'to rescue' or perhaps fear of becoming 'involved'. Often in our culture it is assumed that parents are more likely to be right than the child.

In the Summer of 1987 (*Daily Mail*, 25 June 1987, p. 1) in Britain a crusade was launched by a national newspaper to protect 'THESE INNOCENT PARENTS' from the attention of two paediatricians. They had diagnosed a large number of possible physical and sexual abuse cases in a particular geographical region. The newspaper, with its banner headline, *automatically* judged the parents 'innocent'. The authors believe that children need the protection of authorities and then, after adequate consideration of the circumstances and proper guidance, the child's welfare is sometimes best served by providing them with a person who will hear the truth of their experience and amplify it enough so that they can hear their own pain and transform their rage into life-affirming energy.

Psychological treatment of children 'for their own good' is not only confined to physical or sexual abuse as Garbarino *et al.* (1986) point out, but also manifests in 'the psychological battering of children' by parents terrorising, isolating, ignoring, rejecting or corrupting the small human beings in their care.

In his book, *Taking Care, an Alternative to Therapy*, Smail (1987) expresses his belief that human beings are in pain because we do damage to each other, and we shall continue to suffer pain as long as we continue to do damage. He emphasises 'taking care of people', treating them as plants, rather than relying on therapy as if people were faulty machines that can be repaired:

The profoundly sinister, largely unseen but enormously complex apparatus of nuclear warfare, the South African policeman almost frenziedly whipping a peaceful demonstrator, and the father who regards with stony hatred the despair of a daughter he cannot love, are not separate phenomena, but together speak to the way in which we have become caught up in issues of power and competition beyond our immediate comprehension or control. Any improvement in this state of affairs will depend on a great deal more than our merely 'working on our relationships'.

(Smail, 1987: 121)

Ultimately, Symington (1986) as has been pointed out before suggests we need to move to what he terms the 'tragic position', the existential realisation that we all – children, parents and healers alike – share *la condition humaine*. This is surely the true ground of the I'm OK, You're OK basic existential life position.

Chapter 11

The psychotherapist in training, supervision and at work

Helena: What I can do no hurt to try,
        Since you set up your rest 'gainst remedy.
        He that of greatest work is finisher,
        does them by the weakest minister.
                (Shakespeare, *All's Well that Ends Well* II. i. 133–6)

TA TRAINING

Introduction

This section provides an outline of curriculum and training-programme design which has proved very successful both in training Certified transactional analysts and in providing a framework for mental health professionals which they use to integrate TA principles and practice into their existing work.

Loria (1983) and Cornell and Zalcman (1984) have contributed valuable perspectives on educational design and the development of professional standards of competence for practising professionals. However, the last outline of a training programme *per se* to appear in the TA literature, was Berne's Chapter 7 in *Principles of Group Treatment* (Berne 1966). The outline provided in this chapter will necessarily not be detailed or comprehensive enough to explicate the finer points. Also, it is vital to keep in mind that the training format is highly responsive to the dynamics of the different training groups and to individual need. This, in turn, is monitored by the efficiency in task achievement (reaching learning goals) of the whole group and personal satisfaction, so that self, peer and trainer evaluation is ongoing and regularly structured into the training.

At *metanoia* Psychotherapy Training Institute, a comprehensive, in-depth 4-year programme extends over 10 weekends (of 12 hours each) per academic year, i.e. 120 advanced training hours each year (see Table 11.1). Course participants for each year work together in selected, closed training groups at comparable levels of development.

Individuals may join the programme at the start of any academic year providing they meet the entry requirements for that particular year level. They may take

Table 11.1 metanoia TA training programme syllabus

Year 1	
Introduction to ITAA and	Theory and
EATA Contracts and case studies	Application
Structural analysis	
Transactional analysis	
Games analysis	
Racket analysis	
Script analysis	
Group dynamics	
Child development	
Psychopathology	
Self- and peer assessment	
Year 2	Concepts and
Supervision and treatment planning	Techniques
Structural analysis	
Transactional analysis	
Games analysis	
Racket analysis	
Script analysis	
Group treatment and systems principles	
Child development in TA	
Psychopathology	
Self- and peer assessment and exam procedures	
Year 3	
Contracting and case-studies review	Theory and
Cathexis I	supervision
Cathexis II	
Redecision therapy	
Classical school	
Integrative psychotherapy and personal style	
The therapeutic relationship (transference and countertransference)	
Comparative group therapy	
Ethics and professional responsibility	
Exam preparation and self- and peer assessment	
Year 4	
Contracting and treatment planning	Comparative
Maintenance procedures of a psychotherapy practice	theory and
Psychotherapeutic emergencies	case
Treatment of the neuroses	presentation
Treatment of the schizophrenias	
Treatment of the primary affective disorders	
Treatment of the borderline personality disorders	
Treatment of the narcissistic disorders	
Treatment of the character disorders	
Cure and termination	

Notes: 1 Topics in Year 4 will all have been covered to some extent in the training programme but are now subjected to in-depth critical and comparative analysis
2 This programme is regularly reviewed and may be different by the time of publication

'time out' from the course to attend applied transactional analysis workshops, (e.g. on sexuality, health and healing, TA and family therapy, etc.) or trainees can simultaneously do this whilst continuing with the core programme depending on individual levels of speed, commitment and energy. Any trainee taking 'time out' may subsequently rejoin the programme. Individuals may choose to do their Certification exams at any time depending on their readiness. Several professionals may complete part or all of the training without doing this examination.

Training philosophy

Honouring the spirit of the original Latin root of the word 'education' – which means 'to lead forth' – this programme aims to provide a graduated training for mental health professionals which is based on responsibility for own learning and provision of high-quality input and learning opportunities which are stimulating enough for the most advanced participants and structurally sound enough for people who learn at a more gradual pace. The teaching, besides being didactic, simultaneously seeks to model, by the trainer's behaviour: (a) contractual relationships, (b) emphasis on personal responsibility, (c) the assumption of OKness of both trainers and trainees, (d) colleagial co-operation, (e) openness to experimentation and investigation of the technical culture, the group etiquette and the group character (Berne, 1963).

Overall programme structure

Each year is designed to meet certain training objectives and each workshop aims to address in addition to the overall aim some aspects of theory and practice.

Overall workshop structure

The working weekend is divided into eight 90-minute slots with breaks for tea and lunch, etc. The first slot of any weekend is usually devoted to individuals sharing their professional achievements and/or concerns since the last meeting, e.g. articles published, groups started, and leaving jobs; as well as group process related to management and development of the group imago (Berne, 1963).

Slots 2–7 involve didactic input, experiential exercises and peer or individual supervision/technique-coaching/exam preparation, etc. as appropriate for year level.

The last period, slot 8, of any training weekend is devoted to contract-completion, feedback for self, others and trainers and evaluation. This ranges through informal feedback, structured written scoring forms and planning/contracting for learning, reading, supervisory and psychotherapy foci for the following month.

On Saturday night there is the opportunity to attend a seminar. Because many people travel long distances to attend these weekends, it is most convenient to arrange the seminars at this time. Attendance and presentations here are voluntary and not a compulsory part of the training programme. Also no fee is charged. One or more members of the training groups prepare a communal meal after a rest period and everybody shares expenses for food and drink.

Summary of training methods

These include – didactic lectures; experiential exercises done individually, in pairs and in small groups; projects; and accelerated learning techniques (Rose, 1985). The accelerated learning techniques used include imparting information to trainees while relaxed and with specially selected music, encouragement to read books from the book lists and partake in teaching selected segments of material, using NLP principles in ensuring that audio, visual and kinaesthetic learning preferences are catered for, use of films and video and of course, audio feedback from tape-recorders. Throughout the training year and each weekend the trainers work consciously at encouraging, managing and monitoring the developmental stages of the group process, e.g. at the first meeting of the year, dealing with the hopes, the anxieties and projective expectations, introductions and concerns which form part of the provisional group imago and termination issues nearer the end of the year, etc. The aim is that through effective management of the training group-process and modelling, people develop awareness and learn skills which they can apply to their ongoing therapy and training groups.

All Level I trainees need to arrange for special extra-curricular training in: (a) counselling skills, (b) child development by placement in nursery and/or apprenticing regressive therapy workshops and/or relevant university courses, (c) psychiatric treatment by attachment to a hospital or hostel with attendance at ward rounds and supervision from medical staff as available, (d) an additional training in group dynamics e.g. as provided by the Tavistock Clinic at the Leicester Conference or the annual Group Relations Training (which is part of the Consultation Course at the Tavistock).

It is also important to note the requirement that all trainees continue in personal psychotherapy for the duration of their training. This is considered ethical and responsible as well as a primary avenue of learning 'the inner map', which we believe psychotherapists require to move into depth psychotherapy which has both 'cure' and 'the facilitation of growth through adult developmental stages for all of our lives' as goals.

Furthermore, several national bodies concerned with psychotherapy have recommended that psychotherapists undergo personal therapy of a frequency and duration similar to the clients they would be expected to treat. So personal psychotherapy for the duration of training (individual, group and/or in intensive psychotherapy or regressive marathons), similar to that which they would eventually offer, is part of meeting the requirements for parity with most other respected schools of psychotherapy.

Detailed programme structure

Year 1 – A Foundation Course in TA

Prerequisites are the attendance at a 101 course, the completion of the 101 exam, a recognised qualification in one of the helping professions and current opportunity to apply TA *theory* in thinking about their work.

Contents of Year 1 The overall intent of the first year is to provide a thorough grounding in all the major TA concepts covered in the 101 syllabus as well as the basics of group dynamics, child development and psychopathology. See Table 11.1. Upon completion of the first year's training all participants will usually be able to integrate TA into their ongoing work as one of their helping tools. For some individuals this meets their contract. Others who wish to pursue further TA training will be willing to adjust to the demands of the second year or will decide in conjunction with the trainer to 'take time out' to meet other requirements, e.g. extended professional training on a psychiatric ward. These individuals may, over this period, attend sporadic training workshops offered by this institute or with other local and visiting trainers to broaden their scope before they make a commitment to proceed with their TA training.

The first weekend only, will be summarised: please use the syllabus outline (Table 11.1), for the topics of the other weekends. The first or orientation weekend is devoted to group introductions, clarification of learning and training contracts with self, others and trainers. An exercise using guided fantasy and a questionnaire are used to identify past experiences of optimal learning and people contract to arrange for, negotiate or plan to recreate these.

All participants are also provided with a 'TA Training Starter Pack' (thanks to Val Chang for her example of such a pack). This consists of the table of contents listed in Table 11.2, which is worked through with special attention to the role and function of the ITAA, ethical and professional responsibilities, as well as the importance of the techniques of contracting and experiential exercises.

Furthermore, at some points during the year all participants are contracted to contribute a case study and/or a description of an incident or tape recording and this is subjected to scrutiny by the group, focusing on a particular TA concept, e.g. a transcript of a client interview by a social worker (trainee) who is experimenting with the application of the identification of ego states to real-life working situations, or the report of a series of organisational development interventions to ground learning about group dynamics. This 'application' work, which may include supervision in the more usual sense, comprises at least 45 per cent of the content of the course. The purpose is twofold. First, to provide learning material from actual working situations in order to facilitate the generalising effect of the input. Second, to get participants familiarised with sharing their work with peers in this setting so that some of the principles and responsibilities involved in effective supervision are modelled and trainees can begin to experiment with and internalise the building of confidence and skills (Erskine, 1982).

Table 11.2   TA foundation course: starter-pack list

Administration	Application for new Associate Regular Membership EATA
	101 Exam Questions EATA
	Booklist with bookstores' addresses
	Trans Pubs Order Form
	New ITA Membership Application Form
	Certified Member Training Contract Level I
	Registration of Training Contract form
	EATA Statement of Ethics
	Revised Professional Practices Guidelines (Script)
Examination	COC New Examination Rules & Guidelines for Clinical Case Presentation (Clarkson)
	EATA - Summary of requirements for Level I Examination
	Bibliography for written exam
	CTA and SFTA written examination
	Guidelines for clinical examination
	Level I Oral Exam – BOC
	List of Eric Berne Scientific Memorial Award Winners (TSC ITAA)
Supervision	Short Script Questionnaire (Clarkson)
	Reading List
	Tape Supervision (Barnes, Johnson and Holloway)
	Clinical Supervision Preparation – Guideline form
	Presentation of Material at Supervision/Consultation Group (Clarkson)
	Therapist Evaluation & Treatment Plan
	Clinical Tape Supervision (Chang)
	Record of Supervision (a) trainee
	Record of Supervision (b) supervisor
	Client Information pages 1 and 2
	Diagnosis sheet pages 1 and 2
Teaching	Clinical Applications of TA Theory (Based on *Concepts and Techniques* – Zalcman with additions and modifications by Clarkson)
	Structural analysis
	Transactional analysis proper
	Game analysis
	Racket analysis
	Script analysis
	Group treatment
	Child development (Clarkson)
	Psychopathology (Clarkson)
	Assessment (Clarkson)

Year 2 or Intermediate Year

Prerequisites   In addition to the first-year requirements, the trainees need to: be seeing clients or running group(s); have approximately 120 hours of Advanced TA Training completed on this or other programmes; be engaging in regular, ongoing personal therapy and have a contract for ongoing, regular supervision with an accredited TA supervisor from this or another programme. (Participants who may have received most of their supervision on the course in the first year usually need additional regular supervision structured outside the training group.)
Contents of Year 2   The second year's first weekend, (supervision treatment planning), see Table 11.1, covers the most important aspects of maximising the value of supervision for the supervisee and supervisor, with demonstrations and experiential work around regrettable or valued supervisory experiences. Personal responsibility for the process, different methods of preparing supervisory material and in-depth coverage of several approaches to treatment planning are also dealt with.

Weekends 2–7 are based on the concepts and techniques framework provided by Marilyn Zalcman (personal communication). Each major TA concept is reviewed in depth with practice of the relevant techniques which have been identified in TA literature e.g. with script analysis we review all the concepts and approaches to script and participants practise and receive coaching in the use of the techniques.

Weekend 8 on child development follows a similar format but is based on a development of the concept and technique approach to child development from a TA perspective.

Weekend 9 focuses in depth on psychopathology and diagnosis with extensive practice in using DSM-III-R categories on prepared and unprepared case material.

Weekend 10 involves the evaluation of each trainee by self, peers, and the trainer based on submissions of audio or video tapes, practice portfolios (e.g. TA and art therapy) and/or case studies.

Year 3

Prerequisites   Approximately 240 hours of Advanced TA Training with this or other programmes; active clinical or special fields practice; ongoing personal therapy and supervision contracts as well as completion of written CM exam for certification.
Overall goals   Gaining facility with a multi-theoretical framework in trans-actional analysis, effective self-supervision, ease with comparative TA theory and familiarity with different approaches. The development of peer supervision proceeds in and outside of the training structure/format in small supervisory groups. Several guest trainers identified with 'different schools' are invited to teach and do representative demonstration supervisions with training-group participants throughout the course. Trainees are encouraged to attend the workshops of visiting or local trainers in addition to their core training at

metanoia depending on their level of development and ability to integrate material. This year, our training programme, however, focuses on the deliberate inclusion of visiting trainers to show their integrative potential, intentionally meet and provide support for working with other trainers and model co-operative colleagial relationships. Several trainees will be preparing for the Level I exams and the group will be used to assist in supervision, to support, critique and learn from the open preparation process which takes up some 25 per cent of the time over the weekend. For syllabus see Table 11.1.

Year 4

Prerequisites   Extensive training in any recognised approach to psychotherapy; regular supervision and ongoing personal therapy; a commitment to comparative psychotherapy supervision; an undertaking to present major blocks of input on comparative psychotherapeutic approaches to the different disorders as well as present fully developed case studies.

Overall goals   The focus is on facility in the use of multi-theoretical frameworks of TA *and* other psychotherapeutic approaches; skill and reliability in differential diagnosis, treatment planning and assessment as well as the effective management of their psychotherapy practice and themselves.

The aim is to develop well-rounded and well-grounded ethical clinicians. A great deal of responsibility is devolved onto the training group members who have acquired considerable skills in self-awareness, peer and self supervision, processing of group-dynamics material and teaching.

Several people use this year as a Level I exam preparation year – some have already completed the exam, some are Provisional Training Members (PTMs) – while others use it to integrate their learning over the last few years with no intention of going to examination. Teaching input and supervision of case-study material is substantially done by Provisional Teaching Members in training with the Senior Trainers. The aim of the year for the Provisional Teaching Members is to provide a refinement of comparative psychotherapeutic theory review for the TA Level II exam on theory, organisation and ethics, as well as for clinical refinement in different diagnostic categories and treatment approaches. Supervision of their supervision and of their teaching on the course forms an integral part of preparation for the Teaching Membership exams.

Other PTM training   Training in curriculum design, teaching and supervision is additionally provided individually by visiting the training programmes of Provisional Teaching Members of their supervision groups and supervising occasional workshops. They can come on longer placements e.g. apprenticeship to one of the training 'years' or shorter ones for a couple of months, e.g. joining one of the ongoing supervision groups which are scheduled weekly or fortnightly in addition to the training weekends. They can, of course, also do the contractual supervision of teaching on an individual appointment basis or as part of the ongoing events organised in conjunction with other TMs.

In summary, this section provides an abbreviated outline of curriculum and TA training-programme design as available at *metanoia*.

Post Level I clinical certification training

The TA training period of three to four years includes several hundred hours of theory, supervised clinical work, specialised training in group dynamics, psycho-pathology and child development as well as placement in a psychiatric ward or hostel where this is appropriate (Clarkson, 1986b). It is also required by EATA (the European Association for Transactional Analysis), ITA and ITAA that trainee psychotherapists undergo personal psychotherapy for the duration of their training. Clinical Membership of the International Transactional Analysis Association and EATA carries an international accreditation which is considered to be a model of a competency-based psychotherapy examination by the United States Commission for Health Certifying Agencies (Zalcman and Cornell, 1983).

Level I certification

For many people this is the achievement of a major goal at considerable cost of time, money, effort and emotional investment. In our opinion people should be supported and celebrated in the maintenance and continued development of their clinical practice if they should choose to do so. It is important to note that other professional societies such as the British Association for Counselling require as condition for continuing membership (a) regular ongoing supervision as well as (b) a demonstrated and documented commitment to continual personal and professional development.

The maintenance and development of clinical competence and expertise may be a completely satisfactory life choice for many TA practitioners and is after all the major focus for all our professional activities.

Naturally some people hold influential positions in EATA, ITAA and ITA who are neither Teaching Members (Level II) nor hold Level I accreditation. This demonstrates that people can be active within the organisation without necessarily following an accreditation process. They may be already otherwise qualified, but seeking professional enrichment by learning and integrating TA into their practice. Of course, they cannot use the words 'TA group' or 'Transactional Analysis treatment' (according to the Professional Practices Guidelines) although their relationship with TA usually and obviously proves mutually rewarding.

Level II certification

Berne makes some interesting distinctions between demonstrators (people with technical virtuosity), consultants (people with specialised knowledge), and supervisors (who combine didactic knowledge, a talent for therapeutic technique, and a clear understanding of specific aspects and situations as well as the ability to take diagnostic and clinical responsibility) (Berne, 1966: 159–61). For some people with the latter proclivity, becoming a trainer is an equally viable professional choice. Transactional analysis responds to this understandable desire by providing a Level II examination for teachers and supervisors. This does not, in our opinion, supersede their responsibility and commitment to ongoing clinical work. In our experience, challenging and demanding clinical work provides a thorough ongoing developmental matrix for the teaching clinician without which their teaching and supervision can easily become sterile and incongruent with the poignant realities of everyday psychotherapeutic practice with a mixed client population.

Transactional analysis is one of the few systems of psychotherapy which overtly and categorically acknowledges that good and competent clinicians are not automatically skilled teachers or effective supervisors. It requires of its teachers and supervisors extensive knowledge of comparative psychotherapy, i.e. not only in teaching comparative transactional analysis theory in depth, but also transactional analysis as compared with other psychotherapeutic systems. A deep and adequately-demonstrated knowledge at this level facilitates cross-referencing and cross-fertilisation with other systems of psychotherapy as well as mutual peer recognition and respect in important psychotherapeutic policy-making forums.

We believe that TA provides a unique system of training, supervising and accrediting trainers and supervisors of psychotherapists. Hardly any other psychotherapy training organisation takes this process so seriously and professionally. It examines its trainers and supervisors (by specially selected and trained examination boards) on the basis of written submissions, *viva voce* theory examination and live observation of teaching and supervision. 'This person has a sense of the comparative and integrative aspects of TA within its own theoretical boundaries and in relationship to other theoretical and practical approaches. In addition, a Teaching Member is someone who has a command of all the aspects of supervising practitioners as well as supervisors of practitioners' (TM Exam Format, January 1985).

The Level II examination process is held before evaluating boards of three or four Teaching Members in each of three sections: (1) theory, organisation and ethics; (2) prepared and unprepared teaching; and (3) supervision of a Clinical candidate and a PTM candidate. A pass in section 1 (Theory) is required before doing either section 2 (Teaching) or 3 (Supervision) since an adequately demonstrated knowledge of advanced TA theory and its relationship to other psychotherapeutic systems is a necessary prerequisite for the competent teaching or supervision of trainees, practitioners of TA and Provisional Teaching Members.

The Training Endorsement Workshop (TEW)

A Provisional Teaching Member is a person who takes responsibility for providing training or supervision or both to others under the supervision of qualified Teaching Members. In order to move from being an internationally acknowledged competent TA practitioner to becoming endorsed as a Provisional

Teaching Member, a Level I practitioner needs to undergo the 'rite of passage' (*The Script* Vol. XI, No. 9, November 1981) of a training endorsement workshop. These are held regularly at the major conference sites in Europe and America. It is important to know in advance that endorsement to provisional Instructor, or Supervisor or both is not automatic, since excellent clinicians or 'demonstrators' (Berne, 1966) are not necessarily competent teachers or supervisors. Therefore, some TEW candidates may not be endorsed as Instructors and Supervisors or either of these two, but they may be recommended a further preparatory period.

In the experiences of many trainers and trainees, an interim period between achieving Level I certification and applying for endorsement as a Provisional Teaching Member is considered beneficial. For one thing, a person gets to enjoy and consolidate clinical skills without the awareness of exam requirements, formal reportage or the acquisition of another goal, too close for comfort, on the heels of the first. For another thing, motives may be mixed. It has also proved advantageous for trainees to have some specific training and experience in teaching and supervising before attendance at TEW workshops. Training in these skills, relevant coaching and curriculum may or may not have been part of pre-examination programmes and specific preparation may need to be arranged.

At an evaluation workshop (Training Endorsement Workshop), senior trainers and supervisors assess the candidate's suitability to become a supervisor or trainer on the basis of (a) observing their teaching of a group of colleagues; (b) live observation of their supervision; and (c) a written submission covering ethics, supervision philosophy, professional practices, etc. These outline questions which may be important and interesting for prospective trainees and prospective trainers are available from the ITAA offices. If the candidate is successful, he or she becomes endorsed as a Provisional Teaching Member (Instructor and/or Supervisor). Provisional Teaching Members then sign a contract with a Certified Teaching Member. All Provisional Teaching Members are required to have regular supervision of their teaching and regular supervision of their supervision by Certified Teaching Members within their speciality. They also need to be accumulating at least 100 hours of continuing education by attending courses or training events (subsequent to Level I certification) and to present at conferences and professional meetings.

Level II (Teaching Members) ongoing responsibility

Recommendations being considered by the Singapore meeting of the ITAA Board of Trustees are as follows:

The ITAA in cooperation with the BOC (Board of Certification) has the highest standards for the advanced membership of any professional organisation related to human development and behaviour. In order to maintain these high standards and ensure the quality of services provided by its members, the ITAA requires all advanced members to participate in a minimum number of continuing education experiences. This is consistent with national, organisational and state licensing trends to require a minimum number of continuing education units over a specified number of years. For example: the State of Florida requires all individuals licensed in a mental health-related field to accumulate a minimum of 40 hours of CEUs during a two year period; the National Board of Certified Counsellors requires that each certified counsellor be recertified every five years by either completing 100 CEUs or by re-examination.

(CEU = Continuing Education Units)

TM evaluation

It is also recommended by the Training Standards Committee of the ITAA that Certified Teaching Members also be continually evaluated according to the following standards (modified respectively for Supervisors and/or Instructors).

Trainers who are involved in the sponsorship of advanced members (CM, PTM, Instructor/Supervisor) will have their training evaluated through a feedback process. The feedback process will be based on evaluations of their trainees who are examined by the Board of Certification (BOC) or the Council of Certification (COC). The evaluations will be structured so that trainers might know the areas where their trainees show strengths, show effective abilities or show needs for further growth and learning.

The areas which will be evaluated are:

1 History of TA
2 Basic theory
3 Advanced theory
4 Use of supervision
5 Supervisory skills (when appropriate)
6 Intuitive skills
7 Teaching skills (when appropriate)
8 Therapeutic skills (when appropriate)
9 Organisational skills (when appropriate)

The trainer will receive feedback on each trainee who is examined.

The subcommittee of evaluation will develop a record-keeping system on trainers who are regularly training and review annually the evaluation of that trainer's trainees. Trainers who have trainees who are showing significant needs for further growth and training will be asked to evaluate in writing the remedial steps they will have to take to improve the quality of their trainees. The Training Standards Committee will offer a workshop annually that will focus on improving quality of training for all trainers and will request attendance of those trainers who have a significant number of trainees who need assistance.

A CTM (Instructor/Supervisor) who does not submit remedial steps to improve the quality of trainees or does not attend a TSC workshop, or both, may be required to attend a Training Endorsement Workshop (TEW). Provisional

Teaching Members (PTMs) will have their training evaluated in the same way as CTMs Instructor/Supervisor. Any member who chooses none of the above options will have their advanced membership reviewed.

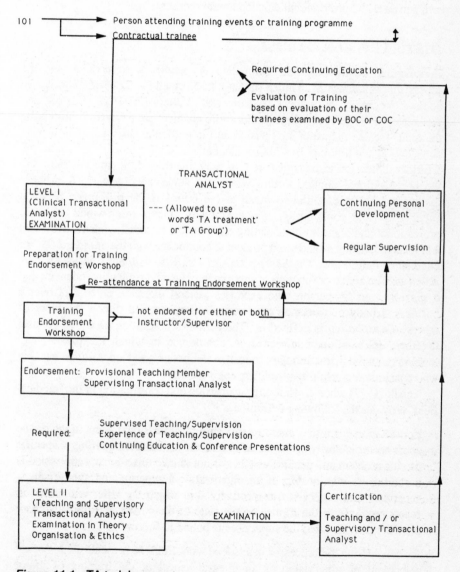

Figure 11.1 **TA training map**

In conclusion

I refer you to the flowchart (see Figure 11.1) which outlines the processes described. It may appear complicated at first glance. However, it represents one of the most dedicated and sincere attempts in the psychotherapeutic world to develop and maintain high standards of practice, teaching and supervision at standardised international levels. Please use this to develop your own thinking; question trainers and trainees; and particularly use it to act as a mirror to your own personal and professional developmental processes.

THE SUPERVISION PROCESS

Considerable controversy has surrounded the nature of supervision and the supervisory relationship, so much so that it has formed the focus of authoritative books concerning the subject (Ekstein and Wallerstein, 1972; Kaslow and Associates, 1977). Within these works entire chapters are devoted to discussing the multi-faceted nature of supervision and in particular distinguishing it from consultation and training. In addition Ekstein and Wallerstein (1972) contribute a further dimension to be considered, namely, the role of the administrator and the organisational context within which the supervision occurs. A primary distinction that is essential to make at the outset is the difference between supervision and consultation. Since much of this is intertwined with the professional and organisational setting e.g. medical or social work (Kaslow and Associates, 1977), it would seem prudent to commence with the *Standard Oxford Dictionary* definitions. *The Shorter Oxford English Dictionary* defines *supervision* as 'The action or function of supervising; oversight, superintendence'; and a *supervisor* as 'A person who exercises general direction or control over a business, a body of workmen etc.; one who inspects and directs the work of others'. *Consultation* is defined as 'The action of consulting or taking counsel together; deliberation, conference. A conference in which the parties, e.g. lawyers or medical practitioners, consult or deliberate'; and a *consultant* as 'One who consults. A consulting physician, engineer etc.'

Kutzik (1977) when considering supervision and consultation in the 'medical field' provides the following definitions:

> Consultation is a time limited relationship of professional peers in which the consultee voluntarily seeks the advice of the consultant regarding a specific case or problem and decides whether or not to take this advice; supervision is a continuous relationship of an organizational superior and subordinate – supervisor and supervisee, respectively – in which the latter is required to report regularly to the former on the state of their work and the supervisor provides direction that the supervisee is bound to follow.

When considering the processes in a 'social work field' he presents the historical development of supervision as an integral aspect of the training of junior colleagues, with the concomitant hierarchical power distribution within the relationship between supervisor and supervisee. Kutzik (1977: 54) also comments on the frequent overlap between supervision and consultation (where the relationships are more of a 'peer-group' or 'colleague-collaborator' with a sharing of decision-making responsibility). Kutzik (1977: 55) also introduces the concept of 'case conferences' as 'regular nonadministrative group meetings of professional staff to share knowledge and skills regarding how to deal with specific cases'. He regards 'case conferences', 'consultation' and 'supervision' as three different ways of 'increasing skills and providing controls to the activity of the social work practitioner' (National Association of Social Workers, 1973: 8). Kutzik concludes, however, that even though there has been confusion in both medicine and social work regarding the nature of supervision and consultation, that 'whatever the confusion and however mislabelled, the appropriate process has generally taken place for the appropriate personnel in response to their needs and in accord with their statuses and the requirements and structure of their profession and/or organization' (Kutzik, 1977: 57).

Ekstein and Wallerstein (1972) discuss a basic model for the supervision of psychotherapists and present their theory concerning 'The clinical rhombus'

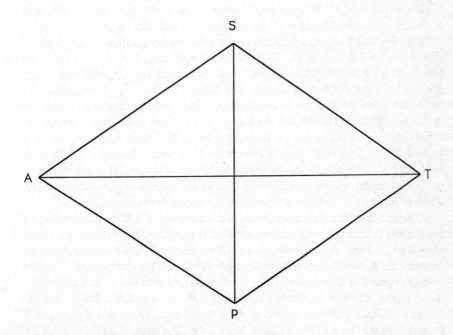

Figure 11.2 The clinical rhombus
Source: Ekstein and Wallerstein, 1972: 11

which is a diagrammatic representation of the many-faceted and interactive relationships occurring within the context of supervision (see Figure 11.2). Each corner of the rhombus represents the four basic facets or components to supervision, namely, the roles of the 'therapist' (T), the 'supervisor' (S), the 'patient' (P) and the 'administrator' (A); and the connecting lines indicating the different relationships involved e.g. S-T (the relationship between the supervisor and the therapist), S-P (the relationship between the supervisor and the patient), etc. All relationships are present within 'supervision' all the time although the emphasis of each on the supervision process will vary from time to time depending on the context.

In summary, therefore, it is clear that supervision is a special, contractual, multi-faceted relationship between two people (the supervisor and the supervisee) or between one person (the supervisor) and a group of people (the supervisees) which exists for the explicit purpose of providing a supportive forum for both the training and control of the work of the supervisee by the supervisor. This relationship must include a code of practice for the particular profession, a code of ethics and the organisational and administrative requirements of the context within which the supervision takes place.

Structure of supervision

Having considered the philosophical nature of the supervision relationship it is necessary to delineate some of the structural boundaries to this relationship, namely, the frequency and duration of sessions, the preparation required of the supervisee for the session, the focus of the session, the goals of the supervision (this includes both the sessional goals and the overall and longer-term training goals of the supervisory relationship), the manner in which any interruptions are to be dealt with, the payment of any fee if applicable, the method to be employed in the supervision process and the format of the supervision (i.e. whether the supervision is to occur on an individual basis or within a group). In both individual and group settings it is customary for a variety and range of methods to be used (case presentations, presentation of particular clinical problems, audio and video tapes, role play, sculpting, Gestalt techniques (e.g.two-chair work), and live supervision involving both the supervisee and the client).

Although the theoretical framework of the supervision will vary depending on the context (e.g. psychoanalytic, humanistic, behavioural, medical model, social case-work, eclectic or any combination of a variety of these) there are general considerations which are independent of the theoretical framework. Erskine (1982) provides a useful model for supervision and presents it as occurring in three stages, namely, a 'Beginning Stage', an 'Intermediate Stage' and an 'Advanced Stage'; and he considers the focus of supervision and the aims of it to be different in each of these stages. During the 'Beginning Stage' the goals are concerned with the development of skills, the provision of information, the creation of a sound theoretical framework and the building of confidence. During the 'Intermediate Stage' the goals are concerned with building the trainee's identity as a counsellor/therapist, enhancing the knowledge possessed by the trainee, the development of more refined skills and treatment-planning acumen, therapy for the trainee to enhance their sense of an 'integrated self' and deal with any personal issues that might impede the therapeutic relationship that the trainee has with his/her client. During the 'Advanced Stage' the goals are concerned with the development of a multi-theoretical framework, the development of skills in selecting and using alternative approaches in treatment planning and working with clients so as to enhance trainee flexibility and promote awareness of the notion that there are different approaches to the same clinical problem. Erskine (1982) also introduces a distinction between 'observations' (essentially historical facts, symptoms, signs or direct observations of the behaviour of the client) and 'theoretical constructs' or hypotheses to explain the 'observations'. He also makes the important distinction that there will always be a number of different hypotheses possible to explain the same 'observations' and that each of these hypotheses will have their own treatment planning and interventions associated with them.

Supervisory tools

Supervision has been described as 'a relationship between a supervisor and a therapeutic relationship' (Finch, 1977). Supervision is a vast, complex and ever-growing field of investigation, practice and discovery. The heart of the supervisory partnership is probably the longitudinal unfolding of a developmental process facilitated by the relationship with a colleague.

We propose to outline briefly two supervisory tools developed by the author, which are designed to facilitate aspects of the supervisory process. The first 'tool' is used to identify priorities or key issues in a supervision session; the second provides a checklist of supervisory criteria for assessing supervision.

A tool for identifying and prioritising categories or bands of key issues in supervision

The scheme outlined below provides a checklist for pinpointing the category or 'band' of key issues in a particular supervision session or at a particular stage in a trainee's development. The choice of such a 'band' enables the supervisor to focus the supervision in the area which he/she considers crucial and most relevant at a specific time.

Contract

1 Diagnosis and treatment planning
2 Strategies and intervention techniques
3 Parallel process (reflection or mirroring)
4 Pro-active countertransference – supervisee's personal issues
5 Ethics and professional practice

Context: relationship

Theory is implicit in all of these.

Diagnosis and treatment planning   Accurate diagnosis is intimately related to effective short- and long-term treatment planning. The focus here is on stages of treatment and the choice of therapeutic techniques appropriate to the client both in terms of diagnosis and stage of treatment. A trainee may lack an awareness of overall treatment planning whilst focusing too narrowly on a particular aspect of the client's functioning.

Strategies and intervention techniques   Training in particular treatment strategies and therapeutic techniques forms the focus in this 'band' of supervision. At certain points, the trainee's primary need may be the acquisition of new techniques or the reinforcement of techniques already learned but not sufficiently internalised. A trainee may be using the same technique or intervention strategy again and again because of the lack of a wider repertoire of choices and options in his/her therapeutic 'tool kit'.

Parallel process (reflection and mirroring)   The beginning therapist in particular seems prone to focus on those problems in the client that highlight his/her own difficulties in learning which are of course mirrored in the supervisory relationship. It is as though the therapist and client are constantly working on similar issues. As the trainee is helped to resolve his or her own difficulties both in the supervisory setting and through personal psychotherapy, she/he will be able to see the problems of the client more objectively and work appropriately with these.

Countertransference   Certain basic difficulties in the therapeutic relationship may be due to the trainee's own unresolved issues from the past which are interfering with the smooth flow of therapy. An identification of such issues and a commitment to resolve these in personal psychotherapy will be an important goal for the developing therapist. Countertransference reactions, if clearly understood as such, can be used to gain insights which can prove useful in helping the client.

Ethics and professional practice   This supervision 'band' embraces issues of professional practice and of ethics as these relate to the trainee in his/her relationships with clients and with professional peers. A spectrum of problems, e.g. confidentiality with clients, how to deal with advertising a practice or difficulties in dealing with a professional colleague, may take priority here as the focus of supervision. The supervisor will ensure that the trainee both knows and implements the Professional Practices Guidelines and the Code of Ethics.

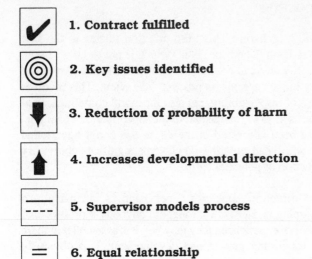

Figure 11.3   Brief supervision checklist

Self-supervision or assessment of supervision

There is a multitude of models of supervision and as many ways of assessing the effectiveness of any supervisory activity.

What we offer here may be helpful for self-supervision or for training supervisors on some occasions (see Figure 11.3). This checklist of some supervisory criteria can be used for assessing individual supervision sessions in the context of the trainee's overall development. Each has a visual aid to accompany it which distils the essence of each aspect symbolically.

The contract fulfilled   The first criterion refers to the central transaction in TA – the contract made with mutual consent, appropriate consideration, competency and lawful object (Steiner, 1974). The relevance of the particular contract in the overall supervision context is of primary concern. For example, even though the trainee may be requesting recognition of work well done, the supervisor must be alert to other supervisory issues of importance and ensure that these issues are covered contractually. If the contract has been fulfilled a check mark is used.

Key issues identified   The second criterion has already been indicated under *Bands of Supervision*. The supervisor's ability to assess, discriminate and identify the major issues in supervision is the focus here. For example, the trainee may present a problem regarding a client's non-payment of fees but from the supervision it may become clear that the key issue is more likely to be the trainee's personal issues of self-worth.

A target with an arrow head in the bull's eye encapsulates symbolically the essence of this supervisory activity.

Reduction of the probability of harm   This third criterion relates to the first principle of the Hippocratic Oath (Thomson, 1988) which is not to inflict harm. In supervision this specifically refers to not inflicting harm or causing harm to be inflicted on the third party in the supervision process – the client. This involves not only the legal mandates of responsibility, but also the moral consequences of bystanding behaviour (Clarkson, 1987) on the part of the supervisor. For example, if suicidal issues have not been addressed in the client this could have lethal consequences. An arrow with head pointing downwards signifies supervisory activity towards such reduction of potential harm.

Increased developmental direction   Because supervision is intrinsically a method for continuing learning and growth throughout anybody's professional career (no matter how senior or experienced they may be), it is assumed that there will always be potential for further growth and development. This obviously should not prevent celebration and validation of accomplished skills where appropriate. However, we consider it the supervisor's responsibility to offer challenges, direction or support for extending the trainee's horizons. An arrow with head pointing upwards signifies supervisory activity towards enhanced development.

Supervisor models process   As we know from Berne's third rule of communication, the outcome of any transaction is determined at the ulterior or psychological level. Therefore the most effective way of supervising is through modelling the desirable process. For example, to instruct someone in an authoritarian manner not to be so directive with a client may well defeat the purpose. Equally to invite the trainee to be more assertive in an apologetic manner is not likely to achieve the desired outcome. This is symbolised by parallel divided and undivided lines showing matching and congruent social and psychological levels of communication.

Equal relationship – I'm OK – You're OK   Since the basis of transactional analysis is an I'm OK – You're OK relationship, this also forms the foundation of an effective supervisory partnership. This does not mean that the supervisor supports or approves all of the trainee's behaviour, but rather that feedback is given in the context of acceptance of the trainee as a valuable and important person. This refers to the vital distinction between 'being' and 'doing' and emphasises that in true existential sense the relationship can be characterised by an equal sign.

BURN-OUT – TYPICAL RACKET SYSTEMS OF PROFESSIONAL HELPERS

Introduction

Since Freudenberger's (1975) pioneering work on 'Burn-out' among people in the helping professions, there has been a virtual explosion of interest in, and research about this particular syndrome. *The Oxford Dictionary* defines burn-out: 'to fail, to wear out, or become exhausted by making excessive demands on energy, strength or resources'. Maslach (1976: 18) defines it as: 'The loss of concern for the people with whom one is working ... [including] physical exhaustion ... [and] characterised by an emotional exhaustion in which the professional no longer has any positive feelings, sympathy or respect for clients or patients.'

There is much concern in the literature and the professions about the prevalence of this burn-out syndrome among caring workers, since it leads to temporary or permanent incapacitation e.g. exhaustion, loss of creativity and enthusiasm for their work, drug dependence, depression, somatic symptoms and even death, e.g. heart attacks.

In this chapter it is suggested that the three not-OK life positions on Ernst's (1971) OK Corral resemble the three personality types Freudenberger (1975) identified as being sensitive to burn-out. (Administrators or professionals can burn out in a similar way whichever of these positions they habitually occupy under stress.)

Freudenberger's classification is: (a) the dedicated and committed worker; (b) the worker who is overcommitted and whose outside life is unsatisfactory and, (c) the authoritarian personality. These three personality types are then related to their respective positions on the OK Corral (see Figure 11.4).

Erskine and Zalcman define a racket system as 'a *self-reinforcing, distorted system of beliefs, thoughts and actions maintained by script-bound individuals*. The Racket System has three inter-related and interdependent components: the *Script Beliefs and Feelings*, the *Rackety Displays* and the *Reinforcing Memories*' (1979: 53).

Based on the author's clinical experience of training and working with large numbers of professional helpers, three distinct characteristic racket systems are also identified. Each of the three characteristic racket systems seem to be associated with one of the not-OK positions on the OK Corral, which in turn correlate with the Freudenberger typology. Such divisions are obviously based on the identification of general types. This kind of categorisation therefore implies both the advantages and disadvantages of stereotyping. It assists professionals to communicate effectively, generalise and teach from their experience of frequently occurring patterns. However, it is in no way meant to be used in a reductionistic way which deprives individuals of their existential uniqueness.

I'm not O.K. – You're O.K. Dedicated and Committed (Overadaptive)	I'm O.K. – You're O.K.
I'm not O.K. – You're not O.K. Overcommitted and work enmeshed	I'm O.K. – You're not O.K. Authoritarian and/or Patronising

Figure 11.4   OK Corral illustrating 'burn-out personality types'

As a format for exploration, these three generalised racket sytems have proved helpful for clients, trainees and workshop participants who are concerned with burn-out phenomena in the helping professions. Psychiatrists, clinical psychologists, social workers, psychotherapists and others use this format to identify their own particular predispositions to 'burn out' in terms of their existential life positions and to make the necessary changes to their scripts and their lives. It is also useful for managers, teachers and supervisors of professional helpers.

The 'dedicated and committed' personality (Freudenberger, 1975)

A dedicated and committed worker, Sally, constantly pushes herself to work harder in an attempt to meet the ever-increasing demands made upon her, not questioning, nor effectively protesting the right of the clients or the institution to make such escalating demands (see Table 11.3). Sally, a social worker of deep conviction, cannot say 'no' because of a basic existential belief system which holds that others (and their needs/demands) are worthwhile (OK). Her own needs to protect herself and her psychophysiological resources, and to live a happy, guilt-free life are fundamentally negated (I am not OK). She seeks to earn her OK-ness by her service to others – 'I am only OK if I can help you'.

When her efforts meet with less and less success, she works even harder. Despite her decreasing cost-effectiveness, she continues to believe that with longer hours, more dedication, and greater intensity she can make a genuine difference to the flood of demands from the people in the deprived neighbourhood in which works.

Freudenberger describes this as follows:

> What happens is that the harder he works the more frustrated he is, the more exhausted, the more bitchy, the more cynical in outlook and behaviour – and, of course, the less effective in the very things he so wishes to accomplish.
>
> (Freudenberger, 1975: 37)

This vicious cycle compounds Sally's guilt, her feelings of worthlessness, and further depletes her intrapsychic and interpersonal resources.

A recurrent motivating dynamic of such personality types is their identification with the victim – the sexually abused girl, the battered wife, the jobless husband caught in a poverty trap, and the person suffering from a physical handicap. By taking care of the hurt child in others, they vicariously seek some solace for the hurt child in themselves. They attempt to be the understanding, generous parent for others which they never experienced. Out of awareness they may have the hope that if they do this long enough, well enough, the grateful client will return their favours. At the very least, the client may demonstrate the love or admiration which they would have wanted from the original parent.

The repressed feeling for people like Sally is frequently that of pain of loss which is enacted by their inability to establish mutually rewarding, protective, challenging and nourishing relationships with others over the long term.

A fairy story or a story which frequently figures prominently in the childhood of people who are committed and dedicated in this way is that of *The Water Babies*. The principal female character, Mrs Do-as-you-would-be-done-by, represents a position of kindness, consideration and unconditional acceptance of other people, particularly of the small or the defenceless. Tom learns through her to be as kind to others as he would like them to be towards him (Kingsley, 1982).

The overcommitted and work-enmeshed personality

Freudenberger (1975) identifies this person as being overcommitted and with a subsatisfactory outside life (see Table 11.4). Work is their only stroke source. Their professional and personal lives have merged to the extent that there is no longer any boundary between the two. This is the 'I'm not-OK – You're not-OK'

Table 11.3 Typical 'committed and dedicated' racket system

Script beliefs/feelings	Rackety displays	Reinforcing memories
Beliefs about:	Behaviour: Dedicated and committed. Preferred helping style: empathy	Early experiences of being:
Self: I am not OK unless I help others. I must try harder. I am worthless		Social level: Rescuer
Others: are OK (worthwhile), are better/more important than me	Reported internal experience: worry, then guilt	Psychological level: Victim
		Existential level: Persecutor
	Predominant Child ego-state cathexis	
Quality of life: there but for the grace of God go I		
	Fantasy: I will be loved/appreciated in the end Fairy story: Mrs Do-as-you-would-be-done-by (Kingsley, 1982)	(2nd order symbiosis with early caretaker) (explained in Chapter 7) Helping game: 'They'll be glad they knew me' (in the end)
Repressed feelings: sadness, loss		

position on the OK Corral. It is easy to become over-involved in a children's home, a free clinic, the crisis intervention unit, or a particular ideology such as TA.

The atmosphere and satisfactions can be so seductive that the person finds herself spending even her free time there. But I view this over-involvement as a real danger sign indicating that the worker has given up trying to find meaningful outside activities and relationships (cf. Freudenberger, 1975: 39).

John's belief is that service to others is the meaning of life and holds its own ultimate reward. He does not value himself nor does he deeply believe that his clients or patients can ultimately become independent and autonomous. The task of individuation and separation may be for ever avoided.

The motivating dynamic of people in this quadrant of the OK Corral may be that sharing the misery and unhappiness and poverty of their clients they can promote a feeling of closeness, family and belonging. Their fantasy may be that by merging their personal and professional selves, they will for ever be at home. They will certainly *not* be lonely. Of course, since the client's capacity and ability to be independent necessarily has to be devalued in this collusive bind, these workers are fundamentally at home with people who do not have many other options for friendship. If the clients were to get well the worker might be deserted and might lose his or her job, status and *raison d'être*.

Because of their over-dedication to their work, these workers may lack the energy and creativity for a satisfactory outside life. This life then fails to provide them with sufficient satisfaction and reinforcement and they hyper-invest back into work. The repressed feeling is despair – 'the world is a lost cause and all that can be hoped for is to share one another's misery in this vale of tears and oppression'. Nobody can be relied upon to help – least of all people in authority who control the resources (such as management or government). Both professionals and clients are construed as powerless to change the situation.

Thidwick, the Big-Hearted Moose, is a character from a children's story who was described as 'over-kind'. He possessed a fine set of antlers and agreed to let a small bug hitch a ride in them. However, the bug then invited a spider to move in and a bird, and although Thidwick found this burdensome he was a good sport and put up with it as well as with a woodpecker, a squirrel family, a bobcat and other animals who all moved in until they became so heavy that he sank to his knees (Seuss, 1968).

Table 11.4 Typical overcommitted and work-enmeshed racket system

Script beliefs/feelings	Rackety display	Reinforcing memories
Beliefs about:	Behaviour: Overcommitted, life unsatisfactory	Early experience of being: Social level: Victim
Self: I'm not OK. I am lonely and unlovable. I am miserable and needy. Powerless	Preferred level: helping style: 'Reality'-type therapy	Psychological level: Rescuer Existential level: Persecutor
Others: You are not OK	Reported Internal Experience: frustration, Impotence (powerlessness)	
Quality of life: greater love hath no man than to give his life ...	Alternating Parent and Child ego-state cathexis	Helping game: Busman's holiday. I'm only trying to help you. Look how hard I'm trying
Repressed feeling: despair	Fantasy: I/we will survive (It's you and me, babe, against the world)	
	Fairy story: *Thidwick, the Big-Hearted Moose* (Seuss, 1968)	

Authoritarian and/or patronising personality

This is the kind of person 'who so needs to be in control that no one else can do any job as well as he can' (Freudenberger, 1975: 39) (see Table 11.5). This person believes that 'only I can do things right around here' and feels they have to control the budget, the work, the belief systems, even the personal lives if possible, of everybody associated with the institution. The assumption is that other people are essentially not-OK and do not have the intelligence, the education, the capacity, the ego strength, etc. to evolve really satisfactory life styles for themselves. The current government or psychosociological environment are also seen as not-OK. The quality of life would be fine if 'I were in charge of the institution, the country, the world!'

This person's predominant ego state tends to be that of an introjected other, frequently a domineering parent with whom the child made a collusive pact. As a child, this kind of person frequently identified with the aggressor, believing that by taking on parental definitions of reality, he or she could permanently control life and other people. This survival solution is an attempt to sustain a precarious sense of personal OKness.

The fantasy is 'if the world would listen to me and obey my instructions, we could all be happy. Until then, it is somebody else's fault.' The repressed feeling is one of terror – the fear is that nobody really knows the answers. No matter how domineering or dominant the parental figure and its pronouncements, they only

Table 11.5 Typical authoritarian/patronising racket system

Script beliefs/feelings	Rackety display	Reinforcing experiences
Beliefs about: I'll get it right. I'll save the day	Behaviour:	Early experiences of being:
Self: I'm OK	Authoritarian	Social level: Persecutor
Others: You are not OK, are inadequate, stupid, incompetent, need controlling	Preferred helping style: confrontation, potency	Psychological level: Rescuer Existential level: Victim
Quality of life: If you can't stand the heat get out of the kitchen, or The weakest go to the wall	Reported internal Experience: Irritation; self-righteousness. Frequent Parent ego-state cathexis	Helping game: 'I told you so' NIGYSOB Blemish
Repressed feeling: terror/scare	Fantasy: I will be right in the end	
	Fairy story: *The Wizard of Oz* (Baum, 1982)	

succeed in creating an imposing Wizard of Oz behind which shelters a rather scared and inadequate person. 'The Wizard turns out to be a little, old, bald-headed man who admits to being a fraud' (Eyles, 1985: 37).

SUMMARY

Observation of several hundred members of helping professions such as doctors, psychologists, social workers, nurses, psychiatrists and clinical psychologists, strongly suggests that there are three frequently occurring and characteristic types of script-bound personalities which may be pre-disposed to 'burn-out' as described in the previous section.

Since the racket system is viewed as characteristic of script-bound individuals it is assumed that 'script-free' individuals will *not* have a 'characteristic racket system' susceptible to burn-out. It is the author's opinion that script-free individuals may have predispositions towards these particular types of manifestation, but will have made the necessary redecisions, integrations and mature developments which would render full-scale activation of any of these racket systems impossible. Because such individuals will be spontaneous, aware and pro-active in the work situation from moment to moment, their behaviour may at times resemble that of any of the three racket systems described, because they will not be exempt from pain, frustration or doubt. Individuals who are mostly in Integrated Adult and who have freed themselves from the more severe stringencies of their scripts, and who are living in concert with the changing demands of the moment-by-moment existential encounter, cannot be fitted into a system. Autonomy, spontaneity and intimacy cannot be mapped, they can only be lived. The effective management and resolution of these non-productive or destructive (third-degree) script decisions as they are presented in terms of the currently fashionable concepts of burn-out, are no different from those which are used for any other kind of symptomatology in transactional analysis.

Freud was once asked by a journalist what he considered to be the two most important things in life. He answered: 'to love and to work.' Discovering and celebrating the fluctuating rhythm between these two may take a lifetime.

ETHICAL ISSUES AND PROFESSIONAL RESPONSIBILITIES OF THE PSYCHOTHERAPIST AT WORK

Ethical considerations are clearly an important element of both the training programme and supervision and, in as much as such issues are concerned with professional responsibility to oneself, others and the world at large, are implicitly referred to in the preceding section on burn-out. A burnt-out psychotherapist is not acting responsibly to him/herself, to the clients or to the world at large and working with clients from within one's own racket system and from one of the three not-OK life positions is not only irresponsible but potentially harmful and damaging. For this reason, trainees and practising TA psychotherapists are ethically bound by their adherence to the Professional Practices Guidelines and the Statement of Ethics (see Appendix C, p.321) to ensure that they are demonstrably committed to continued professional and personal development and provide their best possible services to their clients.

For beginning psychotherapists it may be important to accept the strictures of the ethical codes governing their practice according to their profession, their training institution, national policy, and international standards and conventions. In our experience many beginning psychotherapists need to be told what not to do – 'Do not take on your best friend as a client' – since through their excitement and enthusiasm, or 'furor therapeuticus' (Rycroft, 1972: 55) they may err through lack of caution. At such periods, a clear, almost unquestioning, application of an ethical code may be important. It is as if the beginning therapist can benefit from the safety net of blanket applications while gradually evolving his/her own more finely tuned sense of moral and ethical values which he/she will certainly need as a practising psychotherapist.

Thus, an important part of the education of the psychotherapist is to become aware of the enormous complexity and profoundly disturbing ambiguities with which ethical practice confronts the psychotherapist day after day.

For instance, how does a psychotherapist treat someone who has been referred to them for treatment because they are refusing to fight a war, for example, in South Africa, when on the psychotherapist's report will hang the decision for him to go to psychiatric hospital or prison – or should the psychotherapist stand in line with the conscientious objector?

Equally, how should a client who suspects that the 7-year-old boy next door is being sexually abused by his father respond when taking such action overtly could endanger her as her father is already threatening and abusive to her and that, for her, this would be a repeat of her childhood experience of being punished whenever she tried to get help for herself. How should the psychotherapist deal with such an issue?

Clearly there are often no hard-and-fast rules. Ethical considerations are rarely simple Parental precepts to be followed but rather they are complex, multi-faceted, often paradoxical, existential dilemmas which need to be grappled with a spirit of humility, compassion and integrity.

As an integral part of the training programme, trainees are presented with situations where ethical issues and dilemmas (many of which have been faced in reality by psychotherapists) are confronted. The following is but a small sample of the types of situations clients may bring to their psychotherapist and for which answers, solutions, decisions, or negotiations may be extremely difficult to attain.

Ethics questionnaire

Please consider each of these situations. What ethical considerations are involved in each? How do you think about it? What course of action, by whom, is appropriate?

1 Young gay man has frequent promiscuous sexual encounters but is 'too scared' to go for an HIV blood test. He mostly has 'safe sex' but occasionally gets drunk and forgets.

2 Wife of your client phones to report that he is threatening suicide and asks for your advice. She doesn't want you to mention to him that she called and told that he has been hoarding pills.

3 You have been seeing a woman with five children. She has had problems dealing with them. One of them is already in therapy with another therapist and your client (mother) called in to consult with the other therapist about the child. That therapist then advised the client (mother) to terminate therapy with you because you don't understand about bringing up children since you are not a parent yourself.

4 Your client is on social security but she tells you that she also earns considerable money from working at a market stall. What is your responsibility?

5 You saw a woman client (Client 1) for a period of six months and terminated with her. Then after several months, a new woman client (Client 2) came to see you. She was in the process of a divorce and her husband was involved with someone else. You see her for several months. Your original client calls you to say she in need of further assistance. You agree to see her and in the course of the first consultation, you realise that she is the person who is involved with the husband of your second client. You now have both clients in treatment; what do you do?

6 You have a woman client who reports that her husband regularly beats their adopted son of 10. He has recently sustained an injury to his anus and had to be treated medically. How do you think about this and what do you do, as the woman is your client, not the husband and the son?

7 Your client tells you that a therapist colleague of yours is having a sexual relationship with a client who is also a friend of hers. She wants you to keep this confidential.

8 You have a client who is a medical doctor. He confesses that he gave his mother an overdose because she was suffering from terminal cancer and pleaded with him to do this. Now that he has told you, what is your ethical course of action?

9 During a piece of work in a group-psychotherapy session it emerges that a client killed a man several years ago in order to get drugs from him. As a prostitute she was also involved with the chief of police who refused to investigate.

10 Your supervisor has obviously been tired for several months and looks run down. He is getting more and more irritable and has lost a great deal of weight. What are the ethical considerations in such a situation?

11 You discover that one of your clients is taking amphetamines which she obtains from several GPs. What is involved here, how do you think about it, and what should be done by whom?

12 You know that a colleague has several black clients. At a social gathering you hear this therapist speaking in a derogatory and generalised way about black people to friends.

(Clarkson and Gilbert, 1987)

As can be seen from the preceding examples, there is an ethical perspective which, by its very nature, is intrinsically contained within the therapeutic relationship as well as in the wider human context – that of the 'Bystander' role (Clarkson, 1987).

Definition

A bystander is considered to be a person who does not become actively involved in a situation where someone else requires help. In the literature, the concept of the Bystander is consistently applied to describe the behaviour of people in emergencies, such as the Kitty Genovese murder, where several people witnessed a violent assault without any effective intervention (Latane and Darley, 1970). Where one or more people are in danger, Bystanders therefore could, by taking some form of action, affect the outcome of the situation even if they were not able to avert it. Thus, by definition, anyone who gets actively involved in a critical situation, whether we describe this choice as pathological (scriptbound) or autonomous, is not a Bystander.

In his article on 'Autocratic power', Jacobs correctly suggests that 'by far the largest group in the entire system are the bystanders' (Jacobs, 1987: 68). He cites the case of public protest against the euthanasia programme in Germany in 1939 as an example of how the Bystanders have great power in situations where they choose to exert this power, since they make a considerable contribution to crowd motion. We know from systems theory that a change in any part of the system will affect the rest of the system (Watzlawick *et al.*, 1974). Therefore, if the Bystanders in a system change their behaviour, the rest of the sociocultural system will be affected.

Many people may participate passively in violent or oppressive situations. By not challenging or intervening they give tacit permission to the abuse of power occurring in their environment. 'According to folk wisdom, each of us must decide to be either a part of the problem or the solution and not to decide is to decide' (Roberts, 1984a: 229).

Individual moral choices are exceedingly complex and based on family and cultural scripting as well as environmental trauma. Passing judgement on the existential or script-bound solutions an individual arrives at under extreme stress requires caution and empathy. However, the author questions whether even understandable pressures exonerate an individual from his or her share of the collective responsibility. For example, psychotherapists cannot responsibly avoid considering the implications of their work for individuals or groups by affecting a value-free stance.

If transactional analysts are to be significant agents of change, if we are to offer significant medicine to our communities and to the world community, we need to move beyond issues of individual survival and well-being. We need to engage ourselves and others in a broader sense of purpose.

(Cornell, 1984: 242)

Bystander behaviour in situations where others are at risk or being harmed may be understandable but not necessarily excusable in individuals or groups adhering to the humanistic psychology tradition. In this sense TA is a major example of a humanistic psychology which mandates, by its assumptions, active involvement in the plight of the less fortunate as well as in attending to the welfare of our clients.

Despite some of Berne's prejudices and blind spots, TA has a tradition rich in social awareness, a commitment to changing the world in which we live, and continuing emphasis by some clinicians and trainers throughout the world in broadening our individualistic concerns with the compromises and conventions of everyday life towards an action-orientated commitment to the planet which is ours, and the plight of all its peoples.

(Clarkson, 1986a: 4)

Review of critical choice points in bystanding situations

Latane and Darley (1970) cite five critical steps in the process of participation in 'bystanding' situations: (1) *notice* that something is happening; 2) *interpret* the situation as one in which help is needed; (3) *assume* personal responsibility; (4) choose a form of assistance; and (5) *implement* the assistance.

There is significant correspondence between these five critical steps and the discounting matrix: (1) discounting existence of problem; (2) discounting significance of problem; (3) discounting solvability of problem; (4) discounting own ability to cope with or solve problem (Schiff *et al.*, 1975). Based on a synthesis of these two sources, the five following questions can guide appropriate self-questioning for both psychotherapist and client.

1 Am I aware of what is happening in my environment?

To notice that something is happening is to account for the existence of a problem, for example, *noticing* that a friend at a party is drunk enough to be potentially dangerous to self or others. Not to confront that friend as they leave to drive home is to commit 'bystanding' (doing nothing relevant to solve the problem). 'We feel and act as if we are in fact disconnected physically, spiritually, ecologically and morally from ourselves and from the universe. We behave as if we were each isolated and separate' (Rinzler, 1984: 233).

There is an increasing awareness of the psychotherapist's responsibility to invisible third parties to the therapeutic contract with the client. It is important to recognise the impact of problems such as long-lasting depression or severe anorexia on a client's children, spouse, students or employees and initiate appropriate action with the client and/or other relevant parts of the system.

2 Is help needed?

Schiff's (Schiff *et al.*, 1975) concept of accounting for the significance of a situation is close to interpreting the situation as one in which help is needed. An example of this concerns accurately assessing whether a child screaming in the flat upstairs is genuinely ill or being abused. The potential Bystander needs to decide whether this situation requires investigation to determine if help is needed. Another example reflects how therapeutic neturality may be lethal as in the case of a promiscuous client who may not be aware of the need to take precautions against contracting AIDS.

Another example involves a woman who reveals in psychotherapy that her son beats her daughter to the point of unconsciousness. The woman fails to understand or acknowledge this as a potentially homicidal issue because it 'does not seem serious'.

Another similar instance arises in the course of social interaction, for example between professionals at a party. An acquaintance who is a general practitioner mentions in passing that she has been giving her 5-year-old daughter anti-depressant medication for the past year because the daughter is 'difficult'. Non-contractual intervention by the clinician as a professional and as a person is sometimes essential and frequently justified without being labelled as 'rescuing'.

3 Is it my responsibility?

To assume personal responsibility means to account for the existential fact that you are personally involved in a situation and are able to influence it. For example, how many people in oppressive situations (e.g. South Africa) claim they are not personally responsible for the surrounding injustice and persecution while continuing to benefit financially from the situation? If Jews, disabled elderly people or blacks are being persecuted in my organisation or my country, how can I sustain psychological wellbeing in that culture? If plants react at cellular levels when other plants are injured, how can human beings be exempt from visceral empathy? (Watson, 1974). If a colleague is working 70 hours a week without rest, is it not my responsibility to discuss this with them? If a TA trainer is propagating anti-homosexual prejudice, is it not my responsibility to seek ethical redress on behalf of the community at large?

4 What are the viable options for taking action to change the situation?

Possibilities for change can be developed by generating viable options and then choosing a form of assistance to the person or persons being threatened. For example, people in groups or crowds may participate collectively in bystanding even when one of their own is persecuted (e.g. Nazi Germany or Chile). Fear of personal survival or the welfare of family sustains their passivity. Bystanders in such situations frequently justify not intervening by believing that the situation cannot change, the problem cannot be solved or that no other viable option for action exists. Likewise, many people claim that they personally have no ability to affect the likelihood of a nuclear holocaust.

Assuming individual responsibility should not depend on a successful outcome to one's efforts. Personal responsibility constitutes a commitment to right action regardless of whether the commitment attains the desired short-term results.

5 What action am I taking?

This question is designed to focus on immediacy of action – the opposite of perpetuating and/or endorsing passive behaviour. For example, people may recurrently get into states of agitated depression about the nuclear threat without taking appropriate action related to the problem. Instead of using their biologically appropriate anger to impact on the situation, they become self-condemning and depressed while remaining passive. Incapacitation, such as fainting or hysterical amnesia, in the vicinity of someone abusing their power or authority is another example of bystanding as passive behaviour (if no action follows either at the time or later).

Fighting the oppressor is one solution. Making a moral choice to withdraw and allow the interested parties to fight or negotiate their own battles is another. Human beings can develop many creative alternatives. For example, a South African artist is recording the historical events of her country through her paintings at a time when emergency laws prohibit freedom of the press. Her task is to find a way of being an involved witness that is compatible with her survival and her conscience.

The undiscovered fourth role in the Karpman Drama Diagram

In his 1968 article Karpman identifies the three drama-triangle roles of Persecutor, Victim and Rescuer. However, he does not allow for the fact that the drama almost always has an *audience of Bystanders* (see Figure 11.5). The audience is both affected by the play and also has a profound effect on what transpires. At the simplest level, whether or not the play continues is determined by the audience. It may show displeasure by booing or leaving the theatre, or demonstrate its pleasure or acquiescence by applause. By their very presence, the members of the audience also agree, consent and participate response-ably.

Audience is another word for Bystander, especially in its dictionary definition 'a looker on' (Macdonald in *Chambers Twentieth Century Dictionary*, 1972: 178). Just as another role in the drama triangle is an attempt to discount aspects of self, others or the reality situation (Schiff *et al.*, 1975), so, too, the Bystander can be considered a phoney drama role involving such discounting which, through passivity, perpetuates offensive acts.

Like other role behaviours, unaware or unquestioned bystanding behaviour interferes with full and complete integrated Adult functioning. By avoiding autonomous goal-directed action, bystanding often does violence to both the ethos and pathos aspects of a mature human being as well as limiting the scope, richness, range and effectiveness of intelligent reality processing (Berne, 1980/1961).

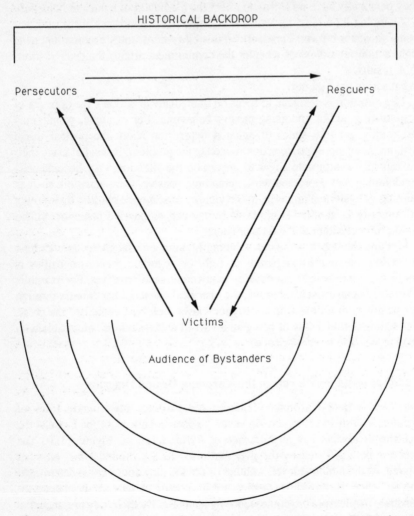

Figure 11.5 The Karpman drama diagram incorporating the Bystander role in sociohistorical context

Although the roles of Victim, Persecutor and Rescuer can all be phoney or taken on in bad faith, these dramatic functions can also be authentically chosen responses to a given situation. In a profound sense the authentic 'looker on' can be 'the witness', as were some people in Nazi Germany who made drawings of the atrocities for posterity. Regardless of the option selected, one cannot *not* choose.

Furthermore, these choices are made against the changing backdrop of history or the circumstances of the time (see Figure 11.5). This is sometimes used to excuse or to justify immoral behaviour. At a certain point in history the use of torture in Algeria was claimed to be justified on the basis of national security. An awareness of ourselves choosing our actions in historical context can help us make choices which will bear the scrutiny of future generations. It is often effective to ask oneself and/or one's client:

> In thirty years time what will you wish you had done now? Would you be happy for your grandchildren to judge the commitments you are making or avoiding here and now? Man makes himself; he is not found ready-made; he makes himself by the choice of his morality, and he cannot but choose a morality, such is the pressure of circumstances upon him. We define man only in relation to his commitments.
>
> (Sartre, 1970: 50)

This view coincides with an idea that is frequently articulated in third-force psychology: that all actions or non-actions involve a commitment to implicit or explicit values (Maslow, 1962). The value of self-survival can also be a position of 'good faith' – an authentic choice genuinely embraced and honestly acknowledged.

Responsibility

The concept of responsibility in existential and humanistic philosophy is *not* meant to impose on others the edict '*you* are responsible'. Rather, to accept responsibility for oneself and to invite others to do the same forms an authentic and potent foundation for personal and social change (Smail, 1978).

Personal responsibility is often avoided by complying with an internalised Parent that prohibits questioning or effectively challenging authority. An example of this is the people who obediently 'follow orders' to torture others even though these acts do violence, at least initially, to their own values and/or visceral empathy.

One would hope that, during the course of becoming conscious (e.g. exposure to minorities, psychotherapy, spiritual awakening and sincere work and reparation), we as psychotherapists and people will develop greater congruity, authenticity and courage to act on behalf of ourselves and others in unjust or violent situations. Indeed, several investigators have suggested that self-actualising individuals have strong value systems which they enact in their daily lives, sometimes at the expense of their own comfort or wellbeing (Cornell, 1984).

As David Boadella says, psychological health includes the 'courage to act in defence of what one believes to be right, even when there is danger' (Boadella, 1986: 5).

> Obviously, freedom as a definition of a man does not depend upon others, but as soon as there is a commitment, I am obliged to will the liberty of others at the same time as mine. I cannot make liberty my aim unless I make that of others equal in my aim.
>
> (Sartre, 1970: 52)

Bystanding is predicated upon the denial of obligation and such responsibility for others. It is the moral obligation of psychotherapists to accept responsibility for themselves, to invite their clients to do likewise, and to recognise their responsibility by avoiding and assisting their clients to avoid the bystanding role within the therapeutic situation and beyond.

This chapter has focused on the TA psychotherapist in the work situation. It has been concerned with training, supervision, ethical issues and the responsibilities of the working professional psychotherapist towards him/herself and towards the client. It is the author's opinion that the professional standard of competence of practising professionals who have undertaken TA training, supervision and (very importantly) their own personal psychotherapy and who are committed to ongoing supervision and further education in psychotherapy, is very favourably comparable to other psychotherapy trainings.

Chapter 12

A multiplicity of therapeutic relationships as a principle of integration

We therefore define psychotherapy in the broadest terms as: *the systematic use of a relationship between therapist and patient – as opposed to pharmacological or social methods – to produce changes in cognition, feelings and behaviour.*

(Holmes and Lindley, 1989: 3)

There has been a long tradition in transactional analysis of recognising that there are several possible therapeutic relationships available in the psychotherapist/ patient dyad (Berne 1980/1961). Since Berne, there has continued to be explicit or implicit acknowledgement of the particularly effective existence of multiple therapeutic relationships (Schiff *et al.*, 1975; Goulding and Goulding, 1979; and Barr, 1987).

It is the intention of this chapter to illustrate theoretically and by examples from dreams and clinical practice, five different kinds of therapeutic relationship. These are: The I–You relationship; the working alliance; the transferential/ countertransferential relationship; the developmentally needed relationship; and the transpersonal relationship. This grid adds two to those collated by Barr[†] which have been recognised in transactional analysis. These five modalities can act as an integrative principle within transactional analysis itself as it brings together different 'schools' or traditions disciplined by the demands of treatment design. This model also acts as an integrative framework for different traditions (or approaches) of psychotherapy notwithstanding apparent schisms or popular stereotypes and explores the metaphor of psychotherapy as the assumption of a voluntary relationship with the client.

Relationship can be defined as 'The state of being related; a condition or character based upon this; kinship' (Onions, 1973: 1786). Relationship is the first condition of being human. It circumscribes two or more individuals and creates

---

[†]Barr (1987) uses a different classification system and focus from the one presented here by diagramatically focusing on how the relationship (caretaker/baby dyad) gets represented intrapsychically (through internalisation of this relationship) and replicated interpersonally (through the enactment of the transference in psychotherapy)

a bond in the space between them which is more than the sum of the parts. It is so obvious it is frequently taken for granted, and so mysterious that many of the world's greatest psychologists, novelists and philosophers have made it a lifetime's preoccupying passion. Of all the forces in nature, it is our familial relationships which serve to cause the most damage, according to the received wisdom of the late twentieth century. Statistically you are more likely to be killed by a relation than by a stranger.

According to the great existentialist psychotherapist, Medard Boss, all illness and treatment develop out of the patient's disturbed human relationships. 'In focussing on the physician–patient relationship, Freud called attention to the true locus of all therapeutic efforts, whether they were surgical, internal or psychotherapeutic' (Boss, 1979: 257).

This chapter reaches for an elucidation of relationship, the betweenness of people. It is common knowledge that ordinary human relationships have therapeutic value. The old structure of religion, accepted moral order and extended family networks used to provide supportive relationships and healing matrixes for people. These appear to have started to crumble in the twentieth century. Indeed it is possible that psychotherapy as an institutionalised profession has become necessary as a consequence of such a decline in society and in the quality of healing relationships which were available in previous centuries. One way of conceptualising the psychotherapeutic relationship is to conceive of it as the psychotherapist voluntarily entering into a kinship relationship with the patient. This in some views recapitulates the early familial maladaptions and in many perspectives is construed as providing an arena for reparation or healing. Fundamentally, if a psychotherapist can establish a relationship with someone who has lost the capacity for relationship (such as a schizophrenic individual), the client has been retrieved in their relatedness with others. Thus they can begin to rejoin the family of man.

Most forms of psychotherapy use this state of kinship or relationship more or less consciously and more or less in awareness. Indeed there is growing recognition that patient characteristics and the helping relationship are the most significant components of successful treatment. Research results consistently show that the choice of a particular therapeutic method appears to have little discernible influence. That is, success in therapy can best be predicted by the properties of the patient and of the therapist and their particular relationship (Norcross, 1986).

If indeed the therapeutic relationship is one of the most, if not the most important factor in successful therapy, one would expect that much of the training in psychotherapy would be training in the *intentional* use of relationship. Some psychotherapies claim that psychotherapy requires use of only one kind of relationship or at most two. In transactional analysis the real relationship or person-to-person relationship is probably best represented. Some specifically exclude the use of certain kinds of relationship; for example the Gouldings (1979) minimise the use of transference whereas Moiso (1985), also in transactional analysis, sees it as a central focal point of classical Berneian psychotherapy. Some psychotherapeutic approaches pay hardly any theoretical attention to the nature of the relationship and they may be entirely free of content (e.g. in some approaches to hypnotherapy or NLP, therapeutic changes can be made by the patient without the practitioner necessarily knowing what these changes may be). In some of course, stated policy and actual practice often diverge. As we shall see later, even the actions of Freud (speaking perhaps louder than his words) often belied the assumed orthodoxy of psychoanalytic practice.

So the first question is: what differentiates an ordinary relationship from a psychotherapeutic relationship? This chapter reaches for an elucidation of relationship, the _betweenness_ of people. It is common knowledge that ordinary everyday human relationships can have therapeutic value. Indeed it is possible that psychotherapy as an institutionalised profession has became increasingly important as the old structures of religion, the moral order and the extended family networks started crumbling as support and healing structures for many people in the twentieth century.

In the psychotherapeutic literature existentialists such as May (1969) are concerned with the nature of therapeutic relationships. So are such recent psychoanalysts as Klauber:

> The most neglected feature of the psychoanalytic relationship still seems to me to be that it is a relationship: a very peculiar relationship, but a definite one. Patient and analyst need one another. The patient comes to the analyst because of internal conflicts that prevent him from enjoying life, and he begins to use the analyst not only to resolve them, but increasingly as a receptacle for his pent-up feelings. But the analyst also needs the patient in order to crystallize and communicate his own thoughts, including some of his inmost thoughts on intimate human problems which can only grow organically in the context of this relationship. They cannot be shared and experienced in the same immediate way with a colleague, or even with a husband or wife. It is also in his relationship with his patients that the analyst refreshes his own analysis.
>
> (Klauber, 1986: 200–1)

The psychotherapeutic relationship is characterised by the facts that: it is paid for according to a contractual agreement; one of the parties in the relationship has been specifically trained to take part in it; and the stated goal is the amelioration of psychological problems or the improvement of mental health of the paying partner in the task; and finally, the psychotherapist is willing to commit him/herself to the welfare of another human being in this way.

THE WORKING ALLIANCE

One of Berne's most enduring emphases was on the importance and quality of the working relationship between therapist and client. He operationalised this in the therapeutic contract (1980/1961). Other transactional analysis psychotherapists such as Steiner (1971), Holloway and Holloway (1973) and James (1977) have all underlined the crucial importance of establishing a working relationship of trust and respect with the client. Without such a working alliance, psychotherapy is certainly limited in its goals and restricted in scope. This working alliance is represented by the client's or patient's willingness to engage in the psychotherapeutic relationship even when they at some archaic level may no longer wish to do so.

In TA, the working alliance is conceptualised as a contract or agreement between the Adult of the psychotherapist and the Adult of the client. In psychoanalysis, 'it is the part of the patient–analyst relationship that enables the patient to identify with the analyst's point of view and to work with the analyst despite the neurotic transference reactions' (Greenson, 1967: 29). The attitudes and character traits which further the development of the transference neurosis are, basically antithetical to those which further the working alliance (Stone, 1961; Greenson, 1965; 1967). Which one is allowed to become figure, or focus, must depend on the nature of the psychotherapeutic task at a particular time with each unique patient. Other modes of therapeutic relationship may also be present, but more part of the background at a particular time.

For many psychotherapists, the working alliance is the crucial and only necessary relationship for effective therapy (Dryden, 1984). It certainly represents the essential co-operation that even the general practitioner requires. For example, the patient actually takes the medication that the doctor prescribes. Research has shown that this working alliance is frequently missing in general practice (Griffith, 1990). Bordin (1979) differentiated goals, bonds and task – three aspects of the working alliance which seem to be required for any form of therapy to be successful.

> The therapeutic alliance is the powerful joining of forces which energizes and supports the long, difficult, and frequently painful work of life-changing psychotherapy. The conception of the therapist here is not of a disinterested observer-technician but of a fully alive human companion for the client. In this regard my view is in marked contrast to the traditional notion of the therapist as a skilled but objective director of therapeutic processes.
>
> (Bugental, 1987: 49)

> Several studies emphasize the importance of such common factors. Among the common factors most frequently studied have been those identified by the client-centred school as 'necessary and sufficient conditions' for patient personality change: accurate empathy, positive regard, nonpossessive warmth, and congruence or genuineness. Virtually all schools of therapy accept the notion that these or related therapist relationship variables are important for significant progress in psychotherapy and in fact, fundamental in the formation of a working alliance.
>
> (Lambert, 1986: 444–5)

In response to the client asking 'How are you?' the psychotherapist in working alliance mode is likely to make any reply which will enhance optimum conditions to accomplish the stated therapeutic task. For example the therapist may say, 'Fine and how have you been?' or 'As you can hear from my husky voice, I am having a bit of a cold, but I am quite well enough to work with you today.'

The following dream encapsulates symbolically the person's previous engagement with her mother (script) contrasted with the working alliance, the current choice with the psychotherapist.

I was with you and we were working – or engaged in something serious but having an enjoyable time. My mother was coming at 3 o'clock and I had an arrangement to meet her. You didn't know that and you said: I am available at three o'clock – why don't we carry on then? I thought, Oh, God, If I stay with my therapist then I won't be there for my mother, if I go I may lose the connection with you – I might break this thing that felt so good. It wouldn't actually be disastrous, since we would continue working again the next day, but it would be like breaking the energy. It is so pleasurable, the work is so good, we're both getting something from it. My mother is more of a shadowy figure than you are. I then decided to do neither and went off for a walk on my own, doing my own thing. In this way I wouldn't be choosing one person or the other. I would be choosing myself. You would agree with that. If I went with my mother you would say you needed to do that, but it would be less wise, but you would absolutely appreciate me for doing my own thing.

In kinship terms, the relationship of working together can be likened to that between cousins. According to Debrett's the word 'cousins' has loosely indicated uncle/aunt/niece/nephew relationships as well as cousin relationships. The notion is meant to convey a distance from the family of origin (different parents) but tribal loyalties to each other's welfare so that it is possible to have a blend of subjective altruism and an objective capacity which may make that relationship constructive.

THE TRANSFERENTIAL/COUNTRANSFERENTIAL RELATIONSHIP

Another mode of therapeutic relationship which has been written about most extensively in psychoanalysis is that of transference. It is important to remember that Freud did not intend psychoanalysis to be a cure but rather a search for understanding and frowned upon people who wished to change instead of analyse. So the transference relationship is an essential part of the analytic procedure since the analysis consists in inviting the transference and gradually dissolving it by means of interpretation.

Laplanche and Pontalis describe the transference as follows:

For psycho-analysis, a process of actualisation of unconscious wishes. Transference uses specific objects and operates in the framework of a specific relationship established with these objects. Its context *par excellence* is the analytic situation.

In the transference, infantile prototypes re-emerge and are experienced with a strong sensation of immediacy. As a rule what psycho-analysts mean by the unqualified use of the term 'transference' is *transference during treatment*.

Classically, the transference is acknowledged to be the terrain on which all the basic problems of a given analysis play themselves out: the establishment, modalities, interpretation and resolution of the transference are in fact what define the cure.

(Laplanche and Pontalis, 1988: 455)

'Transactionally, this means that when the patient's Child attempts to provoke the therapist's Parent, it is confronted instead by the therapist's Adult. The therapeutic affect arises from the disconcertion caused by this crossed transaction' (Berne, 1980/1961: 174). While the patient continues to act according to outdated patterns, the analyst's reaction conforms strictly to the actual therapeutic situation.

Freud went so far at one point as to suggest that the analyst model himself on the surgeon, put aside his human sympathy, and adopt an attitude of emotional coldness (Freud, 1912b). 'This means that the analyst must have the ability to restrain his therapeutic intentions, must control his urge for closeness, and must "blanket" his usual personality' (Stone in Greenson, 1967: 389). In that same paper Freud (1912b) advocated that the analyst should refrain from intruding his personality into the treatment, and he introduced the simile of the analyst being a 'mirror' for the analysand.

However, I do not believe this to be an accurate picture of what Freud had in mind. In my opinion, he stressed certain of the 'unnatural' aspects of psychoanalytic technique because they were so foreign and artificial to the usual doctor–patient relationship and the customary psychotherapy of his day.

For example, in a paper written in the same year as the one where he cites the recommendations for emotional coldness and the mirrorlike attitude, Freud stated:

Thus the solution of the puzzle is that transference to the doctor is suitable for resistance to the treatment only in so far as it is a negative transference or a positive transference of repressed erotic impulses. If we 'remove' the transference by making it conscious, we are detaching only these two components of the emotional act from the person of the doctor; the other component, which is admissible to consciousness and unobjectionable, persists and is the vehicle of success in psycho-analysis exactly as it is in other methods of treatment.

(Freud, 1912a: 105)

Alexander and French expressed the psychoanalytic principle as follows:

The old pattern was an attempt at adaptation on the part of the child to parental behavior ... The analyst's objective, understanding attitude allows the patient ... to make a new settlement of the old problem. ... While the patient continues to act according to outdated patterns, the analyst's reaction conforms strictly to the actual therapeutic situation.

(Alexander and French, 1946: 66, 67)

The patient's question 'How are you?' may often be met with analytic silence. Alternatively the analyst may reply, 'I wonder what prompts your concern for me? It may be that you are anxious again, like you were with your mother, that I will not be able to withstand your envy towards me.'

This transferential therapeutic relationship can be compared to that of stepparent or godparent. Negative transference connects with the former (the witch of many traditional fairy tales, for example, Hansel and Gretel) and idealising positive transference connects with the godparent or fairy godmother relationship in that a putative family connection exists but it lacks the immediacy of a real parent. Whether or not the psychotherapist identifies with such projections, and how he or she handles them, may destroy or facilitate the therapy.

A narcissistic, apparently generous but dynamically retentive patient whose mother overfed him physically while never responding to his real feelings of isolation, abandonment or rage reports the following dream:

I am at a sumptuous banquet which is presided over by you (therapist). I take the food from the table, but I don't eat it. I put it in a plastic bag so that you won't see and I throw it in a wastepaper basket. I want to continue to be invited, but not to have to eat the food.

The great importance of the transference has often led to the mistaken idea that it is absolutely indispensable for a cure, that it must be demanded from the patient, so to speak. But a thing like that can no more be demanded than faith, which is only valuable when it is spontaneous. Enforced faith is nothing but spiritual cramp. Anyone who thinks that he must 'demand' a transference is forgetting that this is only one of the therapeutic factors.

(Jung, 1966: 172)

THE REPARATIVE/DEVELOPMENTALLY NEEDED RELATIONSHIP

The reparative/developmentally needed relationship is another therapeutic relationship mode which occasionally can be differentiated from the others. This is the intentional provision by the psychotherapist of a corrective/reparative or replenishing parental relationship (or action) where the original parenting was deficient, abusive or overprotective. The cathexis approach of Schiff *et al.* (1975) focuses (arguably more than any other in transactional analysis) on providing the therapeutic relationship most needed by the individual patients in terms of their developmental stages.

The following dream shows a client separating out a developmentally needed relationship (for the client's future) provided by the therapist from the transferential relationship (based on the client's past).

He dreams about two psychotherapists, both called the same name as his therapist. The one psychotherapist says to him in the dream: 'How could you make such mistakes, this is terrible, you ought to be punished.' The other psychotherapist says, 'Look, I myself have received a D in this subject. I was not very interested in it and you can see that you don't have to be perfect in all things.' The first psychotherapist responds with anger and accusations of unethical conduct saying, 'How could you say such things, you are just encouraging him to make mistakes and setting a very bad example!' The client himself then steps in to arbitrate and explains to the first psychotherapist: 'Actually she is right. You have to understand what she is saying in the right spirit. This is what I need to hear.'

Dreams often act as unconscious communication about the progress of the therapy from the unconscious of the client. In this dream he is clearly telling me what he needs developmentally – what was absent in the original relationship where he veers between being the saintly clean little boy who has to play without getting dirty and the dirty disgusting child who causes embarassment and shame to his family if he as much as gets his hands dirty. (In life he veers between saintly self-sacrifice and secret addictions.) The client is also communicating a most significant fact – not only has he internalised the psychotherapist and distinguished the two personifications of the person of the same name, but happily he is siding with the therapist who has his best interests at heart and least resembles the tranferential parent who would 'write him off' for the smallest misdemeanour or shame him for not getting the best marks in every subject regardless of his true interests. (Even the D is still a passing mark!)

The developmentally needed relationship, as indicated in the cited dream, refers to those aspects of relationship which may have been absent for the client at particular periods of his or her life and which are supplied by the therapist usually in a contracted form (at their request or with their agreement) during the psychotherapy. Sandor Ferenczi (1980/1926) (one of Freud's early followers) attempted this early in the history of psychoanalysis. He departed from this neutrality and impassivity in favour of giving nursery care, friendly hugs or management of regression to very sick patients, including one whom he saw any time, day or night, and took with him on his holidays. Ferenczi held that there needed to be a contrast between the original trauma in infancy and the analytic situation so that remembering can be facilitative instead of a renewed trauma for the patient.

The advocacy relationship proposed by Alice Miller (1983, 1985) can be seen to be the provision of the developmentally needed force in a child's life which should have been provided by a parent or other significant caretakers but which the therapist ultimately has to provide. The holding environment of Winnicott (1958) is another example of such provision, as are the reparenting techniques of Schiff *et al.* (1975) in transactional analysis.

All of our patients have unmet needs from early on in life where normal cognitive and affectual development was thwarted. Their level and kinds of functioning are often equivalent to that of a child. In planning an environment to provide sufficient support for such individuals, we have found it advantageous to set expectations according to the patients' capacity for healthy functioning and not their chronological age.

(Schiff *et al.*, 1975: 99)

Freud prescribed a mirrorlike impassivity on the part of the analyst, who should himself be analysed, who should not reciprocate the patient's confidences and not try to educate, morally influence or 'improve' the patient, and who should be tolerant of the patient's weakness. In practice, however, Freud 'conducted therapy as no classical Freudian analyst would conduct it today' writes Janet Malcolm (1981) in *Psychoanalysis: The Impossible Profession*, shouting at the patient, praising him, arguing with him, accepting flowers from him on his birthday, lending him money, and even gossiping with him about other patients! Among Freudian analysts today, the analyst generally confines himself to listening to the patient, offering sparse interpretations of the unconscious meaning of his communications (Friedman, 1985: 169).

The psychoanalyst Sechehaye (1951) was able to break through the unreal wall that hemmed in her patient Renee and bring her into some contact with life. In order to do this, Sechehaye not only took her on holiday to the seashore, as Ferenczi had done with one of his patients, but also took her into her home for extended periods. She allowed Renee to regress to the point where she felt she was re-entering her mother's body. Sechehaye became one of the first of those therapists who have undertaken literally to 'reparent' schizophrenic clients. She allowed the patient to lean on her bosom and pretended to give milk from her breasts to the doll with whom Renee identified (Sechehaye, 1951).

That Sechehaye was far more involved personally than even the most humanistic of therapists usually are we can infer from the accounts of how she gave instructions for her meals, saw to her baths, and in general played for Renee the nourishing mother that she had been denied as an infant. That this took an emotional toll far beyond the ordinary is evident from Renee's own account that 'Mama was extremely upset' or that she regained consciousness and found Mama weeping over her.

(Friedman, 1985: 188)

The psychotherapist's reply to the client who asks 'How are you?' in this kind of relationship will be determined by the specific needs that were not appropriately responded to by their caretakers in childhood. In response to the adult who as a child was never allowed to show her care or love for the parent the therapist may reply 'I'm fine thank you and I appreciate your caring.' Alternatively, in response to the adult who as a child was burdened with parental intimacies a therapist may reply 'It is not necessary for you to worry about me, right now I am here to take care of you and I am ready to do that.'

In the developmentally needed relationship the metaphoric kinship being established is clearly closer to a real parent-and-child relationship than any of the other forms of bonding in therapy. In the words of J. Schiff:

> I am as much part of the symbiosis and as vulnerable as any parent. While my attachments don't occur at the same kind of depth with each youngster, they have not been selective in favor of those kids who were successful, and several times I have experienced tremendous loss and grief.
>
> (Schiff, 1977: 63)

In view of the regressive nature of this kind of work and the likely length of time involved, the professional and ethical responsibilities of the therapists are also concomitantly greater and perhaps so awesome that many therapists avoid them. It is certainly true that this depth of long-standing therapeutic relationship is more frequently reported between therapists and more severely damaged patients as in the cathexis school where it is primarily used for working with schizophrenics.

THE I–YOU RELATIONSHIP

The relationship modality which shows most continuity with the healing relationships of ordinary life is that which Buber called the I–You relationship to differentiate it from I–It or I–Thou relationship. The I–You relationship is elsewhere referred to in psychotherapeutic literature as the real relationship or the core relationship (Barr, 1987). It is very likely that those ordinary relationships which human beings have experienced as particularly healing over the ages have been characterised by the qualities of the I–You relationship (Buber, 1970).[†]

With Freud's discovery of the importance of the transference relationship came deep suspicion of the real relationship – the part of the therapy relationship most similar to ordinary healing human-to-human relationships. Certainly for some decades the psychoanalysts' emotional reactions to their patients were usually understood to be a manifestation of the analysts' unresolved conflicts. It is only comparatively recently that countertransference reactions have been seen as valid and important sources of information. However, here as earlier (see Chapter 7), we are still not speaking of informative reactive countertransference which serves as information to be used in the psychotherapy.

Object-relations theorists have offered psychotherapy profoundly useful concepts and theoretical understandings, but the I–You therapeutic relationship is the opposite of an object relationship. For Buber, the other is a person, not an object.

[†] The author agrees with the Buber translator, Kaufmann, that I–You more accurately represents the person-to-person intention and the lack of formality rendered in the German *Du* and which is not captured in English by the more formal thou (Kaufman in Buber, 1970: 14).

Whoever says You does not have something for his object. For wherever there is something there is also another something; every It borders on other Its; It is only by virtue of bordering on others. But where You is said there is no something. You has no borders. Whoever says you does not have something; he has nothing. But he stands in relation.

(Buber, 1970: 55)

The emotional involvement in this relationship between psychotherapist and patient is that between *person-and-person* in the existential dilemma where both stand in a kind of mutuality to each other. Indeed, as Friedman (1985) points out, it is a kind of mutuality because the psychotherapist is also in role.

However, in the immediacy of the existential encounter, the mutuality is almost complete and the self of the therapist becomes the instrument through which the healing evolves.

An intuitive introverted patient sadly remembers difficulty with right or left, physical discomfort in the real world, and incomprehension when required to learn kineasthetically. The psychotherapist bends down to show the scar on her leg which she used as a little girl to help her decide which side was left. The moment is unforgettable, the bonding person-to-person. Yet it is enacted by a professional who at that very moment has taken responsiblity for that self-disclosure in the psychotherapy, judging it appropriate and timely to trust or delight the patient with a sense of shared personhood, siblings in incomprehension, and siblings in discovery, siblings in the quest for wholeness.

Such self-disclosure needs of course to be done with extreme care and in its worst abusive form has been an excuse for acting out of the therapist's need for display, hostility or seductiveness. Genuine well-judged use of the I–You relationship is probably one of the most difficult forms of therapeutic relating. Doubtless this was the very good reason behind the early analysts regarding it with extreme suspicion. Also, of course, it is in the name of I–You relationship that many personal relationships have been destructive. It probably requires the most skill, the most self-knowledge and the greatest care because its potential for careless or destructive use is so great. Yet there are not many trainings which specifically address this either experientially or theoretically. Sometimes lip service is paid to the I–You, person to person concept as if we know what it's about or it is 'outlawed' in the analysis – as if this were possible.

There can be no psychoanalysis without an existential bond between the analyst and the analysand. This means that to imagine there can be analysis without countertransference, without involvement and response on the part of the analyst, is an illusion. The analyst can deny but cannot avoid having an emotional relationship with the analysand: even the objectifying attitude of indifference is a mode of emotional relating.

(Friedman, 1985: 79)

The I–You relationship is characterised by here-and-now existential encounter between the two people, participation in the process and recognising that each is changed by the other and that the real person of the therapist can never be totally excluded from an interactional matrix of therapy.

It is good for analyst and patient to have to admit some of the analyst's weaknesses as they are revealed in the interchange in the consulting room. The admission of deficiencies may help patient and analyst to let go of one another more easily when they have had enough. In other words, the somewhat freer admission of realities – but not too free – facilitates the process of mourning which enables an analysis to end satisfactorily. The end of analysis is in this way prepared from the beginning.

(Klauber, 1986: 213)

To Fromm-Reichmann (1974/1950), Sullivan's concept of the therapist as 'participant observer' included spontaneous and genuine responses on the part of the therapist and even, in some cases, reassuring touch and gestures of affection. This does *not* include transforming the professional relation into a social one or seeking personal gratification from the dialogue with the patient. But it does include confirmation of patients as worthy of respect and 'meeting them on the basis of mutual human equality'.

Guntrip (1961) as well rejected the traditional restriction of the functions of the therapist to the dual one of a screen upon which the patient projects his fantasies and a colourless instrument of interpretative technique. Instead, he saw the personal relationship between patient and analyst as the truly therapeutic factor on which all others depend.

True psychotherapy only happens when the therapist and patient find the person behind each other's defences. Deep insight, as Fairbairn (1952) points out, only develops inside a good therapeutic relationship. What is therapeutic, when it is achieved, is 'the moment of real meeting'. This experience is transforming for both therapist and patient because it is not what happened before, i.e., transference, but what has never happened before, a genuine experience of relationship centred in the here-and-now.

Confusion and lack of clarity abounds when types of therapeutic relationship are confused with each other or the validity of one is used as necessarily substituting for the other. My belief is that human beings need all these forms of relating and that psychotherapists with flexibity and range can become skilful in the appropriate use of all of them, although not all are required in all psychotherapies.

To illustrate: what Freud calls 'transference' Boss (1979) describes as always a genuine relationship between the analysand and the analyst. Despite the difference in their positions the partners disclose themselves to each other as human beings. It seems that Freud and Boss are describing different therapeutic-relationship modalities which are intrinsically different in intent, in execution and in effect, not merely a semantic blurring.

Of course, the humanistically orientated psychotherapies, such as Gestalt which emphasises here-and-now *contact* as a valid form of therapeutic relating, have greatly amplified the value and use of the person-to-person encounter in psychotherapy. For Rogers and Stevens (1967) the establishment of a relationship of congruence, respect and empathy became the cornerstone condition for facilitating human growth and development.

> The details of technique vary, but the strategy is always to keep a steady, gentle pressure toward the direct and responsible I–thou orientation, keeping the focus of awareness on the difficulties the patients experience in doing this, and helping them find their own ways through these difficulties.
>
> (Fagan and Shepherd, 1971: 116)

In transactional analysis, Berne first identified elements of this in the notion of the relationship between the Child and the psychotherapist and the Child and the client – a spontaneous natural sharing of intimacy without games pretence or inauthenticity.

In psychoanalysis, even Anna Freud called for the recognition that in analysis two real people of equal adult status stand in a real personal relationship to each other. 'There are differences in the ways in which we receive and send off patients, and in the degree to which we permit a real relationship to the patient to coexist with the transferred, fantasied one' (Freud, 1968: 360). It is the neglect of this side of the relationship, and not just 'transference', that causes the hostile reactions analysts get from their patients. In 1961 Leo Stone expressed concern lest the analyst's unrelentingly analytic behavior subvert the process by shaking the patient's faith in the analyst's benignity. A failure to show reasonable human response at a critical juncture can invalidate years of patient, skilful work, Stone declared.

According to Malcolm (1981) honesty and spontaneity can correct the patient's transference misperceptions and make the therapist's responses unpredictable and therefore less likely to be manipulated by the patient. The patient's distrust may be relieved, and the therapist provides the patient with a model of authentic being with which he can identify. Such authenticity on the therapist's part may mean that the therapeutic relationship changes the therapist as much as the patient. Both Jourard (1971) and Jung (1966) held this as a central truth in all healing endeavour. Searles (1975) also believed that the patient has a powerful innate striving to heal the analyst (as he or she may have desired to heal the parents) which can and does contribute to greater individuation and growth for the therapist as they are both transformed in the therapeutic dialogue.

'What is confirmed most of all is the personal "realness" of the therapist that has arisen from and been brought into the therapeutic relationship' (Archambeau, 1979: 141–58). I also quote the psychoanalyst Greenson directly: 'A certain amount of compassion, friendliness, warmth, and respect for the patient's rights is indispensable. The analyst's office is a treatment room and not a research laboratory' (Greenson, 1967: 391).

Greenacre (1959) and Stone (1961) are clear that the analyst must be able to become emotionally involved and committed to his patient. He must like the patient; prolonged dislike or disinterest as well as too strong a love will interfere with therapy. He must have a wish to help and cure the patient, and he must be concerned with the patient's welfare without losing sight of his long-range goals.

The kinship quality of the person-to-person relationship is analogous to that of siblings – the shared empathic understanding from a similar inherited frame of reference; although they are different, they are equal and share the ambiguous and ambivalent legacy of existence.

In answer to the patient's question: 'How are you?' the psychotherapist may well reply: 'Physically I am fine; but lately I have been wondering about the helpless feeling I sometimes experience when you talk about the death of your baby. I guess it reminds me of losing my husband, and the fact that we are both grieving for loved ones in the same year.' Equally the reply may be much shorter, for example: 'Great – how about you?'

In all cases the person-to-person relationship will be honoured by truthfulness or authenticity – not at the expense of the client but in the spirit of mutuality. According to Buber (1970) the genuine psychotherapist can only accomplish the true task of regenerating the stunted growth of a personal centre by entering as 'a partner into a person-to-person relationship, but never through the observation and investigation of an object' (p. 179). Buber further acknowledges the limited nature of the psychotherapeutic person-to-person relationship:

> Healing, like educating, requires that one lives in confrontation and is yet removed .... Every I–You relationship in a situation defined by the attempt of one partner to act on the other one so as to accomplish some goal depends on a mutuality that is condemned never to become complete.
>
> (Buber, 1970: 179)

THE TRANSPERSONAL RELATIONSHIP

This refers to the spiritual dimension of relationship in psychology. If the analyst has been moved by his patient, then the patient is more aware of the analyst as a healing presence' (Samuels, 1985: 189). The transpersonal relationship is potentially present in all healing encounters in individual psychotherapy. It is characterised by its timelessness, a sense of numinousness and in Jungian thought is conceived of as the relationship between the unconscious of the analyst and the unconscious of the patient (Guggenbuhl-Craig, 1971).

> The therapist and the client find themselves in a relationship built on mutual unconsciousness. The therapist is led to a direct confrontation of the unreconciled part of himself. The activated unconsciousness of both the client and the therapist causes both to become involved in a transformation of the 'third'. Hence, the relationship itself becomes transformed in the process.
>
> (Archambeau, 1979: 162)

There is suprisingly little documented about the transpersonal relationship in psychotherapy. Scott Peck (1978) mentions the concept of grace (as has Buber before him) as the ultimate factor which operates in the person-to-person encounter and which may make the difference between whether a patient gets better or not. Berne, too, was aware of it when he quoted the following: '*Je le pensay, & Dieu le guarit* ... we treat them, but it is God who cures them' (Agnew in Berne, 1966: 63).

The nature of this transpersonal dimension is therefore hard to describe, because it is both rare and not easily accessible to the kind of descriptions which can easily be used in discussing the other forms of therapeutic relationships. The '*numinosum* is either a quality belonging to a visible object or the influence of an invisible presence that causes a peculiar alteration of consciousness' (Jung, 1969: 7). It is also possible that there may be a certain amount of embarassment in psychotherapists who have to admit that after all the years of training and therapy and supervision, ultimately we still don't know precisely what it is that we are doing or whether it makes any difference at all. This is the kind of statement one can only be sure of having understood correctly by experienced psychotherapists who have been faced repeatedly with incomprehensible and unpredictable outcomes – the person of whom you despaired suddenly and sometimes inexplicably gets well, thrives and actualises beyond all expectation and the person for whom you had made an optimistic prognosis reaches a plateau from which in effect they never move and the analysis is abandoned with a lingering sense of potential glimpsed, but never to be reached.

Samuels acknowledges that 'The psychology of the soul turns out to be about people in relationship' (Samuels, 1985: 21). The relationship which characterises this 'emptying of the self' and the creation of space between the therapeutic partners is that of the marital pair and indeed in Jung's work on the transference the sexual relationship is used to represent the alchemical process (Jung, 1966).

It is quite possible that psychotherapists may be deluding themselves in ways which may be dangerous for themselves and their clients if they mistakenly, prematurely or naively focus on the transpersonal and, for example, overlook or minimise transferential phenomena.

The transpersonal relationship is characterised by its lack of person-to-person connectedness. It is rather as if the ego of even the personal unconscious of the therapist is 'emptied out' of the therapeutic space, leaving the room for something numinous to emerge in the 'between' of the relationship. This space can then become the *temenos* or 'the *vas bene clausum* inside which the transmutation takes place' (Adler, 1979: 21). It implies a letting go of skills, of knowledge, of experience, of preconceptions, even of the desire to heal, to be present. It is essentially allowing passivity, receptiveness for which preparation is always inadequate since it cannot be made to happen, it can only be encouraged in the same way that the inspirational muse of creativity cannot be forced, but needs to have the ground prepared or seized in the serendipitous moment of readiness. What can be prepared are the conditions conducive to the spontaneous or spiritual act.

A trainee reports:

When I first started learning psychotherapy it was like trying to learn a new language, say French, but when I saw a very experienced therapist working it appeared to me that she was speaking an entirely different language such as Chinese. The more I have learnt the more I have come to realise that the training therapist does indeed speak French, she speaks it very well. And sometimes she speaks Chinese.

The context from which this comment arose is his perception of the supervisor as at times intuitively knowing facts, feelings or intentions of patients without there being any prior evidence to lead to the conclusions. It is these intuitive illuminations which seem to flourish the more the psychotherapist dissolves the individual ego from the therapeutic container, allowing wisdom and insight and transformation to occur as a self-manifesting process.

The transpersonal relationship is the metaphorical Chinese in the psychotherapy. In response to the client's question 'How are you?' the therapist's reply may be nothing or any of the above examples. The essence of the communication is in the heart of the shared silence of being together in a dimension which is impossible to articulate exactly, too delicate to analyse and yet too pervasively present in psychotherapy to ignore.

Another trainee in supervision brought as an ethical problem the fact that he had seen a particular client for several years, the client was seriously disturbed and showed no sign of improvement. Indeed she refused to form any working alliance in the shape of an agreed goal for her psychotherapy. It was exceedingly uncertain what benefit there could be for her, yet she continued coming because (we speculated) this was the one, single human relationship which was alive for her in a physically and emotionally impoverished life.

The psychotherapist responsibly questioned whether the client should be referred to another treatment facility. Yet he feared that she would experience this as an abandonment. In our supervision we explored the possibility that he should let go of expectations that she should be different from the way she was. The therapist was willing and able to even let go of the healer archetype, allowing himself to become an empty vessel, a container wherein which healing could have space to manifest or beingness could be validated without any expectation even of acceptance of the acceptance. This needs to be truly done in good faith and not based on the trickery of paradoxical interventions where expectations are removed in order for the patient to change. The atmosphere is more a trance-like meditation the quality of which is conveyed by the 'being with' of highly evolved therapists with patients who are in acute psychosis such as Gendlin (1967) who affirm the spiritual diversion in psychotherapy.

The transactional analysts, James and Savary (1977: 325), contributed the notion of a third self created in the dimension of betweenness when the inner-core energies of the dialoguing partners merge (this has been described in Chapter 8).

'Third-self sharing, perhaps the most complete form of sharing, involves not only self-awareness (of the individual self) and other-awareness (of the relating self), but together-awareness (of the third self); the self created between psychotherapist and client.'

I think this is the archetype of the self which Jung refers to as the person's inherent psychic disposition to experience centredness and meaning in life, sometimes conceived of as the God within ourselves. Buber was essentially concerned with the close association of the relation to God with the relation to one's fellow men, with the I–You which issues from the encounter with the other in relationship. This dimension in the psychotherapeutic relationship cannot be proved and can hardly be described. 'Nothing remains to me in the end but an appeal to the testimony of your own mysteries' (Buber, 1970: 174).

CONCLUSION

This chapter has briefly described five kinds of therapeutic relationship available as potential avenues for constructive use, indicated some characteristics of each and hopefully begun an effort to clarify, specify and differentiate more acutely in theory and practice the nature and intentions of the multiplicity of therapeutic relationships available and often present simultaneously in the consulting room.

It is perhaps time that we acknowledged explicitly that these five forms of relationship are intentionally used in TA as an integrative, humanistic approach to psychotherapy. This is based on recognition that in an integrative, humanistic approach to psychotherapy training, experience and supervision are required in distinguishing between different forms of therapeutic relationship and assessing and evaluating the usefulness of each at different stages of therapy or for individuals with different characteristic ways of relating so that there is not a slipshod vacillation due to error or neurotic countertransference.

Integration of a multiplicity of therapeutic-relationship modalities does not mean eclectic or unconscious use. Indeed if such is the declared field, the responsiblity is awesome. Freedom does not mean that we forgo discipline.

Confusion and lack of clarity abound when types of psychotherapeutic relationship are confused with each other or the validity of one is required to substitute for another. It is possible that human beings need all of these forms of relating, and that psychotherapists with flexibility and range can become skilful in the appropriate use of all of them, although not all are required in all psychotherapies, or for all patients.

The far-ranging implications of this perspective for psychotherapy research, assessment and treatment need to be developed further. Courage in actively embracing the fullest range of potentials of the self, theory or the *numinosum* needs to be accompanied form of testing and forged anew with each client from moment to moment no matter what the prescriptions or proscriptions of theoretical orthodoxy. The more modalities a psychotherapist uses consciously, the more trained, the more supervised, the more physic they need to be. Courage in actively embracing the fullest range of potentials of the self, theory or the *numinosum* needs to be accompanied by the severest form of testing and forged anew with each client from moment to moment.

Appendix A
A comparative TA view of child development

David Schofield

TA views of child development are briefly compared in terms of ego-state formations and the consequences of incomplete development in the various stages with reference to the works of Erikson (1950), Freud, A. (1968), Freud, S. (1905), Melanie Klein (1949), Mahler *et al.* (1975) and Sheridan (1973) (see Figure A.1). Most TA authors agree that the Child ego state (C_2) is on its own initially. Before much Parent and Adult has emerged, the infant has already taken their existential position (3 years) and formed their script (4–7 years); Parent (P_2) emerging about 5–7 years and Adult (A_2) from 8 years or so onwards. Whilst there is this general agreement about the main ego-state developmental phases, there is considerable variation about the initial stages of each ego-state development.

At birth the baby is a physically and emotionally dependent individual, the somatic Child C_1. With no linguistic skills bar crying and no locomotor ability, the mother has to ensure the survival of the baby. This is the stage Anna Freud referred to as the oral libido, all pleasures coming from the mouth. The baby is totally uninhibited, spontaneous and self-centred (Klein, 1949). The mother, or rather her breast, is seen by the baby to be part of itself. Mavis Klein (1980), Jacqui Schiff *et al.* (1975) and Pam Levin-Landheer (1982) all believe the first six months are involved with Child ego-state development (C_1). After this period they see A_1 developing. However, a baby can be seen at three months to smile when he recognises preparation for feeds or bath. This shows some learning process and infers at least A_1 development.

Harris states that ego states develop from birth to 5 years. He states the importance of mobility by crawling at 10 months for the development of Adult. Up to 10 months, he conceives the presence of Child and Parent ego states. The 10 month old, he states, 'is able to do something which grows from his own awareness and original thought. This self-actualisation is the beginning of Adult' (Harris, 1973: 28).

Berne (1972) does not make precise time reference to the development of the ego state. He says, in reference to Child ego state, that the important factor is age.

Mahler *et al.* (1975) noted the steps towards separation–individuation and considered that from 3 to 8 months the baby learns to differentiate between his

Comparative Chart of Psychological Theory

AGE	NEURODEVELOPMENTAL	PSYCHOLOGICAL	PSYCHOANALYTICAL			
	MARY SHERIDAN Developmental Milestones The Development of Infants and Young Children: DHSS Report No. 102 (HMSO)	JEAN PIAGET The Origin of intelligence in the Child 1952 (NY Int Univ Press)	SIGMUND FREUD Collected Works	ANNA FREUD The Concept of Developmental Lines 1963 (Psychoanal. Study Child)	MELANIE KLEIN The Psychoanalysis of children 1932 (Hogarth)	ERIK ERIKSON Childhood and Society 1950 (Norton)
6 weeks	Smiles	SENSORI-MOTOR	Pleasure- pain principle Primary - process thought Primary Narcissism	Mother experienced as part of self ORAL LIBIDO	Fantasy of PART OBJECT images produced within baby and projected outwards when threatening	Lives and loves through mouth contact with mother
3 months	Grasps	Things out of sight don't exist	ORAL drives	Mouth used for explorations as well as libidinal satisfaction	PARANOID - SCHIZOID Fearful, attacking, retaliatory objects projected out	BASIC TRUST V. MISTRUST
6 months	Sits	Environment unpredictable	Main defence is projection and fantasy Sexuality is auto-erotic	Objects important only as satisfying needs	DEPRESSIVE POSITION When baby becomes aware that he is origin of fantasy	
1 year	Walks	9 months looks for hidden objects Recreates object (A-B error)	Oral non-nutritive sucking	Objects gradually given increasing importance	PRIMARY ENVY - fears of parental retaliation for such envy	Can I trust the source of giving?
18 months	Single words	Object permanence	ANAL	OBJECT CONSTANCY Ambivalent object relations	Attempts to balance Paranoid - schizoid and depressive positions and to manage anxiety produced by fantasy	AUTONOMY V. SHAME & DOUBT
2 years	Phrases Temper tantrums Bowel control	Development of mastery over musculature and use of senses	Sadism and wish to control Thinking is still Primary process with omniscience and omnipotence in fantasy	Anal sadism Ego attitudes of clinging, controlling, torturing?		Holding on & letting go Self-control without loss of self-esteem
3 years	Make believe Plays with others Shares Past & Present understood			Objects move to become centre of libidinal striving		Keep rival out Jealous rages
4 years	Bladder control at night Past, present & future Cooperates Takes turns Shows concern	PRE-OPERATIONAL	PHALLIC - OEDIPAL Differentiation of sexes Penis envy Castration anxiety Can delay gratification in response to demands of reality - secondary process thought	Admiration Sexual exhibitionism		INITIATIVE V. GUILT
5 years	Chooses friends Time & rules understood Comforts others			SEXUAL IDENTITY		Potential human glory

Figure A.1 Comparative chart of psychological theory – child development

Age	Physical Development	Cognitive (Piaget)	Psychosexual	Superego Structuring	Psychosocial
6 years	Smooth, efficient physical skill; Bat and ball games	CONCRETE OPERATIONS	LATENCY	End of Oedipal phase; SUPEREGO STRUCTURING	Potential total destruction
7 years	Joined up writing				INDUSTRY V. INFERIORITY
8 years	Efficient at household tasks	Conservation of quantity not understood	Turns to peers and extra-familial figures in response to Oedipal disappointment	Capacity to sublimate	
9/10 years	Peer group; Full reading skills	May make logical inferences but unable to use this ability efficiently	SUPEREGO develops in direction of accepting adult ideals and demands	Internalisation of conflicts with parents	Develops and learns fundamental technology of the culture
11 years	Rapid physical growth	FORMAL OPERATIONS		Capacity to co-operate with peers and teachers	May consider self a failure and doomed to mediocrity and inadequacy
12 years	Puberty; Muscular strength develops			Can work and play	
13 years	Interest in physical appearance in girls and boys	Thinking is free from environmental constraint; Experiments Hypotheses Deductions	ADOLESCENCE	PRE-ADOLESCENCE	IDENTITY V. IDENTITY DIFFUSION; Who am I?
14 years	Stop growing	Can predict possible futures	GENITAL SEXUALITY	Psychological preparation for physical changes	What kind of person will I be?
15/16 years			All drives reappear and move towards adult sexuality (genital) and altruistic love	ADOLESCENCE	Experimentation with roles; Rejections
17/18 years	Physical Development Complete			Repressed Oedipal longings return and are directed towards peer group, same sex and opposite sex	Over-identifications; Exclusion of those who are different
Maturity					

Source: © Magner, 1985

CHILD DEVELOPMENT

TRANSACTIONAL ANALYSIS

AGE	MAVIS KLEIN (Lives People Live 1980 (Wiley))	JACQUI SCHIFF, et al. (Cathexis Reader 1975 (Harper & Row))	PAM LEVIN (Cycles of Power 1980s and Becoming the Way We Are 1974 (Health Communications))			AGE
			EGO STATE	NEEDS	AFFIRMATIONS	
6 weeks	NATURAL CHILD C_1 — Given biologically self-centred loving spontaneous honest uninhibited lovable	I exist	NATURAL CHILD (Early oral)	Feeding Stroking	FOR BEING — OK to be you	6 weeks
3 months		ME NOT ME			You have a right to be here	3 months
6 months		By 5 months can get strokes intentionally C_1 (A_0 P_0 C_0)	C_1	Immediate response to crying signal	OK to be OK to be boy/girl	6 months
1 year	ADULT IN CHILD LITTLE PROFESSOR C_1 A_1 — Intuition, hypotheses insight, creativity	WHAT CAN I DO? A_1 Start of "Little Professor"	LITTLE PROFESSOR (Oral exploratory)	Exploring and doing things	FOR DOING THINGS — OK to explore/experiment OK to initiate OK to be curious	1 year
18 months	Parents impose restraints in interests of socialisation DEVELOPMENT OF AC (P1)		A_1	2 'Yesses' for every 'No'		18 months
2 years	C_1 A_1 — FC = C1 = A1 Practical skills developing	WHAT DO OTHERS DO? A_2	ADULT (Anal) A_2	Time and information Reasons	FOR THINKING — OK to test out	2 years
3 years	C_1 A_1 P_1 A_2 — FORMATION OF A2 P1 (AC) mostly compliant	TERRIBLE TWOS What to give What to get How to think/adapt A_1/A_2	SUPER-NATURAL CHILD (genital) A_1/A_2	Limits	FOR FEELING — OK to let people know how you feel	3 years
4 years	Increasing skills - A2	TRUSTING THREES Rapid learning Increase in Little Professor P_1	SUPER-NATURAL CHILD	Adequate external supply lines maintained while testing powers	FOR POWER & IDENTITY — You can be powerful and still have needs	4 years
5 years	C_1 A_1 P_1 A_2 P_2 — P2 starts as sharing and caring for others develops	FEARFUL FOURS Fears, questions, misinformation, adaption, self-enforcement by fears and fantasy P_1	P_1		You don't have to be sick to be taken care of	5 years
6 years	Parents teach moral code	Compete for strokes in outside world			OK to imagine	6 years

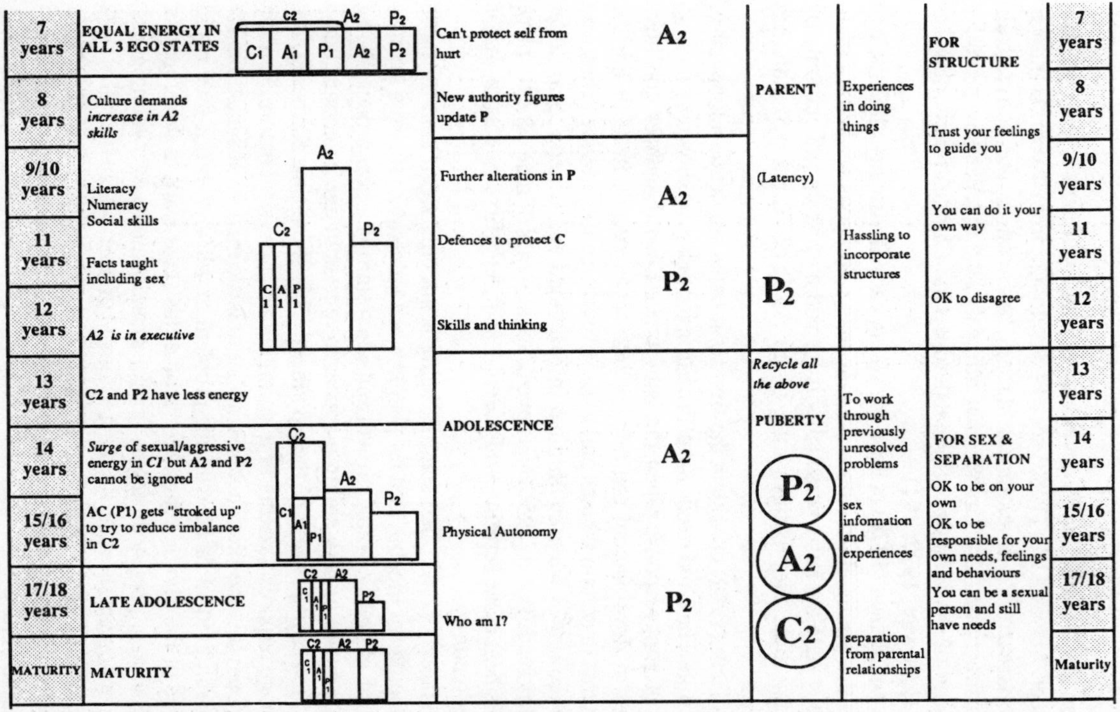

Figure A.1 (continued) — rotated table

Age	EQUAL ENERGY IN ALL 3 EGO STATES		A2 / P2	PARENT		FOR STRUCTURE	Age
7 years	EQUAL ENERGY IN ALL 3 EGO STATES (C1 A1 P1 / C2 A2 P2)	Can't protect self from hurt	A2			FOR STRUCTURE	7 years
8 years	Culture demands *increase in A2 skills*	New authority figures update P	A2	Experiences in doing things		Trust your feelings to guide you	8 years
9/10 years	Literacy Numeracy Social skills	Further alterations in P		(Latency)		You can do it your own way	9/10 years
11 years	Facts taught including sex	Defences to protect C	P2	Hassling to incorporate structures			11 years
12 years	*A2 is in executive*	Skills and thinking	P2	P2		OK to disagree	12 years
13 years	C2 and P2 have less energy	ADOLESCENCE	A2	*Recycle all the above* PUBERTY	To work through previously unresolved problems	FOR SEX & SEPARATION	13 years
14 years	*Surge of sexual/aggressive energy in C1 but A2 and P2 cannot be ignored*	Physical Autonomy	A2	P2 A2 C2	sex information and experiences	OK to be on your own	14 years
15/16 years	AC (P1) gets "stroked up" to try to reduce imbalance in C2	Who am I?	P2			OK to be responsible for your own needs, feelings and behaviours	15/16 years
17/18 years	LATE ADOLESCENCE				separation from parental relationships	You can be a sexual person and still have needs	17/18 years
MATURITY	MATURITY						Maturity

Figure A.1 (continued)

and his mother's body image. This again infers learning and Adult development. Holloway supports this saying that, 'When differentiation of self and others results in purposeful seeking, neopsychic functioning has begun and primitive Adult ego state will be briefly experienced and sometimes observed' (Holloway, 1977: 191).

Schiff *et al.* (1975) conceived the first 6 months were spent dealing with the issue 'I exist' and the problem 'Me–not me'. Schiff suggests that by 5 months a child can get strokes intentionally. This certainly infers Adult development although they (Schiff *et al.*, 1975) see such development as not starting before 6 months.

Schiff *et al.* (1975) hold that P_1 development is delayed until 3 years, as does Levin-Landheer. Mavis Klein (1980) sees P_1 developing from 1 year. Holloway (1977) supports early P_1 development stating, 'As soon as the non-verbally transmitted instructions from mother gain influence, the independent primitive decision-making of the infant primitive exteropsychic (Parent) functioning has also begun' (Holloway, 1977: 191).

Woollams and Brown (1978) believe the young child is virtually all Child ego state and it is this young child who makes the major decisions for getting on in the world. They state the basic personality is formed by 2 years and certainly by 3 years. At this time they believe little or no Adult or Parent ego state has established.

Levin-Landheer (1982) considers the first six months are the development of the Natural Child. The child needs the affirmation for being, as shown by feeling, stroking and prompt response when the baby cries. Levin-Landheer considers that the stages of development can be split into seven stages. In adult life the individual returns to certain themes and issues over the course of time. These are associated to the stages we grew through in childhood and which repeat under specific conditions. Erikson (1950) has devised eight stages of man. The first five of these stages bear close scrutiny with Levin-Landheer's first six stages, that is to the stage of maturity.

Levin-Landheer's (1982) first stage of being is not only significant for those in the first 6 months of life, but also for people when vulnerable, ill, tired at times of personal loss, at times of rapid growth and when starting a new process. Most parents will be aware of how children appear to regress in age behaviour when ill. Spouses often say the same of their partners! This is the time for being, not doing. This stage requires stroking of a warm, intimate, physical nature. Erikson (1950) considered this the first nuclear conflict of basic trust versus mistrust. He considered the individual faced with the problem of whether or not they could trust the source of the giving. Failure to resolve this stage leads to development of paranoid feelings, persistent anger, fear of abandonment, over-humbleness, manipulation or hopelessness. In therapy, a climate of trust, where the client does not fear rejection, is vital. The client should be encouraged to find their own strength, develop their own self-esteem and look at positive and negative feelings towards the same object.

From 6 months to 1 year, Schiff *et al.* (1975), Mavis Klein (1980) and Levin-Landheer (1982) see the energy going towards development of A_1 – 'the little professor'. This is the stage Schiff *et al.* (1975) label 'What can I do?' Mavis Klein sees A_1 development by the observation of intuition and hypothesis-testing taking place. Levin-Landheer puts her second stage between 6 and 18 months as the time for doing. It coincides with the child's ability to move independently, eventually by walking. Speech develops and the infant is in a phase of intense curiosity. Levin-Landheer believes her second stage is significant also for people after they have been nurtured a while, for people in a new physical setting, as part of a creative process or as a prelude to developing a new level of independence. This phase overlaps the late oral and early anal phase of Freud.

Mahler's (Mahler *et al.*, 1975) second stage in the separation–individuation process is from 8 to 15 months and is termed 'practising'. At this stage the infant is already exploring new opportunities in the world about him or her and seems oblivious to mother.

From 18 months to 3 years the child gains bowel control, has temper tantrums, begins to share and play with others and make-believe is important. This is the stage Levin-Landheer sees as the power of thinking. It is also significant for people changing agreements, learning new information or breaking out of dependency. It is the time to make room for ourselves, to be different, unique. This will require some rebellious spirit – 'No' and 'I won't' are commonly used. Schiff *et al.* (1975) refer to the terrible twos as A_1 and A_2 are developed.

From 1 year to 3 years, as mobility increases, the parental figures impose restraint and P_1 emerges. Much energy, Klein believes, is still with A_1 and C_1 though P_1 and also A_2 are developing. Three years marks the end of Erikson's second stage (Erikson, 1950). The fight of autonomy versus shame and doubt is very much associated with bowel control and P_1 development. Willpower and self-control emerge if the stage is successful. If unsuccessful, perfectionism, obsessional traits, inability to let go, inability to take risks, tendency to be overcritical, overprotective, inability to relax or play, explosive anger or over-conforming will be exhibited. The therapist needs to avoid becoming an authority figure and help the client to be his or her own authority. The client may be fearful of criticism from the therapist. The client needs to express those feelings he or she believes to be bad and to differentiate between appropriate and inappropriate guilt.

Erikson's (1950) third stage of initiative versus guilt from 3 to 7 years compares closely with Levin-Landheer's fifth stage from 3 to 6 years. Erikson sees this as the achievement of direction and purpose. Levin-Landheer (1982) sees it as time for power and identity when P_1 is developed. Anna Freud (1968) and Levin-Landheer see this as a time for sexual identity. Fantasy is now separated from reality. The infant is fascinated by its ability to affect other people. Levin-Landheer sees this stage as significant for people developing a new identity, renegotiating a social contract or seeking a new relationship. The individual needs to know it is OK to be powerful and still have needs. If this stage is inadequately accomplished, jealousy, fear of rivalry or competition, poor sexual identity or inadequate feelings may develop. Explorations of sexual feelings and triangular relationships would be important for the client.

Between 3 and 5 years, Schiff (Schiff et al., 1975) sees the trusting threes and fearsome fours, when P_1 develops further. Mavis Klein (1980) considers that from 3 years there is increasing development of A_2. P_2 development in caring for others also commences. The main energy is still with C_1, A_1, P_1. This is the time parental figures teach moral codes.

Between 6 and 12 years is the fifth stage of Levin-Landheer (1982). The period of P_2 development concerns the power of being skilful. This compares with S. Freud's latency stage of 5 to 12 years when energy is directed to peers. Anna Freud considers this the period of sublimation. Seven to 12 years is the time Erikson (1950) saw as the conflict between industry and inferiority, when, if favourable outcome is achieved, a sense of work value, method and competence develops. Klein sees the period 7 to 13 years as a period of A_2 development as social skills, literacy and numeracy, are achieved. Facts are taught and learnt. A_2 is the energised ego state with P_2 C_2 playing minor roles. This appears at variance with Levin-Landheer (1982), who, as stated, sees this predominantly as P_2 development. All authorities see new skills being developed here (A_2). However, Levin-Landheer emphasises that this is the time we decide on values which are consistent with our goals. To do this we argue and hassle with others' morals and methods, often wanting to do things our own way and no other. This would indicate P_2 development.

Schiff (Schiff et al., 1975) sees 5 to 8 years as predominantly A_2 development, 8 to 12 years encompassing both P_2 and A_2.

Between 12 years and maturity, there is a unifying of the ego state with the healthy, mature individual showing full development of P_2, A_2, C_2. Levin-Landheer (1982) believes sex and separation are the key issues to this, her sixth stage. This view is mirrored by S. Freud's phase of genital sexuality, 12 to 16 years. Levin-Landheer sees this stage as an also significant stage for people preparing to leave a relationship, for those ending any process or for those who have developed new morals and skills. The need is for permission to be responsible for our needs, feelings and behaviour. It is OK to be sexual, OK to have a place amongst grown-ups and OK to succeed.

Erikson's (1950) fifth stage, 12 to 18 years, is a conflict of identity with identity diffusion. The question 'Who am I?' arises and, if this stage is traversed successfully, the favourable outcome is devotion and fidelity. Schiff (Schiff et al., 1975) also sees this as identity-crisis time with further development of A_2 and P_2.

Physical maturation with improved dexterity, locomotor and linguistic skills has an easily observed effect on promoting curiosity, assertiveness, competence and identity establishment. These abilities in turn reflect the developing ego state.

Whilst physical abilities and social skills can be observed and dated with close consensus of opinion, there appears not to be the same closeness of opinion about ego-state development. This is particularly so for the early stages of each ego-state growth. This suggests that ego-state identification and subdivision is more complicated than first introductions to TA may convey. Once we realise that many authorities place in C_2 'all our yesterdays', we realise that today's C_2 holds yesterday's A_2. The problems of ego-state identification and their date of development become more apparent. Despite this problem, TA writers have contributed greatly to our knowledge of child development, in particular the psychosocial modalities that individuals require to achieve, either in their own childhood development or later, in therapy.

Appendix B
Addresses of transactional analysis organisations

These TA organisations may be contacted to learn current addresses of regional TA associations.

European Association for Transactional Analysis (EATA),
Case Grand-Pré 59,
CH-1211 Genève 16,
Switzerland

Institute of Transactional Analysis (ITA),
BM Box 4104,
London WC1N 3XX,
England

International Transactional Analysis Association (ITAA),
1772 Vallejo Street,
San Francisco,
California 94123,
USA

All the trainers and supervisors and most of the psychotherapists associated with the TA programme at *metanoia* are members of and/or accredited by the above organisations. Like the ITA, *metanoia* is also a member of the United Kingdom Standing Conference on Psychotherapy. Transactional analysis is one of several other approaches to psychotherapy and organisational consultancy which is available in services, supervision and training directly from *metanoia* Psychotherapy Training Institute, 13 North Common Road, London W5 2QB.

Appendix C
ITAA statement of ethics

Recognizing that professional ethics are a series of Parent rules as to what is right and wrong, the ITAA's Statement of Ethics seeks to promote, in addition, the development of Adult processing in the field of ethics with particular emphasis on establishing a clear Adult contract.

We recognize that through our certification process, the ITAA establishes a social contract that invites the public to trust that Certified Members and Regular Members of the ITAA acknowledge and adhere to the ethical premises and principles in this document.

We also recognize that members do not always utilize these ethical principles and, therefore, that confrontation of a member is sometimes desirable and/or necessary.

We further recognize that should an individual's behaviour show a lack of integration or consistency with these principles, his/her certification, training contract and/or membership may be suspended by the ITAA until such time as that integration is assured.

These principles represent a concensus of Parent values, Adult data and Child rights:

1 An ITAA member acknowledges the dignity of all humanity regardless of physiological, psychological, sociological or economic status.
2 Members of the ITAA shall in their public statements, whether written or verbal, refrain from derogatory statements, inferences and/or innuendoes that disparage the standing, qualifications or character of members, bearing in mind their responsibility as representatives of ITAA and of Transactional Analysis.
3 It is the primary protective responsibility of members of the ITAA to provide their best possible services to the client and to act in such a way as to cause no intentional or deliberate harm to any client.
4 Members of the ITAA should strive to develop in their clients awareness of and functioning from a position of dignity, autonomy and personal responsibility.

5 The ethical practice of Transactional Analysis involves entering into an informed contractual relationship with a client which the member of the ITAA and the client should have the competence and intent to fulfil. When a client is unable or unwilling to function autonomously and responsibly within this contractual relationship, the member of ITAA must resolve this relation- ship in such a way as to bring no harm to the client.

6 A member of ITAA will not exploit a client in any manner, including, but not limited to, financial and sexual matters. Sexual relations between ITAA members and their clients are prohibited.

7 Members of ITAA will not enter into or maintain a professional contract where other activities or relationships between ITAA members and client might jeopardise the professional contract.

8 The professional relationship between a member of ITAA and the client is defined by the contract, and that professional relationship ends with the termination of the contract. However, certain professional responsibilities continue beyond the termination of the contract. They include, but are not limited to, the following: a) maintenance of agreed-upon confidentiality; b) avoidance of any exploitation of the former relationship; c) provision for any needed follow-up care.

9 Members of ITAA will operate and conduct services to clients with full responsibility to existing laws of the state and/or country in which they reside.

10 In establishing a professional relationship, members of the ITAA assume responsibility for providing a suitable environment, including such things as specifying the nature of confidentiality observed, providing for physical safety appropriate to the form of activity involved, and obtaining informed consent for high-risk procedures.

11 If members of the ITAA become aware that personal conflicts or medical problems might interfere with their ability to carry out a contractual relation- ship, they must either terminate the contract in a professionally responsible manner, or ensure that the client has the full information needed to make a decision about remaining in the contractual relationship.

12 Members of ITAA accept responsibility to confront a colleague whom they have reasonable cause to believe is acting in an unethical manner, and, failing resolution, to report that colleague to the appropriate professional body.

We affirm these principles as common to the practice of those certified by the ITAA unless a member of ITAA explicitly states in writing his/her differences from these positions. In such an instance, the client's attention to any such differences must also be noted in writing as part of their contract setting process.

Bibliography

Adler, G. (1979) *Dynamics of the Self*, London: Coventure.

Aggleton, J. and Mishkin, M. (1985) 'The Amygdala: sensory gateway to the emotions', in R. Plutchik and H. Kellerman (eds) *Emotion: Theory, Research, and Experience*, 3, New York: Academic Press.

Alexander, F. and French, T.M. (1946) *Psychoanalytic Therapy*, New York: Ronald Press.

Altorfer, O. (1977) 'Group dynamics: dealing with agitation in industry groups', *Transactional Analysis Journal*, 7 (2): 168–9.

American Psychiatric Association (1987) *Diagnostic and statistical manual of mental disorders*, Washington, DC: APA, 3rd edn revised.

Amundson, N.E. (1978) 'Developmental principles and TA with children', *Transactional Analysis Journal* 8 (2): 142–3.

Anderson, W. (1975) 'J.L. Moreno and the origins of psychodrama: a biographical sketch', in I.A. Greenberg (ed.) *Psychodrama Theory and Therapy*, London: Souvenir Press, pp. 205–11.

Anzieu, D. (1984) *The Group and the Unconscious*, London: Routledge & Kegan Paul.

Archambeau, E. (1979) 'Beyond countertransference: The psychotherapist's experience of healing in the therapeutic relationship', San Diego: California School of Professional Psychology, doctoral dissertation.

Aristotle (1963) *Poetics* (J. Warrington, trans.), London: Dent & Sons Ltd.

Aristotle (1970) *Physics* Bks I & II (W. Charlton, trans.), Oxford: Clarendon Press.

Aristotle (1971) *Metaphysics*, Bks I–IX (H. Tredennick, trans., G.P. Goold, ed.), Cambridge, MA: Harvard University Press.

Armstrong, L. (1978) *Kiss Daddy Goodnight: a Speak-out on Incest*, New York: Hawthorn.

Assagioli, R. (1965) *Psychosynthesis: A Collection of Basic Writings*, New York: Viking Compass.

Axline, V. (1964) *Dibs: In Search of Self*, Harmondsworth: Penguin Books Ltd.

Babcock, D. and Keepers, T. (1976) *Raising Kids OK*, New York: Grove Press.

Bach, G.R. and Goldberg, H. (1975) *Creative Aggression*, New York: Doubleday.

Balint, M. (1959) *Thrills and Regressions*, London: Hogarth Press.

Barnes, G. (ed.) (1977) *Transactional Analysis after Eric Berne: Teachings and Practices of Three TA Schools*, New York: Harper's College Press.

Barr, J. (1987) 'Therapeutic relationship model', *Transactional Analysis Journal* 17 (4): 141.

Baum, F.L. (1982) *The Wizard of Oz*, Harmondsworth: Puffin (first published in 1900).

Bee, H. (1985) *The Developing Child*, New York: Harper Row, 4th Edition.

Bellucci, M.T. (1975) 'Treatment of latency-age children and parents', *Social Casework* 56 (5): 297–301.

Bendell, D. and Fine, M. (1979) 'Increasing personal responsibility in acting-out boys', *Transactional Analysis Journal* 9 (4): 301.

Bentovim, A., Barnes, G.G. and Cooklin, A. (1982) *Family Therapy*, Vols 1 & 2, London: Academic Press.

Bergin, A.E. and Lambert, M.J. (1978) 'The evaluation ot therapeutic outcomes', in S.L. Garfield and A.E. Bergin (eds) *Handbook of Psychotherapy and Behaviour Change*, New York: Wiley, 2nd edition, pp. 139–89.

Berne, E. (1957) 'Ego states in psychotherapy', *The American Journal of Psychotherapy* 11: 293–309.

Berne, E. (1962) 'In treatment', *Transactional Analysis Bulletin* 1 (2): 2.

Berne, E. (1963) *The Structure and Dynamics of Organisations and Groups*, New York: Grove Press

Berne, E. (1964) *Games People Play*, New York: Grove Press.

Berne, E. (1966) *Principles of Group Treatment*, New York: Grove Press.

Berne, E. (1971) 'Away from a theory of the impact of interpersonal interaction on non-verbal participation', *Transactional Analysis Journal* 1 (1): 6–13.

Berne, E. (1972) *What Do You Say After You Say Hello?* New York: Bantam Books.

Berne, E. (1977) *Intuition and Ego States*, New York: Harper & Row (first published in 1957).

Berne, E. (1980) *Transactional Analysis in Psychotherapy*, London: Souvenir Press (first published in 1961).

Berne, E. (1981) *A Layman's Guide to Psychiatry and Psychoanalysis*, Harmondsworth: Penguin Books (first published in 1969).

Berry, J. (1981) *Permission to Live*, Sussex: New Horizon.

Bettelheim, B. (1982) *Freud and Man's Soul*, New York: Vintage.

Beutler, L.E., Pollack, S. and Jobe, A. (1977) 'On "accepting" patients vs. "accepting" therapists', paper presented at the Ninth Annual Meeting of the Society for Psychotherapy Research, Madison, Wisconsin, June 1977.

Bion, W.R. (1961) *Experiences in Groups*, New York: Basic Books.

Bloch, D. (1979) *So the Witch Won't Eat Me*, London: Burnett Books.

Boadella, D. (1986) 'Energy and character', *The Journal of Biosynthesis* 17 (2): 1–23.

Bollas, C. (1987) *The Shadow of the Object*, London: Free Association Books.

Bordin, E.S. (1979) 'The generalizability of the psychoanalytic concept of the working alliance', *Psychotherapy: Theory, Research and Practice* 16 (3): 252–60.

Boss, M. (1979) *Existential Foundations of Medicine and Psychology*, New York: Jason Aronson.

Boyce, M. (1970) 'TA and children', *Transactional Analysis Bulletin* 9 (33): 18.

Boyd, H.S. and Cowles-Boyd, L. (1980) 'Blocking tragic scripts', *Transactional Analysis Journal*, 10 (3): 227–9.

Boyers, R. and Orrill, R. (1972) *Laing and Anti-psychiatry*, Harmondsworth: Penguin Books.

Bridges, W. (1980) *Making Sense Of Life's Changes*, Reading, MA: Addison-Wesley.

Brill, H. (1967) 'Nosology', in A.M. Freedman and H.I. Kaplan (eds) *Comprehensive Textbook of Psychiatry*, Baltimore: The Williams & Wilkins Co, pp. 581–9.

Buber, M. (1970) *I and Thou* (W. Kaufmann, trans.), Edinburgh: T & T Clark (first published in 1923).

Bugental, J.F.T. (1987) *The Art of the Psychotherapist*, New York: W.W. Norton.

Burchfield, R.W. (1976) *A Supplement of the Oxford English Dictionary*, II, Oxford: Oxford University Press, p. 911.

Campos, L.P. (1986) 'Empowering children: primary prevention of script formation', *Transactional Analysis Journal*, 16 (1): 18–23.

Capra, F. (1978) *The Tao of Physics*, London: Collins.

Capra, F. (1983) *The Turning Point*, London: Fontana.
Carroll, L. (1986) *Through the Loooking Glass and What Alice Found There*, London: Gollancz (first published 1892).
Carroll, L. (1987) *Alice's Adventures in Wonderland*, London: Chancellor Press (first published 1865).
Casement, P. (1985) *On Learning From The Patient*, London: Tavistock.
Childs-Gowell, E. and Kinnaman, P. (1978) *Bodyscript Blockbusting: A Transactional Approach to Body Awareness*, San Francisco: Transactional Pubs.
Clarke, J. I. (1978) *Self-esteem: A Family Affair*, Minneapolis, Winston Press.
Clarkson, P. (1986a) 'Peace and the social responsibility of the integrated adult', *ITA News* 15: 4–5.
Clarkson, P. (1986b) 'Training in Gestalt psychotherapy and Transactional Analysis', The British Psychological Society Counselling Psychology Section Review 4 (2): 34–6.
Clarkson, P. (1987) 'The Bystander role', *Transactional Analysis Journal* 17 (3): 82–7.
Clarkson, P. (1988a) 'Ego state dilemmas of abused children', *Transactional Analysis Journal* 18 (2): 85–93.
Clarkson, P. (1988b) 'Script cure? – a diagnostic pentagon of types of therapeutic change', *Transactional Analysis Journal* 18 (3): 211–9.
Clarkson, P. (1988c) 'Crisis and aspiration', *ITA News* 21: 12.
Clarkson, P. (1989) 'Metanoia:, a process of transformation', *ITA News* 23: 5–14.
Clarkson, P. (1990) 'A multiplicity of psychotherapeutic relationships', *British Journal of Psychotherapy* 7: 148–63.
Clarkson, P. and Fish, S. (1988) 'Rechilding: creating a new past in the present as a support for the future', *Transactional Analysis Journal* 18 (1): 51–9.
Clarkson, P. and Gilbert, M. (1987) *Ethics Questionnaire*, Metanoia House Publications, London: Metanoia Psychotherapy Training Institute.
Clarkson, P. and Gilbert, M. (1988) 'Berne's original model of ego states', *Transactional Analysis Journal* 18 (1): 20–9.
Clinebell, H.J. (1966) *Basic Types of Pastoral Counselling*, Nashville, TN: Abingdon.
Conway, A. and Clarkson, P. (1987) 'Everyday hypnotic inductions', *Transactional Analysis Journal* 17 (2): 17–23.
Cooper, D. (1978) *The Language of Madness*, London: Cox & Wyman.
Cornell, W.F. (1984) 'Teaching people what matters', *Transactional Analysis Journal* 14: 240–3.
Cornell, W.F. (1988) 'Life script theory: a critical review from a developmental perspective', *Transactional Analysis Journal* 18 (4): 270–82.
Cornell, W.F. and Zalcman, M. (1984) 'Teaching transactional analysts to think theoretically', *Transactional Analysis Journal* 14 (2): 105–13.
Crossman, P. (1966) 'Permission and protection', *Transactional Analysis Bulletin: Selected Articles from Volumes 1 through 9*, 1976, San Francisco: TA Press.
cummings, e. e. (1987) *73 poems*, London: Faber & Faber, (first published 1964).
Dashiell, S.R. (1978) 'The Parent resolution process: reprogramming psychic incorporations in the Parent', *Transactional Analysis Journal* 10 (4): 289–94.
Davidson, V. (1981) 'Psychiatry's problem with no name: therapist–patient sex', in E. Howell and M. Bayes (eds) *Women and Mental Health*, New York: Basic Books.
Debretts (1989) Personal communication by Charles Kidd.
de Chardin, T. (1959) *The Phenomenon of Man*, London: Collins.
Drego, P. (1981) 'Ego state models', *Tasi Darshan* 1 (4): 1, New Delhi.
Dryden, W. (ed.) (1984) *Individual Therapy in Britain*, London: Harper & Row.
Dryden, W. (1987) *Counselling Individuals: the Rational–Emotive Approach*, London: Taylor & Francis.

Drye, R.C., Goulding, M.M. and Goulding, R.L. (1978) 'Monitoring of suicidal risk', in *The Power is in the Patient*, San Francisco: TA Press.

Dusay, J. (1966) 'Response to games in therapy', *Transactional Analysis Bulletin: Selected Articles from Volumes 1 through 9*, 1976, San Francisco: TA Press.

Dusay, J. (1972) 'Egograms and the constancy hypothesis', *Transactional Analysis Journal* 2 (3): 37.

Duval, S. and Wicklund, R.W. (1972) *The Theory of Objective Self Awareness*, New York: Academic Press.

Edinger, E.F. (1957) 'Some manifestations of the transference phenomena', *Spring*, 32–45.

Edwards, P. (ed. in chief) (1967) *Encyclopedia of Philosophy*, New York: Macmillan.

Ehrenreich, B. and English, D. (1978) *For Her Own Good*, New York: Anchor Press/Doubleday.

Einstein, A., Podolsky, B. and Rosen, N. (1935) 'Can quantum-mechanical description of physical reality be considered complete?' *Physical Review* 47: 777–80.

Ekstein, R. and Wallerstein, R.S. (1972) *The Teaching and Learning of Psychotherapy*, Madison, CT: International Universities Press.

Eliot, T.S. (1970) *Collected Poems 1909–1962*, London: Faber & Faber.

Ellis, A. (1962) *Reason and Emotion in Psychotherapy*, Secaucus, NJ.: Citadel Press.

Emerson, P. (1979) 'Changing your own children's script', *Transactional Analysis Journal* 9 (2): 119–21.

English, F. (1969) 'Episcript and the "hot potato" game', *Transactional Analysis Bulletin* 8 (32): 77–82.

English, F. (1971) 'Rackets and real feelings, part I', *Transactional Analysis Journal* 1 (4): 27.

English, F. (1972) 'Rackets and real feelings, part II', *Transactional Analysis Journal* 2 (1): 23.

Erickson, M.H. (1967) *Advanced Techniques of Hypnosis and Therapy*, New York: Grune & Stratton.

Erickson, M.H. (1980) *Innovative Hypnotherapy*, (E.L. Rossi (ed.)) New York: Irvington Publishers

Erikson, E.H. (1950) *Childhood and Society*, New York: Norton (revised edn 1963).

Erikson, E.H. (1968) *Identity, Youth and Crisis*, New York: Norton.

Ernst, Jr. F.H. (1971) 'The OK Corral: the grid for get-on-with', *Transactional Analysis Journal* 1 (4): 33–42.

Erskine, R.G. (1974) 'Therapeutic intervention: disconnecting rubberbands', *Transactional Analysis Journal* 10 (3): 7–8.

Erskine, R.G. (1980) 'Script cure: behavioural, intrapsychic and physiological', *Transactional Analysis Journal* 10 (2): 102–6.

Erskine, R.G. (1982) 'Supervision of psychotherapy: models for professional development', *Transactional Analysis Journal* 12 (4): 314–21.

Erskine, R.G. and Moursund, J.P. (1988) *Integrative Psychotherapy in Action*, Newbury Park, CA.: Sage.

Erskine, R.G. and Zalcman, M.J. (1979) 'The Racket System', *Transactional Analysis Journal* 9 (1): 51–9.

Erskine, R.G., Goulding, R., Clarkson, P., Groders, M.G. and Mois, C. (1988) 'Excerpts from the 1987 ITAA summer conference round-table discussion on ego state theory: definitions, descriptions and points of view', *Transactional Analysis Journal* 18 (1): 6–15.

Eyles, A. (1985) *The World of Oz*, Harmondsworth: Penguin.

Eysenck, H.J. (1968) *Handbook of Abnormal Psychology*, London: Pitman Medical Publishing Co. Ltd.

Eysenck, H.J. and Rachman, S. (1965) *The Causes and Cures of Neurosis*, London: Routledge & Kegan Paul.

Fagan, J. and Shepherd, I.L. (eds) (1971) *Gestalt Therapy Now: Theory, Techniques, Applications*, New York: Harper & Row (first published 1970).

Fairbairn, W.R.D. (1952) *Psycho-analytic Studies of the Personality*, London: Tavistock.

Federn, P. (1977) *Ego Psychology and the Psychoses*, London: Maresfield Reprints (first published 1953).

Ferenczi, S. (1980) *Further Contributions to the Theory and Technique of Psycho-analysis*, London: Maresfield Reprints, Karnac Books (first published 1926).

Ferrucci, P. (1982) *What We May Be*, Wellingborough: Turnstone.

Finch, W.A. (1977) 'The role of the organisation', in F.W. Kaslow and Associates *Supervision, Consultation, and Training in the Helping Professions*, San Francisco: Jossey-Bass.

Fine, R. (1986) *Narcissism, the Self and Society*, New York: Columbia University Press (first published 1914).

Folkart, L. (1967) 'Some problems of treating children in the in-patient setting', *Journal of Child Psychotherapy* 2: 46–55.

Fordham, M. (1947) 'Integration and disintegration and early ego development', *Nervous Child* 6: 266–77.

Fordham, M. (1957a) 'Notes on transference', in *New Developments in Analytical Psychology*, London: Routledge & Kegan Paul, pp. 62–104.

Fordham, M. (1957b) 'Biology theory and the concept of archetypes', in *New Developments in Analytical Psychology*, London: Routledge & Kegan Paul.

Fordham, M. (1958) *The Objective Psyche*, London: Routledge & Kegan Paul.

Foulkes, S.H. (1951) 'Concerning leadership in group-analytic psychotherapy', *International Journal of Group Psychotherapy* 1: 319–29.

Frank, J.D. (1979) 'The present status of outcome studies', *Journal of Consulting and Clinical Psychology* 47: 310–16.

Frank, J.D. (1982) 'Therapeutic components shared by all psychotherapies', in J.H. Harvey and M.M. Parkes (eds) *The Master Lecture Series, vol. 1, Psychotherapy Research and Behaviour Change*, Washington, DC: American Psychological Association.

Frankl, V. (1969) *Man's Search for Meaning*, London: Hodder & Stoughton.

Freed, A.M. (1971) *TA for Kids*, Sacramento: Jalmar Press.

Freed, A.M. (1976) *TA for Teens and Other Important People*, Sacramento: Jalmar Press.

Freedman, A.M., Kaplan, H.I. and Sadock, B.J. (1975) *Comprehensive Textbook of Psychiatry – II*, Baltimore: The Williams & Wilkins Company.

Freud, A. (1968) *Indications for Child Analysis And Other Papers 1945–1956, The writings of Anna Freud, vol. IV*, New York: International Universities Press.

Freud, S. (1900) 'The interpretation of dreams', in J. Strachey (ed.) *The Standard Edition of the Complete Psychological Works of Sigmund Freud*, London: Hogarth Press, 1: 281–397.

Freud, S. (1905) 'Three essays on the theory of sexuality', in *The Standard Edition of the Complete Psychological Works of Sigmund Freud*, London: Hogarth Press, 7: 45–171.

Freud, S. (1912a) 'The dynamics of transference', in J. Strachey (ed.) *The Standard Edition of the Complete Psychological Works of Sigmund Freud*, London: Hogarth Press, 12: 97–108,

Freud, S. (1912b) 'Recommendations to physicians practising psycho-analysis', in J. Strachey (ed.) *The Standard Edition of the Complete Psychologial Works of Sigmund Freud*, London: Hogarth Press, 12: 109–120,

Freud, S. (1961) *Beyond the Pleasure Principle*, London: Hogarth Press (first published 1920).

Freud, S. (1973) 'Introductory lectures on psychoanalysis', in J. Strachey (ed.) and J.

Strachey and A. Richards (ed. and trans.) *The Pelican Freud Library* (vol. 1), Harmondsworth: Pelican (original works published 1915–1917).

Freudenberger, H.J. (1975) 'The staff burn-out syndrome in alternative institutions', *Psychotherapy: Theory, Research and Practice* 12 (1): 35–45.

Friedman, M. (1985) *The Healing Dialogue in Psychotherapy*, New York: Aronson.

Friedman, H. and Shmukler, D. (1983) 'A model of family development and functioning in a TA framework', *Transactional Analysis Journal* 13 (2): 90–3.

Fromm-Reichmann, F. (1974) *Principles of Intensive Psychotherapy*, Chicago: University of Chicago Press (first published 1950).

Garbarino, J., Guttmann, E. and Seeley, J.W. (1986) *The Psychologically Battered Child*, London: Jossey-Bass.

Garfield, S.L. (1978) 'Client variables in psychotherapy', in S.L. Garfield and A.E. Bergin' (eds) *Handbook of Psychotherapy and Behaviour Change* (2nd edn), New York: Wiley.

Gendlin, E. (1967) 'Subverbal communication and therapist expressivity: trends in client-centred therapy with schizophrenics', in C.R. Rogers and B. Stevens (eds) *Person to Person: the Problem of Being Human; a New Trend in Psychology*, Lafayette, CA.: Real People Press, pp.119–49.

Gellert, S.D. (1975) 'Theoretical differences within TA', *Transactional Analysis Journal* 5 (4): 420–1.

Gerstein, A.I. (1974) 'Variations in treatment technique in group activity therapy', *Psychotherapy: Theory, Research & Practice* 11 (4): 343–5.

Gibran, K. (1926) *The Prophet*, London: Heinemann.

Gillespie, J. (1976) 'Feelings in the Adult ego state', *Transactional Analysis Journal* 6 (1): 69–72.

Ginott, H.S. (1958) 'Play group psychotherapy: a theoretical framework', *International Journal of Group Psychotherapy* 8 (4): 410–18.

Gitelson, M. (1952) 'The emotional position of the analyst in the psychoanalytic situation', *International Journal of Psychoanalysis* 33: 1–10.

Gleick, J. (1987) *Chaos: Making a New Science*, London: Heinemann.

Goffman, E. (1962) *Asylums*, Chicago: Aldheim.

Goldfarb, W. (1943a) 'Infant reading and problem behaviour', *American Journal of Orthopsychiatry* 13: 249–65.

Goldfarb, W. (1943b) 'The effects of early institutional care on adolescent personality (graphic Rorschach data)', *Child Development* 14: 213–25.

Golub, S. and Guerriero, L.P. (1981) 'The effects of a transactional analysis program on self-esteem in learning-disabled boys', *Transactional Analysis Journal* 11 (3): 244–6.

Goulding, M.M. and Goulding, R. L. (1975) 'Injunctions, decisions and redecisions', *Transactional Analysis Journal* 6 (1): 41.

Goulding, M.M. and Goulding, R.L. (1979) *Changing Lives Through Redecision Therapy*, New York: Brunner/Mazel Inc.

Graves, R. (1986a) *The Greek Myths: 1*, New York: Penguin Books Ltd.

Graves, R. (1986b) *The Greek Myths: 2*, New York: Penguin Books Ltd.

Greenacre, P. (1959) 'Certain technical problems in the transference relationship', *J. Amer. Psychoanalytic Association* 7: 484–502.

Greenson, R.R. (1965) 'The working alliance and the transference neuroses', *Psychoanalytic Quarterly* 34: 155–81.

Greenson, R.R. (1967) *The Technique and Practice of Psychoanalysis*, vol. 1, New York: International Universities Press.

Griffith, S. (1990) 'A review of factors associated with patient compliance and the taking of prescribed medicines', *British Journal of General Practice*, 40: 114–16.

Groder, M. (1988) 'Ego state theory: definitions, descriptions and points of view', in Erskine, R.G., Clarkson, P., Goulding, R.G., Groder, M. and Moiso, C., *Transactional Analysis Journal* 18 (1): 6–15.

Guggenbuhl-Craig, C.A. (1971) *Power in the Helping Professions*, Dallas, Texas: Spring.

Guntrip, H. (1961) 'Personality structure and human interaction: the developing synthesis of psychodynamic theory', in J.D. Sutherland (ed.) *The International Psycho-analytical Library*, No.56, London: Hogarth Press and the Institute of Psycho-analysis.

Gurowitz, E.M. (1975) 'Group boundaries and leadership potency', *Transactional Analysis Journal* 5 (2): 183–5.

Haley, J. and Hoffman, L. (1967) *Techniques of Family Therapy*, New York: Basic Books.

Hardy, J. (1989) *A Psychology With a Soul*, London: Arkana.

Harlow, H.F. and Harlow, M.K. (1962) 'Social deprivation in monkeys', *Scientific American* 207: 136–46.

Harris, T.A. (1970) *The Book of Choice*, London: Jonathan Cape.

Harris, T.A. (1973) *I'm OK – You're OK*, London: Pan Books.

Harrower, M. (1965) 'Differential diagnosis', in B.B. Wolman (ed.), *Handbook of Clinical Psychology*, New York: McGraw-Hill, pp. 381–402.

Heidegger, M. (1949) *Existence and Being* (R.F.C. Hull, A. Crick, and D. Scott, trans.), Chicago: Henry Regnery.

Heimann, P. (1950) 'On countertransference', *International Journal of Psychoanalysis* 31 (1): 81–4.

Henderson, A.J. (1978) 'Transactional analysis in the learning disability clinic', *Transactional Analysis Journal* 8 (3): 242–4.

Henry, H. (1979) 'Disciplining an inner-city classroom', *Transactional Analysis Journal* 9 (2): 143.

Hess, A.K. (1980) *Psychotherapy Supervision: Theory, Research and Practice*, New York: John Wiley.

Hillman, J. (1975) *Revisioning Psychology*, New York: Harper & Row.

Hinshelwood, R.D. (1989) *A Dictionary of Kleinian Thought*, London: Free Association Books.

Hobbs, N. (1968) 'Sources of gain in psychotherapy', in E. Hammer (ed.) *Use of Interpretation in Treatment*, New York: Grune & Stratton, pp. 13–21.

Holloway, M.M. and Holloway, W.H. (1973) 'The contract setting process', in *The Monograph Series*, Numbers I – X, Ohio: Midwest Institute for Human Understanding Inc.

Holloway, W.H. (1972) 'The crazy child in the parent', *Transactional Analysis Journal* 1 (3): 128.

Holloway, W.H. (1973) 'Shut the escape hatch', in *The Monograph Series*, Numbers I – X, Ohio: Midwest Institute for Human Understanding Inc.

Holloway, W.H. (1977) 'Transactional Analysis: an integrative view', in G. Barnes (ed.) *Transactional Analysis after Berne*, New York: Harper's College Press.

Holmes, J. and Lindley, R. (1989) *The Values of Psychotherapy*, Oxford: Oxford University Press.

Holmes, T.H. and Rahe, R.H. (1967) 'The social readjustment rating scale', *Journal of Psychosomatic Research* 11: 213–18.

Horney, K. (1937) *The Neurotic Personality of Our Time*, London: Routledge & Kegan Paul.

Horewitz, J.S. (1979) *Family Therapy and Transactional Analysis*, New York: Jason Aronson.

Horowitz, J. (1979) *States of Mind*, New York: Plenum Press.

Horowitz, L. (1985) 'Projective identification in dyads and groups', in A.D. Coleman and

M.H. Geller (eds) *Group Relations Reader: 2*, Washington: A.K. Rice (first published 1974).

Houston, J. (1982) *The Possible Human*, Los Angeles: Tarcher.

Jacobs, A. (1987) 'Autocratic Power', *Transactional Analysis Journal* 17: 59–71.

James, J. (1983) 'Cultural consciousness: the challenge to TA', *Transactional Analysis Journal* 13 (4): 207–16.

James, M. (1969) 'Transactional analysis with children: the initial session', *Transactional Analysis Bulletin* 8 (29): 1–2.

James, M. (1974) 'Self-reparenting: theory and process', *Transactional Analysis Journal* 4 (3): 32–9.

James, M. (1977) *Techniques in Transactional Analysis*, Massachusetts: Addison-Wesley.

James, M. (1981) *Breaking Free: Self-reparenting for a New Life*, Phillipines: Addison-Wesley.

James, M. and Jongeward, D. (1971) *Born to Win: Transactional Analysis with Gestalt Experiments*, Reading, Massachusetts: Addison-Wesley.

James, M. and Savary, L. (1977) *A New Self: Self Therapy with Transactional Analysis*, Reading, Massachusetts: Addison-Wesley.

Jongeward, D. (1973) *Everybody Wins: Transactional Analysis Applied to Organizations*, Massachusetts: Addison-Wesley.

Jorgensen, E.W. and Jorgensen, H.I. (1984) *Eric Berne: Master Gamesman. A Transactional Biography*, New York: Grove Press.

Jourard. S.M. (1971) *The Transparent Self*, New York: Van Nostrand Reinhold (2nd edn).

Jung, C.G. (1928) 'Analytical psychology and education', in *Contributions to Analytical Psychology*, H.G. and C.F. Baynes (trans.), London and New York: Trench Trubner & Co.

Jung, C.G. (1966) *The Psychology of the Transference* (R.F.C. Hull, trans.), London: Routledge & Kegan Paul (original work published 1946).

Jung, C.G. (1969) 'Psychology and religion', in H. Read, M. Fordham, G. Adler, W. McGuire (eds), R.F.C. Hull (trans.) *Psychology and Religion: West and East*, C.W. 11, London: Routledge & Kegan Paul.

Jung, C.G. (1971) *Psychological Types*, C.W. 6, London: Routledge & Kegan Paul.

Jung, C.G. (1975) *Letters*, (vol. 2). (G. Adler ed.), Princeton: Princeton University Press.

Jung, C.G. (1986) *Psychology and Religion: West and East*, C.W. 11, London: Routledge & Kegan Paul.

Kahler, T. (1974) 'The miniscript' (original work published 1958) *Transactional Analysis Journal* 4 (1): 26.

Kahler, T. (1978) *Transactional Analysis Revisited*, Arkansas, USA: Human Development Publications.

Kapur, R. (1987) 'Depression: an integration of TA and psychodynamic concepts', *Transactional Analysis Journal* 17 (2): 29.

Kapur, R. and Miller, K. (1987) 'A comparison between therapeutic factors in TA and psychodynamic therapy groups', *Transactional Analysis Journal* 17 (1): 294–300.

Karpman, S. (1968) 'Fairy tales and script drama analysis', *Transactional Analysis Bulletin: Selected Articles from Volumes 1 through 9*, 1976, San Francisco: TA Press, pp. 51–6.

Karpman, S. (1971) 'Options', *Transactional Analysis Journal* 1 (1): 79.

Kaslow, F.W. and Associates (1977) *Supervision, Consultation, and Training in the Helping Professions*, San Francisco: Jossey-Bass.

Kempler, W. (1974) *Principles of Gestalt Family Therapy*, Oslo: A.S Joh. Nordahls Trykkeri.

Kempler, W. (1981) *Experiential Psychotherapy within Families*, New York: Brunner/Mazel.

Kernberg, O. (1980) *Internal World and External Reality*. New York: Jason Aronson.

Kernberg, O. (1982) 'Self, ego, affects, drives', *Journal of the American Psychoanalytic Association* 30: 893–917.

Kiev, A. and Cohn, V. (1979) *Executive Stress: An AMA Survey Report*, New York: Amacom.

Kingsley, C. (1982) *The Water Babies*, London: Hodder & Stoughton.

Klauber, J. (1986) 'Elements of the psychoanalytic relationship and their therapeutic implications', in G. Kohon (ed.) *The British School of Psychoanalysis: The Independent Tradition*, London: Free Association.

Klein, Mavis (1980) *Lives People Live*, London: Wiley.

Klein, M. (1949) *The Psychoanalysis of Children*, London: Hogarth Press.

Klein, M. (1984) *Envy, Gratitude and Other Works*, London: The Hogarth Press and Institute for Psycho-analysis (first published 1957).

Knight, D. (1986) 'Someone to watch over you', *Social Services Insight*, December: 19–26.

Koestler, A. (1972) *The Roots of Coincidence*, London: Hutchinson.

Kohut, H. (1977) *The Restoration of the Self*, New York: International Universities Press.

Kohut, H. (1978) *The Search for the Self*, New York: International Universities Press.

Kohut, H. (1985) *Self Psychology and the Humanities*, London: W.W. Norton.

Kubler-Ross, E. (1969) *On Death and Dying*, New York: Macmillan.

Kupfer, D. and Haimowitz, M. (1971) 'Therapeutic interventions: part 1, rubberbands now', *Transactional Analysis Journal* 1 (2): 10–16.

Kutzik, A.J. (1977) 'The medical field' and 'The social work field', in F.W. Kaslow (ed.), *Supervision, Consultation and Training in the Helping Professions*, San Francisco: Jossey-Bass.

Lacoursiere, R. (1980) *Life Cycle of Groups*, New York: Human Sciences Press.

Laing, R.D. (1965) *The Divided Self*, Harmondsworth: Penguin Books.

Laing, R.D. (1969) *The Politics of the Family and Other Essays*, New York: Pantheon Books.

Laing, R.D. and Esterson, A. (1970) *Sanity, Madness and the Family*, Harmondsworth: Pelican.

Lambert J.J. (1972) 'Transference/countertransference: Talion law and gratitude', *Journal of Analytical Psychology* 17 (1): 29–43.

Lambert, J.J. (1986) 'Implications of psychotherapy outcome research for eclectic psychotherapy', in J. Norcross (ed.) *Handbook of Eclectic Psychotherapy*, New York: Brunner/Mazel, pp. 436–62.

Landfield, A.W. (1971) *Personal Construct Systems in Psychotherapy*, Chicago: Rand McNally.

Landgarten, H.B. (1981) *Clinical Art Therapy*, New York: Brunner/Mazel.

Landman, J.T. and Dawes, R.M. (1982) 'Smith and Glass's conclusions stand up under scrutiny', *American Psychologist* 37: 504–16.

Langs, R. (1976) *The Bipersonal Field*, New York: Jason Aronson.

Langs, R. (1978) *The Listening Process*, New York: Jason Aronson.

Langs, R. (1985) *Workbooks for Psychotherapists*, vols 1–3, Emerson, New Jersey: Newconcept.

Langs, R. and Searles, H.F. (1980) *Intrapsychic and Interpersonal Dimensions of Treatment: a Clinical Dialogue*, New York: Jason Aronson.

Lankton, S. (1980) *Practical Magic*, 1 & 2, California: Meta Publications.

Laplanche, J. and Pontalis, J.B. (1988) *The Language of Psycho-analysis*, London:

Karnac Books (first published 1973).

Latane, B. and Darley, M. (1970) *The Unresponsive Bystander: Why Doesn't He Help?* New York: Appleton-Century Crofts.

Lazarus, A.A. (1981) *The Practice of Multimodal Therapy*, New York: McGraw-Hill.

Levin, P. (1974) *Becoming the Way We Are*, Berkeley, CA.: Pamela Levin.

Levin, P. (1988) *Cycles of Power*, Hollywood, CA.: Health Communications.

Levin-Landheer, P. (1982) 'The cycle of development', *Transactional Analysis Journal* 12 (2): 129–39.

Levine, S. (1960) 'Stimulation in infancy', *Scientific American* 202: 80–6.

Levinson, D.J. (1978) *The Seasons of a Man's Life*, New York: Ballantine Books.

Lewin, K. (1963) *Field Theory in Social Science: Selected Theoretical Papers*, London: Tavistock (original work published 1952). (Published by Harper & Row, 1951.)

Lidz, T., Fleck, S. and Cornelison, A. (1965) *Schizophrenia and the Family*, New York: International Universities Press.

Lieberman, M.A., Yalom, I.D. and Miles, M.B. (1973) *Groups: First Facts*, New York: Basic Books.

Liedloff, J. (1975) *The Continuum Concept*, Harmondsworth: Penguin.

Little, M. (1951) 'Countertransference and the patient's response to it', *International Journal of Psychoanalysis* 32: 32–40.

Loria, B. (1983) 'Beyond training: the education of transactional analysts', *Transactional Analysis Journal* 13 (3): 134–41.

Lowen, A. (1969) *The Betrayal of the Body*, New York: Collier-Macmillan.

Luborsky, L., Singer, B. and Luborsky, L. (1975) 'Comparative studies of psychotherapies: is it true that "Everybody has won and all must have prizes?"', *Archives of General Psychiatry* 32: 995–1008.

Lynch, M., Steinberg, D. and Ounsted, C. (1975) 'Family unit in a children's psychiatric hospital', *British Medical Journal* ii: 127–9.

MacDonald, A.M. (1972) *Chambers Twentieth Century Dictionary*, Edinburgh: T & A Constable.

Maggiora, A.R. (1987) 'A case of severe depression', *Transactional Analysis Journal* 17 (2): 38.

Magner, V. (1985) *Series of Comparative Charts of Psychological Theory, No. 1: Child Development*, London: distributed by Metanoia Psychotherapy Training Institute, 13 North Common Road, London W5.

Mahler, M.S., Pine, F. and Bergman, A. (1975) *The Psychological Birth of the Human Infant*, London: Hutchinson.

Main, F.T. (1958) 'Mothers with children in a psychiatric hospital', *Lancet* ii: 845–7.

Malan, D.H. (1979) *Individual Psychotherapy and the Science of Psychodynamics*, London: Butterworths.

Malcolm, J. (1981) *Psychoanalysis: The Impossible Profession*, New York: Knopf.

Mannel, S.B., Piehl, W. and Edwards, M. (1968) 'TA with children and adolescents', *Transactional Analysis Bulletin* 7 (28): 84–5.

Maslach, C. (1976) 'Burned-out', *Human Behaviour* 5 (9): 16–22.

Maslow, A.H. (1962) *Toward a Psychology of Being*, Princeton, NJ: Van Nostrand.

Massey, R.F. (1983) 'Passivity, paradox and change in family systems', *Transactional Analysis Journal* 13: 33–41.

Massey, R.F. (1985) 'TA as a family systems therapy', *Transactional Analysis Journal* 15 (2): 120–41.

Masson, J.M. (1985) *The Assault on Truth: Freud's Suppression of The Seduction Theory*, Harmondsworth: Penguin.

Masterson, J.F. (1985) *The Real Self: A Developmental, Self, and Object Relations Approach*, New York: Brunner/Mazel.

Matthews, C. (1986) *No Longer a Victim*, Canberra: Acorn Press.

May, R. (1969) *Love and Will*, New York: W. W. Norton.

McClendon, R. and Kadis, L.B. (1983) *Chocolate Pudding*, California: Science and Behavior Books.

McNeel, J. (1976) 'The Parent interview', *Transactional Analysis Journal* 6 (1): 61–8.

Mellor, K. (1979) 'Suicide: being killed, killing, and dying', *Transactional Analysis Journal* 9 (3): 183–8.

Mellor, K. (1980) 'Impasses: a developmental and structural understanding', *Transactional Analysis Journal* 10 (3): 213–20.

Mellor, K. and Andrewartha, G. (1980a) 'Reparenting the Parent in support of redecisions', *Transactional Analysis Journal* 10 (3): 197–203.

Mellor, K. and Andrewartha, G. (1980b) 'Reframing and the integrated use of redeciding and reparenting', *Transactional Analysis Journal* 10 (3): 204–12.

Meltzoff, J. and Kornreich, M. (1970) *Research in Psychotherapy*, New York: Atherton.

Melzack, R. (1965) 'Effects of early experience on behaviour: experimental and conceptual considerations', in P.H. Hoch and J. Zubin (eds) *Psychopathology of Perception*, New York: Grune & Stratton, pp. 271–99.

Miller, A. (1983) *The Drama of The Gifted Child and The Search for The True Self*, London: Faber.

Miller, A. (1985) *Thou Shalt Not Be Aware: Society's Betrayal of The Child* (H. and H. Hannum, trans.) London: Pluto Books (original work published 1981).

Miller, A. (1986) *The Drama of Being a Child*, London: Virago.

Miller, A. (1987) *For Your Own Good*, London: Virago (first published 1980).

Miller, W.C. and Seligman, M.E.P. (1975) 'Depression and learned helplessness in man', *Journal of Abnormal Psychology* 84: 228–38.

Minuchin, S. (1974) *Families and Family Therapy*, Massachusetts: Harvard University Press.

Misel, L.T. (1975) 'Stages of group treatment', *Transactional Analysis Journal* 5 (4): 385–91.

Mishkin, M., Malamut, B. and Bachevalier, J. (1984) 'Memories and habits: two neural systems', in, G. Lynch, A. McGaugh and N. Weinberger (eds) *Neurobiology of Learning and Memory*, Guildford: The Guildford Press.

Mitchell, A. (1983) 'Parent grafting', *Transactional Analysis Journal* 13 (1): 25–7.

Moiso, C. (1985) 'Ego states and transference', *Transactional Analysis Journal* 15 (3): 194.

Moore, B.F. and Fine, B.D. (eds) (1968) *A Glossary of Psychoanalytic Terms and Concepts*, New York: American Psychoanalytic Association.

Moreno, J. (1965) 'Therapeutic vehicles and the concept of surplus reality', *Group Psychotherapy* XVIII: 213.

Moustakas, C. (1966) *Existential Child Therapy*, New York: Basic Books Ltd.

Moustakas, C. (1967) *Creativity and Conformity*, Toronto: Van Nostrand.

National Association of Social Workers (1973) Standards for Social Services Manpower, New York: National Association of Social Workers.

Neill, J.R. and Kniskern, D.P. (1982) *From Psyche to System: The Work of Carl Whittaker*, New York: The Guilford Press.

Neumann, E. (1954) *The Origins of the History of Human Consciousness*, Princeton, N.J.: Princeton University Press.

Norcross, J.C. (1986) *Handbook of Eclectic Psychotherapy*, New York: Brunner/Mazel.

Novellino, M. (1984) 'Self-analysis of transference: In integrative transactional analysis', *Transactional Analysis Journal* 14 (1): 63–7.

Oaklander, V. (1978) *Windows to Our Children*, Utah: Real People Press.

Onions, C.T. (ed.) (1973) *The Shorter Oxford English Dictionary*, Oxford: Clarendon Press.

Ornstein, R.E. (1972) *The Psychology of Consciousness*, San Francisco: Freeman.

Osnes, R.E. (1974) 'Spot reparenting', *Transactional Analysis Journal* 4 (3): 40–6.

Ounsted, C., Oppenheimer, R. and Lindsay, J. (1974) 'Aspects of bonding failure: the psychopathology and psychotherapeutic treatment of families of battered children', *Develop. Md. Child Neurol.* 16: 447–56.

Padel, J. (1986) 'Ego in current thinking', in G. Kohon (ed.) *The British School of Psychoanalysis*, London: Free Association Books, pp. 154–72.

Parloff, M.B., Waskow, I. and Wolfe, B.E. (1978) 'Research on therapist variables in relation to process', in S.I. Garfield and A.E. Bergin (eds) *Handbook of Psychotherapy and Behaviour Change*, 2nd edn, New York: Wiley.

Paulsen, L. (1956) 'Transference and projection', *Journal of Analytical Psychology* 1 (2): 203–7.

Pavlov, I.P. (1927) *Conditioned Reflexes*, New York: Oxford University Press.

Peck, H.B. (1978) 'Integrating transactional analysis and group process approaches in treatment', *Transactional Analysis Journal* 8 (4): 328–31.

Peck, S. (1978) *The Road Less Travelled: a New Psychology of Love, Traditional Values and Spiritual Growth*, New York: Simon & Schuster.

Penfield, W. (1952) 'Memory mechanisms', *Arch. Neurology & Psychiatry* 67: 178–98.

Penfield, W. (1975) *The Mystery of the Mind*, New Jersey: Princeton University Press.

Perls, F.S., Hefferline, R.F. and Goodman, P. (1969) *Gestalt Therapy*, New York: Julian Press (first published 1951).

Perls, L. (1977) 'Comments on the new directions', in E. Smith (ed.), *The Growing Edge of Gestalt Therapy*, New Jersey: Citadel Press, pp. 221–6.

Pickett, L. (1986) 'The integrative classroom', *Transactional Analysis Journal* 16 (4): 241–6.

Piehl, W. (1969) 'TA with children', *Transactional Analysis Bulletin* 8 (32): 98.

Pine, F. (1985) *Developmental Theory and Clinical Process*, New Haven: Yale University Press.

Pokorney, J. (1959) *Indogermanisches etymologisches Wörterbuch*, Berne: Franke.

Professional Practices Guidelines, San Francisco, CA: ITAA.

Proust, M. (1919) *A la recherche de temps perdu*, 3, (Bibliothèque de la Pleiade) Paris: Gallimard.

Provence, S. and Lipton, R.C. (1962) *Infants in Institutions*, New York: International Universities Press.

Racker, H. (1982) *Transference and Countertransference*, London: Maresfield Reprints (original work published 1968).

Riesen, A. (1965) 'Effects of early deprivation of photic stimulation', in S.F. Osler and R.E. Cooke (eds) *The Biosocial Basis of Mental Retardation*, Baltimore, MD: Johns Hopkins Press.

Rinzler, D. (1984) 'Human disconnection and the murder of the earth', *Transactional Analysis Journal* 14: 231–6.

Roberts, D. (1984a) 'Contracting for peace – the first step in disarmament', *Transactional Analysis Journal* 14: 229–30.

Roberts, D. (1984b) *Able and Equal: a Gentle Path To Peace*, Culver City, CA: Peace Press.

Rogers, C. (1986) *Client-centered Therapy*, London: Constable.

Rogers, C. and Stevens, B. (1967) *Person to Person: the Problem of Being Human: a New Trend in Psychology*, Lafayette, CA.: Real People Press.

Romanini, M.T. (1982) 'Personal transactional analysis of some cases of infant autism', *Transactional Analysis Journal* 12 (2): 100.

Rose, C. (1985) *Accelerated Learning*, Dun Laoghaire, Ireland: Topaz Publishing Limited.

Rosenthel, R. and Jacobson, L. (1968) *Pygmalion in the Classroom: Teacher Expectations and Pupils' Intellectual Development*, New York: Holt Rinehart & Winston.

Rowan, J. (1988) *Ordinary Ecstasy: Humanistic Psychology in Action*, London: Routledge.

Runes, D.D. (ed.) (1962) *Dictionary of Philosophy*, Totona, N.J.: Littlefields, Adams & Co.

Ryce-Menuhin, J. (1988) *The Self in Early Childhood*, London: Free Association Books.

Rycroft, C. (1972) *A Critical Dictionary of Psychoanalysis*, Harmondsworth: Penguin (first published 1968).

Salters, D. and Clarkson, P. (1988) *Series of Comparative Charts of Psychological Theory – no 2: Adult Development*, London: Metanoia Psychotherapy Training Institute, 13 North Common Road, London W5.

Samuels, A. (1985) *Jung and the Post-Jungians*, London: Routledge & Kegan Paul.

Samuels, A. (1989) *The Plural Psyche*, London: Routledge.

Sargant, W. (1957) *Battle for the Mind*, London: Heinemann.

Sartre, J.P. (1970) *Existentialism and Humanism*, Paris: Les Editions Nagel.

Satir, V. (1976) *Peoplemaking*, California: Science and Behavior Books Inc.

Schaefer, C.E., Millman, H.L., Sichel, S.M. and Zwilling, J.R. (1986) *Advances in Therapies for Children*, London: Jossey-Bass.

Schaffer, H.R. (1965) 'Changes in developmental quotient under two conditions of maternal separation', *British Journal Soc. Clin. Psychology* 4: 39–46.

Schiff, A. and Schiff, J. L. (1971) 'Passivity', *Transactional Analysis Journal* 1 (1): 71.

Schiff, J.L. (1969) 'Representing schizophrenics', *Transactional Analysis Bulletin* 8 (31): 47–63.

Schiff, J.L. (1977) 'One hundred children generate a lot of TA', in G. Barnes *Transactional Analysis After Eric Berne*, New York: Harper's College Press.

Schiff, J. L. and Day, B. (1970) *All My Children*, New York: Pyramid Publications.

Schiff, J.L., with Schiff, A.W., Mellor, K., Schiff, E., Schiff, S., Richman, D., Fishman, J., Wolz, L., Fishman, C. and Momb, D. (1975) *Cathexis Reader: Transactional Analysis Treatment of Psychosis*, New York: Harper & Row.

The Script, November 1981, XI (9): 6.

Searles, H. (1975) 'The patient as therapist to his analyst', in P.L. Giovacchini (ed.) *Tactics and Techniques in Psychoanalytic Therapy*, vol II, New York: Aronson, pp. 94–151.

Sechehaye, M. (1951) *Reality Lost and Regained: Autobiography of a Schizophrenic Girl, with Analytic Interpretation by M. Sechehaye* (G. Urbin-Ralson, trans.), New York: Grune & Stratton.

Segal, H. (1986) *Introduction to the Work of Melanie Klein*, London: The Hogarth Press (first published 1964).

Selye, H. (1957) *The Stress of Life*, London: Low & Brydone Ltd.

Seuss, Dr (1968) *Thidwick, the Big-Hearted Moose*, London: Collins.

Shakespeare, W. *The Complete Works* (P. Alexander, ed.), London: Collins.

Sheridan, M.D. (1973) *Children's Developmental Progress*, Windsor, Berks: NFER Publishing.

Sinclair-Brown, W. (1982) 'A TA redecision group psychotherapy treatment program for mothers who physically abuse and/or seriously neglect their children', *Transactional Analysis Journal* 12 (1): 39–45.

Skinner, B.F. (1953) *Science and Human Behaviour*, New York: Macmillan.

Sloane, R.B., Staples, F.R., Cristol, A.H., Yorkston, N.J. and Whipple, K (1975), *Short-term Analytically Oriented Psychotherapy Versus Behaviour Therapy*, Cambridge, MA: Harvard University Press.

Smail, D.J. (1978) *Psychotherapy: a Personal Approach*, London: J.M. Dent.

Smail, D.J. (1987) *Taking Care, an Alternative to Therapy*, London: J.M. Dent.

Smith, M.L., Glass, G.V. and Miller, T.I. (1980) *The Benefits of Psychotherapy*, Baltimore, MD: Johns Hopkins University Press.

Solzhenitsyn, A. (1974) *The Gulag Archipelago*, Glasgow: Fontana.

Spinelli, E. (1989) *The Interpreted World: an Introduction to Phenomenological Psychology*, London: Sage.

Spitz, R. (1945) 'Hospitalism: genesis of psychiatric conditions in early childhood', *Psychoanalytic Study of the Child* 1: 53–74.

Steere, D.A. (1982) *Bodily Expressions in Psychotherapy*, New York: Brunner/Mazel.

Steiner, C.M. (1966) 'Script and counterscript', *Transactional Analysis Bulletin*, p. 18.

Steiner, C.M. (1971) 'The stroke economy', *Transactional Analysis Journal* 1 (3): 9.

Steiner, C.M. (1974) *Radical Therapist/Rough Times Collective: The Radical Therapist*, Harmondsworth: Penguin.

Steiner, C.M. (1975) *Scripts People Live*, New York: Bantam (original published in 1974).

Steiner, C.M. (1984) 'Emotional literacy', *Transactional Analysis Journal* 14 (3): 162–73.

Stern, D.N. (1985) *The Interpersonal World of the Infant*, New York: Basic Books.

Stern, E. (ed.) (1984) *TA: the State of the Art*, Dordrecht: Foris Publications.

Stewart, I. (1989) *Transactional Analysis Counselling in Action*, London: Sage.

Stewart, I. and Joines, V. (1987) *TA Today: a New Introduction to Transactional Analysis*, Nottingham: Lifespace Publishing.

Stone, L. (1961) *The Psychoanalytic Situation*, New York: International Universities Press.

Strachey, J. (ed.), in collaboration with Freud, A. (1966) *The Complete Psychological Works of Sigmund Freud*, London: Hogarth Press.

Stuntz, E.C. (1973) 'Multiple chairs technique', *Transactional Analysis Journal* 3 (2): 29.

The *Sun*, October 29, 1986, p.7.

Symington, N. (1986) *The Analytic Experience*, London: Free Association Books.

Symonds, M. and Dawson, E.S. (1974/5) 'The co-therapist approach to group treatment with institutionalised early adolescent girls', *Groups: A Journal of Group Dynamics & Psychotherapy* 6 (1): 27–36.

Szasz, T.S. (1961) *The Myth of Mental Illness: Foundations of a Theory of Personal Conduct*, New York: Hoeber-Harper.

Tennyson, A., Lord, (1869) 'In Memoriam, prologue', in *The Oxford Dictionary of Quotations*, 2nd edn, Oxford: Oxford University Press.

'These innocent parents' June 25, 1987, *Daily Mail*, p.1.

Thomas, A.L., Chess, S. and Birch, H. (1977) *Temperament and Development*, New York: Brunner/Mazel.

Thomson, G. (1988) personal communication.

TM Exam Format, San Francisco: ITAA, January 1985.

Training Standards Committee (1987) Recommendations to the ITAA, January.

Trautmann, R. and Erskine, R.G. (1981) 'Ego state analysis: a comparative view'. *Transactional Analysis Journal* 11 (2): 178–85.

Truax, C.B. and Mitchell, K.M. (1971) 'Research on certain therapist interpersonal skills in relation to process and outcome', in A.E. Bergin and S.L. Garfield (eds) *The Handbook of Psychotherapy and Behaviour Change*, New York: John Wiley, pp. 299–344.

Tuckman, B.W. (1965) 'Developmental sequence in small groups', *Psychological Bulletin* 63 (6): 384–99.

Tuckman, B.W. and Jensen, M.A.C. (1977) 'Stages of small group development', *Journal of Group and Organisational Studies* 2: 419–27.

Watkins, J.G. (1954) 'Trance and transference', *Journal of Clinical and Experimental Hypnosis* 2: 284–90.

Watkins, J.G. (1976) 'Ego states and the problem of responsibility: a psychological analysis of the Patty Hearst case', *Journal of Psychiatry and Law* pp. 471–89, Winter 1976.

Watkins, J.G. (1978) *The Therapeutic Self*, New York: Human Sciences Press.

Watkins, J.G. and Johnson, R. (1982) *We, the Divided Self*, New York: Irvington Publishers Inc.

Watkins, J.G. and Watkins, H.H. (1986) 'Hypnosis, multiple personality, and ego states and altered states of consciousness', in B.B. Wolman and M. Vilman (eds) *Handbook of States of Consciousness*, New York: Van Nostrand Reinhold Company.

Watson, L. (1974) *Supernature*, London: Coronet.

Watzlawick, P., Weakland, J.H. and Fisch, R. (1974) *Change: Principles of Problem Formation and Problem Resolution*, New York: Norton.

Weiss, E. (1950) *Principles of Psychodynamics*, New York: Grune & Stratton.

Whitman, W. (1976) *Leaves of Grass*, Harmondsworth: Penguin.

Wilhelm, H. (1988) (trans.) *The I Ching*, London: Routledge & Kegan Paul (first published 1951).

Winnicott, D.W. (1958) *Collected Papers*, London: Tavistock.

Winnicott, D.W. (1960) *The Maturational Processes and the Facilitating Environment*, London: Hogarth Press.

Winnicott, D.W. (1975) 'Hate in the countertransference', in *Through Paediatrics to Psychoanalysis*, New York: Basic Books, pp. 194–203.

Winnicott, D.W. (1986) *Home is Where We Start From*, Harmondsworth: Penguin Books.

Woodmansey, A.C. (1988) 'Are psychotherapists out of touch?' *The British Journal of Psychotherapy* 5 (1): 57–65.

Woollams, S. and Brown, M. (1978) *Transactional Analysis*, Ann Arbor, Michigan: Stan Woollams.

Woollams, S. and Brown, M. (1979) *TA: the Total Handbook of Transactional Analysis*, Englewood Cliffs, NJ: Prentice-Hall.

Worden, J.W. (1983) *Grief Counselling and Grief Therapy*, London: Tavistock.

World Health Organization (1978) *Mental Disorders: Glossary and Guide to Their Classification*, Geneva: WHO.

Wundt, W. (1861) *Lectures on Human and Animal Psychology* (E. Creighton and E.B. Titchener, trans.), London: Swan & Somenschein, 1984.

Yalom, I. (1980) *Existential Psychotherapy*, New York: Basic Books.

Zalcman, M. (1990) 'Game analysis and racket analysis: Overview, critique, and future developments', *Transactional Analysis Journal* 20 (1): 4–19.

Zalcman, M. and Cornell, W. (1983) 'A bilateral model for clinical supervision', *Transactional Analysis Journal* 13 (2): 112–23.

Zdenek, M. (1986) *The Right-brain Experience*, London: Corgi Books.

Zohar, D. (1990) *The Quantum Self*, London: Bloomsbury.

Index

UNIVERSITY OF WOLVERHAMPTON
LEARNING RESOURCES